The

Politics

of

Change in

Georgia

A Political

Biography of

Ellis Arnall

The

University

of

Georgia

Press

Athens

and

London

The
Politics
of
Change
in
Georgia

A
Political
Biography
of Ellis
Arnall

Harold
Paulk
Henderson

© 1991 by the University of
Georgia Press
Athens, Georgia 30602
All rights reserved
Designed by Richard Hendel
Set in Galliard
The paper in this book meets
the guidelines for permanence
and durability of the
Committee on Production
Guidelines for Book
Longevity of the Council on
Library Resources.

Printed in the United States
of America
95 94 93 92 91
5 4 3 2 1

Library of Congress
Cataloging in
Publication Data
Henderson, Harold P.
    The politics of change in
Georgia: a political biography
of Ellis Arnall / Harold Paulk
Henderson.
        p. cm.
    Includes bibliographical
references and index.
    ISBN 0-8203-1306-8
(alk. paper)
    1. Arnall, Ellis Gibbs, 1907– .
    2. Governors—Georgia—
Biography. 3. Georgia—
Politics and government—
1865–1950. 4. Georgia—
Politics and government—
1951– I. Title.
F291.A7H46   1991
975.804'092—dc20
    [B]   90-48689
                CIP

British Library Cataloging in
Publication Data available

TO THE MEMORY OF

George Washington and Luna Paulk Paulk

Edward Crawley and Mamie Gray Henderson

Frances Elizabeth Roland

James Elmo Harris

Contents

Preface   ix

Chapter One
Governor You Will Be   1

Chapter Two
This Splendid Young Man   17

Chapter Three
The 1942 Governor's Race   33

Chapter Four
The 1943 Legislative Session   51

Chapter Five
Georgia's Smelly Penal Muddle   63

Chapter Six
A New Constitution   77

Chapter Seven
State Finances and Services   97

Chapter Eight
The Freight Rate Controversy   116

Chapter Nine
The Race Issue   137

Chapter Ten
Political Adversities   152

Chapter Eleven
The Three-Governor Controversy   171

Chapter Twelve
Federal Service, Law, and Business   190

Chapter Thirteen
Arnall and State Politics, 1947–1962   208

Chapter Fourteen
Arnall's Last Hurrah   223

Chapter Fifteen
A Mover and a Shaker   243

Notes   255

Bibliography   309

Index   331

Preface

Ellis Gibbs Arnall served as governor of Georgia in the 1940s. He rose to political power in a time when some of the state's most colorful and flamboyant politicians—Gene Talmadge, Ed Rivers, and Roy Harris—strutted across Georgia's political stage. Arnall proved to be just as dynamic a political personality. He became governor of a state that was rural, poor, underdeveloped, provincial, and a source of ridicule by the national media and northern liberals. Arnall undertook a plan of progressive reform in a state dominated by rural interests. He replaced the state's Tobacco Road image with that of a progressive and forward-looking state. Many of his positions on public policy and his favorable coverage by the national media alienated the conservative rural voters—the strongest defenders of the status quo. In their view, Arnall had moved the state too far and too fast and had enhanced his national popularity by airing Georgia's dirty linen. Unlike most of his predecessors, Arnall had not performed the politically safe role of being a defender and maintainer of the status quo. Clearly Arnall achieved a significant record as governor and had a positive impact on his state.

There is a dismal absence of published scholarly studies of twentieth-century Georgia politicians. The purpose of this biography is to fill a portion of that gap. It traces the evolution of a major Georgia politician from a supporter of one of the state's most famous demagogues, Eugene Talmadge, to one of the state's best-known reformers. Ellis Arnall presented the voters of Georgia with an alternative to Talmadge's status quo politics. He promised the politics of the New South—biracial voting, governmental reform, economic development, an improved standard of living for all Georgians, and an end to demagoguery. Arnall's speedy rise to political power in Georgia and his political demise merit study, for his politics eventually prevailed.

I first became interested in the political career of Governor Arnall while writing a master's thesis on the 1946 governor's race. Some years later, I wrote a doctoral dissertation about the 1966 gubernatorial campaign. Arnall played a significant role in both of those controversial elections. Our paths crossed again during a symposium held at Abraham Baldwin Agricultural College in the fall of 1985. On that occasion, scholars evaluated the administrations of the nine men who held the governorship of Georgia from 1943 to 1983. I had the opportunity of writing papers on two of these governors. While interested in the political careers of all of them, I selected Governor Arnall as the subject of my first essay. As the work on the paper progressed, Arnall suggested that it be expanded into a full-scale biography. After much thought, I agreed to undertake such a project.

The governor, an author himself, has been most cooperative and supportive in my efforts. He has been articulate in presenting his views as well as trying to influence my interpretation of his governorship. I undertook this project with the clear understanding with the governor that the biography would be a scholarly endeavor with the author having absolute control over content and interpretation. He has graciously abided by that ground rule.

Writing a biography requires the assistance of numerous individuals and I am most appreciative for the help I have received. Wayne C. Curtis, who served as president of Abraham Baldwin Agricultural College at the inception of this project, was very supportive. The college's academic dean, James A. Burran, likewise has been cooperative and understanding. One of the strongest supporters of this project has been the chairman of the college's Social Science Division, Gary L. Roberts, who served with me as codirector of the governors' symposium and coeditor of the publication of the proceedings of the symposium. He has read the entire manuscript and has made numerous suggestions for its improvement. Charlotte S. Pfeiffer, professor of English at Abraham Baldwin, has rescued me on numerous occasions from the thicket of improper grammar. The keen eye and professionalism of Debra Winter as copyeditor has greatly improved the manuscript. I am greatly indebted to the two typists for their efforts: my wife, Teena Ann, who typed the rough draft of the manuscript, and Wanda Schwartz, the governor's longtime secretary, who typed the final version. I am also appreciative of Sandra G. Hunt, a learning resource specialist on the staff of the library at Abraham Baldwin, for her editorial assistance. Jonathan Walker allowed me to stay with him during some of my research trips to Atlanta, and my sister-in-law and husband, Betsy and Ben Williams, permitted me to stay with them while I was engaged in research at the University of Georgia.

This biography could not have been written without the assistance of the staff at the following libraries: Abraham Baldwin College, Georgia State University, University of Georgia, Emory University, Valdosta State College, Bainbridge College, Harry S. Truman Library, Franklin D. Roosevelt Library, University of Iowa, and Richard B. Russell Memorial Library. I am also indebted to the staffs at the Georgia Department of Archives and History, Georgia State Library, National Archives, Library of Congress, and the Law Library of the U.S. Supreme Court. Several individuals merit special recognition for their help with my research: Brenda Sellers, reference librarian at Abraham Baldwin College; Barbara Rystrom, head of the Department of Interlibrary Loans at the University of Georgia; Sally O'Neal, head of Archives and Contemporary South Georgia History at Valdosta State College; and Cliff Kuhn, assistant director of the Georgia Government Documentation Project at Georgia State University.

One of the major obstacles in writing this biography has been the absence of collections of private papers of the major figures of Georgia politics during the 1940s. At the conclusion of his administration, Arnall had his papers destroyed. Eugene Talmadge, Herman Talmadge, Ed Rivers, Roy Harris, and M. E. Thompson likewise left little in the way of private papers. Moreover, with the exception of Arnall and Herman Talmadge, these individuals who played such a major role in the politics of the state in the 1940s were deceased long before this project was undertaken. I have attempted to compensate as much as possible for the void of these papers in several ways. I have interviewed Arnall on eight occasions and, in addition, have used James F. Cook's interview of the governor that he conducted as part of the Georgia Government Documentation Project at Georgia State University. Melvin T. Steely and Theodore B. Fitz-Simons kindly provided audio recordings of their video interview of Arnall that is part of the Georgia Political Heritage Series at West Georgia College. I have made exhaustive use of both of the Atlanta daily newspapers, which provided favorable coverage of the Arnall administration; Arnall's two books, his numerous published articles, and his many speeches provided a substantial contemporary record of his views.

To gain a critical perspective of Arnall, I have interviewed Herman Talmadge on two separate occasions. In addition, I conducted a lengthy interview of Senator Talmadge as part of the Georgia Government Documentation Project. I also made extensive use of three newspapers that were critical of Arnall. The *Statesman*, a political weekly published by the Talmadges, provided continuous criticism of Arnall. The Augusta *Courier*, published by Roy V. Harris, provided insight from one of Georgia's most capable behind-the-scenes politicians who switched from being a key Arnall supporter to a bitter political foe. The Savannah *Morning News*, the largest daily in the state that opposed Arnall, provided a conservative perspective on the Arnall administration.

In addition to the Arnall and Talmadge interviews, I have interviewed the following individuals to gain their perspective of Arnall: S. Ernest Vandiver, Jr., Lester G. Maddox, Carl E. Sanders, Jr., James H. Gray, Sr., Howard H. Callaway, Ivan Allen, Jr., Garland T. Byrd, and Ford Spinks. I am most appreciative of the many scholars whose writings on Georgia politics have provided me with a better understanding of the subject. Their contributions are cited in the bibliography. In particular, I am indebted to Elkin Taylor, whose master's thesis on Arnall made my task much easier.

The expense of writing this biography has been underwritten by a grant from the Livingston Foundation. I am indebted to the trustees of the foundation for their financial support and their confidence. Appreciation is also extended to Mr. and Mrs. Robert E. Rich, Mr. and Mrs. Eli Broad, and Mr. and Mrs. John B. Amos for their financial assistance. I am also indebted to the board of directors of the Abraham Baldwin Agricultural College Foundation for that foundation's assistance. In particular, I am grateful for the cooperation of the foundation's executive secretary, Melvin L. Merrill.

Finally, a special word of appreciation goes to my wife, Teena Ann, and to my children, Hank and Mara Dare, for their patience, understanding, and moral support.

The

. . . .

Politics

. . . .

of

. . . .

Change in

. . . .

Georgia

. . . .

A Political

. . . .

Biography of

. . . .

Ellis Arnall

. . . .

1

. . . .

Governor

. . . .

You

. . . .

Will

. . . .

Be

. . . .

Newnan, Georgia, lies forty miles southwest of Atlanta. Founded in the 1820s, Newnan was named for General Daniel Newnan, a veteran of the Creek Indian Wars and a prominent Georgia politician. The small community evolved into a typical Georgia county seat complete with the red brick courthouse surrounded by business establishments. By 1940 Newnan, in Coweta County, had grown to a population of over seven thousand. The local newspaper boasted that the city was "the barbeque capital of the world" and that it was one of the wealthiest communities per capita in the United States. Local residents in the unhurried days prior to World War II prided themselves that one of their own, William Yates Atkinson, Sr., had served the state as governor in the 1890s.[1]

Among Coweta County's most prominent and respected families were the Arnalls, who traced their ancestry to Cornwall, England. The Arnalls' long association with Coweta County began when John Gholston Arnall migrated to the county in 1841. He and his wife, Ann Miles Gibbs Arnall of Walton County, Georgia, had three sons, of which the most successful was Henry Clay Arnall, born in 1850. While still a young man, Henry Arnall moved to the small town of Newnan, where he opened a general merchandise store on the courthouse square in 1869. An industrious and hardworking entrepreneur, Arnall expanded his small store into one of the largest mercantile businesses in town—the H. C. Arnall Merchandise Company. Arnall's store sold everything from groceries and horse collars to clothing and farming equipment. Not content with just selling merchandise, Arnall served as an alderman of the City of Newnan and as a member of the Newnan library building committee. He also broadened his business endeavors to become owner of a local textile mill, part owner of another, founder of the Farmers Warehouse Company, organizer of the Newnan Banking Company, and founder of the Coweta Fertilizer Company. Eventually, this enterprising entrepreneur became a prominent businessman in the community. One writer even called him Newnan's "local Rockefellow."[2]

Active in community affairs, Henry Clay Arnall was a founder and faithful member of the Newnan Central Baptist Church. A devout family man, Arnall and his wife, Sarah Catherine, reared four sons and two daughters. When his sons reached maturity, he entrusted each of them with the management of a portion of his business endeavors. One of his sons, Joseph Gibbs Arnall, assumed the responsibility of managing the grocery division of the H. C. Arnall Merchandise Company. A capable businessman in his own right, Joe Arnall exanded the grocery division into a wholesale grocery and then into a chain of stores in the surrounding area. In 1905 this young businessman married Bessie Lena Ellis of Union Springs, Bullock County, Alabama. Arnall's father-in-law, Joseph Mathew Ellis, was like Henry Clay Arnall in that he also was a successful merchant and businessman. In fact, the J. M. Ellis and Sons Company was the largest general mercantile store in Union Springs. In addition, he owned several thousand acres of land. Joe and Bessie Arnall had two sons: Ellis Gibbs Arnall, born March 20, 1907, and Frank Marion Arnall II, born August 12, 1916.[3]

Ellis Arnall grew up in a small town environment as a member of one of the county's most respected and wealthiest families. One writer in a national magazine called Arnall "the American equivalent of the scion of a European noble house." Arnall remembered his childhood as being happy and normal. At the early age of two, the future politician discovered the pleasure of applause. His parents carried their young son to a band concert in front of the courthouse. When the band played Arnall got up and danced to the applause of the audience, which led the young dancer to perform again for more applause.[4]

Arnall's first-grade teacher, Miss Maggie Brown, remembered Arnall as a wavy-haired, chubby child who was a very good mixer and who was well liked by his peers. She also remembered him as an independent thinker and as a student with an analytical mind. She recalled an occasion when Arnall's class was reciting the nursery rhyme about the cow jumping over the moon. After the recitation, young Arnall asked, "Miss Maggie, don't you know that cow's feet hurt her when she landed." An eight-year-old

Arnall perhaps demonstrated the makings of a future politician when he wrote in a letter to Santa Claus, "I hope times are not to [sic] bad for you to come to see me."[5]

Arnall remembered his mother and father as loving parents who "gave me every advantage a young man could have." These advantages included material things such as being sent to Camp Dixie for Boys in the mountains of north Georgia during the summers. His parents provided him with a college education and spending money as well as an automobile while he was in college. But more important, Arnall recalled that his parents gave "of themselves, their counseling, their advice, their guidance." Arnall grew up in Newnan's Central Baptist Church, which his grandfather Arnall had been influential in establishing. After school and during the summers, Arnall worked in his grandfather's store on the courthouse square.[6]

The exceptionally bright Arnall attended the public schools in Newnan where he made good grades with little difficulty. Arnall possessed an inquiring mind and was constantly probing the outer limits of his teachers' knowledge. As a young boy, Arnall developed a love for reading and looked upon books as the key to knowledge. The outgoing Arnall served as president of each of his high school classes and managed to find time to obtain the rank of Eagle Scout. Arnall loved football and quarterbacked his high school team. Such activities provided early indication of his future leadership abilities. Unfortunately, he failed to graduate with his class as a result of his involvement with football. Newnan High School had a good football team during his senior year. Some of the senior players, including Arnall, decided that they would like the opportunity to play one more year in order to have another opportunity to win the state championship. As planned, the conspirators managed to end the school year with insufficient academic credits for graduation. Prior to the next football season, however, several of the conspirators moved out of town while others decided not to return to school. Thus, the dream of the seniors winning the state championship ended in disappointment for Arnall.[7]

Despite his lack of a high school diploma, Arnall entered Mercer University, a small liberal arts Baptist institution in Macon, Georgia, in the fall of 1924. Grandfather Arnall, a supporter of Mercer University, had prevailed upon the university's admission committee to allow his grandson to enroll. Arnall's enthusiasm for college quickly turned to disappointment, however, because to his dismay two of his "college professors" were student-teachers who had been one year ahead of him at Newnan High School.

Arnall concluded that he "knew as much as they did or maybe more" and looked elsewhere for a college education.[8]

Arnall decided to transfer to Vanderbilt University, a private institution, located in Nashville, Tennessee. Fortunately for Arnall, he came from a well-to-do family who could afford to send him out of state to a prestigious private university. During the train trip to Nashville, however, he met several students from the University of the South who persuaded him to visit their school, a small Episcopal liberal arts college located at Sewanee, Tennessee. Impressed by the beauty of the campus atop a Tennessee mountain, Arnall enrolled at the small institution—a decision he never regretted because its emphasis was not on teaching students how to make a living but how to "appreciate life and love life." Arnall even considered becoming a college professor because of the college's impact on his life. Ironically, Arnall—the son and grandson of practical businessmen—soon "fell in love with Greek," which he took as a major. While most of the courses Arnall enrolled in were in the languages, he managed to take a sampling of courses in such areas as economics, philosophy, mathematics, and public speaking. Arnall completed his course work with an 83 average without a great deal of study and graduated with an A.B. degree in Greek in 1928.[9]

While a student at the University of the South, Arnall impressed classmates with his outgoing personality. They described him in such terms as "popular," "big talker," "gregarious," and "jovial." One former classmate remembered Arnall because he "had a definite gift for the use of words." Another recalled Arnall as a popular student who "managed to make all the dances." In addition to perfecting his billiards game, Arnall found time to read the Greek version of the New Testament. Arnall's extracurricular activities included membership in Kappa Alpha social fraternity, Pi Omega, the German Club, and the Georgia Club. Arnall's extroverted and colorful personality, so essential to success in the state's one party and generally issue-less politics, began to emerge during his years as a student at the University of the South.[10]

After graduating, Arnall entered the law school at the University of Georgia. He had decided upon a legal career—a decision which his father wholeheartedly endorsed. Arnall, already envisioning a political career, selected the practice of law as "the best avenue to politics possible." Classmates at both the University of the South and the University of Georgia remembered his boasting that he would be governor some day. Arnall conceded that while at Athens, he "made no bones" about his desire to eventually occupy the governor's office. The politically ambitious Arnall saw active participation in campus activities as an asset to his gubernatorial plans. He reasoned that the friends he made while involved in campus affairs would later become community leaders who would be beneficial to his future political career.[11]

Consequently, Arnall participated in extracurricular activities at a whirlwind pace. He continued his membership in Kappa Alpha and successfully campaigned for the presidency of the Pan-Hellenic Council. As president of the council, Arnall held one of the most visible and prestigious positions on the campus. The council served as the governing body of the social fraternities and the sponsor of fraternity social activities. Other campus activities included his serving as president of the international legal fraternity, chief justice of the Hill Law Club, and the first chief justice of the Law School Honor Court, a body that Arnall had successfully urged the faculty to create. Arnall also served as president of the Sphinx, Gridiron Club, Pelicans, Ravens, Junior Law Class, and Cavalier Club. His wide range of activities received the attention of the 1931 edition of the university annual. The publication had a section entitled "Views of Prominent People" in which a photograph showed a neatly dressed Arnall sporting a three-piece suit, a hat, and mustache. The annual even called Arnall "one of the greatest politicians who ever entered the University." Former law school classmates remembered Arnall as "ambitious," "a born politician," "popular," and "a leader." [12]

In the midst of his politicking at the University of Georgia, Arnall found time to take some law courses. The exceedingly bright Arnall, however, found the study of law to be "slow and boring" and "very easy." So easy that Arnall never bought a textbook but borrowed "books occasionally to see what it was all about." With a minimum of effort, Arnall graduated with an LL.B. degree with honors in June 1931. Arnall summed up his stay at Athens with the statement: "I had a good time at the University." [13]

With his diploma in hand, the young attorney returned to Newnan to practice law first with an uncle, Alvan Freeman, and later with another young struggling Newnan attorney, Stonewall H. Dyer. Both Dyer and Arnall were intelligent, young, and politically ambitious. In May 1932, Arnall, at twenty-five years of age, announced his candidacy for one of the two seats that Coweta County had in the Georgia House of Representatives. His partner, Dyer, announced for the other position.[14]

In retrospect, it seemed inevitable that Arnall would embark upon a political career. His father loved politics and encouraged his son in that direction. Joe Arnall was himself a politician, who had served on the Newnan Board of Aldermen and as chairman of the Coweta County Commission. Arnall's mother was very active in church and civic affairs. One of Arnall's uncles had served as mayor of Newnan and in both houses of the state legislature. Arnall's paternal great-grandfather had served in the state senate. His grandfather Ellis had served in the Alabama House of Representatives. Thanks to his grandfather Ellis, Arnall served as a page in the Alabama legislature when he was only eight years old. Arnall believed that his entry into politics was preordained. He recalled that his first-grade teacher had written the names of occupations on slips of paper and that he had drawn a slip which stated: "Governor you will be." [15]

Arnall's first political campaign was conducted during the worst economic crisis ever to confront the nation. The agricultural South had been in a state of depression since the end of World War I as a result of the collapse of agricultural prices. The economic crisis of 1929 only added to the plight of the farmer in Georgia. Agriculture dominated the state's economy, and cotton was the major cash crop in Georgia, providing 53 percent of the state's farm income in 1930. Unfortunately, the price of cotton had dropped from thirty-five cents a pound in 1920 to less than six cents per pound in 1931. Along with this drastic decline in prices, Georgia farmers witnessed a decline in the value of farmland. Because of the economics of the situation, more and more farmers moved from the status of farm owner to that of farm tenant.[16]

It was under such conditions that Commissioner of Agriculture Eugene Talmadge along with nine other hopefuls entered the governor's race in 1932. Most of the candidates promised the same solutions to deal with the economic crisis—reduce taxes, cut services, economize in government spending, and improve governmental efficiency. Talmadge, who had been commissioner of agriculture since 1927, quickly emerged as the leading candidate. Denounced by critics as the "wild man from Sugar Creek," Talmadge espoused a political philosophy of low taxes and few governmental services. He extolled the virtues of thrift, hard work, and rural living. Unfortunately for Georgians, Talmadge's concept of negative government offered few solutions to the plight of his fellow citizens other than cutting taxes, reducing governmental services, lowering the price of automobile tags, and reorganizing the highway department.[17]

Avoiding taking sides in the gubernatorial race, Arnall concentrated on his own campaign. The young candidate espoused the prevailing conservative philosophy in state government of retrenchment of state services and reduction of taxes as the best way to cope with the economic crisis. Arnall, sounding like Talmadge, contended that the people wanted relief from excessive tax burdens, and for the state government "to get back to the fundamentals—the protection of life, liberty and property with equal opportunity for all." Arnall undertook a vigorous personal campaign to get his name and message to the voters.[18]

Five candidates including the incumbents qualified for the two state representative positions from Coweta County. At that time, voters voted for two candidates, with the two receiving the highest number of votes being elected. Arnall led the contenders while his law partner came in second. He attributed his victory to his vigorous personal campaign, his vast family connections, and his lack of a political record.[19]

Though the youthful Arnall looked forward to serving in the state legislature, he had already set his sights on higher public office—the governorship. His election to the House was just a step toward that goal. He had no intentions of making a political career by serving in the legislature, nor did the ambitious Arnall have any intentions of being a typical freshman legislator. At first, he contemplated seeking the speakership—the highest elective position in the House—a bold undertaking for a freshman solon. Nevertheless, the extremely self-confident Arnall, who had never held public office, had no doubts about his ability to be speaker. Arnall discovered, however, that another ambitious politician, Eurith D. "Ed" Rivers, had his eye on that post as well. Rivers, twice an unsuccessful gubernatorial candidate, had won election to the House in 1932, and let it be known that he intended to seek the speakership as a stepping-stone to the governor's office. Perhaps fearing defeat by the more experienced and better known Rivers, Arnall decided to seek the second highest elective position in the House—the speaker pro tempore.[20]

Just as he had in his legislative race, Arnall undertook a vigorous personal campaign for that office. Prior to the opening of the General Assembly in January, Arnall visited with each member of the House in his home county to solicit votes for the legislative position. Though his father approved of the unusual statewide campaign for a legislative position, other members of the well-to-do Arnall family disapproved of one of their clan rambling around the state in a "battered jalopy." Arnall's mother even feared that her son would eat something that might be harmful to him. In spite of such objections, a determined Arnall temporarily left his law practice with Dyer and undertook his campaign. Anyway, Arnall confessed, "There was very little for a young lawyer to do in a tranquil and non-litigious Coweta County." He recalled that "the members of the House were very amused and very kind, and if they laughed at a brash boy who wanted to be an officer of the legislature, they also agreed to vote for me." In 1932 few Georgians or, for that matter, few members of the legislature could claim to have visited every county in Georgia. Arnall's campaign began his effort to make personal friendships and to build political alliances in every county in the state, which was essential for Arnall's future political career.[21]

Although three other representatives sought the position of speaker pro tempore, Arnall easily won on the first ballot. Arnall credited the victory to his personal visits with the representatives. He quickly became close friends with Rivers, who had been elected speaker, and Roy V. Harris, Talmadge's floor leader in the House. Both played major roles in Arnall's future political career, and the trio later became leaders in the anti-Talmadge faction that existed in Georgia state politics for almost two decades.[22]

Soon after its formal organization, the House of Representatives, under the leadership of Rivers, set about to try to enact laws to carry out the campaign pledges of Governor Talmadge. Rivers assigned the choice committee chairmanships to Talmadge supporters. Although the speaker did not give Arnall a chairmanship, the young legislator received good committee assignments. These committees included Rules, Ways and Means, and Banks and Banking. Arnall also served as secretary of the Rules Committee, which was chaired by the speaker.[23]

In keeping with his negative state philosophy, Governor Talmadge requested little in the form of legislation from the 1933 session. His requests included reorganization of the highway department, reduction of utility rates, reduction of state taxes, retrenchment of state services, and lowering of the cost of automobile tags to three dollars. Perhaps the latter issue created the most excitement in the 1933 session. Arnall supported Talmadge's request and served as a leader in the fight for the bill. Even though Arnall conceded that the bus and large trucking companies would be the greatest beneficiaries of the three-dollar tag, Arnall believed that the reduction would benefit poor Georgians who otherwise could not afford to purchase tags. Despite Arnall's efforts, the legislature failed to lower the price of automobile tags.[24]

Arnall also joined in the unsuccessful efforts to divert funds from the state highway department—the recipient of over half the state's revenues. He cosponsored a Talmadge bill to reorganize the highway department that passed the House but was killed in the Senate. While the supporters of the highway department succeeded in turning back these efforts, Arnall's willingness to take on the largest and most powerful agency in state government seemed unusual for a freshman legislator.[25]

A proposed sales tax supported by Speaker Rivers also generated great controversy in the legislature. On this issue, Arnall sided with Talmadge against Speaker Rivers and Harris. Rivers had long advocated a sales tax instead of the property tax as the best means of financing state government. The question of a sales tax became a burning issue when the state auditor issued a report during the legislative session that revealed a substantial drop in state revenue. Rivers argued that such a drastic reduction made a sales tax inevitable. Talmadge opposed the sales tax, fearing that the increased revenue would lead to an increase in the size of state government. Arnall joined the governor in opposition but for different reasons.[26]

Arnall, who led the fight against the sales tax, defended the existing ad valorem tax system as being fairer than a sales tax. Instead of seeking additional revenue, Arnall called for "drastic tax reductions and thrift" to compensate for the decline in state revenue. Moreover, he reminded his fellow lawmakers that the "mighty state highway machine rolls on, absorbing 53 cents out of every tax dollar paid in Georgia." Arnall argued that the state's budget could "be balanced by retrenchment and economy measures and temporarily diverting highway funds." Despite Rivers's personal pleas from the floor, the House defeated his sales tax proposal. While Talmadge prevailed on this issue, the legislature enacted few of his legislative requests.[27]

While Arnall had no difficulty in getting his local bills enacted, he, like Talmadge, had little luck in getting his bills of a statewide nature passed. One of these proposals required an annual license to operate a motor vehicle in the state. Even though the bill received support from the American Legion, numerous civic organizations, and the Atlanta *Constitution,* the House killed it. Despite some opposition from rural legislators, the House managed to pass an Arnall-sponsored bill that required lights on the rear of vehicles drawn by a horse or mule which operated on the public highways at night. The bill, however, died in a Senate committee.[28]

Additional Arnall-sponsored bills that were never enacted included bills abolishing county game wardens, establishing a state board of examiners for accountants, and creating a state department of banking. Arnall, who had taken on the highway department, now urged the dismantling of the agriculture department—another powerhouse in state politics. He contended that the department was nothing more than "a great patronage department and its necessary functions, which are few, could be transferred to other state agencies and bring about a great savings of the taxpayers' money." Revelations of alleged wrongdoing of Commissioner of Agriculture G. C. Adams aided the cause of those seeking to abolish the agency. According to Dyer, Arnall played no role in the effort to impeach Adams, fearing involvement might prove to be detrimental to his gubernatorial ambitions. However, Arnall voted "yes" in the unsuccessful effort to impeach Adams. The bill to abolish the department never reached the floor—perhaps due to the anticipated hostility of rural lawmakers and former commissioner of agriculture Talmadge, who now occupied the governor's office. Nevertheless, Arnall's challenge to the agriculture department confirmed the fact that he was not a typical freshman lawmaker.[29]

Although the 1933 legislature passed over two hundred bills, the state press condemned the session as a dismal failure. Even the New York *Times* lambasted the session for its "stupidity, selfishness and lack of purpose." Even though the Newnan *Herald,* Arnall's hometown paper, joined in the press's condemnation of the legislature, it nevertheless praised Arnall and Dyer for their "hard work coupled with intelligent attention to duty."[30]

Despite failure to get his legislative proposals enacted, Arnall's achievements in the 1933 session merited praise. His colleagues in the lower house had elected him to the body's second highest position even though he was one of the youngest members. Arnall, in untypical freshman style, received considerable attention in the Atlanta papers as a result in part of his outgoing personality and some of the bills that he introduced. Arnall refused to play a back-bench role during his freshman term. Nor did he quietly defer to the judgment of the senior members of the House. Instead, Arnall vigorously fought for his bills or those of the governor in committees and on the House floor. On occasion, he differed with the speaker and demonstrated a willingness to do battle with the highway department and the department of agriculture—two of the state's most powerful bureaucracies. While not able to command the focus of attention bestowed upon a governor or a speaker, the freshman legislator nevertheless had made his presence known in Atlanta.

Talmadge, having little success in getting his legislative program enacted, moved decisively after the legislature adjourned to carry out his campaign promises. He lowered the price of license tags by executive order. When the commissioner of motor vehicles balked at selling tags at the reduced price, Talmadge threatened to fire him. The beseiged commissioner quickly saw the error of his ways and agreed to sell tags at the reduced price. When the Public Service Commission, whose membership was elective, refused to lower utility rates as requested by Talmadge, the governor replaced the entire commission with his own appointees. The newly constituted commission immediately lowered rates. Talmadge then challenged the highway board by ordering it to fire five of its engineers. When two of the board members refused, Talmadge ordered the National Guard to physically remove them from their offices and replaced them with Talmadgites.[31]

While critics expressed shock at Talmadge's methods, his supporters throughout the rural areas of the state applauded his decisive leadership. Talmadge carried out most of his 1932 campaign promises by executive action. Moreover, his actions, condemned by critics as dictatorial, were upheld in the courts. Talmadge emerged from his bureaucratic battles as the strongest governor Georgia had seen since Reconstruction.[32]

In 1934 Talmadge sought reelection by campaigning on the slogan that "Talmadge keeps his promises." Arnall had not campaigned for Talmadge in 1932, but he did this time. Perhaps Arnall's willingness to become active on behalf of Talmadge in 1934 may be attributed to the fact that Arnall ran unopposed for reelection and that Talmadge looked like an easy winner. Certainly the 1934 election, in which Talmadge carried all but three counties, marked the high point of his political popularity. The editor of the Athens *Banner* concluded that "the masses are with him and his policies."[33]

The 1935 legislature, in response to the election results, demonstrated more sympathy for the governor's legislative program than had its predecessor. The legislature approved Talmadge's reshuffling of the Public Service Commission, the reduction of the price of tags, and a Talmadge-supported constitutional amendment creating the office of lieutenant governor. In fact, the legislature passed all of the Talmadge-sponsored bills with the exception of one allowing the governor to call and limit the duration of extra sessions.[34]

Arnall again sought the position of speaker pro tempore, which he won with Talmadge's endorsement and no opposition. The press considered Arnall a Talmadge leader in the House, but the youthful lawmaker did not blindly follow the governor as demonstrated by their differences over an issue involving the Board of Regents. Despite Talmadge's opposition, the board had successfully negotiated a loan and grant from the federal Public Works Administration. Talmadge requested that the legislature enact a law prohibiting the board from borrowing money. Arnall opposed the governor on this issue, leading a reporter to wonder whether Arnall was still a Talmadge loyalist. A compromise bill providing for a special appropriation for the university system in return for the regents refusing the PWA money finally passed the legislature with Arnall's support.[35]

With his brief platform enacted, Talmadge believed that the legislature had done what was necessary for relieving the depression in the state and therefore should adjourn. Rivers, Harris, Arnall, and others in the legislature differed with the governor on this point, believing that legislation should be enacted to permit Georgians to participate in New Deal programs. Talmadge's view of a negative government contrasted sharply with President Roosevelt's positive state philosophy. An example of this difference occurred over the issue of old-age pensions. Arnall cosponsored a constitutional amendment permitting the levying of taxes for the state's contribution to the old-age pensions system. The legislature overwhelmingly passed the proposed amendment. Talmadge, however, vetoed it, contending that he was opposed to all pensions except those for veterans. The governor warned that an old-age pension would be a step toward destruction, for it would make the people dependent upon the government. Despite the governor's warning, the House overwhelmingly overrode the veto with Arnall voting with the majority.[36]

Rivers revived his proposal for a sales tax that had been defeated in the 1933 session. Arnall denounced the tax calling it a plan to shift the tax burden "from the shoulders of the wealthy onto the backs of the poor." Instead of a sales tax, Arnall contended that an income tax would be a better replacement for the state's ad valorem tax system. Rivers, realizing that he did not have the votes necessary for passage, withdrew the sales tax bill from consideration. Arnall publicly congratulated the speaker for his decision.[37]

During the 1935 session, Arnall sponsored or cosponsored over thirty bills and resolutions of statewide importance—about twice as many as he had in the 1933 session. Arnall again demonstrated great interest in highway safety. He reintroduced his bill requiring a light on the rear of a horse- or mule-drawn vehicle used on state highways at night, but his bill was withdrawn after a similar bill had passed both houses. Arnall reintroduced a bill providing for the issuance of licenses to operate motor vehicles that was tabled. The legislature also failed to pass Arnall's bills to allow bail for motor vehicle violators and to provide eligibility rules for licenses for disabled veterans. However, the legislature passed an Arnall-sponsored bill establishing procedures concerning highway law violators. Arnall expressed the hope that the state would "take her place along with other progressive states by affording her citizens adequate safety legislation and highway traffic regulation."[38]

Arnall also proposed several bills of a relatively minor nature in the area of judicial organization and procedure. Arnall successfully cosponsored a bill that provided for the sterilization of criminally insane inmates in state institutions. Talmadge, however, vetoed the bill because, as he told his adjutant general, "you and I might go crazy one day, and we don't want them working on us."[39]

While Talmadge sought to reduce governmental services and regulations, Arnall introduced legislation to increase the functions of government—an indication of Arnall's difference with Talmadge's political philosophy. Arnall unsuccessfully cosponsored a bill to create a state agency to regulate accountants in the state and to create a state department of insurance. The legislature enacted a bill cosponsored by the young legislator establishing a system of farmers' markets throughout the state. Another Arnall bill, to regulate collection agencies, however, met defeat in a Senate committee.[40]

Perhaps Arnall's most interesting proposal in the 1935 session was one to create a unicameral legislature. Arnall joined Dyer in cosponsoring a proposed constitutional amendment creating a unicameral legislature. "We believe," Arnall contended, "that if the membership is cut down and each district given its representation, much more can be accomplished for the good of the State." Under the Arnall-Dyer plan, the legislature would have consisted of fifty-two members who would serve four-year terms. Even though the bill passed the committee stage, it was tabled when it reached the floor of the House. Arnall's plan revealed a willingness to challenge the status quo by reforming state government—an attitude that would later characterize his tenure as governor.[41]

While Arnall demonstrated a progressive philosophy of government for a Georgia politician in the 1935 session of the legislature, he also demonstrated that he, like Talmadge, could appeal to the fears and prejudices of his fellow Georgians as well. Arnall conceded that he "did a lot of things in those days that were purely political," such as cosponsoring a resolution condemning communism and advocating the immediate deportation of alien enemies. In a similar vein, Arnall cosponsored a resolution inviting the staunchly anti-communist William Randolph Hearst to address the House. Appealing to the isolationist feelings in the state, he cosponsored a resolution urging Georgia's United States senators to vote against America's coming under the jurisdiction of the World Court. Arnall also cosponsored a resolution condemning a proposed federal anti-lynching law as a violation of states' rights.[42]

During the 1935 session, Arnall emerged as a defender of the state against an alleged onslaught of modern-day carpetbaggers infiltrating Georgia through the ranks of federal employment. He cosponsored a resolution condemning the practice of filling administrative positions of federal agencies in Georgia "with non-resident persons who are mostly of Republican and Progressive party affiliation." In an emotional speech to the House, Arnall charged that federal agencies in Georgia were recruiting "as far away as Salt Lake City to get people to come here for jobs that Georgians need and could fill." He charged that the director of the Federal Emergency Relief Administration in Georgia was not even a Georgian but, of all things, a "New Yorker." He concluded that federal hiring practices were "nothing more nor less than carpetbagging, except that the old carpetbaggers drove the south around with bayonets while the present ones are using federal money in an effort to undermine the south." Moreover, Arnall claimed that white employees in one federal agency had been told to address black employees as "Mr., Miss or Mrs."[43]

Although Arnall's resolution passed the House unanimously, several prominent ministers issued a statement condemning Arnall's resolution and his speech. The statement contended that the overwhelming majority of employees in the FERA in Georgia were Georgians and condemned the use of "the time-worn, but ever-ready skeleton, the race issue, in an effort to incite prejudice and fear." Arnall quickly responded that the ministers' attack showed "clearly that they condone the teaching of racial equality and Yankee Republican carpetbag rule in Democratic Georgia." He urged the ministers to devote more time to preaching the gospel than to meddling in politics.[44]

In the midst of defending the state from creeping carpetbaggism, Arnall had the honor of becoming the first Georgian to receive the Distinguished Service Cross of the United States Junior Chamber of Commerce. Arnall, who served as president of the Georgia Junior Chamber of Commerce, responded at the awarding presentation that he hoped to continue in "un-selfish service to my people." Arnall, however, had no intention of con-tinuing this "unselfish service" in the legislative halls of his state. Already holding the second highest elective position in the House of Represen-tatives, Arnall had no desire to become speaker. After two terms, Arnall decided to leave the House, claiming that the major factor in his decision was economics. Arnall complained that his legislative service "required me to spend a great deal of my time doing favors for constituents for which there was no compensation." Arnall revealed the major reason for the ter-mination of his legislative service when he confessed that he "had gotten out of the legislature about all that it could offer me toward my ambition. I had met people from every crossroads in Georgia and had a nucleus of a good political organization."[45]

During the 1935 legislative session other interests besides politics com-peted for the attention of the young bachelor lawmaker from Newnan. It began with the request of his law school roommate to be a groomsman in his wedding. Arnall, who by this time was growing weary of performing such duties, postponed a decision. He finally resolved the issue by the toss of a coin with the option of being a groomsman prevailing. So, Arnall went to Orlando, Florida, to participate in one more wedding. Little did he real-ize the importance of the coin toss. He fell in love at first sight with one of the bridesmaids, Mildred Delaney Slemons, who was a beautiful and per-sonable society editor of an Orlando newspaper. After a short, whirlwind courtship, Arnall and Slemons were married on April 6, 1935.[46]

The newly married couple moved into a house next to his parents in Newnan after returning from a Caribbean honeymoon cruise. They con-structed their home with the city's first federally insured home loan on a lot purchased with money borrowed from Arnall's mother. Almost three years later, their first child, Alvan Slemons, was born. A second child, Alice Slemons, became part of the Arnall family in 1945. The Arnalls were de-voted parents and remained happily married until Mildred's death in 1980. Mildred Arnall disliked politics but tolerated her husband's interest out of love for him. Throughout their marriage, she refused to play an active role in her husband's political activities. In spite of this difference, the Arnalls shared many common interests. Both enjoyed movies, dancing, and in par-ticular taking trips together. Each summer after their marriage, they man-aged to take an extended trip. Though Mrs. Arnall liked to play golf and bridge, her husband had minimal interest in either. Occasionally, he could be coaxed into a game of gin rummy. Arnall continued to enjoy reading books and, like his father, enjoyed smoking a good cigar.[47]

Arnall rightly received praise for his service in the legislature. Roy McGinty, the editor of the Calhoun *Times,* observed that "members of the House respect him for his tact, for his knowledge of government, and for his progressive view point." His hometown paper, the Newnan *Herald,* praised Arnall for his constructive role in the legislature and even endorsed him for the lieutenant governorship in the 1936 election. A reporter for the Atlanta *Journal* agreed that Arnall was a "logical contender" for the office of lieutenant governor. The *Constitution* concluded that Arnall's record of achievement during his short public career was "not only impressive but presages broader service and greater honors from his fellow citizens. Keep your eye on Ellis Arnall!"[48]

Clearly, the happily married Arnall had political ambitions beyond service in the legislature. He possessed a level of self-confidence and motivation that was unusual even for a politician. As a legislator, Arnall demonstrated a willingness to assume the role of reformer and, by the end of his legislative career, had aligned himself with the more progressive wing of the state's Democratic party. At the same time, however, Arnall displayed a willingness to protect his political base by catering to the conservatism of his constituents by his anti-communism, his opposition to a federal anti-lynching law, and his Talmadge-like attack upon modern-day carpetbaggers. As the legislative stage of his political career drew to a close, Arnall looked forward to new opportunities of service to aid his determined quest for the governorship. The Atlanta *Constitution* had correctly urged Georgians to keep an eye on the youthful, energetic, and politically ambitious resident of Coweta County.

2

This

Splendid

Young

Man

The 1936 primary provided Georgians a rare opportunity to choose between conflicting philosophies of government. Eugene Talmadge, the foremost critic of the New Deal in Georgia, ran for the U.S. Senate that year. He ran as a staunch foe of the New Deal against the incumbent senator, Richard B. Russell, Jr., who campaigned as a New Dealer. Charles Redwine carried the banner of Talmadgeism in the governor's race, while Ed Rivers opposed him by promising the voters a "Little New Deal."[1]

Arnall contemplated entering the 1936 primary as a candidate for lieutenant governor. Governor Talmadge had successfully persuaded the legislature in 1935 to propose a constitutional amendment creating the office of lieutenant governor with the voters determining the amendment's fate in the 1936 general election. Arnall, however, had reservations about an office in which "you only preside over the Senate and wait for the governor's heart to stop beating." The voters also had reservations about the lieutenant governorship because they overwhelmingly failed to ratify the amendment. After deciding not to seek public office in 1936, Arnall actively supported Rivers's successful gubernatorial candidacy.[2]

The decisive triumph of Rivers and Russell in 1936 heralded the reemergence of bifactionalism in the state's Democratic party. Prior to the Civil War, Georgia had experienced a two-party system in which whites divided over issues. After Reconstruction, however, white Georgians united in the Democratic party in order to maintain white supremacy. Despite occasional challenges from disgruntled Georgians such as the Populists in the 1890s, political warfare took place within the confines of the Democratic party.[3]

Early in the twentieth century the state's electorate had divided into the Hoke Smith and Clark Howell factions. By the 1920s, however, that bifactionalism had been replaced by multifactional politics. Eugene Talmadge's entry into gubernatorial politics in 1932, however, changed the nature of Georgia's political system back to one bifactional in nature. V. O. Key, Jr., attributed the reemergence of bifactionalism to Talmadge's personality as well as his race and class appeal. Ironically, the leaders of the anti-Talmadge faction—Rivers, Arnall, and Harris—had once been supporters of Talmadge. The two factions provided a degree of choice to the voters, with the Talmadge faction offering the most conservative programs and policies.[4]

The anti-Talmadge faction won its first electoral battle with Rivers's election as governor in 1936. Because of Arnall's support in that campaign, Rivers offered Arnall a position in his administration. Arnall had long viewed the attorney generalship as a stepping-stone toward the governor's office. Unfortunately for Arnall, Manning J. Yeomans, who had been first elected attorney general in 1932, gave no indications of retiring. In fact, the elderly but well-liked gentleman had just been reelected in 1936. Unable to assume the top position in the state's law department, Arnall asked Rivers to appoint him to the position of assistant state attorney general. At that time, a governor could appoint several assistants to the attorney general.[5]

Arnall anticipated that the elderly Yeomans would not seek reelection in 1938. As a candidate with experience in the law department, Arnall reasoned that he would be in an advantageous position in running for Yeomans's position in 1938. Rivers agreed and appointed Arnall assistant state attorney general in January 1937. The Newnan *Herald* observed that the appointment "comes as no surprise to those familiar with the state's political picture."[6]

As an assistant state attorney general, Arnall assumed the role of liaison between the governor and the attorney general in legal matters. Rivers had grown dissatisfied with the elderly Yeomans's slow pace of rendering opinions. Because of the increase in legislation and guidelines relative to New Deal programs, requests for legal opinions from the attorney general's office had increased substantially. Both Rivers and Arnall saw Yeomans as struggling with the increased workload, forcing Arnall to assume more of the responsibility of writing opinions relative to New Deal activities.[7]

Despite his age and his discontent with the legal work generated by the New Deal, Yeomans decided to seek a fourth term in 1938. Although he had strong opposition from former congressman John S. Wood, the voters reelected Yeomans. Rivers, also reelected in 1938, encouraged Arnall to persuade Yeomans to retire as attorney general in return for an appointive position in the administration. Arnall successfully persuaded the attorney general to assume the directorship of the State Hospital Authority, a state agency recently created. Arnall argued that the directorship paid more than the attorney generalship and that it was an appointed rather than an elected office, which meant that Yeomans would not have to undergo the ordeal of periodically campaigning to stay in public life. Following the resignation of Yeomans, Governor Rivers appointed Arnall attorney general on February 2, 1939.[8]

According to Arnall, Yeomans was "so glad to get out of this New Deal stuff that he accepted the directorship." Margaret Yeomans, however, claimed that her husband's resignation was primarily due to his failing health and the necessity of lightening his official duties. Arnall, at thirty-one years of age, became Georgia's and the nation's youngest attorney general. The Atlanta *Constitution* observed that Arnall "brings to his important duties an experience, ability and knowledge of the law that foreshadows a highly satisfactory tenure." Congratulations on Arnall's appointment even came from Talmadge, who praised "this splendid young man whose career began in my administration when he was elected speaker pro tem." In fact, Talmadge had given Arnall his first political appointment when he had designated him a special assistant attorney general in 1935 to oversee the liquidation of a bank in Coweta County.[9]

Arnall believed Rivers appointed him attorney general because of his innovativeness shown as an assistant attorney general. Arnall demonstrated an "inventive and innovative nature" in the creation of the State Hospital Authority. A pressing need for additional facilities at the state mental hospital in Milledgeville had existed for years. Rivers had promised in his gubernatorial campaigns to bring about improvements at the hospital. Federal matching funds for public works projects existed, but a financially strapped state lacked the money to match federal grants. In addition, the state constitution prohibited the state government from borrowing.[10]

Arnall claimed credit for suggesting a way out of the dilemma by creating an independent corporation that would have the authority to sell self-liquidating bonds, the proceeds of which would go to matching federal grants. The proposal did not create a state debt since an independent entity was selling the bonds instead of the state nor did the proposals pledge the credit of the state to underwrite the bonds. When Arnall's efforts to sell the bonds to skeptical financiers in New York failed, the Reconstruction Finance Corporation, with the encouragement of President Roosevelt, purchased them. The revenue generated by the bonds allowed the State Hospital Authority to construct several new buildings at the hospital, one of which was later named after Arnall.[11]

Arnall ran for reelection in 1940 unopposed. He attributed the lack of opposition to his using "every minute to strengthen my political position." In addition to numerous speaking engagements he had undertaken while in office, Arnall recalled that he

> had a press service, a clipping service, and we took every paper in Georgia, every rural paper, every county paper, every daily paper, and we clipped everything having to do with local people. For example, if a man became president of a bank—he got a letter from me, a personal letter on attorney general stationery commending him and wishing him much success and happiness as president of the Bank of Chattooga County. If there was a death in the family, they heard from me . . . if a man was elected county commissioner, he heard from me; mayor, he heard from me. And I built up a local contact following that was very powerful.[12]

The voters reelected Arnall in 1940 and also returned Talmadge to the governor's office. Some speculation arose that Arnall and Talmadge had made a political deal in which Arnall would not actively support a candidate against Talmadge while a Talmadge candidate would not enter the race against Arnall. The attorney general denied any arrangement with Talmadge because "it was not necessary to deal," contending that no one could have defeated him for the attorney generalship in 1940. Herman Eugene Talmadge, his father's campaign manager in 1940, denied knowledge of any deal between Arnall and his father.[13]

Arnall held the office of attorney general for almost four years. He generally rendered legal opinions based on what he considered to be the intent of the legislature, court decisions, or the state constitution. On one occasion, state superintendent of schools M. D. Collins had asked Arnall whether the department of education had the authority to furnish textbooks and teachers to children in a private charity hospital. Citing a law that limited such services to the public schools or institutions operated by the state, Arnall held that the department had no such authority to provide textbooks to the hospital even though it was a "most worthwhile institution."[14]

In another opinion, Superintendent Collins asked Arnall whether the department of education could allow children of defense workers who had temporarily moved to Georgia from another state to attend the state's public schools. Arnall held that the children's parents had to establish a domicile in the state and pay taxes for the support of the public schools in order for them to attend public schools in Georgia. Arnall also ruled that the state had no obligation to furnish free textbooks or library books to temporary residents. On another occasion, the superintendent of a local public school system asked Arnall whether denominationalism could be taught in public schools. Citing a provision of the Georgia Constitution that prohibited public funds from being used "directly or indirectly in aid of any church, sect or denomination," Arnall ruled that state school funds could not be used to teach denominationalism in the public schools.[15]

During his term as attorney general, Arnall appeared as a protector of individual rights in several opinions. In one case, a county board of education had prohibited married females of school age from attending schools under its jurisdiction. Superintendent Collins inquired of Arnall as to the legality of such a policy. Arnall noted that appellate courts in Georgia had never ruled on the question but that the supreme court of Mississippi had. While conceding the Mississippi case was not binding on Georgia's courts, he concluded that it was "most likely" that such a policy would be invalidated if adjudicated in Georgia. Arnall therefore ruled that a policy making marriage the sole grounds for denying a child of school age to attend the public schools "unreasonable and void." In another case, a police chief asked Arnall to rule on the validity of a city ordinance that made it a misdemeanor to drive "in such a manner as to indicate either a willful or wanton disregard for the safety of persons or property." Arnall replied that "from a legal standpoint, this ordinance would be too vague and indefinite to be enforceable." Arnall also held that drug addicts could not be admitted to the state hospital for the insane or to penal institutions solely because of drug addiction.[16]

As attorney general, Arnall upheld the racial status quo. When asked about the constitutionality of the poll tax, Arnall rendered an opinion upholding the tax. At least on two occasions Arnall issued opinions pertaining to school segregation. On the first occasion, Superintendent Collins asked Arnall whether a white teacher could teach blacks in the public schools of the state. Arnall ruled against such a policy on the basis that the state constitution mandated segregated schools. A second ruling arose out of a controversy whether school buildings used by whites could be used to provide vocational training for blacks. Citing the constitutional provision requiring segregated schools, Arnall stated that the Georgia constitution "effectively prohibits the comingling of the races in the schools of Georgia and forestalls any attempt to use white schools for negroes."[17]

Nor did Arnall demonstrate a liberal attitude toward the rights of aliens. In 1938 the legislature passed a law that prohibited the state or local governments from employing an alien until a thorough investigation had been made and it was determined no qualified American citizen was available to fill the position. Shortly after Arnall became attorney general, the president of the University of Georgia inquired whether an alien, who had applied for but had not yet been granted citizenship, could teach at the university. Arnall responded that an application for naturalization did not change the status of an alien.[18]

In May 1940 Arnall sent an opinion to all state department heads reminding them that those in authority who did not comply with the 1938 law would be subject to removal by the governor. He praised state and local officials for their cooperation "in the campaign to eliminate un-American activities in our state." In the same month Governor Rivers issued an executive order requiring all aliens residing within the state to register with law enforcement agencies and be fingerprinted. While Arnall agreed with the order, the American Civil Liberties Union criticized it. Arnall cautioned against the anti-subversive campaign developing into a witch hunt and stated that his investigation of disloyalty would be conducted in a calm manner and would not turn into a campaign of fear. Although he solicited information about un-American activities, Arnall warned against providing information based on ill will or prejudice.[19]

Undeterred by ACLU criticism, Rivers continued his campaign against aliens by issuing an executive order requiring them to apply for citizenship in order to retain their occupational and professional licenses. Shortly after the order was issued, the U.S. Supreme Court struck down a state law restricting the right of aliens to work in New York. Arnall pointed out that since 1886, the Supreme Court had been ruling that aliens were entitled to the same constitutional privileges and immunities as citizens. He suggested an amendment to the U.S. Constitution limiting constitutional privileges and immunities to U.S. citizens. Congress never took action on his proposal. Arnall met with greater success in his effort to keep communist candidates off the ballot in the 1940 election in Georgia.[20]

During Rivers's first term, the philosophy of state government in Georgia shifted from one of providing minimal state services to one in which the state assumed greater responsibility for improving the quality of life of its citizens. Under Rivers's leadership, the state participated in numerous New Deal programs—an involvement that former governor Talmadge had opposed. Among other things, the General Assembly passed legislation allowing Georgia to receive federal funds for dependent children, the blind, and the aged. For the first time, Georgians participated in federal unemployment and workman's compensation programs. Expenditures for public health, highway construction, and education increased substantially. The Rivers administration instituted a program of free textbooks, provided state funds for a seven-month school term, reformed the state's penal system, and created five new state agencies.[21]

Unfortunately for Rivers, though, he had not sought additional revenue in his first term to finance his "Little New Deal." After his reelection in 1938, Rivers unsuccessfully sought to raise additional revenue. After the legislature rejected his efforts in the 1939 session, he asked Arnall whether the governor could submit a sales tax referendum to the voters without legislative authorization. Arnall responded that a governor had no such power. Lacking sufficient revenue to finance the "Little New Deal," Rivers had the unpleasant task of cutting back state services and reducing the number of state employees.[22]

By the latter half of 1939, the state owed teachers several million dollars in unpaid salaries. When two teachers filed suit to obtain their back salaries, Arnall ruled that teachers had no legal recourse because the state lacked revenue to pay the back salaries. Arnall cited section 26 of the General Appropriations Act of 1937 as the basis for his ruling. That section provided for a pro rata reduction of state spending when revenues fell below that needed to fully fund the appropriations act. Due to the specific language of the law, Arnall concluded the teachers could not use the courts to gain their unpaid salaries. Though he conceded that the state had a moral obligation to pay the teachers, Arnall suggested that teachers seek a legislative rather than a legal remedy for their money problems.[23]

Rivers envisioned section 26 as a partial solution to his revenue problems. That section, more commonly known as the "grandfather clause," applied only to state agencies funded from the general fund. The appropriations act specifically exempted several state agencies including the highway department from the grandfather clause. These agencies received their monies from allocated funds that had been earmarked for their use. The highway department, for example, received four of the six cents of the state gasoline tax. The General Appropriations Act of 1937 specifically stated that allocated fund agencies could not have their funding cut more than 3 percent during the fiscal year.[24]

In the previous fiscal year, the appropriations of the general fund agencies had been reduced to 60 percent of their original appropriation. In contrast, the allocated fund agencies received 97 percent of their appropriation. Had the grandfather clause applied across the board, all state agencies would have received almost 82 percent of their appropriations. Rivers saw the extension of the grandfather clause as a way to distribute inadequate state revenue on a more equitable basis to all state agencies. He asked Arnall for an opinion whether the grandfather clause applied to all governmental agencies. The attorney general held that the language of the law pertaining to the grandfather clause clearly limited its application to general fund agencies. Arnall expressed regret to Rivers that "I cannot agree with the construction that you would place upon the law in this instance."[25]

As Rivers's financial problems mounted, he increasingly looked to the revenue of the largest and most powerful state agency—the highway department. Rivers sought an official opinion from Arnall whether he could withhold alloated funds from the highway department. Arnall held that Rivers, by virtue of his power as governor and as director of the budget bureau, had the legal authority to withhold any funds that he believed should not be spent. Consequently, Rivers withheld the department's allocated funds. He justified his actions as necessary to conserve the revenues of the agency, which, if need be, could be diverted to other state agencies.[26]

The chairman of the highway board, M. L. Miller, became concerned over Rivers's interference in the affairs of his department and called upon Arnall for an official opinion regarding Rivers's control of the highway department. Arnall responded that the state constitution limited the attorney general to issuing official opinions to the governor only and then only when the governor made such a request. Arnall further added that he had "no desire" to be involved in a controversy between the governor and one of his appointees.[27]

The controversy intensified in September 1939 when state school superintendent Collins requested funds from the governor to pay teachers' salaries for the month. In response to the request, Rivers issued an executive order diverting almost two million dollars in highway funds to pay the teachers' salaries. Miller feared such diversions would jeopardize federal highway financial assistance. Relations between the governor and the chairman reached a crisis stage when Miller gave a speech denouncing Rivers as a dictator. Rivers responded by issuing an executive order removing Miller from the highway board.[28]

When Miller refused to leave, Rivers had him physically removed from his office. Rivers ignored a court injunction prohibiting him from interfering with Miller's conducting the duties of his office. The governor, in Talmadge-like fashion, declared martial law and used National Guardsmen to deny Miller entrance to his former office. Miller then obtained an injunction against the Georgia National Guard, which Rivers ignored. A superior court judge held the state's adjutant general in contempt of court and sentenced him to a jail term. Rivers promptly granted the adjutant general a pardon. In the meantime, a superior court held that Miller was still on the board and still chairman. Rivers ignored the decision.[29]

During the midst of this controversy the federal government stopped all federal highway aid to Georgia until the status of the highway board was cleared up. In response to an inquiry from Rivers, Arnall ruled that two members of the three-member highway board "irrespective of which two that may be, hold a legal and valid title of their offices and constitute a quorum." Arnall carefully avoided ruling on the sticky question of who was chairman. Arnall and Rivers finally persuaded the Federal Works Administrator to release the federal funds for Georgia. Arnall expressed his gratification that Georgia would "not suffer loss of federal funds by reason of the unfortunate highway row." [30]

Since the governor chose to ignore the orders of the state's superior courts, Miller turned to the federal courts. Federal District Judge Bascom S. Deaver of the Middle Georgia District Court held that Miller had been deprived of his constitutional rights without due process of law. In February 1940 Judge Deaver ordered the governor to comply with the state courts' orders. Rivers refused to abide by Deaver's order, and the National Guard continued to deny Miller admittance to his office. Deaver then ordered Rivers to appear before him to show cause why he should not be held in contempt. On the night of March 15, 1940, a federal marshal arrested Rivers after he had given a speech in Macon. Rivers was released on his own recognizance. Two days later Arnall issued a statement that he was not "officially interested" in who was right in the Rivers-Miller dispute but that he was "officially and tremendously interested when the Governor of Georgia, whoever he may be, is threatened with fine or imprisonment by a federal judge because he, as Governor, undertakes to do what he conceives to be his duty, no matter how misguided or mistaken he may be." Arnall appealed Judge Deaver's decision to the U.S. Court of Appeals for the Fifth Circuit in New Orleans, which held that the federal courts lacked jurisdiction in the case. Arnall expressed delight that the federal court believed "that internal political affairs of Georgia are not subject to regulation and control by the federal judiciary."[31]

In the meantime, the Georgia Supreme Court unanimously held that Miller was the rightful chairman of the highway board. Upon assuming his former position, Miller discovered that the other two members of the board had stripped him of his powers and had passed a rule permitting two members of the board to transact business. Arnall upheld the board's actions, leading Miller to charge that Arnall's opinion defeated "by evasion the clear intent of the Supreme Court." Although Rivers won the final battle in his lengthy confrontation with Miller, he lost the battle of public opinion. His defiance of the courts, his proclamation of martial law, his use of the National Guard, and his arrest had severely damaged Rivers's standing with the voters, who had turned to him in 1936 as an alternative to similar tactics by Talmadge. The press generally condemned Rivers's conduct in the Miller controversy.[32]

In the spring of 1940 federal investigators conducted a thorough investigation of the highway department, which resulted in four indictments by a federal grand jury. One of the indictments was against Hiram W. Evans, a former imperial wizard of the Ku Klux Klan and a close friend of Rivers. The indictment charged that Evans, an asphalt dealer, had violated federal antitrust laws by conspiring to monopolize the sale of asphalt to the state. Evans pleaded nolo contendere in federal court in January 1941 and was fined $15,000. In March 1941 Arnall, contending the price fixing had damaged the state, announced his intention to sue Evans under the Sherman Antitrust Act to recover the damages that the state had suffered. Under existing state law, however, Arnall needed the permission of the governor to file suit in federal court. Talmadge, who had been elected to a third term in 1940, readily gave his permission for a suit against a friend of Rivers.[33]

Arnall charged in federal district court that Evans had engaged in a conspiracy to control the sale of asphalt in violation of the Sherman Antitrust Act. The suit alleged that the state had been damaged in the amount of $128,027.13 through the payment of excessive prices for asphalt purchased.

Under the Sherman Act, any person, firm, or corporation could sue to recover three times the amount of the alleged damages. Arnall therefore sued
for $384,801.39. Arnall's suit, however, faced difficulties as a result of a re-
cent U.S. Supreme Court decision, *United States v. Cooper Corp.*, in which
the court held that the Sherman Antitrust Act did not include the federal
government as a "person" for the purposes of seeking damages. Citing the
Cooper case, the district court held that Georgia was not a "person" entitled
to bring suit under the Sherman Antitrust Act. A federal appellate court affirmed the lower court's decision, and Arnall appealed the case to the U.S.
Supreme Court.[34]

At the time, Arnall served as vice chairman of the National Association
of Attorneys General. He contacted every attorney general in the nation,
requesting that their state join Georgia by filing amicus curae briefs in the
Supreme Court urging reversal of the lower federal courts' decision. The
Supreme Court issued its opinion in April 1942. Associate Justice Felix
Frankfurter, who wrote the court's opinion, commented that the importance of the case was demonstrated by thirty-four states filing amicus curae
briefs supporting Georgia's arguments. In an eight to one decision, the
court held that a state was a "person" under the Sherman Antitrust Act
and therefore Georgia could bring suit under the law. Arnall contended
that this victory, which was the first time a state had won an antitrust case
in federal court, was precedent setting in that it gave political entities "the
protection given individuals and corporations."[35]

While Arnall was attorney general, an incident arose that he believed had
the potential of damaging his political future. Two young college students,
Richard G. Gallogly and George R. Harsh, had been sentenced to life imprisonment in 1928 for the murder of a drugstore clerk in Atlanta. Gallogly
came from a prominent Atlanta family who owned controlling interest
in the Atlanta *Journal*. Nevertheless, governors Russell and Talmadge had
refused to commute Gallogly's sentence. In October 1939, Gallogly took
matters in his own hands by escaping and fleeing to Texas, where he turned
himself in and pleaded for "Texas justice."[36]

Arnall would ordinarily have sent an assistant to seek the extradition of
a fugitive from Georgia's legal system. Prior to his association with the
state's law department, however, Arnall had unsuccessfully pleaded Gallogly's case for clemency. In addition, Arnall's former law partner, Stonewall Dyer, represented Gallogly in a clemency case before Governor Rivers
in May 1939. That request had been withdrawn before Rivers had made a

decision on its merits. Arnall feared suspicions would be raised about his commitment to returning Gallogly to prison if an assistant attorney general failed in the extradition effort. Cleburne E. Gregory, Jr., an assistant attorney general under Arnall and later one of his law partners, recalled that the attorney general "felt that his political future was at stake" in the outcome of the extradition hearing. As a result, Arnall concluded that he had to go personally to Texas and obtain the extradition of Gallogly.[37]

Whether Arnall succeeded depended upon the decision of the governor of Texas—W. Lee "Pass the Biscuits, Pappy" O'Daniel. Two prominent Texas attorneys represented Gallogly in his fight to remain in Texas, one of whom, state senator Jess Martin, served as the governor's floor leader in the Texas Senate and was a close personal friend and political ally of O'Daniel. The Texas newspapers provided extensive coverage of the case, and numerous stories appeared about Gallogly's alleged mistreatment while in custody in Georgia. Senator Martin even compared Gallogly's plight to that of Robert E. Burns, another well-known fugitive from Georgia justice. In that case, New Jersey's governor had refused to honor Georgia's extradition request.[38]

Gallogly's attorneys argued that Gallogly had been fraudulently induced to accept a life sentence for a pardon that never came and had been severely mistreated while in prison. Senator Martin complained of Georgia's system of "injustice." Gallogly personally made an emotional plea during the hearing in which he urged the governor not to extradite him to an uncertain future and possible death.[39]

Arnall effectively countered the arguments of Gallogly's attorneys. But more important, Arnall argued that Governor O'Daniel had only two questions to decide—whether Gallogly was a fugitive and whether Georgia's extradition papers were in order. Governor O'Daniel agreed with Arnall and ordered Gallogly to be returned to Georgia. While Gallogly's attorneys praised Arnall for the "brilliant way" in which he represented Georgia at the hearings, a bitter Gallogly criticized the attorney general. The case of Richard Gallogly faded as a potential issue in Georgia politics when Governor Rivers pardoned him on the last day of his administration.[40]

As attorney general, Arnall remained loyal to the man who had appointed him to head the state's legal department. Arnall differed, however, with Rivers on several occasions. Perhaps their biggest disagreement was over the prosecution of John E. Whitley. Shortly after Arnall's appointment, Rivers discussed with the new attorney general the possibility of the state's filing suit against Whitley, a LaGrange contractor and a close personal friend of Talmadge. Rivers believed that Whitley had overcharged the state in his selling of asphalt to the highway department. Arnall persuaded the governor that the state did not have a sufficient case against Whitley. As a result, Rivers dropped the matter, but later, without consulting Arnall, publicly announced that he had authorized the filing of a suit against Whitley for overcharging the state in asphalt sales. Arnall publicly complained that Rivers had the suit filed without his knowledge or approval as required by law. Arnall announced his intention to have the suit dismissed contending that "as long as I am Attorney General of Georgia, I propose to be Attorney General and matters of public import that involve the state's legal affairs shall be submitted to me." An embarrassed Rivers conceded that Arnall had the right to dismiss the suit. A reporter for the Atlanta *Constitution* speculated that the attorney general's action did not mean a political split had occurred between the attorney general and the governor. Rather, he viewed the episode as "a new display of the political independence Arnall has shown since his entry into political life."[41]

Despite such demonstrations of independence, however, Arnall generally sided with Rivers on legal questions. Certainly an adversarial relationship between Rivers and Arnall did not exist. Arnall, who served as attorney general during the third Talmadge administration (1941–43), frequently clashed with Talmadge. Arnall, the young, upcoming, and ambitious politician, yearned for the governorship. He had earlier differed with Talmadge as a representative in the 1935 legislative session and had supported Rivers against the Talmadge-backed gubernatorial candidate in the 1936 election. Arnall owed his position as attorney general to Rivers, who had made Talmadge the major issue in his 1936 race. Talmadge viewed the attorney general as a leader of the anti-Talmadge faction and as a potential gubernatorial opponent. While Talmadge stood as the leading anti-New Dealer in the state, Arnall had emerged as an enthusiastic supporter of Franklin Roosevelt. Recognizing their numerous differences, Talmadge generally ignored or bypassed the attorney general when he needed legal advice.[42]

The most important confrontation between Attorney General Arnall and Governor Talmadge occurred in 1941 over the membership of the Board of Regents. Talmadge had unsuccessfully attempted to persuade the board to fire Marvin S. Pittman, president of Georgia Teachers College, and Walter D. Cocking, dean of the College of Education of the University of Georgia. After being rebuffed by the board, Talmadge moved to change its membership. An assistant attorney general, Carlton Mobley, who had been appointed by Talmadge and was assigned to the governor's office, provided the governor with a legal opinion that three of the members of the board had to resign because they had been improperly appointed by Talmadge. The governor confessed that he had unknowingly violated a 1937 law which limited the number of alumni from one school on the Board of Regents to seven. Since ten of the regents were graduates of the University of Georgia, Talmadge stated that he had to remove three of these regents to comply with the law. Talmadge requested the resignation of three of his own appointees. The trio refused to resign, contending that the various schools that comprised the university had customarily been considered separate entities. Under such an interpretation, they reasoned that their appointments complied with the law. Arnall, who was vacationing when Mobley rendered his opinion, quickly overturned his subordinate's ruling in an opinion requested by the chairman of the Board of Regents. In that opinion, Arnall stated, "You may be assured that as long as I have the honor to serve as attorney general of my native state, I propose actually to be attorney general and will not allow any subordinate to speak for the Law Department without my approval, consent or concurrence."[43]

Arnall ruled that the regents involved did not have to resign because their appointments did not violate the 1937 law. Arnall concluded that the university consisted of four separate schools, a position held by governors and the legislature since the creation of the Board of Regents in 1932. Since no more than five of the present members of the board were alumni of any one of the four schools at the university, Arnall concluded that a violation of the law had not occurred. Talmadge, dismissing Arnall's ruling because he had not asked for it, charged Arnall with being "headed in the wrong direction on a one-way street." Although Arnall had temporarily stalled Talmadge's drive to control the board, Talmadge eventually prevailed. He obtained the resignation of three board members and the newly constituted board agreed to Talmadge's request to fire Pittman and Cocking.[44]

The strained relationship between the governor and the attorney general continued to deteriorate. In October 1941 the state Board of Education created a special committee to determine if the state could take over a vocational school in Monroe that was operated by a close friend of the governor. Superintendent Collins insisted that a legal opinion should be obtained prior to committee action. To satisfy Collins, Talmadge requested an opinion from assistant attorneys general Linton S. Johnson and Andrew J. Tuten, both of whom he had appointed. Without discussing the matter with Arnall, they ruled that the state could take over the school but could not assume its debts. Collins then requested an opinion from Arnall, who held as Johnson and Tuten had. An irritated Arnall wrote a blistering letter to the assistant attorneys general in which he stated that if any of them would rather take direction from the governor than from him, they should resign. Arnall announced his intentions of preventing the governor from taking over the law department as he had with other departments.[45]

Late in 1941 Arnall and Talmadge clashed over another issue—the renewal of the license of state-owned radio station WGST. Talmadge, bypassing Arnall again, appointed John E. McClure special assistant attorney general to represent the state in the proceedings. In an appearance before the Federal Communications Commission, however, Arnall argued that he rather than McClure should be representing the state in the matter. Arnall filed a formal motion with the FCC that he be recognized as chief counsel for the state. Unless granted that status, he threatened to file suit in federal court to obtain the right to represent the state. Arnall charged that McClure's appointment was made without consultation with him and was a political appointment. An irritated Talmadge appeared before the FCC to defend his appointment of McClure. Arnall contended that the Reorganization Act of 1931 gave the attorney general complete and exclusive jurisdiction in this case. The FCC finally compromised by accepting Arnall and McClure as cocounsel in the case for the state.[46]

While Talmadge increasingly viewed the attorney general with disdain and suspicion, others viewed Arnall in a more favorable light. At the close of the 1941 session, the Georgia House of Representatives unanimously passed a resolution praising Arnall for his faithful and unselfish service to the House and to the state. *Future,* the official publication of the U.S. Junior Chamber of Commerce, selected the youthful attorney general as one of the ten outstanding men of the nation in 1939. The House Economy and Efficiency Committee commended Arnall in 1939 for his efficient and economical management of the state's law department while the young executive editor of the Atlanta *Constitution,* Ralph E. McGill, praised Arnall's office for turning "out work on time and in an efficient manner." Arnall's office rendered almost 5,000 opinions and handled 780 cases, of which it won 687 for the state. His fellow state attorneys general even elected him vice chairman of their organization, the National Association of Attorneys General.[47]

Arnall effectively used his tenure as attorney general to continue to develop political alliances and to broaden his connections throughout the state. While remaining supportive of the progressive governor who gave him the opportunity to become attorney general, he continued to demonstrate a spirit of independence that had revealed itself in his legislative career. Arnall grew disenchanted with the darker side of the Rivers administration, such as the controversy with the highway board, the resort to martial law, the defiance of the judiciary, and the Evans controversy.

By the time Arnall assumed the office of attorney general, he had already broken politically with Talmadge. The relationship between the two strong-willed personalities continued to deteriorate during the governor's third term with both viewing the other as a future political adversary. Arnall realized that the governor remained the dominant political personality on the state's political horizon because of his strong support from the all-important rural voters. A successful challenge to Talmadge in a future gubernatorial race depended upon an issue that could undermine that strong support. In the spring of 1941 Talmadge provided Arnall with such an issue when he had President Pittman and Dean Cocking fired.

3

The

1942

Governor's

Race

In describing the 1942 Democratic gubernatorial primary, the Atlanta *Constitution* editorialized that "rarely, in all her history, has Georgia witnessed a more hotly contested election." Lillian Smith called it "one of the hottest, dirtiest races Georgia has ever experienced." Adding to the excitement of the campaign was the fact that the voters had recently approved a Talmadge-sponsored constitutional amendment changing the governor's term to four years effective in 1943. Talmadge wanted the distinction of being the first to serve a four-year term. Arnall, however, had other plans. The race pitted two of the state's most colorful and exciting political personalities against each other. But more important, the candidates differed sharply on a number of major issues.[1]

As part of his strategy to keep other contenders on the sidelines, Arnall entered the race early. In June 1941 he announced his intentions not to seek reelection as attorney general and denounced Talmadge as an "imitation Hitler"—an indication of the theme of his campaign. In November 1941 Arnall announced his intention of becoming a candidate in the 1942 gubernatorial primary. When qualifications closed, only two candidates—Arnall and Talmadge—had entered the race.[2]

At first glance, the odds seemed to favor Talmadge in that he had been successful in three previous bids for the office. In the 1940 primary he had won 132 of the state's 159 counties. He entered the 1942 campaign as an incumbent governor with numerous advantages. He controlled state patronage and dominated the state's budgetary process. Many observers believed the three-term governor to be at the height of his political power. One of his biographers concluded that Talmadge dominated the "political structure as few. men have done in any state's history." One historian called Talmadge "the most dynamic force in Georgia since the Populist demagogue, Thomas E. Watson." Several months before Arnall's entry in the race Ralph McGill, editor of the Atlanta *Constitution,* even predicted Talmadge's reelection because of the "great record" he had achieved during his third term as governor.[3]

In addition to the power of incumbency, Talmadge had another major advantage—campaigning experience. The governor had conducted eight statewide campaigns since 1926; Arnall had run in only one and then without an opponent. Talmadge had been elected three times as governor and three times as commissioner of agriculture. Although Talmadge had been defeated in races for the U.S. Senate in 1936 and 1938, he had never been defeated in a gubernatorial campaign. Some speculation even arose that Talmadge might seek election to the U.S. Senate in 1942 rather than seek another term as governor. If Talmadge entered the senate race, however, he would run against Senator Russell, who had given Talmadge the worst defeat of his political career in 1936. Russell, a popular former governor, had built a strong statewide political organization. Talmadge wisely entered the governor's race.[4]

Talmadge came into the campaign with a hard-core constituency of about one hundred thousand, mostly low-income farmers. To these "wool hat boys" a biographer noted, "Gene Talmadge was almost a deity." McGill maintained that the Talmadge faithful "would follow him to hell." Herman Talmadge, Eugene's son, concluded that about one third of the voters would indeed follow his father to hell while a like number wanted him in hell. The younger Talmadge observed that only Tom Watson and Eugene Talmadge enjoyed that degree of loyalty and hatred in Georgia politics.[5]

In an era when political rallies were the political and social events in a state where over 60 percent of the residents were classified as rural, Talmadge had few peers as a stump speaker. Appearing before an audience of farmers, Talmadge conveyed the impression that he was one of them—and he was. Talmadge, reared on a farm and a farmer himself, never forgot or let the farmers forget his rural heritage. The farmers believed him when he told them that he was battling their common enemies. He once bragged that the "poor dirt farmer ain't got but three friends on this earth: God Almighty, Sears Roebuck and Gene Talmadge." His political rallies, always entertaining in a time of economic stress for farmers, featured a lengthy address by old Gene himself and country music by Fiddlin' John Carson and "Moonshine" Kate, along with an abundance of good food.[6]

Talmadge's political career benefited from Georgia's unique system of nominating state officials. Instead of nominations being determined by statewide popular vote, the Georgia Democratic party had used the county unit system of nomination for decades. Each of the state's 159 counties had two county unit votes for each representative in the state House of Representatives. Representation in the lower house, however, was not based upon population. Instead, the eight most populous counties had only three representatives and six unit votes each. The next thirty most populous counties had two representatives with four unit votes each while the remaining 121 counties had one representative and two county unit votes each. In order to be nominated, a gubernatorial candidate had to receive a majority (206) of the 410 unit votes. Under the unit system, the rural and small-town counties had thirty-six more county unit votes than were needed to win. While these counties contained less than 40 percent of the adult white population, they possessed 60 percent of the county unit vote in 1940. However, the eight most populous counties, with 34 percent of the adult white population, had less than 12 percent of the county unit votes.[7]

The system significantly diminished the influence of the most populous counties and maximized the influence of the sparsely populated rural counties. It permitted the voters with the most conservative political views— white rural and small-town residents—to dominate the nomination process. The system ensured that gubernatorial candidates who hoped to be victorious had to cater to the wishes and prejudices of the voters in the small rural counties.[8]

Like his political hero Tom Watson, Talmadge appealed for votes in the rural idiom and championed the farmer. He extolled the virtues and values of rural life—individualism, hard work, and frugality as well as belief in God and white supremacy. Talmadge once boasted that he did not want to carry any county in which there were streetcars. Once he even pastured a cow on the lawn of the executive mansion in Atlanta. On another occasion, to the disgust of his well-to-do neighbors, Talmadge had a barn and a hen house built on the grounds of the mansion. While many of the more respectable members of Georgia society expressed shock and dismay at such activities of the "wild man from Sugar Creek," his rural supporters delighted in such antics.[9]

Despite his championing of the downtrodden farmers, his conservative policies and belief in negative government did little to relieve their economic stresses. Rather, he fulfilled their psychological needs in making the farmers feel important in a time when they were experiencing economic hardship and witnessing significant change. At the same time Talmadge's conservative economic and political philosophy endeared him to many of the commercial and industrial interests of the state. Although fearful of the "wild man" when he first entered the governorship, they soon grew to appreciate him because of what he stood for: low taxes, economy in government, balanced budgets, and negative government. In addition, his bitter criticism of the New Deal attracted the support of many of the state's businessmen. Key, in his classic study of southern politics, concluded that Talmadge's "strength was drawn from the upper and lower reaches of the economic scale. Industrialists, bankers, corporation executives provide funds. Poor farmers provide votes." Certainly Talmadge's 1942 campaign had ample financial support from big business interests in the state.[10]

Despite his numerous advantages—incumbency, political experience, a large number of loyal supporters, the county unit system, and adequate financial support—Talmadge entered the campaign with some notable liabilities. The issue that became the greatest hindrance to his reelection was the education issue—an issue which he had created. The controversy centered around two administrators in the University System of Georgia—Walter D. Cocking and Marvin S. Pittman. Cocking held the position of dean of the College of Education at the University of Georgia and Pittman served as president of Georgia Teachers College. In the process of upgrading the college of education, Cocking had alienated some personnel, including Sylla Hamilton, a distant Talmadge relative, who had not been rehired by Cocking. Shortly after Talmadge's inauguration in 1941, Hamilton informed Talmadge of a staff meeting that she had attended concerning the building of a demonstration school to allow graduates of the college of education to practice teach. According to Hamilton, Cocking stated that the school "was to be for both blacks and whites in order to uplift the state of Georgia." Hamilton's allegations gained the prompt attention of Talmadge, who resolved to deal with this "threat" to the racial status quo.[11]

At the May 1941 meeting of the Board of Regents, Talmadge, an ex officio member, objected to the rehiring of Cocking and Pittman. He accused Cocking of favoring racial coeducation and Pittman of engaging in local partisan politics. The regents, most of whom had been appointed by Talmadge, agreed with the governor not to rehire the two educators. However, at the insistence of Harmon W. Caldwell, president of the University of Georgia, the board agreed to allow Cocking a hearing at the next board meeting in June. At that hearing only Hamilton testified against Cocking. In contrast, several prominent Georgians, including the presidents of Emory University and Agnes Scott College and a former chairman of the board of regents, testified on Cocking's behalf. In addition, sixteen of the faculty of the college of education who had attended the 1939 staff meeting made sworn affidavits that the dean had not made the statements alleged by Hamilton.[12]

By a close vote, the board voted to reappoint Cocking and agreed to hold a hearing for Pittman at the July meeting. Stunned by the board's action, Talmadge moved to overturn the vote by changing the membership of the board. He attempted to gain the resignation of three regents who had supported Cocking. Backed by an opinion from Attorney General Arnall that upheld their right to remain on the board, they refused to resign. Eventually Talmadge managed to obtain the resignation of two regents and persuaded the board to remove another. Talmadge replaced these three members, all of whom had voted for Cocking, with appointees who shared Talmadge's views toward Cocking. With three new members on the board, Talmadge believed he had the votes to remove Cocking at the next board meeting.[13]

However, James S. Peters, an influential Talmadge supporter, attempted to persuade the governor to drop his efforts against Cocking. He feared the removal of the educators could lead to disaccreditation of the university system and to Talmadge's defeat in 1942. Both Talmadge's wife and son also attempted to dissuade the governor from his course of firing Cocking. Herman Talmadge recalled, "I knew he was making a drastic political mistake. So did my mother. We both tried to persuade him but no way on earth could you have changed his mind when he made his decision and planted his feet firmly in concrete." Eugene Talmadge had made up his mind: Cocking had to go.[14]

Talmadge justified the removal of Cocking and Pittman because he viewed them as part of a conspiracy to destroy white supremacy in Georgia. He believed that the Rosenwald Fund, a philanthropic endeavor that had been established by Julius Rosenwald, had spent millions of dollars in the South to undermine southern traditions and customs. He accused Cocking of being sent to the University of Georgia by the Rosenwald Fund for the purpose of breaking down the state's racial barriers. Talmadge viewed both Cocking and Pittman as being unsafe on the race issue.[15]

Even though Cocking had been reemployed at the regents' June meeting, Talmadge informed the dean that he should be at the hearing in July. Following two hours of hearings, the board overturned the June decision concerning Cocking and voted not to reemploy the dean. The board further voted not to reemploy Pittman on the basis of testimony that he favored racial equality, taught communism, and profited from the operation of the Georgia Teachers College farm. After several temporary setbacks, a determined Talmadge had finally removed Cocking and Pittman.[16]

Talmadge's effort to remove undesirables from the system did not stop with these two educators. The regents in the next few months removed eight other employees of the system in a manner that violated established academic procedures. Talmadge also had the state's public school system investigated to determine the extent of the Rosenwald Fund's influence there. In the July 1941 meeting of the state Board of Education, the board elected Talmadge its chairman, who appointed a special committee to investigate subversive books in the state's school system. The committee found twenty-three such books, which were promptly banned by the state Board of Education. The influence of Governor Talmadge, an ex officio member of the Board of Regents and chairman of the Board of Education, dominated the state's educational system.[17]

The removal of the two educators received almost unanimous condemnation from the state's press. The Calhoun *Times* reported that only five newspapers supported the governor on this issue. The Meriwether *Vindicator* called the hearing "the most farcical and disgraceful proceeding ever enacted in Georgia by men in high station." The Cobb County *Times* editorialized that "justice was publicly raped under the very dome of the Capitol"; the Atlanta *Constitution* called the removal of the two educators "the saddest day in Georgia's history in many, many years." Despite such condemnation, Talmadge's office was swamped with letters of support from the "wool hat boys."[18]

In an earlier term as governor, Talmadge had replaced the entire membership of the elected Public Service Commission. On another occasion, he had both the state treasurer and state comptroller removed from their offices. When the state highway department board had opposed him, he used the National Guard to remove uncooperative members. In these and other confrontations Talmadge had somehow managed to prevail. Why should his domination of one more state agency be any different? Unfortunately for Talmadge, he underestimated the power of the educational accrediting associations.[19]

Two days after the Cocking-Pittman hearings, the Southern Association of Colleges and Secondary Schools appointed a committee to investigate political interference in the University System of Georgia. The committee, concluding that the university system had suffered from "unprecedented and unjustifiable political interference," recommended that ten white units of the system be removed from the association's accreditation list. At the annual Southern Association meeting in December 1941 delegates accepted unanimously the committee's recommendation. The delegates, however, voted to delay implementation until a date a week prior to the Democratic party's 1942 gubernatorial primary. The resolution suggested that suspension would not occur if reforms were instituted to ensure the future independence of the Board of Regents. Other accrediting agencies, however, took immediate action. The University of Georgia's College of Medicine and Law School lost their accreditation. The Association of American Universities dropped both the University of Georgia and Georgia Tech from membership. Other accrediting associations followed suit.[20]

Students, educators, parents, and alumni expressed concern over the loss of accreditation. Harmon Caldwell, president of the University of Georgia, warned that if the university remained unaccredited "our beloved institution will be threatened . . . with disintegration." Chancellor Steadmon V. Sanford warned of the collapse of the university system unless it was reaccredited. Regents Chairman Sandy Beaver warned that "the accreditation question overshadows every other issue in Georgia today."[21]

In addition to the education issue, Talmadge had other problems. Critics charged him with abusing the clemency power—a power that had been bestowed upon the governor's office by the state constitution of 1877. During his first two terms, Talmadge had granted over 660 pardons; his successor, Ed Rivers, granted over 1,600 pardons. During his third term, however, Talmadge granted over 3,000 pardons, leading McGill to accuse him of holding the record among governors for issuing pardons. The Gainesville News attributed the opposition of many Georgians to Talmadge to his pardoning record. More than seventy-five grand juries throughout the state had gone on record supporting a reform of the existing clemency system. Talmadge, instead of conceding that reform of the system was needed in an effort to deflate a rising tide of criticism, vigorously defended his clemency record.[22]

In addition to the pardon racket charge, Talmadge had the liability of a long-standing strained relationship with President Roosevelt. By Talmadge's second term, the conservative Georgian had become one of the leading critics of the New Deal. Talmadge had lead the opposition to Roosevelt's renomination in 1936 and had run for the U.S. Senate that year as an anti-New Dealer. Some observers even believed that Talmadge had intended to run on an anti-New Deal platform in 1942 until the Japanese bombed Pearl Harbor. Despite his repeated claims throughout the campaign of promised cooperation with Roosevelt in fighting the war, many still suspected Talmadge of being anti-Roosevelt.[23]

Although Talmadge had enjoyed some strong support from the state's newspapers in earlier campaigns, the state's press overwhelmingly opposed Talmadge in 1942. The Atlanta *Journal* claimed that ninety-seven newspapers supported Arnall, but only eighteen endorsed Talmadge. The *Journal,* one of the governor's most adamant critics, contended that Talmadge should be defeated because he had never represented "the Georgia that stands for freedom, enlightenment and progress." The Thomaston *News* reminded Georgians that Talmadge had issued thousands of pardons, had vetoed the free schoolbook law, the old-age pension law, and the seven-month school law, and had always fought President Roosevelt. A south Georgia daily, the Americus *Times-Recorder,* editorialized that the issue was whether the state wanted democracy or rule by "a dictatorial demagogue"; the Cordele *Dispatch* concluded, "GENE IS SYNONYM FOR ILLITERACY AND STUPIDITY." The Moultrie *Observer* opposed Talmadge because of "his deep-rooted objection to orderly government." The Vidalia *Advance* believed that Arnall should be elected in order to "restore decency, dignity, and democracy in Georgia." The Augusta *Chronicle* warned Georgians not to lose sight of the paramount issue in the campaign—Talmadge had brought about the loss of accreditation of the university system.[24]

In addition to these problems, Talmadge's campaign experienced organizational difficulties as well. Throughout the election, some prominent Talmadge supporters publicly defected from the ranks of the governor. Several resigned from positions in the government; others resigned from the governor's staff. The newspapers revealed almost on a daily basis the desertion of former Talmadgites for various reasons. Two defectors in particular damaged the Talmadge candidacy. Sandy Beaver, a longtime Talmadge supporter and friend, resigned from his positions as chairman of the Board of Regents and as the governor's chief of staff. Beaver publicly blamed Talmadge for the loss of accreditation of the university system. Commissioner of Agriculture Tom Linder, a powerful Talmadge supporter since 1926, also broke with Talmadge. Linder had planned to run against Senator Russell in 1942. Talmadge, though, feared a Linder campaign against Russell might result in Russell supporters voting against Talmadge in the governor's race. Despite Talmadge's concern, Linder let it be known that he still intended to take on Russell. Talmadge then had the state Executive Democratic Committee issue a rule that an office holder had to resign from his office if he sought election to another office. Linder, with two years left in his term as commissioner of agriculture, decided not to contest Russell's seat. A hurt and bitter Linder then endorsed Arnall. Linder's defection damaged Talmadge's candidacy because the commissioner, like Talmadge, had his strongest support in the rural counties.[25]

In addition to these defections, Talmadge experienced problems with the "courthouse rings"—those local politicians and leaders essential to electoral success in the county unit system. A gubernatorial race under the county unit system actually consisted of 159 separate races for the unit votes in each county. In the rural counties that generally had small electorates, Key concluded that "two or three local politicos may be able to determine who wins the county's plurality and under the county unit system plurality determined who received the county's unit vote." Talmadge tended to neglect the local politicos. "I don't worry about leaders," Talmadge once boasted; "If the people are for me, the leaders will be for me." Herman Talmadge agreed that his father tended to ignore the local political bosses.[26]

Despite Talmadge's claims of ignoring the local bosses, he did distribute money for services and promised roads and jobs in an effort to gain their support. One political scientist concluded, however, that Talmadge "failed to employ these techniques systematically, or to do so on a scale comparable with some opposition leaders." One of Talmadge's biographers also suggested that the governor in his third term had "left patronage problems except for major appointments to certain of his friends, wholly unacquainted with politics." As a result, many county leaders who had been ignored in patronage matters turned to Arnall. Thus, while Talmadge had a strong personal following, he had a weak political organization—in fact, one of the weakest of any major politician in the state's history. Despite numerous liabilities of the Talmadge candidacy, the "wild man" still remained the Goliath of Georgia politics.[27]

Arnall, hoping to become the David of Georgia politics, entered the campaign with several major advantages, foremost of which was the accreditation issue. Without such an issue, Arnall conceded that he would never have entered the race but would have waited until later to run. Arnall correctly viewed Talmadge's firing of Cocking and Pittman to have been the "worst mistake" of the governor's political career. Seeking to capitalize on that mistake, Arnall entered the campaign, promising to free Georgia's educational system from political interference. To do that, Arnall proposed the creation of constitutional state boards to oversee the state's educational systems. Arnall contended that accreditation could be restored only by making the regents a constitutional body. If elected, he assured Georgians that the first act of his administration would be to restore accreditation in order to preserve the academic credits of students and "save the investment parents have made in their children."[28]

The loss of accreditation had, in Arnall's opinion, "aroused the people" throughout the state. He believed that many of Talmadge's loyal supporters would desert him on this issue. One Talmadge supporter lamented, "The main complaint that I hear is that Talmadge is responsible for the schools of Georgia losing their credits." The Augusta *Chronicle* reminded "parents who have worked and slaved and saved and sacrificed practicing frugality and self-denial so that your children could be educated" that diplomas from the university system would no longer be accepted outside of the state. One Arnall political advertisement stated, "If you love your Boys and Girls, vote for Ellis Arnall & Save Georgia Schools." Under such attack, Talmadge found himself on the defensive for the first time in a gubernatorial campaign.[29]

Understandably, Arnall's candidacy gained the enthusiastic support of college students desirous of accreditation being restored. One historian estimated that more than 90 percent of the almost thirteen thousand students in the university system supported Arnall. The Augusta *Chronicle* called the students "the most zealous workers" in Arnall's campaign because they viewed him as their "white knight in armor." College newspapers endorsed the Arnall candidacy and Arnall for governor clubs sprang up on college campuses throughout the state. In April 1942 a statewide student political organization, the Student Political League, came into existence. The league, committed to removing political interference in the operation of the state's educational system, supported Arnall. While most students could not vote since the state's minimum voting age was twenty-one, they nevertheless played a key role in the election. Arnall observed that students "found time to canvass thousands and thousands of Georgia homes and ask neighbors and relatives and friends, and strangers they had never seen before, to vote for me." Allen L. Henson, Talmadge's sympathetic biographer, complained that colleges "practically closed while students rang doorbells, drumming up anti-Talmadge votes." [30]

Leading educators, including the presidents of Georgia Tech and the University of Georgia, Chancellor Sanford, and former regents chairman Beaver, supported Arnall. The president of the Georgia Education Association stated that teachers intended to do what they could "to preserve Georgia's educational system and its standards." Although Arnall could expect strong support from educators because of the accreditation issue, he sought to solidify that backing by promising them a "reasonable" retirement system and a salary increase. During the campaign, he urged Talmadge to increase teachers' salaries and reminded teachers that Talmadge had vetoed the free textbook and the seven-month school term bills.[31]

Throughout the campaign, Arnall feared the possibility of Talmadge's apologizing to the state for damaging the university system and promising never to interfere in the education system again. "If he had done that, he would have won," Arnall concluded. However, a stubborn Talmadge boasted late in the campaign that his packing of the Board of Regents was "the greatest service I ever rendered the state of Georgia." Arnall breathed a sigh of relief. He still had his issue undiluted by a remorseful Talmadge.[32]

Arnall's candidacy benefited from the fact that only two candidates had entered the race. Talmadge had never been in a two-man gubernatorial campaign. He had always benefited from a split in the anti-Talmadge vote with his supporters providing him pluralities in many counties. Under the county unit system, plurality rather than majority vote determined which candidate received a county's unit vote. Arnall believed that he had to be the sole challenger in order to defeat Talmadge. In an effort to establish himself in that position, Arnall announced his candidacy ten months in advance of the primary. He then undertook a campaign to ward off other potential candidates by warning that a third candidate would be put in the race by Talmadge in order to split the anti-Talmadge vote.[33]

Arnall's efforts almost collapsed when former governor Rivers and former commissioner of agriculture Columbus Roberts considered entering. Rivers blamed Talmadge for his indictment by a Fulton County grand jury early in 1942. Some observers saw Rivers running against Talmadge as a means of clearing his name. Rivers, however, announced in July 1942 that he would not enter the race and threw his support to Arnall. Roberts, who had run a strong second to Talmadge in 1940, seriously considered entering the race. Arnall dispatched Roy V. Harris to persuade Roberts not to enter. The former commissioner finally decided not to run. He later endorsed Talmadge's candidacy. Much to Arnall's relief, the race remained a two-man affair.[34]

Arnall had a significant advantage in that he assembled a political organization that compensated for his lack of experience in running a statewide campaign. William Y. Atkinson, Jr., a close personal friend from Newnan, directed Arnall's campaign with the assistance of Revenue Commissioner Melvin E. Thompson. The Arnall campaign had the backing of two of Georgia's most adept county unit politicians—Rivers and Harris. Although discredited in the eyes of many Georgians, Rivers still had supporters and county leaders loyal to him throughout the state. Rivers actively supported his former attorney general, causing Talmadge to complain that Rivers was "out working for Ellis Arnall and hitting every spot he can." Harris proved to be even more indispensable to Arnall's candidacy. In fact, one observer called him "the most important man—outside of Arnall—in the attorney general's campaign." Harris knew county unit politics and county leaders better than anyone else in Georgia. McGill called him the best political organizer in the state. Arnall agreed, calling Harris "the best politician I have ever known." Harris had managed Rivers's successful gubernatorial campaign in 1936 and had played a major role in Senator George's defeat of Talmadge in 1938. With both Rivers and Harris actively working on his behalf with the county leaders, Arnall enjoyed a significant advantage. An indication of Talmadge's difficulty with county leaders came when Arnall gained the endorsement of two of the state's best known political organizations: the Cracker party in Harris's home county of Richmond and the Democratic party organization in Chatham County. Both had supported Talmadge in 1940.[35]

Arnall had not been politically idle while attorney general but had used that time to make political contacts in every county in Georgia. He spoke at numerous school functions and civic clubs throughout the state. Arnall also employed a clipping service of all the state's newspapers that "clipped everything having to do with local people." Using that information, Arnall sent out numerous congratulatory and sympathy letters on attorney general stationery. In addition, the attorney general mailed five thousand postcards every Christmas to supporters and county leaders throughout the state. He also corresponded frequently with influential local leaders. Arnall even hired two men who sold supplies to local governments to find out who local politicians supported in the governor's race. "As they would feed me these names—the ones for me—I would write them a letter or call them on the telephone and tell them I had heard they were for me and how much I appreciated it."[36]

Arnall—energetic, enthusiastic, and twenty-three years younger than his opponent—ran a vigorous campaign against the fifty-eight-year-old Talmadge. He carried his message to the people by giving numerous speeches throughout the state and by holding weekly statewide radio broadcasts. One reporter wrote that Arnall "conducted the most extensive handshaking campaign ever undertaken by a gubernatorial candidate, going into almost every county . . . and speaking in more than half of them." Arnall presented an appealing image of a youthful reformer committed to restoring democracy and good government to Georgia. Arnall also demonstrated during the campaign that he, like Talmadge, could excite an audience with his oratory. Arnall's campaign appearances drew large crowds. At his kickoff rally, fourteen thousand of his supporters descended upon Newnan and consumed one hundred pit-barbequed pigs and twelve hundred gallons of Brunswick stew.[37]

Arnall's campaign had sufficient financial resources. In fact, he claimed that he didn't worry about money because his key financial supporters told him to "get out and win the election. We will finance you." Although Talmadge enjoyed the support of Georgia Power Company, highway contractors, and many textile and railroad officials, Arnall's financial support included backing from banking and insurance interests, oil companies, friends of the university system, and the Coca-Cola Company. Arnall's ability to raise money was aided by the fact that he was the only anti-Talmadge candidate in the race, and that he had a good issue to use against Talmadge.[38]

In addition to having adequate finances, Arnall had the overwhelming support of the Georgia press. The Atlanta *Journal* claimed that over 85 percent of the state's newspapers that had taken a stand in the race supported Arnall. The Vidalia *Advance* believed Arnall could "restore Georgia to the place she so rightfully and richly deserves." The Atlanta *Constitution* argued that "the Arnall platform promises redemption of Georgia from all the harm done the state during the Talmadge administration"; the Moultrie *Observer* predicted that the election of Arnall "would be the dawning of a new day in Georgia politics." Another paper, the Brunswick *News,* concluded that Arnall should be elected because the time has come to retire Talmadge from public life. The Augusta *Chronicle* believed Arnall's election would restore the state's dignity and good name, which had suffered because Talmadge had "made Georgia the laughing stock of the nation."[39]

During a time when the nation was fighting dictatorial regimes overseas, Arnall effectively used the dictatorship issue against Talmadge. The attorney general proclaimed that a major issue in the election was democracy versus tyranny and presented his campaign as "a crusade to uproot dictatorship here and to redeem the reputation and honor of our state." Arnall warned Georgians that the "Hitler pattern" of government had already taken shape in Georgia with Talmadge's reckless abuse of gubernatorial power. Arnall proposed a reform program "to destroy the Georgia gubernatorial dictatorship." As the central plank in his program, he proposed the creation of a constitutional Board of Regents and a constitutional state Board of Education to remove gubernatorial domination of the state's educational system. He also called for the creation of a constitutional board to take over gubernatorial clemency power. Other proposed reforms included removing the governor from governmental boards, stripping the governor of the power to remove the comptroller-general and the state treasurer from office, transferring the power to appoint the state auditor from the governor to the legislature, and denying the governor the power to fire state employees.[40]

Arnall promised not only to restore democracy to Georgia's state government but to return honesty and efficiency to the state capitol as well. Challenging Talmadge's claim of economical and fiscally conservative management of state finances, Arnall charged the Talmadge administration with hiring more state employees and spending more money than any administration in the state's history. He charged Talmadge with numerous violations of good government practices such as abusing the pardoning power, forcing state employees to make political contributions, using state employees for partisan political activities, and practicing nepotism. Arnall accused the Talmadge administration of being tainted by its association with undesirables such as "political racketeers, Atlanta underground characters, gamblers, pardon brokers, and clemency merchants." According to Arnall, public policy was not made in the capitol but "in hotel rooms filled with stuffy cigar smoke, around tables filled with liquor bottles in the late hours of the night." In place of such a corrupt regime, Arnall promised "a decent administration injected with a big dose of common honesty." He further promised an economical administration in which new or higher taxes would not be needed.[41]

Arnall also sought to capitalize on Talmadge's well-known opposition to President Roosevelt. Despite the voters' rejection of the Roosevelt candidate in the 1938 senatorial race in Georgia and the leftward leanings of the New Deal, President Roosevelt's personal popularity remained high in the state. Unlike Talmadge, Arnall had been closely associated with the president, having served as state director of the Roosevelt-Wallace clubs in Georgia in the 1940 presidential election. In February 1942 candidate Arnall visited Washington for a well-publicized meeting with Roosevelt. Throughout the campaign, Arnall accused Talmadge of being uncooperative with the president in the war effort. "There will be no sabotage of our war effort," Arnall assured voters if he were elected, "because there will be no sour, captious, contentious, rebellious hater of everything for which Franklin D. Roosevelt has stood." Arnall contended that the governor of the state should be someone who could cooperate with the national administration and "who admires devotedly our commander-in-chief." Although Roosevelt never publicly endorsed Arnall, he provided behind-the-scenes support to him.[42]

In an effort to blunt the Arnall attack, Talmadge stressed his accomplishments, which included reducing the state debt, paying teachers their back pay, reducing state property taxes, cutting utility rates, lowering the price of automobile tags, and accumulating a surplus of $10 million in the state treasury. He promised to continue to operate the "state on a safe, sane, conservative basis" and not to raise taxes. In contrast, Talmadge claimed that Arnall lacked a record of accomplishment and had a "wholly unimpressive career." Talmadge reminded farmers that Arnall had proposed doing away with the state Department of Agriculture while serving in the legislature. The governor accused the attorney general of rendering opinions detrimental to school teachers, counties, old-age pensioners, and the people. Moreover, Talmadge reminded Georgians that the Arnall family wealth was "wrung from the labor of the poor" and that Arnall "was sent to a fashionable play-boy school outside of the state."[43]

Talmadge also sought to link Arnall with the discredited Rivers administration. Talmadge wrote to one supporter, "I am going to hammer 'Rivers-Arnall' and 'Arnall-Rivers' throughout the campaign." In his speeches, Talmadge usually referred to the Rivers administration as the Rivers-Arnall administration, which he claimed had "a program of extravagance which left Georgia in the worst shape, financially and otherwise, in history." He accused the Rivers-Arnall administration of engaging in a spending orgy that left the state with a debt of over $29 million. Talmadge accused Rivers of appointing Arnall attorney general to uphold Rivers's every move. Talmadge charged the attorney general, whom he called "Little Boy Blue" throughout the campaign, of sleeping "through a carnival of sin and corruption and thievery so notorious that the press of the nation have referred to it as the blackest pages of Georgia history." Talmadge tried to paint the election as a choice between financial stability and financial ruin. A Talmadge political advertisement stated, "We know what Arnall-Rivers will do—raise taxes, create debts and close the schools and cut off old age pensions." The newspapers supporting Talmadge generally cited his conservative handling of state finances as a major reason for his reelection.[44]

Throughout the campaign Talmadge belittled the major issue of the race—the question of accreditation. He assured voters that the state could create its own accrediting agency if the need existed and accused the Southern Association of withdrawing accreditation "in an effort to defeat me." After his reelection, Talmadge assured students and parents that "those credits are going to come running back to Georgia so fast that a Greyhound bus couldn't catch them." Moreover, he promised Georgians that his reelection would ensure that the University of Georgia would be the greatest university in the country for white students.[45]

Realizing that the education issue had placed him on the defensive, Talmadge sought to convince the voters that southern traditions and customs rather than education was the main issue in the race. "It is absurd," Talmadge told a statewide radio audience, "to say that there is no movement to promote racial equality in Georgia." He contended that "misguided people" had been trying to impose racial equality on the South since the War Between the States. Talmadge accused Cocking and the Rosenwald Fund of leading the latest assault on the southern way of life. He claimed that Cocking was an employee of the Rosenwald Fund, whose real purpose was "to try to get negroes into the University of Georgia." However, Talmadge reassured the voters that, as long as he were governor, "The niggers will never go to a school which is white." Talmadge proudly designated himself "the champion of white supremacy in Georgia" and called upon the voters to maintain the tradition by returning him to the governor's office.[46]

Arnall undercut Talmadge's white supremacy campaign by stressing his own commitment to the southern way of life. One of Talmadge's biographers concluded that "two racists opposed each other with one identified with closing the colleges, the other with keeping them open and accredited." Arnall reminded voters that he was a native Georgian whose ancestors had lived in the state long "before the ancestors of my opponent came down from New Jersey." The attorney general praised the "wise provision" in the state constitution requiring segregated schools. He assured Georgians that the provision would remain intact in the constitution if he were governor and that southern traditions and customs "will always prohibit co-education of the white and Negro races." He denounced the rumor that he favored coeducation of the races as "the biggest lie and the most bunk and baloney that has ever been thought up." On another occasion Arnall even resorted to demogoguery by telling an audience that "if a Negro ever tried to get into a white school in the section [of the state] where I live, the sun would not set on his head. And we wouldn't call on the governor or the State Guard, either."[47]

Arnall, stressing that white supremacy in Georgia was not threatened by his candidacy, charged Talmadge with raising the race issue in a last ditch effort to hang on to the governorship. Arnall called the race issue a false issue since the state constitution clearly provided for school segregation and because both candidates favored segregation. The leadership of the state's system of higher education—Chancellor Sanford, former regents chairman Beaver, and University of Georgia President Caldwell—also rejected Talmadge's claim of a threat to white supremacy. The former regents chairman contended, "There is not and never has been any danger of co-education of the whites and colored in the University System of Georgia." The press also criticized Talmadge's use of the race issue. "Old Gene must think the people of Georgia are dumbbells," the Thomaston *Times* concluded. The Americus *Times-Recorder* dismissed race as a phoney issue because "Georgians are strongly of the same opinion in regard to the negro question." The Augusta *Chronicle* criticized Talmadge for manufacturing "a racial issue where none existed before."[48]

To the relief of the weary voters, the long and bitter campaign finally ended on September 9, 1942. Arnall received 174,757 votes, or almost 58 percent of the popular vote and 261 unit votes. Talmadge obtained 128,394 votes and 149 unit votes. In order to win the primary, Arnall had to sweep the four-unit and six-unit counties and break even in the two-unit counties. Arnall did exactly that. He carried most of the four-unit counties, all of the six-unit counties, and fifty-six of the 121 two-unit counties.[49]

Several factors accounted for Arnall's victory, the most important one of which was the loss of accreditation of the university system. Both Arnall and Talmadge as well as most observers attributed the election outcome primarily to the education issue. As one historian concluded, the issue "aroused Georgians as no other event had done in Talmadge's long and tumultuous career." In addition, Arnall's candidacy benefited from a unique situation in that the anti-Talmadge vote was not split between several candidates. Arnall had a strong organization, enjoyed adequate financial support, and conducted a well-run campaign. Senator Russell praised Arnall for his campaign that "was intelligently planned and tirelessly and courageously conducted." Arnall's reform campaign also benefited from a rising tide of idealism and commitment to democratic principles of a people at war with dictatorship overseas. His campaign also enjoyed the overwhelming support of both the state's rural and urban press, causing Talmadge to complain after the primary that unfair newspaper coverage put him at a disadvantage in the campaign. He charged the press with creating "a sentiment that Arnall would win, and this put the bandwagon crowd against us." Surely a bandwagon mentality existed among many county leaders, and as Thomas Elkin Taylor observed, "Nobody is fonder of picking a winner than a county political boss."[50]

With the press and a majority of the voters rejecting his call to arms to defend southern traditions and customs, Talmadge ultimately failed to convince a sufficient number of voters that race was the major issue in the campaign. While Talmadge failed in his efforts to persuade enough voters that white supremacy was at stake, Arnall persuaded enough voters that Talmadge presented a clear and present danger to the well-being of education in the state. Talmadge thus returned to his farm on Sugar Creek, and Arnall went to the governor's mansion in Atlanta.

4

The

1943

Legislative

Session

The outcome of the 1942 primary generated widespread comment not only in Georgia newspapers but also in the regional and national press as well. The Pittsburg *Courier*, a black newspaper, optimistically proclaimed, "Talmadge's Defeat Proves Race Issue Is Dead in Dixie." Another black paper, the Chicago *Defender*, hailed Arnall's victory as evidence of a democratic awakening in the South. The Washington *Post* praised the election for ending Talmadge's political career, while the New York *Herald-Tribune* editorialized that Georgia deserved congratulations for denying Talmadge another term. *Time* magazine hailed Talmadge's defeat because it ended the reign of one of the worst dictators in American politics since Huey Long.[1]

Southern newspapers such as the Richmond *Times-Dispatch* and the New Orleans *Times-Picayune* expressed pleasure at Talmadge's political demise. The *Nation,* a liberal publication, agreed that Arnall was preferable to Talmadge but concluded that "this is surely a new low in compliments." In a similar vein, the *People's Voice,* a black newspaper in Harlem, predicted that Arnall's election "will not mean a new birth of freedom for either the poor whites or the blacks of the state." The *Voice* pessimistically concluded that Arnall was "far from the sort of man who can bring Georgia back into the Union."[2]

Within the state, many papers that had opposed Talmadge's election expressed unconcealed pleasure over his defeat. The black-owned Atlanta *Daily World* even concluded that Talmadge's defeat meant white supremacy no longer had an "alluring appeal" among the white rural masses. The Moultrie *Observer* believed Arnall's election had redeemed the state's good name; the Bartow *Herald* editorialized that the state's leadership was passing "from a man who has brought us into nationwide ridicule." The Valdosta *Times* predicted "an era of bigger and better things" for the state under Arnall's leadership, and the Augusta *Chronicle* believed the state would have honest and progressive government under Arnall's direction. The Milledgeville *Union-Recorder* even went so far as to deem Arnall's victory "a great triumph for the forces of righteousness." Many Georgians agreed with a Cobb County *Times* editorial that Arnall would restore dignity to the governor's office.[3]

President Roosevelt took great joy in the outcome of the Georgia election, so much so that he invited Arnall to the White House to personally congratulate him. Arnall then returned to the state to attend the Democratic party's state convention in Macon. After officially being designated the party's gubernatorial nominee, Arnall gave an eloquent acceptance speech. Ralph McGill compared it to those given by such giants of Georgia politics as Robert A. Toombs or Alexander H. Stephens. Arnall promised to inaugurate "a new day for Georgia. A day of understanding, a day of progress, a day of reformation, a day of freedom and development for our people." Arnall boasted that the Talmadge brand of "peanut politics" and "disreputable state government" had been driven from the halls of state government.[4]

On the eve of Arnall's inauguration, the state auditor issued a report that the state had debt of almost $36 million. The governor-elect called the size of the debt appalling and admitted that he had not realized it was so large. In addition to the debt problem, Arnall had to deal with a substantial reduction in state revenue because of the war economy. At that time, a gasoline tax constituted the state's major source of revenue. Federal rationing of gasoline had resulted in a substantial reduction of tax revenue by an estimated $10 million a year. The state also stood to lose a possible $5 million per year because of exemptions granted to Georgians on their federal income taxes. The state auditor warned that Georgia faced "dark days ahead because of the curtailment of revenue." Arnall faced the unpleasant responsibility of having to operate the state as well as to cope with the state debt with declining revenue. Since he had campaigned on the promise of not raising taxes, he conceded, "We are going to have a real job to finance state operations during the next four critical years."[5]

On January 12, 1943, the thirty-five-year-old Arnall took the oath of office as Georgia's seventy-first and the nation's youngest governor. In his inaugural address, Arnall urged the legislature to enact his reform platform and reiterated his campaign pledge to veto any bill raising taxes. Arnall reminded his audience, which included outgoing governor Talmadge, that his election occurred because Georgians wanted good government. He pledged to have an honest administration, requested citizens to inform him of any graft, irregularities, or corruption in state government, and promised swift action to deal with any wrongdoing. Despite numerous problems confronting the state, an optimistic Arnall pledged "to inaugurate a new and better day for Georgia." Throughout the address, a partisan crowd cheered and clapped while a dejected Talmadge looked on.[6]

Arnall realized that the success of his administration depended on the cooperation that his program received from the legislature. Unlike Talmadge, Arnall had served in the General Assembly. His two terms in the House had given him firsthand experience of the workings of the legislative process. Talmadge had usually had an adversarial relationship with the legislature; Arnall desired cooperation. The governor traditionally handpicked the presiding officers of the two houses of the legislature. Arnall continued that practice. He chose former speaker Roy V. Harris, who played a crucial role in his election, as his candidate for speaker of the House. He picked another close supporter, Frank C. Gross, as his candidate for president of the Senate, the presiding officer of the Senate. Both were elected unanimously. The reform-minded governor, totally rejecting the idea of an independent legislature, continued the practice of governors picking the standing committee chairmen. Willingness on the part of the lawmakers led by Harris and Gross to enact Arnall's reform program characterized the spirit of the 1943 legislative session. In contrast, Talmadge could not even obtain permission to deliver a farewell address to the legislature.[7]

The lawmakers quickly began consideration of Arnall's reform program. At his request, the legislature unanimously adopted a resolution of support for President Roosevelt's conduct of the war. The legislature then considered the major plank in Arnall's platform, which called for the abolition of the Talmadge-controlled Board of Regents, the creation of a new board, and the proposal of an amendment changing the board to a constitutional body. The governor insisted that the regents could be insulated from future political interference only by placing the board under the protection of the constitution. Arnall emphasized that such action was needed in order to hasten the reaccreditation of the university system. Both houses unanimously supported House Bill One, which created a new board and removed the governor as a member. The legislation retained the power of the governor to nominate regents subject to senatorial confirmation. The legislature also unanimously voted to submit to the voters an amendment making the board a constitutional body.[8]

On January 22, 1943, Arnall proudly signed House Bill One into law and proclaimed it to be a major victory for education. Shortly thereafter Arnall nominated fifteen members—all white and all male—to the newly created Board of Regents. Although the governor received praise for his nominations, the Atlanta *Daily World* criticized him for not nominating any blacks. The Senate unanimously approved the nominations the governor had made. Eight days after Arnall had signed House Bill One into law, the Executive Committee of the Southern Association of Colleges and Secondary Schools notified Arnall that accreditation had been restored to the University System of Georgia. Arnall quickly expressed gratitude for the action and praised the legislature for its role in the restoration of accreditation. As he promised in the campaign, Arnall also requested the legislature to reorganize the state Board of Education and to make it a constitutional body as well. The legislature unanimously created a new board and proposed a constitutional amendment changing the board to a constitutional body. A proud Arnall praised the legislature for its actions and pledged to continue to champion education because it was "the cure for ignorance, poverty, prejudice, hatred, and demagoguery."[9]

Arnall's reform program called for the legislature to remove from the governor the power to suspend the state treasurer and the state comptroller-general. Under existing statutes, the governor had the power to suspend the two state officials under certain conditions. Arnall recommended that the grant of such power be repealed, and the legislature unanimously agreed. He also requested that the power of the governor to appoint the state auditor be transferred to the legislature. Again the legislature unanimously complied. The lawmakers further agreed without dissent to remove the governor as a member of the governing board of all state agencies. The legislature also unanimously agreed to Arnall's request to remove the power of the governor to arbitrarily strike state employees from the budget.[10]

Arnall further proposed that the legislature abolish the allocations system by which state revenue obtained from certain taxes went to specific governmental agencies. Approximately 60 percent of the state budget was predetermined by the allocation system. Arnall requested the replacement of the allocation system with a system of specific appropriations for each state agency. The legislature unanimously agreed. Arnall submitted two appropriations bills to provide funding to operate the state government and obtained their passage without change and without an opposing vote. He called such action "without parallel or equal in Georgia's long legislative history." [11]

Arnall's reform platform also called for the governorship to be stripped of clemency power. Arnall had criticized Talmadge's abuses of that power and had proposed the creation of a constitutional pardon and parole board which would have clemency power. In response to the governor's request, the Senate unanimously approved the creation of a state Board of Pardons and Paroles. The House, however, made several changes in the bill, leading three senators to vote against the revised bill. Both houses unanimously proposed an amendment making the agency a constitutional board. Arnall praised the legislature for its actions on this request and promised never to ask the new board to pardon or parole anyone. [12]

After obtaining the passage of his reform program, Arnall urged the legislature to consider several other legislative requests. These included creating a teachers retirement system, limiting gubernatorial campaign expenditures, increasing the investigative powers of the state attorney general, creating a "non-political" game and fish commission, and lowering the state's voting age to eighteen. Arnall called for the creation of a teachers retirement system because teachers "certainly deserve special consideration at the hands of the state." With only two dissenting votes, the legislature created the state Teachers Retirement System with the provision that the system would become operational only when the governor or the legislature provided funding. Because of the state's financial difficulties, Arnall made no request in the 1943 session for state funds to implement the system. In order to have a teachers retirement system, the legislature had to propose two constitutional amendments. One provided that the taxing power of the state and local governments could be used for the purpose of paying pensions to teachers. The other authorized the payments of benefits under the retirement system. Both passed with little opposition. [13]

Arnall also asked the legislature to strengthen an office that he had previously held—the attorney generalship. Arnall pointed to a "glaring defect" in the operation of the attorney generalship in that investigations by that office had to be authorized by the governor. Arnall called for the attorney general to have the authority to initiate investigations of alleged irregularities in state agencies. Arnall accused Talmadge in the primary of having a similar bill defeated in the 1941 legislative session. This time the bill received a more favorable reception with only four dissenting votes. The governor still retained the right to order the attorney general to conduct investigations.[14]

Thus far in the legislative session, Arnall's requests had met little resistance. His effort to make Georgia the first state to lower the voting age to eighteen, however, provoked strong opposition. Arnall told the lawmakers that Georgians should be allowed to vote if they were old enough to fight for their country and asked for a constitutional amendment lowering the voting age. The proposal quickly met opposition. Senator W. W. Stark charged that the proposed amendment would enfranchise young blacks and "mix politics up in every high school and college in Georgia." Senator Stark asserted that Arnall never would have been elected if he had advocated such a proposal in the primary. Another senator, Herschel Lovett, warned that "this is a university system bill, and they want the children to control their parents." Despite such criticism, the Senate passed the amendment with three more votes than was needed in order to propose a constitutional amendment.[15]

In the House, however, the amendment encountered stronger resistance. Representative J. Robert Elliott, Talmadge's former House floor leader, led the attack. He denounced the amendment, charging that it had the support of the Communist party. He warned that their amendment would enfranchise all of the state's young people, "regardless of their race or whether they had paid their poll taxes." Another representative feared the amendment would allow the state to become a "hotbed for every subversive influence." Talmadge even came to the legislature to lobby against the amendment. At first the opposition forces prevailed. The proposed amendment fell short by thirteen votes of the required two-thirds majority needed to propose a constitutional amendment. Although Arnall had suffered his first defeat in the 1943 session, the setback proved to be temporary.[16]

The House voted to reconsider the proposal, which it did the following day. Again Representative Elliott led the opposition. He accused the governor of breaking a campaign promise of never dictating to the legislature. "During the past twenty hours, the contrary has taken place," Elliott charged. To ensure approval of the amendment when it was reconsidered by the House, Arnall engaged in a vigorous lobbying campaign. He also arranged for the Veterans Hospital to send to the capitol many busloads of wounded young veterans. Some were in wheelchairs, some were maimed, some were minus arms or legs. These disabled veterans filled the capitol. Arnall then addressed the legislature and said that it was unconscionable to tell these young men under twenty-one that although they had fought for our country and were maimed for life, Georgia would deny them the right to vote at eighteen. The stratagem worked. He prevailed on the second House vote with six votes more than needed to propose the amendment. A pleased Arnall promised to speak in every county if needed to obtain popular approval of the amendment. Several months later, Arnall carried his fight to lower the voting age before a House subcommittee, where he spoke in favor of an amendment to the U.S. Constitution lowering the voting age.[17]

During the election, Arnall had promised to "divorce the governor's office and the State Highway Board." After being elected, Arnall had second thoughts about implementing this reform. Instead, he urged the legislature to replace the existing three-man highway board with a state highway director who would serve at the pleasure of the governor and a twelve-member highway commission to be appointed by the governor. The commission, however, would have only advisory responsibilities to the director. With only seventeen votes in opposition, the legislature approved the governor's request. The pro-Talmadge Macon *Telegraph* chastised the legislature for establishing a "one-man dictator, appointed by the governor and responsible to him alone." Certainly Arnall had not divorced the governor's office and the state highway department nor did he have any intention to do so. Arnall opposed the creation of a constitutional state highway board in the 1943 session, claiming that "highway construction is purely political and it ought to be." Arnall further explained that "what I did was to remove the influence of the governor from the agencies that ought to be left alone and should be based on technical knowledge and expertise—such as the merit system, such as education, such as the prison system."[18]

Other changes in state government occurred. At Arnall's direction, the legislature abolished the existing state planning board that had been created in the Rivers administration and replaced it with the Agricultural and Industrial Development Board, with its membership to be appointed by the governor. At Arnall's request, the legislature abolished and then re-created fifteen of the sixteen state's professional examining boards, a move that allowed Arnall to appoint the membership of the newly created agencies. The legislature also reorganized the state revenue department and proposed a constitutional amendment making the elected Public Service Commission a constitutional body to take it out of politics.[19]

During the session, Arnall supported legislation to create a state merit system. Merit systems for employees in several state agencies had been created during the Rivers administration with each agency having its own system. Arnall supported the consolidation of these various systems into a statewide system to be operated by a state merit system council, which would appoint a director to oversee the operation of the system. The legislature unanimously approved an administration bill authorizing the governor to set up a state merit system, and in May 1943 Arnall implemented the legislation.[20]

Arnall had not requested the legislature to consider constitutional revision in his inaugural address nor was it part of his campaign platform. However, the state's antiquated constitution needed either to be revised or to be replaced. Efforts to replace the Constitution of 1877 had begun at least by the early 1930s. A resolution creating a constitutional revision commission had been vetoed by Governor Talmadge in 1933. After the legislature had enacted his reform program, Arnall stated, "Georgia needs a new constitution and ultimately is going to get one." Instead of convening a constitutional convention to draft a new state constitution, he favored the creation of a commission to revise the state's constitution of 1877. The legislature approved a resolution creating a twenty-three-member constitutional revision commission. The legislature directed the commission to submit a proposed constitution to the 1945 session of the legislature for its consideration.[21]

After seventy days of productive work, the 1943 legislative session adjourned. Arnall had thoroughly dominated the session with every bill which he requested being passed—many of them without any change. The Atlanta *Journal* declared that Arnall had "received the most wholehearted cooperation ever given any chief executive by a Georgia legislature." Arnall agreed and praised the 1943 legislature as "the finest that has ever assembled under the dome of the State Capitol." Certainly Arnall had reason to praise the legislature. A writer in an article in *Collier's* magazine dubbed the governor "Unanimous Arnall" because of his astounding success with the legislature. He called the passage of Arnall's reform platform in twenty-four days a "political record breaker anywhere and a miracle in Georgia."

One historian even compared Arnall's success with the General Assembly to President Roosevelt's success in getting the Congress to pass legislation in the first "100 days" of the 1933 congressional session.[22]

The 1943 legislative session received praise from the state press. The Atlanta *Journal* commended the lawmakers for establishing "a new standard for efficiency" and restoring democratic government to the state. The Atlanta *Constitution* applauded the legislature for its record of accomplishment "that has rarely if ever, been equalled by a previous assembly session." Even the pro-Talmadge Savannah *Morning News* conceded that the record of the session was commendable. The editor of the Calhoun *Times* stated, "No governor ever had smoother sailing in translating his campaign promises into law than Ellis Arnall," while the Augusta *Chronicle* praised the legislature for its "outstandingly progressive work." One out-of-state newspaper, the Cleveland (Ohio) *Plain Dealer,* commented that "both Talmadge's abuses of power and the speedy correction of those abuses are unique in state affairs."[23]

Although Arnall had been successful in obtaining legislative approval of his requests, one obstacle remained before several of his major reforms could take place. Sixteen statewide constitutional amendments had been proposed by the legislature. These amendments included the creation of a constitutional Board of Regents, a constitutional state Board of Education, a constitutional state Board of Pardons and Paroles, a teachers retirement system, and the lowering of the voting age to eighteen. Normally, voters voted on proposed amendments at the general election following the legislative session that had proposed the amendments.

Instead Arnall urged the legislature to call a special election prior to the general election of November 1944 to allow the voters to decide the fate of the amendments. Speaker Harris agreed with the governor's suggestion because it would permit voters to consider the amendments without them becoming entangled in the politics of the 1944 presidential election. The Talmadge forces, however, dissented. Representative Elliott accused the governor of favoring a special election because he knew that such elections traditionally had a low turnout. The legislature overturned such opposition and designated August 3, 1943, as the date to allow the voters to determine the fate of the proposed amendments. To ensure passage, Harris, Gross, and the governor actively campaigned for the adoption of the amendments. Harris and Gross directed the activities of the Georgia Committee for Good Government that had been created to ensure ratification of the amendments. Arnall made speeches throughout the state, delivered radio addresses, and wrote an article in the Atlanta Journal *Magazine* on behalf of ratification.[24]

The Macon *Telegraph*, still a loyal supporter of Talmadge, predicted "no great harm will be done" if all of the amendments were defeated. In particular, the *Telegraph* opposed the teenage vote amendment, fearing it would destroy parental control over their children and divert students' minds from school matters. Arnall, claiming that Talmadge and his supporters had singled out the teenage vote amendment as their object of attack, vigorously defended the amendment. "We need the idealism, the candor, the unselfishness of those young people's influence in our public affairs," Arnall stated in a statewide radio broadcast in which he urged voters to support the amendment. Arnall concluded that the state needed more "of the starry-eyed enthusiasm of youth." The governor urged voters to ratify all of the amendments because they were beneficial and progressive. The Atlanta *Journal* endorsed the amendments as a way to ensure "that never again will there be an attempt to Hitlerize our educational system, or to revive the pardon racket, or to substitute autocracy for representative government."[25]

In a light turnout, voters overwhelmingly approved the constitutional amendments. They ratified the creation of a constitutional Board of Regents, a constitutional state Board of Education, and a constitutional state Board of Pardons and Paroles by affirmative votes of over 80 percent. The amendment lowering the voting age received the support of 68 percent of the votes. Even Talmadge's home county of Telfair approved that amendment by a vote of 72 percent and the amendment conferring constitutional status on the Board of Regents by a vote of 82 percent.[26]

As a result of the 1943 legislative session and the ratification of the constitutional amendments, state government in Georgia underwent significant change. In 1931 Governor Richard B. Russell, Jr., had persuaded the legislature to reduce the state's unwieldy bureaucracy of almost one hundred departments, agencies, commissions, and bureaus to less than twenty. Russell had stressed the need for efficiency and economy as the major reasons for his reorganizational program. Governor Eurith D. Rivers had been elected in 1936 on a platform of providing more state services. Rivers had obtained the creation of several new state agencies to administer the expanding services provided by the "Little New Deal." Arnall had been elected governor on a platform of ending gubernatorial dictatorship in the state. He successfully led the fight to place several major state agencies under the protection of the state constitution to remove them from future gubernatorial domination. Prior to 1943 Georgia did not have any governmental agencies protected by the state constitution. Now it had five—the Board of Regents, Board of Education, Public Service Commission, Game and Fish Commission, and the Board of Pardons and Paroles.[27]

As a result of Arnall's leadership, the governor's office had lost powers that Arnall's predecessors once possessed, such as the power to appoint the state auditor, the power to grant pardons, the power to suspend the state comptroller-general and the state treasurer, as well as the power to fire state employees by deleting them from the state's budget. The governor had also been removed as a member of state boards. Arnall hoped his reforms would prevent gubernatorial domination of these agencies. In the process of doing that, Arnall also purged state government of many high-ranking Talmadge supporters by getting the legislature to abolish state agencies and recreate them with new members or administrators appointed by Arnall. Elkin Taylor concluded that the 1943 legislature "went further than any other Georgia legislature in this century in purging an outgoing administration." Nevertheless, not all Talmadge supporters lost their jobs. Many Talmadge supporters who had not been active against Arnall in the primary retained their positions.[28]

Although Arnall's reforms had taken some powers from the governorship, he had not downgraded the office to one of insignificance. Even after the reforms, Arnall still possessed sufficient power to exercise enormous influence in state government. In his effort to remove politics from the operation of state agencies, Arnall never considered giving up gubernatorial control over that most political of all agencies—the state highway department. He later confessed, "I used that Highway Department to get through a lot of things I couldn't have gotten through unless I controlled it." Nor did his reforms diminish the governor's domination of the state's budgetary process. Arnall willingly gave up some powers that had been abused by some of his predecessors. He gladly surrendered the clemency power that he deemed more of a liability than an asset. He willingly yielded other powers, such as the authority to suspend the state auditor, to suspend the state comptroller-general, to appoint the state auditor, or to serve on the membership of the governing body of state agencies. Arnall never deemed these powers essential to exercising strong gubernatorial leadership. Arnall contended that he removed the governor's office from the operation of state agencies that should be operated on the basis of expertise and technical knowledge. Arnall hoped that the constitutional protection of these boards would prevent future governors from dominating them as Talmadge had. Despite the creation of the constitutional boards, however, Arnall conceded that the governor still retained power over them "through his personal influence and through a large degree of control over the finances of the state."[29]

With the support of the legislative leadership, Arnall completely dominated the 1943 legislative session. The overwhelming ratification of the constitutional amendments on August 3 indicated his continued popular support. In contrast, the political fortunes of Talmadge continued to decline. He could not even convince the voters in his home county to reject the amendment lowering the voting age. By the end of the legislative session, Arnall had emerged as the dominant personality on the state's political scene. His leadership invoked widespread praise. Georgia's senior U.S. senator Walter F. George stated, "When led by men like him with eyes forward but feet on the ground, we can contemplate the future with confidence." McGill detected a new mood and spirit in Georgia's state government. He noted "that visitors, governors, and visiting newspapermen all express amazement at the fact that Georgia has a clean, decent man for governor and a clean, decent government." The Atlanta *Journal* reminded its readers that for the past decade the national press had condemned and ridiculed Georgia for its bad government. The *Journal* boasted, however, that "newspapers throughout the United States have been quick to salute Georgia and to congratulate the new administration." E. Merton Coulter, a prominent Georgia historian, agreed and wrote that

> Arnall was the most dynamically constructive governor Georgia had within the memory of its oldest inhabitants. All too often heretofore the attention of the nation had been directed toward Georgia for her sins and the sins of her leaders, and feature writers in their articles for national magazines had brought Georgia into shame and disrepute. Now the picture was completely reversed. It seemed none came to Georgia but to praise—to praise the state and its governor.[30]

Truly it seemed that a new day in Georgia politics had dawned.

5

Georgia's

Smelly

Penal

Muddle

Six months after the adjournment of the 1943 legislative session, Arnall reconvened the lawmakers in special session to deal with one of the state's most perplexing problems—its infamous prison system. One observer concluded that Georgia's treatment of prisoners ranked "second only to racial problems in causing infamy to be heaped on the state by the northern press." The state newspapers had joined the "northern press" in condemning the state's penal system. The Valdosta *Daily Times* called it "a shame and disgrace to the good name of the state." The Augusta *Chronicle* editorialized that the state's prison system had "brought Georgia nothing but condemnation and shame." An editorial in the Atlanta *Journal* stated, "The Georgia penal system is rotten to the core and has been over a long span of years"; the Meriwether *Vindicator* called the system "a stench in the nostrils of all decency."[1]

Criticism of the state's penal system began shortly after the Civil War when the state established a convict leasing system. Under this system, Georgia leased its prisoners to private interests. Unfortunately, the leased prisoners suffered from improper nutrition, inadequate medical attention, mistreatment, and inhumane living conditions because of a lack of state regulation. Investigations revealed corruption in the awarding of leases and a system that resulted in the degradation of both guards and inmates. Many Georgians, including such prominent political leaders as Thomas E. Watson, Rebecca L. Felton, and William Y. Atkinson, Sr., spoke out against the evils of the system. The legislature eventually abolished the much-criticized leasing system in 1908, and the state regained control of its prisoners from private lessors.[2]

Yet the life of Georgia's prisoners still remained bleak. Most of the state's inmates were farmed out to county work camps, more commonly known as "chain gangs." The state provided a subsidy for prisoners accepted by the counties. In return, the prisoners were required to perform a minimum amount of work for the state. After fulfilling that obligation, state prisoners could be used by counties for local projects. Like the old leasing system, the county camps operated with little state supervision. Since county politicians attempted to hold down expenditures for prison upkeep, many of the inmates suffered from inadequate housing, poor medical treatment, improper diets, and overt cruelty. Inflicting punishment rather than rehabilitation remained the overriding concern of the state's penal system.[3]

In 1932 Robert Elliott Burns published *I Am a Fugitive from a Georgia Chain Gang!*, an exposé of the state's prison system. Burns, who had twice escaped from Georgia's infamous penal system, described in vivid detail life on a Georgia chain gang—the long workday, the inadequate diet, the brutality, and the inhumane living conditions. He compared life in a Georgia chain gang to the "bottomless depths of Hell—a Hell where the inmates received abuse, curses, punishment, and filth."[4]

Georgians sensitive to outside criticism expressed irritation at the national publicity that Burns's exposé received with Governor Richard B. Russell, Jr., dismissing the book as inaccurate. A movie, based on Burns's book, further irritated many Georgians, who had adopted a defensive attitude about their penal system and believed that criticism, especially from the North, was generally inaccurate or unfair. Although this long-existing attitude had hindered reform of the system, some improvements had occurred. The convict lease system had been abolished in 1908, and the beating of prisoners had been prohibited—at least on paper—in the 1920s. From the ending of the lease system until the Rivers administration in the late 1930s, however, no major reform of the system had occurred. Governor Rivers made several recommendations to the legislature to reform the system, most of which were adopted. Unfortunately most of them were never implemented, and only limited improvement in the state's penal system occurred. Prisoner rehabilitation remained a neglected and ignored concern by most legislators, penal officials, and citizens.[5]

When Arnall became governor in 1943, he found a prison system very similar to the one Burns had condemned eleven years earlier. The system consisted primarily of the Tattnall State Prison at Reidsville, thirteen work camps operated by the state highway department, and ninety county work camps. The state prison board, consisting of three elected officials, oversaw the penal system. During the regular session of the 1943 legislature, Arnall requested the lawmakers to take action on only one aspect of the penal system—removing the pardoning power of the governor. After the legislature stripped the governorship of the clemency power, Arnall admitted "that many of us assumed the other ills of the prison system would disappear rapidly." That assumption proved to be incorrect.[6]

Less than a month after the adjournment of the regular 1943 legislature, an event occurred that put the state prison in the headlines for weeks. On April 16, 1943, twenty-five prisoners escaped from Tattnall State Prison. Even though escapes had occurred at the prison before, never had so many inmates sought freedom at one time. An angry Arnall attributed the escape either to the collaboration of prison employees with the prisoners or to the negligence of prison employees. Arnall directed the state prison board to proceed immediately to Reidsville to investigate the escape and provide him with a written report. The governor called for the resignations of the members of the popularly elected board if the board failed to prevent future prisoner escapes. "The people of Georgia," Arnall declared, "will not tolerate the lax prison supervision which has been in effect and is now in effect."[7]

During the Talmadge administration, Roland H. Lawrence, a cousin of Talmadge, served as warden at Tattnall. However, he had been replaced by an Arnall appointee, W. R. Duvall, prior to the escape. As soon as the escape had occurred, news reporters and photographers descended upon the prison to investigate. During Lawrence's tenure as warden, reporters were denied access to the prison. Duvall asked Arnall what course of action he should take concerning the press. Arnall responded, "Let them in. Let them see everything. Let them take whatever pictures they want. Let them have the run of the prison. Let's try to clean up this mess. I have nothing to hide." The Augusta *Chronicle* commented that Arnall had "thrown wide the doors of Tattnall prison and allowed newspaper men to observe everything that goes on there—something that was never permitted during the Talmadge regime." A reporter for the Atlanta *Constitution* speculated that the mass escape focused public attention on a rotten system which would result in the "reformation and rebirth of Georgia's entire prison system."[8]

In addition to the board's inquiry, a Tattnall County grand jury conducted its own investigation. Contrary to the views of the governor, the grand jury absolved prison employees of assisting in the escape. The grand jurors accused one of Lawrence's subordinates of conducting a gambling racket among inmates and selling narcotics to them. The grand jury also charged that during Lawrence's wardenship several liquor stills were allowed to operate "apparently" with his knowledge. J. Henry Kennedy, sheriff of Tattnall County, who had recently been appointed superintendent of the state prison farm, complained of farm mismanagement and improprieties that had taken place during Lawrence's wardenship.[9]

In addition to the prison board and the Tattnall County grand jury investigation, the Senate Penitentiary Committee inquired into the mass escape. While concluding that there was nothing to justify calling for the resignation of members of the prison board, the report indicated a number of problems at the prison that existed under Lawrence's leadership. In particular, the committee charged that prisoners bought drugs, gambled, and consumed moonshine made on the premises. The committee made several recommendations, which included calling for educational and vocational training for inmates, hiring a full-time prison chaplain, and raising the salaries of guards. Following the release of the committee's report, Lawrence issued a lengthy defense of his wardenship from former governor Talmadge's law office in Atlanta. Lawrence bitterly attacked the report for its "gross misstatement of facts."[10]

In the aftermath of the senate committee's report, Arnall concluded that the former warden, who was still on the state's payroll, had outlived his usefulness as a public servant and fired him. An angry Talmadge quickly came to the defense of his cousin, calling him a "capable and competent warden." In addition to firing Lawrence, Arnall moved against another Talmadge loyalist—Royal K. Mann, who had been designated chairman of the state prison board by Talmadge. Governors had the authority to appoint one of the popularly elected members of the board to be chairman for a one-year term. Although Mann's term as chairman had expired in February 1943, Arnall had allowed Mann to continue to serve in that position. In the aftermath of the prison escape, Arnall replaced Mann with Clem R. Rainey, who was not as closely allied with Talmadge.[11]

Arnall also expressed his displeasure at how the board had been carrying out its responsibilities. He encouraged the board members to get out of their offices in Atlanta and "visit the prisons and the highway camps and find out conditions there first hand." The governor threatened to call a special session of the legislature to abolish the board if another mass escape occurred or if the board failed to clean up the penal system. Maintaining that he had the authority to abolish the board, the governor stated that he did "not believe in the principle of wiping out an elective office by executive order."[12]

In August public attention shifted to the state highway department's work camp at Cartersville, where three prisoners cut their heel strings as a protest against alleged cruel treatment. Even prior to that incident, Arnall and State Highway Director Ryburn C. Clay had sent investigators to look into the possibility of cruel treatment at the camp. The camp's warden, A. W. Clay, had earlier been removed as warden of another camp by Governor Rivers after several prisoners had broken their legs in protest against alleged cruel treatment. Upon investigating the situation at Cartersville, Director Clay suspended Warden Clay and a guard on grounds of cruelty to prisoners. Arnall quickly announced his approval of Director Clay's action and ordered a public hearing concerning the cruelty charges.[13]

In the course of the investigation, the prisoners admitted cutting their heel strings to avoid being whipped by the warden. Other prisoners complained of working from sunup to sundown on road gangs with beatings administered by the warden if they did not work hard enough. At least twelve prisoners claimed to have been beaten with rubber hoses. Such revelations led Senator Claude Pittman, chairman of the Senate Penitentiary Committee, to remark, "If there is a hell, and if I were responsible for the operation of the present chain gang system in Georgia, I would expect to go to that hell when I died."[14]

As a result of the Cartersville incident, the governor requested the House and the Senate penitentiary committees to conduct a thorough investigation of the state's prison system and to make recommendations to reform the system. Arnall further requested Speaker Roy Harris and Senate President Frank Gross to investigate penal systems in other southern states and to make recommendations to reform Georgia's system. "I want the public of Georgia to get stirred up about these rotten conditions," Arnall stated, "because our whole system is rotten." Arnall insisted that merely firing wardens would not solve the problems of the state's penal system. Instead Arnall called for a complete reorganization of the system as the only way to reform it.[15]

C. E. Gregory, a reporter for the Atlanta *Journal*, observed that reforming the system would be difficult because "the theory that a convict must be beaten and abused and imposed upon from sunrise to sunset, like a Georgia mule, has prevailed in the state for a long, long time." Nevertheless,

Time believed the Cartersville incident "showed signs of blasting Georgia's prison system out of its antiquated, sadistic, scandal-ridden past." The Augusta *Chronicle* argued that "no institution in our state is so badly in need of overhauling as our disreputable prison system." The Columbus *Enquirer* agreed that prison reform in Georgia was long overdue. While the editor of the Valdosta *Daily Times* claimed that Georgians were overwhelmingly in agreement that prison reform should occur, his counterpart at the Albany *Herald* speculated that the issue had caused more editorial comment in Georgia newspapers than any other in the Arnall administration.[16]

On September 14, 1943, Speaker Harris and President Gross issued their report—a fourteen-page indictment of the penal system. They concluded, after inspecting the penal systems of nine southern states, that Georgia had "the worst system that we have seen anywhere." Only in Georgia did the lawmakers find prisoners wearing leg irons, guards beating inmates, prisoners talking revolt, and inmates cutting their heelstrings in protest against alleged cruelty. The report observed that Georgia, unlike other states, made no effort to rehabilitate prisoners. Moreover, it concluded that the state's penal system was a financial liability unlike the penal systems of surrounding states which generated revenue to pay a substantial portion of operational costs with some of the prisons even reaching self-sufficiency.[17]

The Harris-Gross report made several recommendations for the improvement of the Georgia penal system. It called for the replacement of the prison board with a department of corrections to be headed by a director and for the expansion and improvement of prison industries as well as emphasis on rehabilitation. Other recommendations included the banning of corporal punishment, prohibiting the use of chains and leg irons, discontinuing the use of striped uniforms, providing supervised recreation, and improving food service. Concluding that the state highway camps were a financial liability to the state, Harris and Gross recommended closing them and transferring their prisoners to the state prison. The report, while not favoring abolishing the county work camps, called for the director of corrections to have the authority to issue rules and regulations concerning the operation of the camps. The Columbus *Ledger-Enquirer* praised the Harris-Gross report and called upon Georgians to "face the fact that over many decades we have failed to recognize that we had the 'worst penal system anywhere' and have done absolutely nothing to get a better system." The Columbus paper noted that while Georgians could dismiss criticism of the penal system by "outsiders," they could not ignore calls for reform from such influential Georgians as Harris and Gross.[18]

A House Penitentiary Committee's report further indicted the state's beleaguered penal system by concluding that the majority of the prison camps suffered from poor management, inadequate facilities, and lack of necessary equipment. The committee's report complained that the cruel and inhumane treatment of prisoners "was certainly not conducive to the purpose of rehabilitation." Like the Harris-Gross report, the House report recommended the development of prison industries at Tattnall and called for the creation of a director of corrections to oversee the state's penal system. The report urgently called for the governor to take action "to bring about the correction of the present system." The Senate Penitentiary Committee's report also condemned the state's penal system, and in particular, the widespread practice of beating prisoners. While not calling for a director to oversee the system as had the other reports, the Senate report called for the establishment of statewide penal rules and regulations.[19]

Arnall believed that the time had come to reform the state's disgraceful penal system and replace it with a system in "which the people of Georgia may take pride." To accomplish that task, he presented a lengthy list of proposed reforms to the prison board, foremost of which he requested the board to voluntarily turn over its control of the state's penal system to a director of corrections appointed by Arnall. If the board refused, he threatened to call a special session of the legislature to abolish the board. The governor ordered the board to meet with him in his office to discuss his proposed reforms.[20]

Prior to the meeting, however, Attorney General T. Grady Head rendered an opinion that the board could not relinquish its powers to a director of corrections and that the governor could not create such a position by executive order. According to the attorney general, only the legislature could divest the board of its power or create a director of corrections. Despite the attorney general's ruling, Arnall still met with the board and presented his reform program for its consideration. The program consisted of twenty-seven reforms with the creation of a director of corrections heading the list. Arnall proposed the retention of the prison board in an advisory capacity to the proposed director of corrections. Following the meeting, Arnall told reporters that the board supported his reform program.[21]

In response to the attorney general's opinion, the governor called a special session of the legislature for the purpose of reforming the state's "primitive, inhumane, cruel, and archaic prison system." He concluded that the system had resulted in "much criticism and adverse publicity for the state." In its place, he envisioned "a progressive, economical, modern and humane prison system." The state press generally supported the governor's call for the special session. The Atlanta *Journal* and the Columbus *Enquirer* agreed with the governor that prison reform in the state was long overdue. Noting that the pardon racket had been recently abolished, the Thomasville *Times-Enterprise* asked, "Why not the filthy and cruel methods of handling our prisoners?" The Augusta *Chronicle* expressed the belief that the cost of the session was justified because of the needed reform of "Georgia's archaic and notorious prison system." In fact, the Moultrie *Observer* predicted that penal reform might prove to be the greatest accomplishment of the Arnall administration. However, the editor of the Albany *Herald* warned that it "would take a legislative miracle to get out of 'GEORGIA'S SMELLY PENAL MUDDLE.'"[22]

Arnall's call for a special session received criticism from pro-Talmadge papers and the former governor himself. The Savannah *Morning News* concluded that convening the legislature for the purpose of abolishing the state Board of Prisons "smacks of dictatorship in its most glaring form—the very thing that Mr. Arnall has heretofore denounced." The Macon *Telegraph* also opposed a special session to enact a law giving the governor the authority to appoint a prison director. Talmadge strongly opposed the special session contending that reform could be implemented under existing state law.[23]

The former governor questioned why Arnall wanted to legislate the board out of existence when it supported penal reform. He concluded that Arnall stood to gain financially from abolishing the board and replacing it with his appointed director who would be in charge of buying and selling of supplies for the penal system. The former governor claimed, "A little clique . . . wants to make some millions of dollars out of the present administration in Georgia, and the business of the Georgia penitentiary is too rich a harvest for them to overlook!" The former governor saw no need for penal reform and defended the state's prison system. He claimed that while governor, he "visited practically every prison east of the Rocky Mountains" and that prisoners with whom he talked "were all unanimous in their statement that Georgia gave a convict a better chance, and a more

humane opportunity than any prison they ever served in." Talmadge concluded, "There is nothing on this earth lower than a person who will defile
the good name of his state to build up a hysteria to fix a plan so they can
reap a profit."[24]

The special session convened on September 27, 1943. In a speech to
the lawmakers, Arnall reminded them of the nationwide criticism of the
state's penal system. In an effort to console Georgians offended by such
criticism, the governor conceded that much of the criticism was nothing
more than sensationalism. Nevertheless, Arnall agreed that the "penal system is punitive in purpose, archaic in method, and unnecessarily costly
to our taxpayers." In his address, the governor quoted extensively from
the three legislative reports that had called for reformation of the system.
Arnall praised the reports as "powerful documents, stringent criticism of
a condition that has become intolerable to the citizens of Georgia." The
governor reminded the lawmakers that no true reform of the system had
occurred since the abolishment of the lease system in 1908.[25]

Arnall urged the legislature to create a humane penal system in which
social misfits could "be restored to society as men and women, not wild
beasts." The governor, contending that penal reform could not take place
under existing laws, called for the legislature to create a department of corrections to be headed by a director who would have the authority to make
rules and regulations for the system. Instead of abolishing the Board of
Prisons as two of the legislative reports had recommended, Arnall urged
the lawmakers to retain the board as an advisory body to the director of
corrections. He expressed the view that it would not be "in keeping with
democratic traditions for me" to recommend the abolition of the positions
to which the prison board members had been elected.[26]

Arnall proposed several reforms based upon the three legislative reports. They included prohibiting whippings, doing away with leg irons,
segregating first and youthful offenders from hardened criminals, providing vocational training, eliminating striped uniforms, and segregating the
mentally ill prisoners from other inmates. In addition, Arnall called for
providing religious and educational activities for inmates, improving the
quality of prison food, providing for a receiving and classifying center, and
making the system self-supporting. Arnall urged the legislature to abolish the state highway camps because of the high cost of operating them.
While favoring retention of county work camps, Arnall called for increased

supervision of them by the director of corrections. The governor stressed that penal reformation should lead to the creation of a system emphasizing rehabilitation rather than punishment.[27]

Arnall defended the cost of the special session as minimal and emphasized that, regardless of cost, he would have called the session because "human rights and human needs are above budgets." He emphasized that his proposals would not convert the state prison into a "vacation resort" or eliminate discipline in the penal system. While conceding prison officials had to use firmness, he contended that brutality was no substitute for firmness. Arnall suggested that by reforming the penal system, the legislature would be providing "a service as great as that which liberated education from political interference." In the most eloquent passage of his speech, Arnall told the lawmakers, "We hear a great deal of talk about being practical, being efficient, doing what is wise and prudent. I think it is high time that we talked some once again about doing what is right."[28]

Although the mood of the legislative session favored penal reform, Arnall's suggestion of retaining the prison board in an advisory capacity ran into strong opposition. Both the Harris-Gross report and the House Penitentiary Committee recommended abolishing the board. Representative Ben W. Fortson, Jr., and Senator Pittman led the fight to abolish the board. Fortson argued that the board members would be "doing their worst to nullify every effort made by the director of corrections" if the board were not abolished. Senator Pittman argued that the board should be abolished because it had failed to carry out its responsibilities. Speaker Harris blamed the prison board for the existing penal situation and expressed a willingness to vote to impeach the board members if that was the only way to get rid of them. The legislature abolished the prison board with only sixteen dissenting votes.[29]

A second bill proposed the creation of a department of corrections, a director of corrections, and a commission of corrections. The proposed legislation also contained numerous proposed reforms of the penal system. Under the proposed legislation sponsored by the Arnall administration, the former prison board would become the commission of corrections. However, Representative Fortson offered an amendment to the House bill that deleted the proposed commission of corrections. The House passed the amendment and approved the bill by an overwhelming vote. An effort to restore the commission failed in the Senate, which passed the amended bill that retained the board as an advisory commission with only one dissenting vote. At the urging of Speaker Harris, the House agreed to the Senate-amended bill.[30]

The legislation created the department of corrections and the position of director of corrections, who would be appointed by the governor. The law mandated that the director institute "immediately a program of wise, humane, and intelligent prison administration" in order to rehabilitate the inmates as well as to make the system self-supporting. The director was authorized to issue rules and regulations pertaining to the penal system as he deemed appropriate. The legislature spelled out eighteen specific penal reforms, most of which had been requested by Arnall. Major reform of the state's notorious penal condition had finally taken place.[31]

Arnall praised the lawmakers for their action. The Atlanta *Constitution* optimistically proclaimed that the special session meant that "the archaic Georgia prison system will be transformed immediately into a modern setting." *Life* magazine ran a six-page picture/story article on the reform of the penal system under Arnall's "courageous leadership." Nevertheless, the Atlanta *Journal* cautioned that "the stride forward which Georgia has taken is only the beginning." Arnall agreed and stressed that reformation of the system would not occur immediately because "the mistakes of forty years cannot be corrected overnight." Indeed, he predicted that it would take years to implement all of the reforms enacted by the General Assembly. Nevertheless, under the leadership of the governor, Georgia finally undertook a comprehensive program to clean up its penal system. While conceding that his administration "never completely solved the prison problem," Arnall contended, "we went a long, long way toward its solution."[32]

To implement the reform of the state's penal system, Arnall appointed Wiley L. Moore, a prominent businessman and close political associate, to the position of director of corrections. The governor prevailed upon President Roosevelt to send the director of the U.S. Bureau of Prisons to assist and advise Moore. Arnall also obtained the services of the warden of the Atlanta Federal Penitentiary and several other federal penal experts to assist Moore in undertaking penal reform.[33]

The lawmakers returned home after a productive special session and were not scheduled to reconvene until the next regular session in January 1945. However, action in the U.S. Senate led the governor to call them back to Atlanta. The U.S. Senate had been considering a bill to allow members of the armed services to vote in federal elections. Southern senators opposed the measure, contending it violated states' rights and could lead to enfranchisement of the blacks in the South. They successfully obtained the passage of a substitute bill which recommended that the states pass legislation permitting military personnel to vote in federal and state elections.[34]

Shortly after the passage of the substitute bill, Senator George, the state's senior U.S. Senator, wrote to Arnall to urge him to convene a special session of the General Assembly to implement the Senate's recommendation. Receptive to the suggestion, Arnall stated that he would be delighted for Georgia "to blaze the trail in this as it has been doing in other matters." On January 1, 1944, Arnall issued a proclamation convening a special session to consider a soldiers' voting law. Two days later, Arnall spoke to the legislators and urged them to become the first state legislature to enact a soldiers' voting act. Both Speaker Harris and Senate President Gross endorsed the bill and predicted its speedy enactment. The bill also had the overwhelming support of the state's press. Even the pro-Talmadge Macon *Telegraph* favored the session and urged other states to enact soldier voting laws.[35]

The legislature not only passed a soldiers' voting act but passed it unanimously. The law provided for voter registration and voting by mail for members of the armed services, established a state agency to implement the law, and eliminated the poll tax for military personnel. The ease with which the legislation passed reminded the Savannah *Morning News* "of the early days of the New Deal, when Congress rubber-stamped many pieces of 'must' legislation." The Atlanta *Journal* commended Arnall and the legislators for "A Good Job Well Done," and the Atlanta *Constitution* praised the legislature for "adding another jewel to Georgia's crown." Arnall thanked the lawmakers for their "fine public service" in passing the legislation and estimated that two hundred fifty thousand Georgians in military service would become eligible to participate in the state's electoral process because of the legislature's action. Thus Georgia, in addition to being the first state to lower its voting age to eighteen, also became the first to enact a soldiers' voting law.[36]

Passage of the soldiers' voting act and the reforms of the penal system further enhanced Georgia's progressive and forward-looking image. The Augusta *Chronicle* boasted after the session on penal reform that Georgians would never "have to look shamefacedly while someone writes an article of indictment as 'I-am-a-fugitive-from-a-Georgia-chain-gang.'" Understandably, the author of that indictment, Robert Elliott Burns, had been keeping up with the prison reform efforts in Georgia. While Arnall was in New York in December 1943 to give a speech to the New York Southern Society, Burns met with Arnall. Burns, who had been living in New Jersey following his second escape from a Georgia "chain gang," had remarried, fathered three children, and become a successful businessman and a leader in community and church affairs. Burns requested a pardon in his meeting with Arnall. Convinced that Burns had been rehabilitated, Arnall, upon his return to Atlanta, requested that the state Board of Pardons and Paroles pardon Burns so he could "live as a free citizen and not as a fugitive from the Georgia prison system." The board ruled, however, that Burns had to return to Georgia and surrender to the board before it could consider any official action.[37]

In November 1945 Burns surrendered to Arnall in Atlanta, and the governor appeared before the board to request a pardon for Burns. Arnall told the board that this would be his only request of the board because he wanted "the entire nation to know that the state of Georgia recognizes rehabilitation as the main objective of its prison system." Arnall urged the board to pardon Burns because he had been rehabilitated. Arnall further told the board that the reform of the penal system had restored the "good name" of the state. "If I am to get credit for anything during my administration," Arnall told the board members, "I believe that I have helped the state's reputation abroad." He contended the pardoning of Burns would further enhance the state's image. Following Arnall's presentation, the board commuted Burns's sentence to time already served.[38]

The board's action brought quick response from Talmadge. The former governor accused Arnall of promoting a pardon for Burns in order to obtain publicity to advance his political career. Moreover, Talmadge charged, "There is money behind the deal." Talmadge reminded Georgians that Burns had written a book "defaming and slandering Georgia and holding her courts and public officials up to ridicule and scorn throughout the nation." In contrast, the Atlanta *Journal* praised Arnall's actions which it believed "will rebound far and wide to Georgia's honor and prestige."[39]

Reform had to occur in Georgia's antiquated penal system, with Arnall providing the necessary leadership that hastened the timetable of that needed reform. Under his direction, the legislature enacted the most significant prison reform in the state's penal system since the abolishment of the convict lease system in 1908. The governor realized that the state's penal system—one of the worst in the nation—had to be reformed. He traced his commitment to that goal back to the fall of 1932 when he saw the movie based on Robert Burns's book. After viewing that movie, Arnall vowed that when he became governor, he was going "to reform Georgia's antiquated, iniquitous, and cruel prison system." Arnall did not campaign on that issue in 1942, nor did he urge the regular session of the 1943 legislature to overhaul the state's prison system. However, Arnall had pledged in 1942 to restore the state's tattered image among her sister states. It seemed clear that the image-conscious governor would no longer ignore one of the state's worst image problems—its festering penal system.[40]

The mass escape at Reidsville in April 1943 and the incident at Cartersville four months later aroused public opinion on the subject of penal reform. Arnall called for legislative investigations of the penal system and sent the presiding officers of both houses of the legislature to investigate the penal system of surrounding states. Georgians might dismiss outside criticism of their penal system as false, exaggerated, or biased, but the Harris-Gross report and the House and Senate penitentiary committees' reports were condemnations of the penal system by members of the General Assembly. In one respect, Talmadge had been right. Arnall had carefully cultivated public opinion to the point where citizens demanded penal reform. Politicians, newspaper editors, civic leaders, grand juries—even the state's prison wardens association—called for reform. The demands culminated in legislative action.

Within the span of a year, a regular session and two special sessions of the legislature had overwhelmingly responded to Arnall's leadership. Talmadge had run against Arnall in 1942 and had lost. He had opposed Arnall's legislative reform program in the regular session of the 1943 legislature and had lost. He had fought the ratification of the Arnall-backed constitutional amendments in August 1943 and had lost. On the issue of penal reform, Talmadge had led the opposition and again had lost. While the Talmadge political influence continued to decline, Arnall appeared almost invincible in the arena of Georgia politics. He had replaced Talmadge as the dominant political leader in state politics and become a national recognized reformer. Seldom, if ever, had a Georgia politician been so strongly supported in his home state while at the same time he received such praise from outside of the state.

6

A New

Constitution

Ellis Arnall assumed the governorship under the Constitution of 1877. Like most state constitutions, that document was longer, more detailed, and less flexible than the U.S. Constitution. Georgia, like many states, had replaced and amended her fundamental law on a frequent basis. In fact, the state had gone through six constitutions prior to the Constitution of 1877. By 1943 the U.S. Constitution had been amended only twenty-one times. In sharp contrast, twenty-eight amendments were added to the state's constitution during Arnall's first year as governor. With those amendments, Georgia's constitution had been amended over three hundred times.[1]

The Constitution of 1877 had been written in reaction to the Reconstruction era in Georgia history. Rufus B. Bullock, Georgia's first Republican governor, had been elected in 1868 but was forced to resign three years later in order to avoid impeachment and removal. Bullock later stood trial on charges of embezzlement of state funds but was acquitted. Nevertheless, one historian concluded that Bullock's administration was unique in the state's history for its "fraud, corruption, rascality, and extravagance." In particular, many Georgians criticized the liberal use of the state's bonding authority under the Bullock regime.[2]

Robert A. Toombs, an unreconstructed rebel, led the efforts of the Democrats to cleanse the state of Republicanism. In particular, Toombs objected to the Constitution of 1868, which he called the handiwork of "alien enemies, domestic traitors, and ignorant, vicious, emancipated slaves." Toombs headed a successful effort to call a constitutional convention to give the state another constitution unsoiled by the hands of "domestic traitors." Most of the delegates who attended the convention shared Toombs's conservative economic philosophy and they established frugality as a fundamental principle in the new constitution, which was adopted by the voters in 1877. The new constitution placed numerous restrictions on state and local governments in the area of public finance, taxation, and debt. It limited the taxation power of both state and local governments and provided that their power to tax could be changed only by constitutional amendment. The constitution further prohibited the state from issuing bonds. Toombs proudly told the delegates at the convention of 1877, "You have locked it [the State Treasury], and you have put the key in the pockets of the people, and I thank God for it."[3]

In later years, many Georgians criticized the rigid and conservative Constitution of 1877, which restrained state and local government spending and subjected local governments to the will of the legislature. A 1938 publication of the Citizens Fact Finding Movement of Georgia, an organization of reform-minded citizens, contended that the Constitution of 1877 restricted "governmental action almost to the point of strangulation." So many amendments had been added to the constitution in order to cope with changing conditions and demands upon governments that Arnall dismissed it as nothing more than a "hodge-podge of amendments."[4]

Constitutional reform had been urged at least as early as 1901, when Governor Allen D. Candler called for a constitutional convention to revise the state's fundamental law. Candler's effort failed. Several years later in 1927, Governor Lamartine G. Hardman suggested the creation of a constitutional commission to propose a new constitution because the existing constitution was "not specially fitted for the needs of this state today." Ed Rivers, who at that time was in the state senate, ignored Hardman's call for a commission and instead led the fight for a constitutional convention. Neither Hardman nor Rivers succeeded in their efforts.[5]

In 1930 Charles M. Snelling, chairman of the Institute of Public Affairs at the University of Georgia, appointed a committee to draft a proposed constitution. The committee's constitution proposed several significant changes, such as reducing the size of the legislature, apportioning representation on a population basis, and increasing the governor's term to four years. The committee concluded that Georgia had to have a new constitution in order to assume its rightful place among the other states. The proposed constitution, which would have resulted in major modification of the state's political system, never received serious consideration.[6]

During the 1933 session, the legislature unanimously adopted a resolution creating a constitutional revision commission. The resolution complained of the high number of amendments that had been added to the constitution. Despite the overwhelming support in the legislature for constitutional reform, Governor Eugene Talmadge vetoed the resolution on the grounds that correct legislative procedure had not been followed. However, Talmadge's low-tax philosophy may have been a major factor for the veto. Certainly Talmadge's conservative economic philosophy and the Constitution of 1877 were compatible.[7]

In 1940 the Citizens Fact Finding Movement called for a new constitution or constitutional revision. The group suggested a commission to propose revision rather than a convention as the "more satisfactory method" to achieve constitutional reform. During the heated 1942 gubernatorial primary, Arnall did not make constitutional reform a campaign issue but came out in favor of constitutional revision only after his campaign reform program had been passed in the regular session of the 1943 legislature. Arnall, concerned about what the legislature could do in its 1945 session, "decided that it would be a good idea to bring forth a new constitution since the Constitution of 1877 was out-dated and was not in step with the times and there were so many amendments to it that it was unwieldy and bulky."[8]

Arnall did not favor a complete rewriting of the constitution. Instead, he believed the Constitution of 1877 should be "revised and rewritten to meet changed conditions and to bring harmony to its provisions." To accomplish this task, he advocated the creation of a constitutional revision commission whose efforts would be subject to the approval of the legislature and ratification by the voters. Arnall opposed a constitutional convention out of fear that "the special interests seeking special privilege would take over the convention." By using a much smaller body, Arnall believed he could better control "what was going on."[9]

The legislature, with only five dissenting votes, created a constitutional revision commission. The resolution stipulated that the commission would submit its efforts for revision to the 1945 legislature, which in turn would submit the revised document to a ratification vote of the people. In addition to Arnall's support of the commission method of revising the constitution, another factor aided the passage of the resolution. The Constitution of 1877 stipulated that delegates attending constitutional conventions had to be apportioned on a population basis. It further provided that a constitution written at a convention had to be submitted directly to the voters for adoption or rejection. Rural lawmakers, who dominated the malapportioned legislature, feared any process that allocated delegates on a population basis. The Arnall-backed measure ensured that the commission's proposed constitution had to be reviewed by the legislature prior to its submission to the voters. Under the commission system, the politically powerful rural lawmakers retained final control over what was submitted to the voters.[10]

The legislature charged the commission to better adapt the state's constitution "to the needs and conditions of the people of the State." The resolution created a commission consisting of twenty-three members, including Arnall, who was given the authority to appoint eight members. Arnall's appointees included the only woman on the commission—Beatrice H. (Mrs. Leonard) Haas of Atlanta, who was active in the Georgia League of Women Voters. The resolution designated Speaker Harris and Senate President Gross commission members and stipulated that they would appoint eight members. Since Arnall appointed eight members to the commission, and Harris and Gross, both Arnall supporters, cleared their eight appointments with the governor, the governor had more influence in the body of twenty-three members than he would have had in a convention several times as large composed of popularly elected delegates.[11]

The commission met for the first time in October 1943 and unanimously elected Arnall as its chairman. At the initial meeting, the commission divided itself into seven subcommittees that were charged with making revisions in assigned portions of the Constitution of 1877. The subcommittees filed with Arnall written reports that served as the basis of commission deliberations. The commission held public hearings, and the proceedings were open to the public with representatives from various groups such as the Georgia Bar Association, the American Legion, the Temperance League, the Association of County Commissioners, and the Georgia Education Association appearing before the commission. For advisors to the commission, Chairman Arnall also invited Hatton W. Sumners, chairman of the Judiciary Committee of the U.S. House of Representatives; Frank Bane, executive director of the Council of State Governments; and professors W. Brooke Graves and Walter F. Dodd, both authorities on state constitutional revision.[12]

Arnall told the commissioners in their first meeting that he deemed their efforts to be "the most important undertaking that has yet been made by the present administration." In fact, Arnall declared the revised constitution would be the "capstone of the administration, the lasting monument to this era of government in Georgia." Arnall suggested to his fellow commissioners that the first issue they had to resolve was over what kind of constitution they wished to produce—a simple constitution containing basic principles or one that resembled a legal code. Haas, perhaps the most liberal member of the commission, called upon the commission to demonstrate courage and leadership in revising the constitution. James V. Carmichael urged the commission to revise the constitution "regardless of whether people are going to like it or not, or whether it is going to be popular." Taking a more cautious attitude, Commissioner Hugh J. MacIntyre urged his fellow commissioners to go easy on revising and called for them to leave the nonessentials alone in order to avoid "friction with the Legislature or the voters." Arnall joined in the discussion by stating that though he was an idealist, he was also practical "and very anxious to have a new Constitution."[13]

Arnall favored simplifying the constitution but feared that deleting unnecessary provisions could "create a situation that would enable the critics of the new Constitution to pounce upon them and undertake to mislead and confuse the people." Arnall conceded a willingness to sacrifice simplicity in order to get a new constitution. Haas disagreed. She argued that the people demanded leadership from the commission on this question and it should go as far as "fundamentally necessary in revising the Constitution." Arnall responded that he was

> just as progressive as any person I know, just as liberal, just as anxious for changes to take place, but I recognize the only way you can bring about change is through gradual movement, and not revolution, so to speak; and therefore I have always told you in my judgment at times for expediency sake, we must sacrifice some of the things we would like to do in order to put through the Constitution. Government is a system of compromises and I think we have a compromise right here. I don't think we have to compromise with wrong or evil, but I mean compromise with provisions of the Constitution in that they are non-essential in order that we may carry through on our job.[14]

One of the major controversies the commission dealt with was whether to create additional constitutional boards. Arnall had successfully obtained the creation of five constitutional boards in his first year in office. Commissioner David J. Arnold proposed the creation of another—a constitutional state banking commission. Arnall hesitated to embrace the suggestion and confessed to being in a quandary over the issue. He conceded that sometimes the political pendulum swings too far in one direction and popular disgruntlement forces it back the other way. He cited as an example the situation in New Jersey, where constitutional boards had lost their independence as a result of complaints from the public about bureaucratic inefficiency and lack of popular control. Arnall expressed apprehension that the addition of new offices and departments in the proposed constitution could jeopardize its adoption.[15]

Later during the session, Arnall's doubts about the creation of additional constitutional boards faded. He revived the issue by seeking to establish a constitutional board of corrections to operate the state's penal system. Arnall believed that such a board would provide the penal system with continuity, uniformity, and stability, and remove the operation of the penal system from politics. Arnall defended the existence of the boards as essential for the operation of state government. "I can't speak for other governors," Arnall told the commission, "but this one likes for the Boards to operate." In spite of Arnall's arguments, the commission turned down his efforts to create a constitutional state board of corrections.[16]

Arnall also fought to establish a constitutional personnel board to direct the state's merit system, telling the commission that the establishment of such a board would be one of the most important undertakings of the commission. The governor's proposal resulted in a lengthy and heated discussion with Speaker Harris opposing Arnall's proposal. While favoring a state merit system, Harris believed that it should not be run by a constitutional board because of the lack of popular control over it. Instead, he favored a board accountable to the legislature to ensure popular control. By the end of a lengthy and vigorous discussion of the question, most of the provisions in Arnall's seven-paragraph proposal had been deleted. The commission finally created a state personnel board whose members were to be appointed by the governor and whose duties and powers were to be determined by the legislature.[17]

The governor enjoyed more success with the question of gubernatorial succession. The Constitution of 1877 prohibited a governor from succeeding himself. At the last regular meeting of the commission in November 1944, state Representative Fortson appeared before the body to urge it to permit gubernatorial succession. He contended that the ban on gubernatorial succession violated democratic principle. Speaker Harris and President Gross issued a joint public statement in support of Fortson's efforts. While emphasizing to the commission that he was not a candidate for reelection, Arnall supported Fortson's suggestion claiming the ban violated "the sound principle of democratic government." The commission permitted gubernatorial succession by an 8 to 7 vote.[18]

Arnall also urged the commissioners to remove a constitutional grant of tax immunity for the Georgia Railroad Company. The privilege had been granted to the railroad in the 1830s. Arnall opposed the continuation of this "unfair, unjust discriminatory taxing immunity." He urged the commissioners to either delete the provision or extend it to every business and taxpayer in Georgia. Arnall dismissed concern of several commissioners that the U.S. Supreme Court would not allow the state to revoke the immunity granted because such would constitute a violation of the contract clause of the U.S. Constitution. The former attorney general argued a tax exemption could not be considered a contract since the power of taxation was part of the state's sovereignty and could not be contracted away. According to Arnall, the state could reclaim its sovereignty at any time by revoking that provision of its constitution. He called upon the revocation of the immunity so the Georgia Railroad could pay "its just share of taxes." The commission accepted Arnall's proposal and adopted a provision that voided all tax exemptions for incorporation charters. Arnall conceded that he "had a hard time" revoking the exemption because of the opposition led by Harris, who was from Richmond County, where the Georgia Railroad Company had its headquarters.[19]

Arnall generally played an active role in the deliberations of the commission. On the issue of representation in the legislature, however, he kept unusually quiet. Under the Constitution of 1877, the 121 rural counties with 43.5 percent of the population in 1940 elected 59 percent of the membership of the state House of Representatives. Haas from Atlanta, the state's largest city, proposed that the malapportioned House be reapportioned on a population basis. Her motion failed for a lack of a second. A motion to distribute seats in the lower house on the basis of one representative for each twenty-five thousand residents failed with Arnall voting against it. Arnall justified his vote on the basis that the rural legislators would have defeated such a proposal in the legislature. Arnall, the pragmatic politician, later observed that "there were many things that I thought would have been fine if they had been possible of fulfillment."[20]

While refusing to fight for fairer representation in the legislature, he lead the effort to grant home rule to local governments. Arnall noted that local governments under the Constitution of 1877 were "minutely controlled" by the state to a degree never contemplated in Georgia's previous constitutions. He conceded that these limitations had been placed on local governments "to prevent the corrupt and irresponsible financial transactions that had marked the 'carpetbag' period." Arnall estimated that at least two-thirds of the legislation passed by the General Assembly was local in nature. Of the 323 constitutional amendments that had been proposed to the Constitution of 1877, 63 percent were of a local nature.[21]

The Arnall home rule plan, which had been drafted by the League of Women Voters, provided that local governments could adopt, change, or amend their governments provided the changes did not violate the state constitution and that the changes were approved by a majority of the local voters. The proposal further provided that 20 percent of the local voters could initiate a vote on proposed changes. Arnall believed that home rule would restore democracy at the local level and allow the legislature to devote more time to statewide issues. After lengthy discussion, the commission adopted Arnall's proposal but on the following day the issue was reconsidered. In the give and take of debate, Arnall candidly confessed, "I don't know enough about it now to draw a home rule bill that would work in Georgia." After more discussion, which revealed increasing concern over inserting a home rule provision in the constitution, the commission voted not to mention home rule in the revised constitution. Instead the commission urged the legislature to consider allowing local governments to have home rule.[22]

During the deliberation of the commission, the U.S. Supreme Court handed down a decision that threatened the existence of one of the major political institutions in Georgia—the Democratic party's white primary. Southern Democratic parties had instituted the white primary around the turn of the century as one way to disfranchise black voters. Although the Supreme Court's decision of *Smith v. Allwright* handed down in April 1944 did not involve Georgia specifically, it had implications for the state's primary system. The court had held that the exclusion of blacks from the Texas Democratic primary violated the Fifteenth Amendment. Even though Texas law did not exclude blacks from voting in the state primaries, state Democratic party rules did. The court reasoned that since primaries were regulated in other respects by state law, Texas was in effect enforcing the party's discrimination against black voters. In short, if the Texas

Democratic party could not exclude blacks from voting in its primaries, neither could the Georgia Democratic party.[23]

In a session one week following the Supreme Court's decision, the commission considered a provision in the Constitution of 1877 pertaining to voting in a primary election. Commissioner Warren Grice suggested that the section be deleted from the proposed constitution, contending that the basis of the *Smith* decision was that Texas law had made the primary rules a part of the state's election machinery. Haas feared that deletion would leave the primaries unregulated by the state and subject to corruption and fraud. Despite her objections, the commission voted to delete the section in question from the revised constitution. Governor Arnall differed with Haas on this issue by arguing that the legislature or the political parties could still regulate primaries and prevent fraud. The Atlanta League of Women Voters warned of voting irregularities in primaries if they were not regulated by the state. Arnall disagreed and told the commissioners of his opposition to "any regulation of primaries in the Constitution or on the statute books of this state."[24]

The commission also considered whether to retain the poll tax—a tax that critics claimed contributed to low voter registration in the South. The Constitution of 1877 provided for an annual poll tax of one dollar. Judge Edgar Watkins, a spokesman for a group that favored abolishing the tax, urged the commission to delete the tax from the revised constitution because it was undemocratic. During the 1942 primary, several of Arnall's liberal-minded supporters had urged him to come out against the poll tax. Arnall refused, "Hell, if I do I'll get beat." During the commission's discussion of the tax, Arnall reminded the commissioners of the numerous exceptions to the poll tax—citizens aged eighteen to twenty-one, citizens over sixty, military personnel, and first-time women voters. "I have sometimes wondered," Arnall mused, "who was left to pay poll tax." Arnall admitted, however, that "the Chair has no deep-seated convictions on it" and called for a study to determine the impact of abolishing the poll tax. Despite Judge Watkins's eloquent appeal to abolish the poll tax, the commission voted overwhelmingly to retain the tax with only Carmichael and Haas voting to abolish it.[25]

The commission held its last regularly scheduled meeting on November 14, 1944. While much of the outdated material had been deleted and the language of the document improved, no major revisions had been made.

Arnall's efforts to create a constitutional state board of corrections and a personnel board as well as to provide local home rule had failed. Nevertheless, Arnall told the commissioners of his satisfaction with their efforts. He conceded the likelihood of criticism arising from its failure to provide for substantial reform but commented, "Had we put into this document too many radical departures from customs or procedure, it would have . . . met defeat." The commission under Arnall's direction had written a "new" constitution, but it could hardly be called one that reformed the state's political system.[26]

As Arnall anticipated, the new constitution received substantial criticism. The Georgia League of Women Voters, perhaps the strongest advocate of constitutional reform, had called for eight major changes in the revised constitution prior to the convening of the commission. These included establishing local home rule, reapportioning the legislature on a population basis, reducing the number of counties, providing for jury service for women, providing for a secret ballot, and abolishing the budget allocation system. The revised constitution contained only one of these reforms—the abolishing of the allocation system—and that change had already been made by the 1943 legislative session.[27]

The Atlanta newspapers led the attack on the shortcomings of the commission's effort. The Atlanta *Constitution* criticized the commission for failing to provide home rule, create a constitutional prison board, and establish a constitutional state merit system—all of which Arnall had unsuccessfully fought for in the commission. The Atlanta *Journal* observed that many critics had concluded that the commission "has brought forth a mouse." Jack Tarver, a columnist for the Atlanta *Constitution,* accused the commission of "producing an innocuous document which couldn't possibly offend anyone." C. E. Gregory, a reporter for the Atlanta *Journal,* wondered whether the new constitution was "worth the eighty-nine scraps of paper that it is written on." State Auditor B. E. Thrasher, Jr., a member of the commission, believed the chief accomplishment of the commission was "to compel twenty-three people to read the old constitution in full."[28]

Arnall received hundreds of letters complaining of the commission's work and over thirty-five newspaper editorials criticized the proposed constitution. Arnall publicly conceded that if criticism continued he would call the commission back in session. The criticism continued and on November 25, 1944, Arnall called for the commission to reconvene on December 8 and 9. He concluded that 95 percent of the criticism directed toward the commission was a result of its failure to provide for a constitutional state merit system, home rule, and a constitutional board of corrections. He feared that the commission members had not listened to "the people who really expect us to blaze the trail for better government through a better constitution." The Atlanta *Journal* warned that the people would not adopt the proposed constitution unless it contained a constitutional civil service system, home rule, and a constitutional corrections board. The Albany *Herald* hoped the reconvened commission could get back to work "sans fumbling and dodging of politically red-hot issues." The Augusta *Chronicle* praised Arnall for reconvening the commission after realizing that many of the state's citizenry were not satisfied with its work.[29]

The reconvened commission immediately took up the issue of home rule. Two proposals for home rule emerged. Gross proposed a liberal home rule plan allowing local governments to enact local legislation as long as it was not in violation of the state constitution or in conflict with state law. The Gross plan also provided that local legislation could be enacted by a local government's submitting it to the local voters for approval or rejection. Gross's proposal further provided for local initiative to propose legislation for the legislature's consideration. Harris opposed the Gross plan and in particular the initiative provision. The Carmichael plan proposed that optional plans of local governments would be drawn up by the legislature and be made available to the local voters who would choose one of the options. Arnall, disagreeing with Harris again, favored the Gross plan.[30]

After much discussion, the commission adopted a home rule article provided that the legislature propose optional plans of local government with a majority vote of the local voters determining which plan would be used. The proposed article retained the local initiative and referendum provisions, although it increased the percentage of voters needed to activate the local initiative and referendum provisions. Arnall, who had fought hard for a liberal home rule article in the regular session of the commission, had finally prevailed in the home rule fight with Harris. However, both realized that the proposed article had to survive legislative scrutiny.[31]

Arnall tried again during the reconvened session to obtain the creation of a constitutional state board of corrections. Harris again opposed Arnall's efforts. While the commission finally created a constitutional board of corrections, Harris convinced the commission to allow the legislature to determine the responsibilities of the board. Arnall also clashed with Harris over the creation of a constitutional state merit system. He feared it could lead to "a super-government over the State that is beyond the will of the people." Arnall disagreed and urged the commission to write a detailed merit system in the constitution as the only way to protect it from political interference. Harris successfully moved that the commission stand by its earlier action of refusing to create a constitutional state merit system.[32]

In addition to considering home rule, the merit system, and a state board of corrections, the reconvened commission, at Arnall's insistence, wrote into the proposed constitution a state department of veterans service to ensure the administration of the department on "a non-partisan, non-political basis." The commission voted, as it had in the regular session, to retain the poll tax in the proposed constitution. The question of gubernatorial succession reemerged with Gross expressing reservations about his earlier support for removing the ban. Arnall spoke against reconsideration, and Gross's motion to reconsider failed on a tie vote with Arnall voting against the motion.[33]

The proposed constitution still had to undergo the scrutiny of the General Assembly before being submitted to the voters. The Atlanta *Journal* urged the legislature to accept the recommendations of the commission and in particular those concerning home rule, a state civil service system, and a board of corrections. "These three essentials must be fully guaranteed," the *Journal* asserted, "if we are to have an acceptable constitution." The Georgia League of Women Voters called a vote on ratification "a sheer waste of tax money" if the proposed constitution did not contain those key provisions.[34]

The House Committee on Constitutional Amendments, however, unanimously voted to delete the commission's home rule article. Instead, the committee adopted a proposal authored by Speaker Harris that mandated the legislature to provide for uniform systems of local government and to provide for local initiative, referendum, and recall elections. The House adopted the committee's version of home rule. In the Senate, an effort to restore some of the House-deleted provisions of the commission's home rule recommendations failed. Senator Spencer M. Grayson, a political adversary of the governor, then attempted to amend the House version by making legislative enactment of home rule optional instead of mandatory. The Senate adopted Grayson's amendment. However, a conference committee report, which was adopted by both houses, restored the House version. Although substantially modified from the way it was originally submitted, a system of limited home rule had survived legislative revision.

The articles dealing with a state merit system and a state board of corrections also passed legislative scrutiny.[35]

During the commission's deliberations, the members never discussed the possibility of creating the office of lieutenant governor. However, Arnall, after the House had passed the proposed constitution, requested the Senate to create the lieutenant governorship. The Senate complied with only one dissenting vote. A conference committee incorporated the office in its report—an addition which the House accepted. Georgia would have a lieutenant governor—provided the voters ratified the proposed constitution.[36]

Unlike the lieutenant governorship, the issues of gubernatorial succession and the poll tax had the potential of generating conflict among the lawmakers. Arnall, in his address opening the 1945 legislative session, urged the General Assembly to approve the action of the constitutional commission concerning gubernatorial succession. He qualified his plea for this reform by asking the legislature "to make it effective with the next occupant of the Governor's chair and not with me." Nevertheless, Harris, who had favored the reform in the commission, now feared that the inclusion of such controversial questions in the proposed constitution could "get it all killed." The speaker proposed with Arnall's concurrence that the question be submitted as a constitutional amendment to be voted on separately from the proposed constitution. While Arnall insisted that the amendment should apply to his successors, Harris opposed any amendment that excluded Arnall. The governor finally requested that consideration of the succession issue be postponed until the 1946 session of the legislature. In doing so, Arnall avoided the possibility of entangling the issue of succession with legislative consideration of the constitution and the ratification struggle.[37]

Though the legislature temporarily sidestepped the issue of gubernatorial succession, it took action on the poll tax. The commission had retained the tax in the proposed constitution. According to an Associated Press survey in December 1944, most of the lawmakers favored retention of the tax. In the same month, Arnall called for a year-long study to determine the fate of the poll tax. He promised to take a stand on the issue after examining the findings of the study. Thus, when the legislature convened in January 1945, Arnall had avoided a leadership role on the issue.[38]

In contrast, both Harris and Gross had already indicated their support for repealing the tax. In addition, both of Georgia's U.S. senators favored repeal by the legislature. Unlike some Georgia politicians, these four political leaders didn't see the repeal of the poll tax as a race-related issue. In addition, a new convert, former governor Talmadge, came out in opposition to the tax, contending the tax kept many whites from voting. Talmadge concluded that abolishing the poll tax would not allow blacks to vote in Georgia because they "as a class don't care to vote anyway, unless they are encouraged by some communistic elements." The Atlanta *Journal* concluded that such wide support for ending the tax among the state's political leadership meant that "the days of the poll tax in Georgia are numbered."[39]

Nevertheless, Arnall still refused to take a public stand on the issue. Instead, he urged the legislature in his opening address on January 8, 1945, to "ponder" whether the tax should be retained. He called for the tax's repeal—if the legislature determined it served no useful purpose. Representative Fortson, seeing no need to ponder the issue, introduced a bill providing for veterans' exemption from the tax and another that repealed the tax. Senate President Gross and John R. McGinty cosponsored a bill in the Senate repealing the tax. On January 13 Arnall announced his legislative agenda for the 1945 session, which included a request for the repeal of the poll tax—his first public call for its repeal. Despite Arnall's belated support, the House on January 22 defeated Fortson's bill exempting veterans from the tax by an overwhelming vote.[40]

On the same day the Senate began debate on the Gross-McGinty bill. The upper house postponed a heated discussion on the bill in order to hear an address by Arnall pertaining to the tax. He told a joint session that the tax served "no possible good and should be repealed." The governor confessed to being "tired of seeing my state, the state I love, kicked about in Congress" on the poll-tax issue. Arnall saw "no danger" of blacks voting in Georgia's primary elections as long as the state retained the white primary. If the legislature refused to repeal the poll tax, Arnall threatened to suspend collection of it under an 1821 law. Ironically, former governor Talmadge had resorted to the same law when the legislature refused his request to lower the price of automobile tags in 1933.[41]

Arnall's ultimatum drew swift reaction. In a blistering editorial entitled "Who is Dictating Now?," the Savannah *Evening Press* reminded its readers that Talmadge had been denounced as "a dictator and usurper of authority" when he had issued a similar threat. Senator Grayson declared that Arnall's ultimatum meant that "we might as well abolish the legislature." Representative James Dykes agreed, "If one man is going to countermand the actions of 257 legislators, we might as well go out of business." Even the Columbus *Ledger,* which supported repeal of the poll tax, opposed Arnall's ultimatum "because government by fiat is dangerous no matter how splendid the cause."[42]

The day following the governor's speech, the Senate voted to repeal the poll tax by a 31 to 19 vote. Senator Grayson declared that up until the governor's address, "This bill faced certain defeat in the Senate. The governor's influence and nothing else passed it." The Senate even passed a resolution complaining of the "heat" generated by the governor's lobbying on behalf of repeal. Arnall had engaged in a vigorous lobbying effort to get the tax repealed. Calling groups of legislators into his office, he told them:

> when you adjourn and you haven't done away with the poll tax, then by executive order I can do away with it until the next meeting of the legislature. So you will be running without any poll tax. So when you go to ask somebody to vote for you, they say, "Hell, if it hadn't been for Governor Arnall I couldn't vote, I'm against you." Whereas, if you take full credit on it and you go home and tell it—put it in the local paper that you supported doing away with it—you wanted a broad franchise—you'll get elected.[43]

On January 31 the House considered the Senate bill and overwhelmingly passed it. The Senate version, however, required biennial voter registration, whereas the House had provided for permanent registration. The Senate eventually agreed to the House's version. The legislature later in the session deleted the poll tax as a requirement for voting on the proposed constitution. Under Arnall's leadership, Georgia had become the fourth southern state to abolish the poll tax. Arnall received widespread praise for his role in the elimination of the tax. Two hundred fifty prominent liberals signed a tribute to Arnall commending him for his leadership in bringing about the demise of the tax in Georgia. Signers included the prominent American historian Charles A. Beard, Eleanor Roosevelt, and U.S. Senator Claude D. Pepper of Florida. The Atlanta *Journal* also gave Arnall the major credit for the tax's repeal because of his support for repeal "at the crucial moment when the tides of battle wavered." The Chattanooga *Times* praised the courage of Arnall in leading the successful repeal effort in Georgia. The Nashville *Tennessean* even called Arnall "a statesman of the Jeffersonian mold." Josephus Daniels, writing in the Raleigh *News and Observer,* hailed the repeal as "only one of the progressive measures championed by

Governor Arnall." The liberal *New Republic* praised Arnall's leadership on the poll-tax issue and contended that he "shows more signs of becoming another Hugo Black or another Claude Pepper than any other young progressive in the South today." Clark Foreman, writing in the *New Republic,* hailed Arnall's "bold progressivism." Foreman claimed that Arnall, by leading the fight to lower the voting age and eliminate the poll tax, had "done more to extend the franchise than any other American since women were given the vote."[44]

However, the Savannah *Morning News* contended, "Repeal was the last thing Mr. Arnall dreamed of for this year—until former governor Gene Talmadge forced his hand." Gerald W. Johnson, writing in the American *Mercury,* rejected the views of northern liberals that Arnall's fight to repeal the poll tax was proof of his liberalism, contending that some of the rankest reactionaries in the South opposed the tax. In *The Poll Tax in the South,* Frederick D. Ogden attributed Arnall's study-to-action conversion to a personal plea from President Roosevelt—an allegation that Arnall denied. Arnall insisted that his conversion came about because of his realization that the legislature "was not going to do away with the poll tax unless I got tough." Whatever the reason, Arnall had entered the battle, and his presence made the critical difference.[45]

As the 1945 session drew to a close, the legislature with only twelve dissenting votes adopted a conference committee's report on the constitution. The committee had resolved forty-nine differences between the two houses over the proposed constitution. The legislature also designated August 7, 1945, as the date when the fate of the proposed constitution would be determined by the voters. Although approval of the constitution headed the governor's legislative agenda, Arnall had also requested passage of a number of administration bills. The legislature unanimously approved his request to appropriate one million dollars to fund the Teachers Retirement System. The system had been created but not funded by the 1943 legislature. Lawmakers also agreed unanimously to provide the Department of Education with an additional revenue to increase teachers' salaries for the 1944–45 school year. Both appropriations came from accumulated revenues on hand and not from increased taxation. With only one negative vote, Arnall obtained the establishment of the State Ports Authority, which would have the responsibility of constructing and operating state-owned docks in Savannah and Brunswick. The legislature also passed several administration requests pertaining to veterans.[46]

Though they approved most of the governor's requests, the lawmakers turned down several. These included creating a state version of the federal Reconstruction Finance Corporation, establishing a pension and retirement system for law officers, and expanding state health services. In spite of these defeats, Arnall hailed the 1945 General Assembly as "one of the greatest, if not the greatest, ever to legislate in the interest of the people." He deemed the passage of the proposed constitution as the "greatest accomplishment" of the session. The governor praised the 1945 General Assembly as one of the most progressive in the state's history because of its repeal of the poll tax.[47]

In July 1945 Arnall launched a statewide campaign to gain ratification of the new constitution. Ivan Allen, Sr., a prominent Atlanta businessman, chaired the Committee for Constitution Ratification, which led the fight for ratification. A statewide advisory committee of over eighty leading Georgians assisted Allen's committee. The constitution had the endorsement and active support of former governor Rivers, Speaker Harris, and Senate President Gross. Arnall encouraged state officials and employees "to do everything that the proprieties will permit" to ensure the adoption of the constitution. He undertook a vigorous speaking tour on behalf of ratification that carried him into every section of Georgia. In addition, the governor made several radio addresses, numerous personal contacts, and countless telephone calls to ensure ratification. With the exception of Talmadge, no prominent state politician opposed the constitution.[48]

In addition to having an organizational advantage, the pro-ratification forces had the support of the state press. C. E. Gregory, a reporter for the Atlanta *Journal,* wrote that the press was "almost unanimously supporting ratification." A common theme occurred in their editorials—ratification meant a continuance of the progress made by the state under the Arnall administration. The Milledgeville *Union-Recorder* editorialized that those "who believe in progress will support the new constitution," while the Winder *News* attacked opponents of the constitution as "those who would hinder the progress of Georgia." The Augusta *Chronicle* viewed the constitution as "one of the choicest ornaments in the new House of Progress that has been under construction ever since Governor Ellis Arnall has been in office." The Vienna *News* urged its readers to vote for the constitution in order to be on the side of progressive government. The editor of the Valdosta *Daily Times* urged voter approval "to give our state another boost along the path of progress." The Fitzgerald *Herald* declared the adoption of the constitution would be another effort toward restoring Georgia to her rightful place as the Empire State of the South.[49]

In addition to having the overwhelming endorsement of the press, the proposed constitution enjoyed the strong backing of numerous statewide organizations. These included the Georgia Education Association, Georgia Association of School Administrators, Georgia League of Women Voters, Georgia Junior Chamber of Commerce, Georgia Mercantile Association, Georgia Association of County Commissioners, Georgia Municipal Association, and Georgia Bar Association. The Atlanta *Journal* noted that "no state group has registered opposition."[50]

Despite fighting a lonely battle, Talmadge conducted a vigorous attack on the proposed constitution. He questioned why a constitution should be replaced that had permitted Georgia to have "the best educational system, the best college system and the best penal system in the Union." He dismissed the proposed constitution as "eighty-nine scraps of paper!" The former governor even charged that the method of revision was illegal because the Constitution of 1877 specifically required that it could be replaced only by a constitutional convention. Talmadge warned that the major purpose of revising the constitution was to "get rid of about one hundred counties in Georgia!," abolish the county unit system, and eliminate most of the local school trustees. In short, the proponents wanted, said Talmadge, "to concentrate power! They want to take the authority away from the local governments! This is antidemocratic and pro-New Deal!"[51]

Talmadge also raised the race issue by claiming that the "New Deal Constitution" threatened white supremacy in Georgia. He noted that the revised constitution left out voter qualifications that had been added to the Constitution of 1877 by Governor Hoke Smith to disfranchise blacks. These had been omitted, according to Talmadge, because Arnall was in league with Vice President Henry A. Wallace and U.S. Attorney General Francis Biddle, both of whom advocated racial equality and wanted "negroes holding office in Georgia." Talmadge claimed that if the voters ratified the Wallace-Biddle-approved constitution, the state would "have negro officers in Georgia within less than five years, elected by negro voters!"[52]

While conceding the proposed constitution contained several provisions he disliked, Arnall believed the document stood "over the old constitution like a dollar does to a dime." He dismissed Talmadge's criticism as "based upon fraud and misrepresentation." Arnall argued that instead of

making county consolidation easier as Talmadge charged, the new constitution made it more difficult. Noting that the Association of County Commissioners had endorsed the constitution, Arnall asked why the commissioners would support ratification "if it were possible for the big counties
to gobble up the little ones." Arnall also dismissed as untrue the Talmadge
allegation that the document threatened the county unit system. As for Talmadge's argument against constitutional reform during war time, Arnall
declared, "I think it is our duty to make our state a better place for our
service men and women to come home to."[53]

Former governor Rivers urged "the biggest vote possible" to repudiate
the "reactionaries" opposing ratification. Despite Rivers's plea, the August
election proved to be a typical special election in that less than 20 percent of the registered voters participated. Those who voted ratified the
constitution by a vote of 60,065 to 34,417. Even Talmadge's home county
of Telfair voted in favor of ratification. Arnall praised the vote as "a victory for progressive and forward-looking government." He had scored yet
another political victory over "the wild man from Sugar Creek." In doing
so, Georgia became the first state to use the commission method to replace
its constitution.[54]

After sixty-eight years, Georgia finally had a "new" constitution. One
constitutional scholar, Albert B. Saye, estimated, however, that "fully
ninety percent" of the 1945 constitution had been taken from the Constitution of 1877. Elkin Taylor, in his study of Arnall, deemed the new
constitution "the same sorry material as the 1877 Constitution." Arnall
conceded the constitution was not progressive enough and that it did not
reform enough. However, the new constitution contained fifty changes
over the old constitution, and even Saye conceded that "some of the
changes in structure were of great significance." These changes included
the creation of the office of lieutenant governor, the addition of a seventh
member to the state supreme court to prevent split decisions, the addition
of two positions to the state Senate, and the creation of three constitutional
boards—the State Board of Corrections, the State Veterans Board, and the
State Personnel Board. Thirteen of the fifty changes in the new constitution
occurred in the area of local government. The new constitution permitted
local governments to spend revenues for many new services, made it easier
to pass local bonds, allowed local governments to enact zoning laws without legislative approval, and allowed political subdivisions to contract with
each other for exchange of services. Under the new constitution, counties

gained the power to increase their tax millage and counties assumed greater responsibility in the operation of public schools.[55]

Despite the revisions, the state's political system remained fundamentally unchanged. The major defects of the state's political system—too many counties, the county unit system, malapportionment, denial of equal rights for blacks, a lack of local home rule, and an inflexible constitution—continued after the ratification of the Constitution of 1945. Arnall could have brought about more significant reforms in the new constitution, but in order to do so, he would have had to overcome significant opposition not only in the commission itself but also in the rurally dominated legislature. By 1945 Arnall had carefully cultivated the image of a successful politician leading Georgia down the road to progress. He enjoyed widespread popularity throughout the state and had gained national recognition. Arnall was determined to add a new constitution to a lengthy list of accomplishments. However, he realized that a constitution capable of dealing with the major defects in the state's political system would require a major political struggle, resulting in a loss of political popularity and possible defeat on the issue. The pragmatic Arnall compromised on the issue and opted for a constitution that could be approved by the legislature and ratified by the voters.

Arnall's efforts allowed Georgia to gain an updated version of the Constitution of 1877, but that document did not survive as a "lasting monument" as Arnall had envisioned. Increasing criticism of the Constitution of 1945 led to efforts to replace it. Despite its imperfections, the Arnall 1945 Constitution was an improvement over its predecessor, yet it remained the state's fundamental law for only thirty-one years.[56]

7

State

Finances

and

Services

Ellis Arnall assumed the governorship during a difficult time in the history of the state. The United States was fighting a major war, and Georgians were experiencing numerous hardships and deprivations because of that conflict. More than 320,000 of the state citizenry entered the military service with 6,754 making the ultimate sacrifice. On the homefront, Arnall inherited a huge state debt and a revenue system straining to maintain the existing level of inadequate state services. The prospect of affording the people adequate governmental services in the Arnall administration appeared bleak.[1]

On the eve of his inauguration, a state auditor's report revealed a state debt of almost $36 million. In comparison, the state's revenue from all sources amounted to less than $82 million in the 1942 fiscal year. In addition to the debt problem, the incoming governor had to deal with a substantial reduction in state revenue. Georgia lacked a general sales tax and depended upon a motor fuel tax as its major source of income. The fuel tax provided 31.6 percent of the state's entire revenue in the 1942 fiscal year. Federal rationing of gasoline, however, had reduced revenue from the fuel tax from almost $26 million in the 1942 fiscal year to $18 million in the 1943 fiscal year. The state auditor gloomily concluded that Georgia faced "dark days ahead because of the curtailment of revenue."[2]

Arnall agreed and told the legislature in his inaugural address, "The outlook for a solution of our state's financial plight is indeed dark." The new governor faced the difficult task of maintaining state services and paying the debt with a declining state revenue. Arnall's pledge in his gubernatorial campaign not to raise taxes eliminated that option as a source of needed revenue.

He conceded that it was going to be "a real job to finance state operations during the next four critical years." Resolving the financial crisis while continuing to provide state services loomed as one of the most perplexing problems facing the new administration.[3]

Although Arnall considered himself a liberal on the question of providing governmental services, he deemed himself a conservative in fiscal policy and placed paying off the state debt high on his agenda. He believed the debt, some of which was over a century old, should be paid off because a debt-free state characterized good government. He feared a state debt "behind which mysterious financing projects could hide" to be an invitation to dishonest government. While conceding that public debt per se was not bad, Arnall believed that the state's debts should be liquidated when due. He noted with dismay that some of the state's debts had been refinanced many times, resulting in the interest paid exceeding the principal in many cases. Arnall wanted a debt-free state so that it could emerge into the postwar period in a sound fiscal condition fully able to participate in federal public works programs and to undertake a necessary expansion of state services. Furthermore, Arnall warned, "Industries will not come to a state where the state's finances are chaotic."[4]

When Arnall took office, the funded debt of the state was $25,227,675, plus almost $11 million of outstanding highway contracts. The gross state debt totaled $35,961,630. War conditions assisted Arnall in his endeavor to liquidate the state debt by curtailing highway construction and thus reducing expenditures for the largest department in the state government. State highway construction could not occur in Georgia during the war years without the approval of the federal government, and then only when the construction was related to the war effort. These conditions substantially reduced the demands of highway contractors and politicians for roads.[5]

In his budget message to the legislature in January 1943 Arnall made no request for funds for highway construction and canceled highway projects already awarded. Arnall stated that the state had a responsibility to limit new road construction "to relieve the materials, transportation facilities, and labor for use in the war effort." He stated his preference for reserving that money to start a large road building program after the war to stimulate business and provide employment. Lack of materials and labor also limited the construction of public facilities during the war and a decline in the number of state employees aided Arnall's efforts to cope with his financial crisis.[6]

Despite Arnall's concerns early in his administration, the state's revenue did not suffer as drastic a decline as he had feared. In fact, revenue from state taxation declined in only one year of the Arnall administration. In 1942 state taxes brought in over $58 million. The following year, revenue generated by state taxes declined, but by 1945 this source of revenue had increased to over $61 million and the following year totaled over $80 million. In addition, Arnall began an austerity program to provide additional revenue to pay the state's debts.[7]

Arnall made a decision early in his administration to divert state revenue into sinking funds to pay off state obligations prior to their due dates— an undertaking that reduced the amount of interest the state had to pay. During his term, Arnall committed over $26 million toward paying off the state's debt. The percentage of state revenue spent on debt payment underscored Arnall's commitment to ending Georgia's debtor status. In the 1942 fiscal year the Talmadge administration had committed less than one percent of its tax revenue to public debt payment. The percentages of the four years of the Arnall administration read 14.4, 11.4, 9.0, and 5.1. Because of these efforts, a proud governor announced in December 1945 that the state had paid or had sufficient funds in the treasury to pay all the state's debts and claimed that Georgia was in the best financial shape of any state in the Union. "Today for the first time in more than one hundred years," Arnall told the legislature in its 1946 session, "a Governor can report to the Legislature that Georgia is solvent." State Auditor Thrasher, usually tight-fisted with the expenditure of state funds, spent eight thousand dollars on publishing a financial statement in every county newspaper to inform Georgians of the state's good financial condition. Arnall considered the removal of the debt burden one of the major accomplishments of his administration.[8]

Arnall also took pride in the fact that taxes had not been raised during his governorship. The governor had opposed a sales tax while in the legislature and had promised no additional, increased, or new taxes in his gubernatorial campaign. Arnall throughout his term held to his opposition to an increase in state taxes and threatened to veto any measure increasing taxes. Arnall opposed the general sales tax because of its regressive nature and objected to increasing other state taxes because of the heavy federal taxation already imposed on Georgians due to the war. When support of a general sales tax grew in the latter half of his administration, Arnall stood steadfast against such a tax even though half of the states had a general sales tax, including four southern states.[9]

An increase in one state source of revenue occurred in the Arnall administration. In November 1945 Arnall's revenue commissioner, Melvin E. Thompson, raised the state's warehouse liquor fee from fifty cents to three dollars per gallon. At that time the state required alcoholic beverage distributors to store their liquor in state warehouses. Arnall contended that Thompson had initiated the increase on his own but that he supported Thompson's action. Arnall denied, however, the storage fee increase was a tax increase. The governor used the additional revenue to support an expanded program of state services in 1946.[10]

Despite initial fears that services would have to be cut to survive the financial crisis, spending for state services actually increased in the Arnall administration. The greatest increase occurred in education, which Arnall considered the most important of all state services. He had successfully campaigned on a platform of removing gubernatorial domination over the state educational system. Although he agreed that adequate financial support for education was important, Arnall deemed it secondary to his effort to free the state's educational system from political interference. In his inaugural address, Arnall expressed his belief that education was the hope of the future and pledged to go "all-out" for education.[11]

State spending for education increased significantly during Arnall's governorship. The Department of Education received $15,506,400 from the state in the last year of the Talmadge administration. By fiscal year 1946 the state's appropriation for the public schools had increased 41 percent, and the university system appropriation had increased 131 percent over the last fiscal year of the Talmadge administration. Under the Arnall administration, state spending for the public schools and the university system had increased so that Arnall claimed that the state ranked first in the nation in the percentage of total state income spent on education.[12]

In addition, the Arnall administration secured the creation of a teachers retirement system. The drive for such a system had started in the mid-1930s with supporters arguing for Georgia to join ranks with the majority of other states which had implemented such systems. Arnall agreed and in his 1942 campaign promised to establish a teachers retirement system. The legislature created such a system in 1943, but the state's financial problems delayed its funding until 1945. By fiscal year 1947, the state's annual contribution had grown to over $2 million. In February 1945 in a ceremony in the governor's office, the first recipient of the system proudly received a retirement check. The *Georgia Education Journal*, the official publication of the Georgia Education Association, called the occasion "one of the memorable days in Georgia."[13]

Despite the increase in state spending for education, Arnall conceded that more money was needed. Arnall broke ranks with the states' rights philosophy of most southern politicians by calling for federal aid to education. According to Arnall, state and local governments, especially those in the South, needed federal assistance because they lacked the financial resources to provide an adequate educational system. Arnall further believed federal assistance essential in order to equalize the educational opportunities for all students no matter which section of the country they resided in or what their economic status was. He also called on local governments in Georgia to increase their inadequate financial support of education.[14]

Arnall presided over a state whose educational system had long suffered because of low teachers' salaries. In 1944 the average teacher's salary in Georgia was less than half of the national average, leading the Atlanta *Journal* to claim that low teacher salary was the number one problem of the Arnall administration. Arnall continued the 25 percent salary increase for teachers that Governor Talmadge had initiated shortly before the 1942 primary. He further raised teachers' salaries by gradually extending teachers' contracts from seven months to twelve months by the last year of his term. Despite these efforts, the state school superintendent, M. D. Collins, warned of school closings due to a lack of teachers, which he attributed primarily to low salaries.[15]

At its 1944 state convention, the Georgia Education Association endorsed an additional 25 percent pay increase for teachers. By early 1946 GEA demands had increased to a 50 percent pay raise, which Arnall rejected as "utterly out of the question" because it would require an increase in state taxes. "No amount of political pressure," Arnall declared, "will force me to plunge the state into bankruptcy and debt, as some apparently desire." Arnall qualified his statement by noting that the Budget Bureau which he headed had the authority to allocate surplus revenue and that he would support the allocation of surplus funds to education.[16]

Shortly after Arnall's statement, Eugene Talmadge announced his entry into the 1946 gubernatorial primary. Talmadge's platform included a 50 percent salary increase for teachers. Shortly thereafter, Arnall announced a 50 percent increase in teachers' salaries to take effect in the last four months of his administration. Arnall explained that an estimated increase in state revenue would permit the salary increase without an increase in taxes. He warned that his successor would have to determine whether to continue the pay increase. Teachers' salaries had been increased substantially in the Arnall administration. When Arnall came into office, the average annual teacher's salary was $842.97. The average salary increased by fiscal year 1947 to $1,538.79, an increase of 83 percent.[17]

According to State School Superintendent Collins, the 50 percent salary increase "probably did more to lift the sagging morale of our teachers and send us surging ahead in education than any other single action of recent date." The executive secretary of the GEA called Arnall "the greatest friend of education Georgia has had." The Atlanta *Journal* praised Arnall's commitment to education as "an unparalleled and epoch-making advance in Georgia's educational progress." Marion Smith, the chairman of the Board of Regents, hailed the Arnall administration for its "great progress in the educational work of Georgia along all lines."[18]

Despite Smith's praise, "great progress" had not occurred in the state's education of black Georgians. The state, while rigidly adhering to the segregationist provision of the separate but equal doctrine, had failed to provide any semblance of equal educational opportunities for black Georgians. That discrepancy continued in the Arnall administration. In 1943 a white teacher received an average annual salary of $1,088 while a black teacher averaged $547, a difference of $641. By 1947 teachers' salaries for both races had increased, but the gap between white and black teachers had grown to $701. Inequality also existed in facilities, library holdings, and bus transportation as well as per student spending by the state. In 1945 the state spent $87.29 to educate a white student and only $28.77 to educate a black.[19]

While conceding that blacks had not received adequate educational opportunities in the South, Arnall never urged the legislature to provide funding necessary to upgrade educational opportunities for blacks in Georgia. To do so would have antagonized whites and especially whites in the politically important conservative rural counties who dominated the legislature and the state's electoral system. These voters constituted the most vehement defenders of the racial status quo. Arnall, in order to obtain the passage of his reform program, had to have cooperation of the racially conservative legislature, which would have been hostile to efforts to improve black education. In later years, when the separate but equal doctrine was under challenge in the federal courts, segregationist governors in the South called for upgrading black schools in a desperate effort to save segregation. The federal judiciary posed no threat, however, to segregated schools in Georgia in the Arnall administration. An effort by Arnall to substantially improve black education could be expected to result in a substantial loss of political support especially in the rural counties. Nor could Arnall ignore the staggering financial cost required to upgrade black education at a time of serious financial difficulty for the state. Consequently, Arnall, as governor, never addressed the problem of black education in Georgia as he had other problems of the state such as the penal issue, the poll tax, or constitutional reform. Politically, he could not afford to do so.[20]

Changes in the new constitution improved education in Georgia. Most important, the Constitution of 1945 abolished over twelve hundred local school subdistricts, each of which had its own board of trustees and taxing powers. Arnall, during the deliberations of the Constitutional Revision Commission, favored the elimination of the subdistricts with county boards of education assuming their functions. The new constitution contained such a provision, resulting in the eventual consolidation of thousands of small, substandard schools. The Constitution of 1945 also made it easier for local voters to pass school bond issues, permitted a state-supported twelfth grade, and raised the local taxing authority limit for education from five to fifteen mills. Although they did not get all the reforms they desired in the new constitution, the state's educators supported its adoption. The legislature, with the support of Arnall, also passed a new compulsory school attendance law.[21]

The state made progress in vocational and rehabilitation education during the Arnall administration. The state Board of Education authorized the establishment of the North Georgia Vocational School in 1943. The state's financial difficulties delayed the establishment of a similar school in south Georgia until 1946. The board also authorized a plan to create several area trade schools, but a lack of finances delayed implementation of this program until after the war. Nevertheless, by 1945 Georgia ranked tenth in combined federal-state-local government expenditures for vocational education and fourth in the nation in total enrollment in vocational classes. Arnall praised the state's effort in vocational education as "outstanding in the nation." He also had praise for the state's effort on behalf of vocational rehabilitation, a program that he called the best in the nation. By 1945 Georgia led the nation in the number of persons rehabilitated through the vocational rehabilitation program.[22]

Despite such progress, the state had far to go before it could claim to have an adequate educational system. Two studies conducted during the Arnall administration made that fact clear. Arnall had successfully supported the creation of the Agricultural and Industrial Development Board in the 1943 legislative session. The board divided itself into several panels, one of which was an education panel that undertook an intensive study of the state's public school system. After investigating the condition of school facilities, the panel estimated the expenditure of $83,571,000 would be required to bring the state school buildings up to minimum standards. The report blamed the economic depression of the 1930s and the "virtual cessation" of school construction during the war as the major culprits for the pitiful condition of school buildings in the state.[23]

With the support of Arnall, the legislature created a special committee in the 1946 session to investigate the state's public school system. The resolution creating the committee concluded that the system faced "the worst crisis in its history" despite the "tremendous increase" in state appropriations. The resolution charged the committee with investigating the state public school system and making recommendations to the 1947 legislature to correct the crisis. The committee, chaired by Governor Arnall, made an exhaustive study and presented the lawmakers in 1947 with a 420-page report. The report agreed with the education panel's estimate needed to upgrade the state school's facilities to meet minimum standards. Altogether, the report made over one hundred recommendations for improving education in the public schools. In 1949 the legislature passed the Minimum Foundation for Education Act, which was based on the 1947 report. The program, which had its origins in the Arnall administration, became the foundation of the state's modern educational system.[24]

Highway construction in the state declined during the war years. The federal government, upon the entry of the United States into the war, canceled all construction projects involving federal funds except those considered essential to the war effort. Even state construction projects had to be war-related. With construction curtailed, the highway department paid off a huge debt, accumulated a surplus, and made extensive plans for postwar construction projects. The U.S. Congress enacted the Federal-Aid Highway Act of 1944 to promote postwar highway construction. The law authorized the expenditure of over $1.5 billion to become available at the rate of $500 million annually for the fiscal years 1946 through 1948 with states receiving federal highway construction money on a matching basis. In January 1946 Arnall requested the legislature to appropriate $5,790,512 to match federal funds for the remainder of fiscal year 1946 and over $23 million for fiscal years 1947 and 1948. The legislature approved the request.[25]

In addition, Arnall announced that over $4 million of highway construction projects could be financed by reserves in the state treasury. Arnall proudly claimed that his administration, in the aftermath of the war, was "carrying out the most ambitious road building program ever instituted in the history of Georgia." Arnall estimated the cost of the construction program over the next three years to be approximately $80 million. Georgia certainly needed such a program. Early in 1946 the state highway director complained of the terrible conditions of Georgia highways, attributing the situation to the lack of new construction, heavy war traffic on existing roads, and the worst weather in recent times, which had contributed to the deterioration of the state's roads. In response, Arnall diverted $3 million from his emergency fund for highway repairs.[26]

In August 1946 Arnall announced that he had been informed that federal highway matching funds would not be available for the rest of his administration. He therefore proposed to divert approximately $10 million in state highway matching funds to build roads totally funded by the state. Arnall's proposal drew criticism from Herman Talmadge, who attributed Arnall's proposal to an effort "to fulfill some of the road promises" the governor had made during the recent gubernatorial primary in which he had supported a candidate in opposition to Eugene Talmadge's successful comeback effort.[27]

State Auditor Thrasher, who had been friendly to Arnall throughout his governorship, also took issue with the governor's proposal. He contended that Arnall could not divert the money in question because it had been specifically designated by the legislature to match federal highway construction funds. Arnall had an alternate plan if the money in question could not be used for construction purposes. He suggested spending the state's sinking fund of several million that had been set aside to pay state obligations when they became due. Thrasher found that proposal unacceptable as well, contending that the money had been designated to pay off state debts and not to build highways. Thrasher, who praised Arnall's "good financial record up to now," called both of Arnall's suggestions illegal. Arnall quickly responded that he was not going to do anything illegal. "However, I made commitments," he added, "to build a number of roads if I can do so, and I am going to build them if it is legally possible." The Atlanta *Constitution* urged Arnall to withdraw his proposed expenditure in order not to jeopardize his "splendid record" as governor.[28]

To clarify the issue, Arnall requested a legal opinion from Attorney General J. Eugene Cook on the legality of his proposals. Cook sided with Thrasher and held that Arnall could not use the state matching funds to build highways that were totally funded by the state. Cook further ruled that state money set aside for future debt payment could not be used for highway construction. Expressing regret over the opinion, Arnall nevertheless announced he would comply with the ruling. The Atlanta *Journal,* which had differed with Arnall on the issue, editorialized that the ruling allowed Arnall to "fully redeem his promise to leave the state entirely debt free."[29]

The question of a constitutional state highway board came up in the Arnall administration. Arnall, while favoring constitutional boards to take other state agencies "out of politics," opposed the creation of a constitutional board for the state's highway department, contending highway construction was "purely political." He obtained the reorganization of the highway department in the 1943 legislative session. The reorganization replaced the Talmadge three-man highway board with a director who would be appointed by the governor and serve at his pleasure. A highway board, also appointed by the governor, served in an advisory capacity to the director. Ironically, the legislature had given Arnall more power over the highway department than Eugene Talmadge, whom Arnall had campaigned against as being a dictator.[30]

Unlike Rivers and Talmadge, Arnall had a cordial relationship with the two individuals who ran the department in his administration, Ryburn G. Clay and George T. McDonald, who succeeded Clay in 1945. Arnall, however, had a strained relationship with J. Knox Gholston, whom he appointed to the highway commission. Shortly before the legislature convened for its 1945 session, Gholston publicly charged the department with practicing political favoritism in the distribution of state highway construction and maintenance funds. To correct the situation, Gholston proposed legislation allowing the General Assembly to elect board members who in turn would select a director. Gholston's proposal would substantially curtail gubernatorial influence over the highway department. Arnall defended the highway department and insisted that it operated in an honest and efficient manner and contended that it must remain accountable to the governor in matters of finance. The Senate sided with Arnall and defeated a bill to reorganize the department as suggested by Gholston.[31]

The following year, a persistent Gholston again called upon the lawmakers to create a constitutional highway board. Senators Peyton S. Hawes and B. Warren Hill sponsored legislation creating such a board with members elected by the legislature. Their bill also restored the allocation of revenues obtained from fuel taxes to the highway department, which the legislature in 1943 abolished at Arnall's insistence. Senator Hawes contended that the governor controlled the purse strings of the highway department under the existing appropriation system. The senator claimed that, as a result, the governor would continue to control the highway department and the legislature even if a constitutional board were created. Speaker Harris and several other representatives introduced legislation to create a constitutional board while retaining the existing system of legislative appropriation of highway funds.[32]

Arnall again expressed his opposition and promised not to "sit still and let the legislature take the highway department away from the Governor and put it in worse politics." Speaking before a group of state legislators, Arnall candidly offered to give up control of the highway department "if you members of the legislature will release me from roads I have promised you." Arnall told the lawmakers that either the governor or the highway board had to control the money of the department. "I think it should be the Governor," Arnall declared, "since he is elected by the people and responds to the people and to the legislature."[33]

The lawmakers invited Commissioner Gholston to speak to a joint session of the 1946 legislature. In his address Gholston charged that Arnall had not carried out a campaign promise to straighten out the department and charged its operation to be "the rottenest thing in the state of Georgia." Gholston called upon Arnall to end his dictatorship over the department and urged the legislature to strip the governor of financial control of the department. An angry Arnall defended the highway department from Gholston's "unwarranted attacks." While insisting road construction and repairs should be "on a basis of merit and fairness," Arnall wrote the chairman of the highway commission that he did not want the department "to discriminate against my friends because they are my friends." The highway commission with Gholston present voted to "deplore and condemn" his allegations about the operations of the department made before the legislature.[34]

In the last year of his term Arnall yielded in his opposition to a constitutional board and asked the legislature for such a board in his address to the lawmakers at the beginning of the 1946 session. The House easily passed a Harris measure proposing a constitutional board with members elected by the legislature in the 1946 session. The proposed constitutional amendment, however, failed to receive the needed two-thirds vote in the Senate. Upon reconsideration, the Senate amended the measure by allowing the voters in each congressional district instead of the legislature to elect members of the board. Arnall supported the Senate's position of popularly elected board members, believing the board members should either be appointed by the governor like all other constitutional boards or else be elected by the voters. However, both houses refused to budge from their respective positions, and the proposed amendment failed. In 1950 the legislature created a state highway board whose members were elected by the legislature and voters finally approved an amendment in 1964 giving the board constitutional status.[35]

Administration of the Department of Public Welfare proved to be less controversial. Benefits paid by the department increased each year in the Arnall administration. The state portion of benefits paid by the department for dependent children, the blind, and the elderly increased from $3,461,164 in fiscal year 1942 to $5,126,562 by fiscal year 1946, an increase of 48 percent. The numbers of recipients grew slightly from 79,722 in 1942 to 83,666 by 1946. Arnall praised the department for eliminating the backlog of twenty thousand applicants from the Talmadge administration, reducing the cost of operating the system, increasing benefits, and improving its services to the people of the state. He took issue with the federal system of matching funds by arguing that the system penalized the South because of its poverty. To Arnall it seemed ironic that the southern states, which had the greatest poverty and needed the most federal assistance, actually received the least. Arnall called for a revamping of the federal matching system so that federal grants would be distributed on the basis of need.[36]

Late in his term Arnall attempted to obtain the creation of a constitutional board to run the state's welfare system. The legislature, at the request of Arnall, proposed an amendment creating a constitutional state Board of Public Welfare in its 1946 session. The proposed amendment received only one negative vote. However, by the time of the general election in November 1946, when the people voted on the amendment, state politics had undergone a significant change. A politically revived Eugene Talmadge, who had won the 1946 gubernatorial primary, strongly opposed the amendment. Despite Arnall's support of the amendment, voters turned it down by a two-to-one majority in the general election.[37]

Arnall claimed significant advances had been made in the state's eleemosynary institutions. These included the construction of a new fireproof dormitory at the state's School for Mental Defectives, the provision of a recreation building at the state's Training School for White Girls, and the department taking over the operation of the Training School for Black Girls. In particular, Arnall expressed pride in the progress made at Milledgeville State Hospital. He pointed out that when he came into office hundreds of citizens who were mentally ill were in jails. "Today there is not a single person so confined in Georgia," Arnall boasted. He noted that new buildings had been built, old buildings renovated, and improvements made in the appearance of the hospital as well as in the food service and clothing for the patients.[38]

In September 1945 a joint legislative committee, at Arnall's request, inspected Milledgeville State Hospital. It recommended the expenditure of $6,815,000 to upgrade the facilities. Later in the year Arnall authorized the expenditure of $500,000 for physical improvements at the hospital. Construction on two new buildings began and a third underwent renovation. Fire escapes were installed in buildings that lacked them. In 1946 lawmakers passed and Arnall signed into law authorization for the State Hospital Authority to issue $7 million in bonds for construction at the hospital. Prior to the legislative session, the joint committee made another visit to the hospital and observed numerous improvements. These included the replacement of wooden beds with iron beds, the purchase of new mattresses and pillows, the addition of modern medical equipment, and the employment of additional doctors. Although Arnall could not claim that Milledgeville State Hospital had become one of the best mental hospitals in the South, he could point to significant improvements at the institution.[39]

When Arnall had requested a legislative investigation of the state hospital at Milledgeville, he also urged the legislature to investigate all of Georgia's public institutions. He conceded that wartime conditions prevented major construction projects or the increase of personnel at the state's institutions. After making its investigation, the legislature's Joint Committee on Institutions concluded that it would require almost $28 million to bring the physical properties of Georgia's public institutions "to the same level as those at which our sister Southern states maintain theirs." Arnall suggested the creation of a state development authority to authorize the issuance of $100 million in bonds for a postwar public development program. Among other activities, the authority could construct public buildings, build highways, schools and hospitals, as well as make loans to finance both private and public business enterprises. The legislature failed to act on the suggestion.[40]

The state had an inadequate public health system with only 59 of the state's 159 counties having full-time health departments and 38 counties lacking any public health services. In addition, 142 counties lacked minimum standard hospital facilities, and only 20 counties had enough doctors to meet the minimum needs of their population. To alleviate such a condition of such inadequacy would have required a massive expenditure of financial resources—resources the Arnall administration didn't have.[41]

In 1945 the governor tentatively approved plans at a meeting with the State Health Board to expand state health services at a cost of $5 million. After a session with the state auditor, however, Arnall reversed his position, contending that the state lacked the money for such an undertaking. "I am convinced," Arnall declared, "we have about reached the limit of expanded services without increasing taxes on the people." Arnall expressed the view that the expansion of public health services should be one of the issues in the 1946 gubernatorial campaign. While Arnall favored an improved public health program, he declared, "Georgians must decide freely whether they want it and want to pay for it."[42]

In November 1945 Speaker Harris, an unannounced candidate for governor, unveiled a program for a multimillion dollar expansion of state services. At first Harris proposed financing his program by an expected growth of state revenue and by increasing the state's tax on alcoholic beverages. Due to Arnall's opposition to increasing taxes, however, Harris claimed prior to the 1946 session that an expansion could be financed by increasing the state's liquor warehouse fee and by an anticipated increase in state revenue.[43]

Arnall, in an address before the 1946 legislature, joined Harris in urging an expansion of state services. He requested the expenditure of $9.6 million to pay for the additional services. Like Harris, he claimed that the expansion could be financed by increasing liquor warehouse fees and an anticipated increase in state revenue. Arnall's request included expenditures for paying teachers on a twelve-month basis, increasing spending for public health, increasing spending for state eleemosynary institutions, establishing a permanent improvement and building fund for the state's institutions, and providing additional funds to match federal public assistance funds. The legislature approved the request. In view of Arnall's opposition to increasing state taxes, Harris believed that the legislature had gone as far as it could "in the way of expanded services without increased revenue."[44]

When Arnall assumed the governorship, the state already had a planning board that had been created in the Rivers administration. Rivers's successor in the governor's office, Eugene Talmadge, however, had little use for such an agency, since he was a strong advocate of a laissez-faire approach. Therefore the State Planning Board became inactive during the Talmadge administration. Arnall, however, strongly believed in the need and merit of state planning. He told the legislature in his inaugural address, "We must constantly work for the development of Georgia on a sound and progressive basis." The young governor believed Georgia stood on the threshold of building "an industrial-agrarian economy that will provide a high standard of living for all its citizens." To achieve that goal, Arnall contended two objectives had to be met. The state government had to be put in order by paying off the state debt, promoting efficiency in government, revising the constitution, and reforming state government. In addition, the state had to assume a major role in developing an ordered and comprehensive development plan for the transition into the new industrial-agrarian society.[45]

To develop that plan, Arnall supported the creation of a new state planning agency—the Agricultural and Industrial Development Board. The legislature created the agency in its 1943 session. Arnall believed the board's responsibility of formulating a comprehensive "blueprint for Georgia's future" to be "the biggest job ever undertaken in Georgia." The board consisted of twenty-one members, most of whom were appointed by the governor. The board divided itself into several panels to facilitate the carrying out of its responsibilities. The importance of the board to Arnall is evidenced by the fact it received almost four hundred thousand dollars in state funds during his term of office. In contrast, the legislature only appropriated $23,342 for the state Planning Board in Talmadge's last term. By 1946 the staff of the development board had grown to over fifty compared to five employees in 1942.[46]

While Arnall desired increased industrial development for the state, he realized the state could not ignore agriculture since "approximately two-thirds of our citizens are supported by agriculture." Unfortunately, farming practices harmful to the soil and reliance on cotton had weakened the state's agrarian economy. The value of farm land in the state had declined to one of the lowest levels in the South, and a depressed one-crop agricultural economy had crippled the state's overall economy. Arnall called for diversification of farm production as a means of bringing about higher income for Georgia farmers.[47]

The agriculture panel, chaired by Cason J. Callaway, sought to improve agriculture in the state through the Georgia Better Farms Program. Under the program, seven hundred businessmen invested one thousand dollars each to establish one hundred agricultural corporations with each hiring a farmer to manage a farm of one hundred acres. These corporations, located in over seventy counties, became experimental or demonstration farms to show farmers how to improve marginal farm land as well as to demonstrate the economic benefits of crop diversification. The program received widespread praise, with the Atlanta *Constitution* calling it "the greatest single contribution to the progress and prosperity of Georgia." Acclaim came from such diverse sources as the Wall Street *Journal, Christian Science Monitor,* and *Businessweek.* Even the Savannah *Morning News,* normally critical of the Arnall administration, called the program "a bold and challenging idea!"[48]

The educational panel, chaired by State School Superintendent Collins, proved to be one of the most active panels. It conducted statewide studies in school facilities, pupil transportation, school administration, and teacher education. Many recommendations of the panel made as a result of these studies were either enacted into law by the legislature, adopted as policy by the state Board of Education, or written into the 1945 constitution. Much of the information gathered by the panel's studies were later incorporated in the Special Committee on Education's report to the legislature.[49]

Another panel of the development board, the public health panel had as its major objective the preparation of a comprehensive state public health and medical care program. The panel surveyed existing health and hospital facilities to determine what facilities existed and what was needed. The survey revealed deficiencies in the number of physicians and hospital beds, inadequate county public health departments, and a lack of necessary medical equipment. The health panel recommended the division of the state into nine districts with a health officer for each district and support personnel for each county. While the plan received the endorsement of the General Assembly, lack of revenue prevented the implementation of the program estimated to cost almost $28 million.[50]

The industry panel sought to promote industrial development in the state. The panel established an advisory committee of prominent business and industrial leaders. Meetings were held by the panel in each of the state's ten congressional districts in which approximately eighteen hundred selected business and industrial leaders attended. Those in attendance were encouraged to make plans for industrial development in their communities by organizing local industrial recruitment committees with which the industry panel could work in an effort to promote industrial development.[51]

As a result of the combined state and local effort, Arnall proudly told the legislature in January 1946 that more than three hundred new industries had been established in Georgia in 1945. The July 1946 issue of the *Georgia Progress,* the official publication of the Agricultural and Industrial Board, proclaimed that the cities and towns in Georgia were "pushing a campaign of industrial development which is unprecedented in the state's history." Arnall, the state's most active booster of industrial development, urged industry to come to Georgia where "progress is on the move." At least on one occasion Arnall went north to solicit industry to come to Georgia.[52]

Perhaps most significant to the future economic development of the state was the public works panel's promotion of the Brunswick and Savannah ports. The panel hired a New York City engineering firm to make a detailed study of the two ports. On completion of this study, the Arnall administration supported the creation of a state ports authority to promote, develop, and operate state docks and terminal facilities. With only one dissenting vote, the proposed legislation authorized the issuing of $15 million in bonds to carry out the authority's responsibility.[53]

As the Arnall administration drew to a close, Arnall praised the work of the board. Arnall assured board chairman Blanton Fortson that "no little part of the progress made during the last few years has been due to the efforts of the Agricultural and Industrial Development Board." The governor believed that in future years the state would benefit from "the fruits of the labor this Board has expended." The legislature also praised the members of the board "for their untiring efforts and patriotic service to the great State of Georgia." Certainly, the nationwide praise and attention received by the board enhanced Arnall's national reputation. However, the board suffered a tremendous loss when its chief advocate left the governorship in 1947 and the Herman Talmadge administration replaced the board with the Department of Commerce. Looking back on the board's activities, Arnall declared that his administration had laid out a course for future development of the state.[54]

Arnall's positive attitude toward state planning differed substantially from that of Eugene Talmadge. His views on the subject of states' rights also contrasted sharply with those of his predecessor. While both professed a strong belief in states' rights, Arnall emphasized the responsibilities of states as well as their rights. "One of my ideas," Arnall told a congressional subcommittee in 1943, "is that we have talked too much about State rights and not enough about State responsibilities." The young governor warned of a "dangerous tendency" to use the claim of states' rights as an obstacle to prevent progressive action by the federal government. Arnall concluded that too often "political hacks" had resorted to states' rights "as an excuse for doing nothing." Unlike the negative state attitude of Eugene Talmadge, Arnall believed the people had the right to expect their governments to perform any services that they needed and wanted. He viewed state government as laboratories for progressive government and concluded that "the right to be static" was not one of the rights given by the people to their state governments. He called upon the states to assume their rightful responsibilities of dealing with and solving the problems facing their people. Like President Roosevelt, Arnall believed in experimentation by government in trying to solve the problems of a changing society.[55]

Unlike many liberal Democrats, however, Arnall feared centralization of governmental power in Washington. He saw centralized power as a monopoly that was "dangerous to the liberty of the people." He envisioned effective and responsible state governments as being effective counterweights to centralization of power in Washington. States' rights, in Arnall's scheme of government, meant the states assuming "responsibility for initiating and carrying forward, experimentally if necessary, those programs deserved by the people for their benefits." He warned that "empty phrases" would not solve the needs of the people and predicted the states would "lose their rights just as an individual loses his strength by persistent laziness" if they failed to assume their rightful responsibilities. As he told the legislature in 1944, "The preservation of States' rights depends, I am convinced, upon a ready acceptance by the States of their responsibilities."[56]

When Arnall entered the governorship in 1943, the level of state services was inadequate. When he left office four years later, state services were still inadequate. Nevertheless, progress had been made in spite of wartime conditions inhospitable to the providing of governmental services. Instead of having to reduce funding for state services as feared because of a financial crisis, the Arnall administration increased the state's financial commitment to providing governmental service. By the end of his administration Arnall realized, however, that the state had reached its potential in providing services without increasing taxes. Arnall had not been able to correct all of the shortcomings of the state in providing services in the four years he served as governor. His administration had, however, addressed and dealt with many of the more pressing problems of state government. Progress had been made, but much still remained to be done. Future governors would build upon the groundwork provided by the Arnall administration in improving and expanding state services.

8

The

Freight

Rate

Controversy

As governor, Arnall battled some of the most pressing problems of Georgia's government, such as "gubernatorial dictatorship," an antiquated constitution, an inadequate penal system, a huge state debt, and inadequate state services. Early in his administration, Arnall confronted the problem of economic underdevelopment in Georgia and the South. He saw discriminatory freight rates as the culprit for the South's stunted economic growth. He entered the fray with the same zeal and enthusiasm of his previous political battles. This fight, however, carried him to the highest court in the land and to the halls of Congress.

Even before Arnall became governor, President Franklin D. Roosevelt called the South the "Nation's No. 1 economic problem." President Roosevelt requested the National Emergency Council to prepare a report on southern economic needs. The council responded that "the paradox of the South is that while it is blessed by nature with immense wealth, its people as a whole are the poorest in the country." Efforts had failed in the late nineteenth century and the first part of the twentieth century to end this paradox by remaking the South in the image of the industrialized and more prosperous North. Before World War II, the southern economy remained predominantly agricultural, with the South continuing in its traditional role as exporter of raw materials and importer of finished products. The industrialization that had occurred consisted primarily of low-wage and low-value-creating industries that did little to raise the per capita income of southerners.[1]

Many critics of the southern economic status quo, including Governor Arnall, blamed unfair freight rates as a major reason for the South's lack

of industrialization and poverty. They claimed high rates hampered the development of southern industry and limited the ability of southern manufacturers to sell their products in northern markets. Even before the Civil
War, freight rates in the South had been higher than those in the North
because of the claim that it cost more to haul freight in the South than
in the North. Later, critics charged that northern railroads and industrialists conspired to keep southern rates high to minimize competition from
southern manufacturers.[2]

Before the Civil War, each railroad determined its own freight rates,
but excessive competition and rate cutting threatened the financial sur-
vival of the railroads in the South in the postwar period. In 1875 several
southern railroads and steamship companies created the Southern Railway and Steamship Association, which assumed the authority to make
and enforce rates for its members. Similar rate associations came into existence throughout the country and by 1885 the United States had been
divided into freight-rate territories in which associations of railroad carriers fixed rates.[3]

Five major rate territories had evolved with the Southern Territory consisting of Kentucky and most of the states of the former southern confederacy. By 1940 the Southern Territory contained less than 20 percent of
the nation's population but had only 12.2 percent of its work force employed in manufacturing and had the lowest per capita income of the five
rate territories. In sharp contrast, the Official Territory, containing over
51 percent of the nation's population in 1940, had the largest percentage
of employees in manufacturing and the highest per capita income of any
rate territory. The Official Territory consisted of the northern states east of
the Mississippi including most of the Virginias. The other rate territories
divided up the remaining portions of the United States.[4]

Rates within each territory were called intraterritorial rates and they
varied from territory to territory. The most important of these were the
class rates that were charged to haul manufactured or finished products.
These rates were lowest in the Official Territory and considerably higher
in the other territories. A report issued by the Tennessee Valley Authority
in 1937 revealed that, on the average, manufacturers that shipped goods
by class rates paid 39 percent more in the Southern Territory than manufacturers did in the Official Territory even though the quantity and distance
of the goods being shipped were the same.[5]

Southern and western manufacturers also complained of higher interterritorial rates charged to transport products from one territory to another. Interterritorial rates were generally determined by averaging the rates of the territories traversed with the actual rate, depending upon the proportion of the total distance traveled in each territory. As a result, southern and western manufacturers had to pay higher interterritorial rates for products shipped to the Official Territory because of the higher class rates in their respective territories. Under the existing system, however, the northern manufacturer could ship products into the Southern Territory cheaper than southern manufacturers could ship to customers in their own territory.[6]

Defenders of the system conceded that class rates were higher in the South, but they pointed out that most freight hauled in the South did not use class rates. Instead, southern freight consisted primarily of raw materials or semifinished products that were shipped under commodity rates which were considerably lower than class rates. However, lower commodity rates for goods shipped from the South into the Official Territory benefited the northern manufacturers by providing an inexpensive transportation cost for raw materials. It also perpetuated the South's role as a provider of raw material to northern manufacturers.[7]

One southern governor, Bibb Graves of Alabama, went so far as to proclaim in the late 1930s, "This freight rate business is the heart of the whole Southern problem." Arnall, who increasingly assumed the role as a spokesman for the South on freight rates, agreed that discriminatory rates were the major obstacle to southern economic development. He accused the North of keeping the South in a colonial economic status in which the South served as the "economic doormat of the United States as Ireland was of the United Kingdom." In Arnall's view, economic exploitation of the South had to end.[8]

Perhaps most irritating to Arnall was the fact that railroads were supposedly being regulated by the federal government for the purpose of protecting the public welfare. High freight rates and other abuses by the railroads had resulted in regulation by the states following the Civil War. However, the U.S. Supreme Court limited state regulation in 1886 when it ruled that states could not regulate the interstate operations of railroads. In response to that decision, Congress passed the Interstate Commerce Act of 1887 to protect the public from high and discriminatory interstate rates. The law provided that railroad rates had to be just and reasonable and created the Interstate Commerce Commission to enforce the law. Each railroad initiated its own rates that were filed with the commission; the rates became effective unless an interested party obtained a suspension order from the commission. Arnall claimed, however, that more than 90 percent of the rates filed had become effective without question or challenge.[9]

In 1890 Congress passed the Sherman Antitrust Act, which prohibited combinations in restraint of trade. In the late 1890s the U.S. Supreme Court held the rate-fixing associations of the railroads to be in violation of the Sherman act. However, the ICC permitted the railroad associations to continue rate-fixing on a voluntary basis without legal authority to coerce member carriers to abide by their rate decisions. The reorganized associations resorted to nonlegal means such as economic coercion to ensure compliance.[10]

Criticism had been heard since Reconstruction of freight rates that crippled and retarded southern economic development but by the 1930s that criticism had become a "crusade of great popular appeal" among many southerners. This "crusade" against unfair rates received the support of numerous allies, including President Roosevelt, who believed that freight-rate barriers limited the national market for southern manufactured goods and helped keep the South on a raw-material production economy. The chairman of the Tennessee Valley Authority, Arthur E. Morgan, condemned freight rate barriers as harmful to southern economic development. His agency produced two reports in the 1930s substantiating the allegations of the crippling effect of discriminatory rates on southern economic development. High ranking officials in the Justice Department took a critical position toward the discriminatory rates. Vice President Henry A. Wallace, Harry Hopkins (the head of the Works Progress Administration), and Eleanor Roosevelt also joined in on the attack on unfair rates.[11]

While the ICC had mandated uniformity in class rates in the Southern Territory in the 1920s, it had not required lowering of rates in the South. In March 1934 the Southern Traffic League, an organization of southern shippers, called for lower class rates in the South and a readjustment of southern interterritorial rates. In the same year, Senator George and Georgia congressman Carl Vinson introduced resolutions calling for an examination of rates in the South. In 1935 Senator Russell introduced a resolution that the public would be best served by uniform transportation rates, while the Tennessee legislature passed a resolution petitioning Congress to establish the principle of freight rate uniformity. Also in 1936, the Southern Traffic League joined with the Southeastern Association of

Railroads and Utilities Commissions, an organization of southern public regulatory boards, in requesting the ICC to investigate the "excessive and unreasonable" class rates in the South.[12]

A newly formed organization of southern governors joined in the fight against discriminatory freight rates. Ed Rivers, who was at the time governor of Georgia, played a major role in the creation of the organization in 1937. Rivers, blaming discriminatory freight rates for the lack of southern industrial development, envisioned an organization of southern governors as a vehicle to be used to bring about freight rate equalization. The organization initially came into existence for that purpose and officially called itself the Southeastern Governors Freight Rate Conference. Later, the organization changed its name to the Southern Governors Conference.[13]

The organization elected Governor Graves as its first chairman in 1937, and shortly thereafter Graves filed a complaint with the ICC on behalf of eight southern states. The complaint, which became known as the "Southern Governors Case," charged discriminatory freight rates had been placed on fourteen manufactured and processed articles that were produced in the Southern Territory and shipped to the Official Territory. It alleged that interterritorial freight rates on these products transported into Official Territory were unreasonable and discriminatory and were in violation of the Interstate Commerce Act of 1887. The complaint charged that the rates in question forced southern manufacturers to absorb higher freight costs to compete in the northern market and thus placed the southern manufacturer at a distinct disadvantage.[14]

Attorneys for the Southern Governors Conference accused the northern railroads of forcing the South to pay higher interterritorial rates in order to protect the markets of the northern manufacturers. They claimed the northern railroads controlled the interterritorial rates. The southern governors also attacked the traditional justification for higher rates in the South, which was that the cost of service was higher in the South.[15]

Witnesses representing over thirty southern companies and four southern state regulatory agencies supported the Southern Governors Case in testimony before the ICC. Southern carriers even claimed that they had offered lower interterritorial rates to the North but that their offer had been rebuffed by their northern counterparts. The southern railroads, however, parted company with the governors on the question of operating costs, which they claimed were higher in the South. The northern carriers defended the existing system by claiming that the rates in question were in line with rate decisions that had previously been approved by the ICC. The northern carriers rejected the allegations that the interterritorial rates were prejudicial to the South and that they controlled the making of interterritorial rates.[16]

By June 1938 several southern congressmen, growing impatient with waiting on the ICC, decided to take action on their own. They announced their intentions to reduce freight rates by the legislative process. Congressman Robert Ramspeck of Georgia announced plans to form a southern-western coalition in the House to push for legislation to lower freight rates in the event of further delay by the ICC or an unfavorable decision by that agency. In the opening days of the 1939 congressional session, several southern congressmen introduced resolutions pertaining to freight rates that proposed to amend the Interstate Commerce Act of 1887 by prohibiting discriminatory rates against products manufactured in the South. Other resolutions prohibited regional differences in freight rates and called for the ICC to investigate the rate structure. The House Committee on Interstate and Foreign Commerce held hearings on freight rates in 1939 as part of its consideration of a general transportation bill. A subcommittee of the Senate Committee on Interstate Commerce also held hearings on the question of freight rate discrimination.[17]

In February 1939, while the congressional hearings were being conducted, the board of directors of the Tennessee Valley Authority submitted to President Roosevelt its second study on the interterritorial freight rate question. The study had been prepared under the direction of J. Haden Allredge, who had prepared an earlier TVA report that had been critical of the existing freight rate structure. The more recent report, among other things, revealed that shippers in industrialized portions of eastern Canada actually paid lower class rates on manufactured goods shipped into the Official Territory than did southern shippers.[18]

As a result of the congressional hearings Senator Hill and Congressman Ramspeck introduced resolutions that provided that the ICC investigate interterritorial class rates. The resolutions also proposed to amend the Interstate Commerce Act to prohibit freight rate discrimination against a region or a rate territory. Omnibus transportation bills containing the Hill-Ramspeck resolutions passed both houses. Differences between the two bills necessitated a conference committee, which did not make a report in 1939. However, after House passage of its transportation bill, the ICC announced its intention to investigate class rates east of the Rocky

Mountains. Some observers attributed the ICC's decision as a response to the congressional activity on rates and its "fear of legislative rate making." The ICC had traditionally opposed legislative interference with the rate-making process.[19]

In the meantime, the ICC continued its deliberations on the Southern Governors Case. After more than two years of hearings, the ICC handed down its decision on the complaint in November 1939. By a five to four vote, the ICC ruled in favor of the southern governors and ordered a reduction in rates on ten of the fourteen articles in question. The majority concluded that the desirability of reasonable uniform levels of interterritorial rates was "not open to serious question." It agreed with the southern governors that the challenged rates were unreasonable, unlawful, and unduly prejudicial to southern shippers.[20]

With this decision, the ICC had reversed its traditional stand that higher transportation costs in the South justified higher rates in that region. The majority also disagreed with the northern railroads' argument that they did not control freight rates in the North as "contrary to the facts." The majority agreed with the argument of the southern railroads that lower interterritorial rates to the North had been denied because of the opposition of the northern carriers. The southern governors hailed the decision as a major victory and made plans to broaden their challenge to discriminatory rates.[21]

The following year, Congress passed the Transportation Act of 1940, which contained the provision requiring the ICC to investigate interterritorial rates and to prohibit freight rate discrimination against a region. Despite the congressional mandate and its own announced investigation of class rates, the ICC postponed hearings on its investigation of freight rates until July 1941. The hearings lasted through June 1944, with northern shippers and railroads opposing any revision of the existing rates.[22]

In the South the united front that had generally supported the governors rate case disintegrated. The southern carriers now led the attack against rate revision while the attorneys for the southern carriers argued that the rate system had not damaged or held back southern industrial development. In fact, the southern carriers now argued that the rate system had actually contributed to the region's economic growth and claimed that the South had made more progress in industrialization than any region in the nation. The southern railroads feared lower rates would jeopardize their profitability.[23]

Certain segments of southern industry also opposed rate revision. Shippers of the South's commodities shipped northward favored retention of the rate status quo because they feared revision might jeopardize their low commodity rates. The Southern States Industrial Council, which claimed a membership of almost six thousand large and small southern industries, also opposed rate revision. Other southern businesses opposed to tampering with rates included the Southeast Shippers Conference, Southern Paper Manufacturers Conference, Southern Pine Association, and Southern Traffic League. One student of the controversy concluded that major industries in the South generally opposed rate revision while the small manufacturer and dealers in consumer goods favored a uniform rate structure.[24]

When Arnall assumed the governorship in 1943, the ICC's investigation of class rates had been going on for almost two years. The young governor quickly joined the battle against rate discrimination. Speaking before the Southern Governors Conference in March 1943, he suggested political pressure as a means for the South to end unfair rates. Arnall urged his colleagues to "stand together" politically in order to obtain support from the national Democratic party in their fight against unfair rates. Arnall also suggested resorting to the courts as a means of overturning the unfair freight rate system. Both of Arnall's suggestions failed to receive the support of the southern governors. Ironically, in a meeting of the governors two years earlier, Governor Eugene Talmadge had also recommended legal action as a means of obtaining relief from unfair freight rates. Like Arnall's later plea, Talmadge's suggestion failed to receive the endorsement of the southern chief executives, who viewed the ICC as the proper forum to gain relief against the economic discrimination against the South.[25]

Arnall's call for political pressure and litigation indicated his growing impatience with the slow pace of the ICC's rate investigation. Arnall told his cohorts at the 1943 conference that he would like to see "some immediate hope" of action. Predicting that unfair rates would eventually end, Arnall believed the change had to be made immediately and could not be delayed until after the war so that the South could compete with other regions in postwar economic development.[26]

Several months later, Arnall addressed the freight rate issue at the National Governors Conference. He complained of the lack of war plants in the South, which he attributed to the freight rate differential that made it too expensive to locate war plants in the region. Arnall called for the elimination of the freight rate discrimination that had "impoverished the people of our section." Shortly thereafter, Arnall spoke before a convention of the National Junior Chamber of Commerce in which he told his audience that poverty was the cause of inadequate educational systems, bad health conditions, and poor housing in the South. Arnall predicted that a fair freight rate structure would permit the development of southern industry, which would in turn lead to a more prosperous South.[27]

In September 1943 Arnall continued his freight rate battle at the Western Governors Conference in Denver, where southern governors were meeting with their western colleagues to discuss mutual concerns. In an address to the gathering, Arnall urged the western governors to unite with their southern counterparts to end "the wholly unwarranted discrimination against West and South in freight rates." The western governors, however, seemed unconvinced of the need of such a battle. A reporter for the Atlanta *Constitution* observed that the western governors, most of whom were Republicans, "were more concerned about the national government invading private business and usurping the rights of the states." Arnall, however, told the western governors that the southerners were not present "to argue about states' rights, but to discuss unfair, discriminatory freight rates."[28]

The best that Arnall could obtain from the meeting was a resolution calling for the removal of barriers to the free flow of commerce. Leaving the less-than-receptive West, Arnall and the southern governors switched their efforts to the national level. In January 1944 Arnall, along with the other southern chief executives, met with the southern congressional delegations to discuss freight rates. While in Washington, Arnall conferred with President Roosevelt, after which Arnall reported that the president favored ending the discriminatory rates.[29]

In an address to the southern governors and congressional delegation, Arnall called for the readmission of the South to the Union by removing unfair trade barriers. The southern political leaders ended their conference by signing a joint statement in support of equal freight rates for manufactured and processed goods in all parts of the country. An optimistic Arnall left Washington, believing that the South's fight was "brighter than ever," and even predicted an end to the discriminatory rates "before many more months and years." By May 1944, however, a discouraged Arnall had abandoned hope for favorable action by the "timid, reactionary Interstate Commerce Commission." Arnall, a man of action, had grown dissatisfied with the snaillike pace of the fight for rate equity. Looking for another forum to battle unfair rates, he turned to the U.S. Supreme Court. Arnall later claimed that President Roosevelt had recommended this course of action to force the ICC to take action.[30]

As attorney general of Georgia, Arnall had sued Hiram W. Evans, imperial wizard of the Ku Klux Klan, and several contractors on behalf of the state to recover damages from an alleged conspiracy in the sale of road-building materials. He charged that the conspiracy to defraud the state had violated federal antitrust laws and that Georgia had the right to seek damages in federal court. The U.S. Supreme Court agreed and upheld the right of Georgia to file suit under the antitrust laws. Prior to Arnall's tenure as attorney general, the court had upheld the efforts of Georgia to enjoin a copper company in Tennessee from discharging noxious gas into Georgia. With these two cases in mind, Arnall concluded that the state was "on sound ground legally in asking the Supreme Court to consider a conspiracy to fix freight rates that keeps the economy of Georgia in a state of arrested development."[31]

On May 27, 1944, Arnall ordered state attorney general T. Grady Head to file an original jurisdiction suit in the U.S. Supreme Court on behalf of the state against the Pennsylvania Railroad Company and twenty-two other railroads. Arnall contended in his executive order directing the filing of the suit that interstate rail carriers had engaged in a freight rate conspiracy against the South in violation of the antitrust laws. He further charged the ICC with condoning and being a party to the conspiracy which was harmful to the economy of the state of Georgia.[32]

Arnall conceded that some of his fellow southern governors would criticize him for bringing the suit while the ICC was investigating class rates. At least one southern governor, Millard Caldwell of Florida, stated publicly that he had declined to join Arnall's suit for fear of its adverse effect on the ICC's class rate investigation. Arnall conceded efforts to persuade his fellow southern governors to join him in the suit had failed. He attributed this lack of support to a defeatist attitude and the belief that only the ICC could provide relief. Arnall's independent action, which gave him a great deal of publicity, rankled the other southern governors. The Atlanta *Constitution* conceded that many southern governors believed Arnall's unorthodox method of fighting the railroad rates to be "a personal publicity stunt." Perhaps aware of growing hostility on the part of southern governors toward him because of the suit, Arnall did not attend the 1945 session of the Southern Governors Conference.[33]

Governor J. Melville Broughton of North Carolina, chairman of the freight rate committee of the Southern Governors Conference, publicly announced that Arnall's suit did not reflect the attitude of the Southern Governors Conference. He stressed the conference would continue its fight against freight rates before the ICC. However, U.S. Senator Burnet T. Maybank of South Carolina urged southern governors to follow Arnall's example. Despite Maybank's suggestion, no southern governor sought to intervene in the case on behalf of Georgia until 1947, when James E. Folsom, an admirer of Arnall, assumed the governorship of Alabama and directed his state's attorney general to do so. The Supreme Court, however, refused to allow the state of Alabama to become a party in the case.[34]

On June 20, 1944, Georgia filed a bill of complaint with the Supreme Court seeking an injunction against the continuance of an alleged freight rate conspiracy against the state. The complaint sought $750,000 in damages to the state and $6 million in damages to the shippers of the state from the twenty-three railroads named as defendants. The complaint alleged that the defendants had engaged in a conspiracy to impose arbitrary and noncompetitive rates on the state in violation of federal antitrust laws.[35]

An amended bill of complaint contended that the state could not seek relief from the Interstate Commerce Commission because it had never been given jurisdiction over freight rate conspiracies. The state's complaint emphasized that it was not challenging a specific rate "but a continuing situation, created and maintained by a conspiracy of carriers." According to the state, the existing rate associations had been merged in 1934 into a national system overseen by a newly created organization—the Association of American Railroads—which maintained "complete and arbitrary domination and control over all freight rates." According to the state's complaint, the association supervised a hierarchy of private rate fixing associations, bureaus, and conferences with the association's having final authority over rates. The state further alleged that railroads which belonged to the AAR promised to abide by the rate decisions of the organization. The state charged that failure of a company to adhere to AAR rates resulted in its automatic withdrawal from the association, which resulted "in a crippling isolation of, and the institution and carrying on of a practical boycott against, such offending member."[36]

According to Georgia's argument, the northern carriers dominated the AAR and used its private rate-making machinery to maintain a discriminatory rate structure that prevented "the products of Southern industries from competing on equal terms with the products of Northern industries in markets serviced by Northern defendants." The state argued that northern railroads kept the South in the status of an "undeveloped economic colony" by limiting its industries to the unprofitable production of raw materials. The state accused the railroads of engaging in the "most far-reaching violation of the antitrust laws in the history of the country"—a violation that injured the South's economy and perpetuated the "economic bondage of the South to the North."[37]

On January 2, 1945, the court heard oral arguments in the case. Even though Georgia did not have the support of any other southern state, it had gained one very important ally—the U.S. Government, which had filed an amicus curiae brief. The government's brief concluded that Georgia had presented a justiciable controversy within the original jurisdiction of the U.S. Supreme Court. The government also concurred with Georgia's contention that the alleged conspiracy ranged beyond the jurisdiction of the Interstate Commerce Commission, whose jurisdiction had never been broadened to include regulating rate-fixing. Since no other administrative agency had the authority to regulate rate-fixing, the government agreed with Georgia that only the U.S. Supreme Court could end the injury done to the state by the rate conspiracy.[38]

Arnall, then only thirty-eight years old, decided to make the oral arguments on behalf of the state before the court. He went to Washington several days before the scheduled oral argument to confer with lawyers in the Department of Justice and to work on his presentation. Arnall also received assistance from the department by obtaining from it copies of over sixteen thousand documents from the files of the AAR and other rate-making associations that had been obtained during the department's earlier investigation of rate-fixing against western railroads in the early 1940s. During oral arguments, U.S. Attorney General Biddle and several of his assistants along with Georgia Attorney General Head and several of his assistants sat at the same table with Arnall.[39]

Arnall told the justices that this case was one of the most "far-reaching cases" ever presented to the court. He argued that efforts to promote southern economic development had been hampered by "conspiracy on the part of the railroads to handicap and hamstring the South." Arnall told the justices that all the South wanted was for the court to enjoin the continuation of the rate-making conspiracy, which would force the railroads to once again compete, resulting in a lowering of rates. The governor came in for some sharp questioning by several of the justices as to whether the Supreme Court was the proper forum to resolve the issue. Conceding the court's right to decline to assume original jurisdiction, Arnall vigorously contended however that the state of Georgia had the right to have its case heard by the court. He concluded his argument by expressing his hope that Georgia's returning veterans would "be able to make a living for themselves and their families and find a future unhampered by this conspiracy to retard the growth of Georgia and the South."[40]

Arnall's conduct of the state's case before the nation's highest court received widespread praise. The Atlanta *Journal* commended Arnall for his "eloquent and audacious argument," and the Washington correspondent for the Atlanta *Constitution* wrote that Arnall "drove his arguments home with good skill." Sam Hall Flint, author of an article on the freight rate fight, claimed that the governor "brilliantly argued the case." Elkin Taylor concluded in his study of Arnall that the governor had "stolen the show with his concise presentation." President Roosevelt wrote Arnall, "I hear from all sides that your appearance was excellent in the presentation of the case, and that it created a profound impression."[41]

On March 26, 1945, the court agreed by a five to four vote to accept jurisdiction—a victory for Arnall. The New York *Times* called the vote a "familiar pattern of cleavage between the 'liberals' and the 'conservatives.'" The majority opinion written by Justice William O. Douglas agreed with Arnall's argument that the court should accept jurisdiction, emphasizing that no other remedy existed "which Georgia can apply to eliminate from rate-making the influences of the unlawful conspiracy alleged to exist here." However, the court voided the state's efforts to seek damages by citing an earlier court decision which held that states could not obtain damages under antitrust laws from railroad carriers even though an alleged conspiracy existed. The court agreed with the defendants that it could not accept a case asking to review or to annul a rate decision of the Interstate Commerce Commission. Concurring with Arnall's position, Justice Douglas pointed out that what Georgia sought was a cessation of the alleged rate fixing combination and conspiracy among the defendant carriers.[42]

Arnall reacted to the decision by proclaiming that he was prouder of this victory than of any other achievement of his administration. The decision, in Arnall's opinion, "gave the railroads the shock of their corporate lives" and produced a "little faintness in the offices of the Interstate Commerce Commission." As a result of the decision, Arnall declared that "the door has been unlocked which would allow the South and West to obtain fair treatment in the rate-making process." He predicted that shortly the ICC would hand down a sweeping decision in the Southern Governors Case, which would provide for equality of freight rates. Conceding that the South's battle for rate equality had been long and slow, Arnall predicted that "final and complete victory is now in sight."[43]

Senators J. William Fulbright of Arkansas, Lister Hill of Alabama, and A. Thomas Stewart of Tennessee hailed the decision as a victory for the South. *Time* called Arnall's bold action "characteristic of the 38-year-old fireball." Maury Maverick, chairman of the Smaller War Plants Corporation, stated that the opinion "probably is the most important decision rendered in the history of the court." The South Carolina House of Representatives passed a resolution commending Arnall for his victory, and the Atlanta *Journal* hailed the decision as a victory for Arnall "when few thought he had a chance of success." The Atlanta *Constitution* called the court's acceptance of the case "a great personal victory for Georgia's brilliant young chief executive."[44]

After deciding to accept jurisdiction in the case, the court appointed a special master, Lloyd K. Garrison, to hear the arguments of the parties and to make a recommendation to the court as to its course of action. While the state had won the battle of jurisdiction, it now had the task of convincing the special master that a rate-fixing conspiracy detrimental to Georgia's economy actually existed.[45]

However, a more immediate problem to Georgia's case had emerged. Arnall saw his recent court victory threatened by legislation being considered by Congress. Congressman Alfred L. Bulwinkle of North Carolina had introduced a bill in 1943 permitting common carriers to make rate agreements among themselves without being subject to the antitrust laws. The legislation had been introduced in response to a Justice Department investigation of private rate-making by common carriers and their rate associations. Under pressure from the War Department, which claimed the elimination of private rate-making machinery would be detrimental to the war effort, the Justice Department had curtailed its investigation. In May 1943, however, the department obtained indictments against several truck-

ing companies and lines for engaging in a rate-fixing conspiracy in violation of the Sherman Antitrust Act. As a result, the transportation industry
sought to legalize its private rate-making machinery to make it immune
from the antitrust laws. Several bills, including the Bulwinkle bill, had been
introduced in the 1943 congressional session for that purpose. However,
Congress failed to take action in 1943. An executive order issued by the
chairman of the War Production Board exempting rate arrangements made
by common carriers from antitrust laws for the duration of the war lessened
the demand for the Bulwinkle bill.[46]

Nevertheless, in August 1944 the Justice Department filed a civil suit in
Nebraska against the Association of American Railroads for engaging in
a rate-fixing conspiracy detrimental to the economic development of the
West. Following this action, Congressman Bulwinkle reintroduced his bill
in 1945. Arnall attacked the bill as railroad-sponsored legislation that would
protect the freight rate-fixing conspiracy from antitrust laws. He contended
that, if enacted, the legislation would nullify the recent victory won by
Georgia in the Supreme Court. Noting that one ICC commissioner had
indicated ICC's support of the bill, Arnall publicly denounced the agency
as a "tool of the railroads." He called on the members of the ICC either
to correct the injustice in the transportation system or to resign. Arnall
sent telegrams to the members of the Georgia delegation urging them to
oppose the bill.[47]

In May 1945, less than two months after Arnall's victory in the Supreme
Court and six years after the ICC began its investigation of class rates, the
commission handed down its long-awaited decision. The ICC, in a seven
to two vote, held that class rates east of the Rocky Mountains were unjust,
unreasonable, and violated the Interstate Commerce Act. Concluding that
the class rate structure was detrimental to southern and western economic
development, the ICC called for uniformity in class rates. Conceding that it
would take some time to implement that goal, the ICC ordered an interim
10 percent increase in class rates for all interstate shippers in the Official
Territory and a 10 percent decrease in class rates in the other territories east
of the Rocky Mountains.[48]

Arnall praised the ICC for "mustering up enough courage to throw off
the railroad yoke that had held back economic development of the South
and West." He predicted, "The U.S. Supreme Court, will, in my judgment,
complete the job of freeing the transportation system of America from
monopoly, conspiracy, and fraud." The governor had no doubt that Geor-

gia's victory before the Supreme Court had hastened the ICC's action. The Birmingham *News* concurred, "Perhaps the apples were ready to fall from the tree anyway. Perhaps not. The Supreme Court action gave the tree a strong shake." The Atlanta *Journal* credited Arnall's Supreme Court victory with forcing the ICC decision. The Washington correspondent of the Atlanta *Journal* observed that without the governor's initiative in bringing the suit "the decision of the ICC might have been delayed indefinitely in the opinion of many."[49]

Arnall continued to lead the fight in opposition to the Bulwinkle bill. In October 1945 Arnall wrote President Truman that railroad spokesmen had claimed administration support for the legislation. The governor predicted victory in Georgia's fight against the freight rate conspiracy unless the administration supported the Bulwinkle bill. "If the railroads are successful with the administration's support in exempting their conspiracy from the antitrust laws," Arnall predicted, "other big businesses will secure like exemption with a result that these laws will only apply to the small, the weak, and the uninfluential." Arnall urged the president to oppose the bill to assure the country that "free competitive enterprise reigns in this country and that it is not ruled by J. P. Morgan and Company, Kuhn, Loeb and Company, or its agent, the Association of American Railroads." The president's decision on the bill, Arnall concluded in his appeal, had "grave importance" for the future of the government monopoly policy and for enforcement of antitrust legislation. Truman responded by expressing his belief that "freight rates should be equitable—taking the cost of operation into consideration for the whole country."[50]

Arnall announced his intent early in October 1945 to appear before a subcommittee of the House Interstate and Foreign Commerce Committee, which was holding hearings on the Bulwinkle bill. Arnall never testified, however, and insisted that he had been denied the opportunity. Arnall had been scheduled to testify on October 22, though he had asked for a later date because "pressing official business in Atlanta" prevented him from being in Washington on that date. When told that October 22 was the last day scheduled for hearings on the bill, Arnall questioned why the bill was being hurried through the subcommittee and why only witnesses favorable to the bill had been allowed to testify. Ninety-six witnesses representing 148 organizations had testified in favor of the bill. In addition, the subcommittee received communications from almost one thousand organizations—governmental, shippers, carriers, industrial, commercial, and agricultural—in favor of the bill. No witness appeared in opposition and only communications from Arnall and the U.S. attorney general opposed the bill. The committee reported the bill favorable to the House, which passed it by an overwhelming vote in December 1945.[51]

In 1946 the Senate Interstate Commerce Committee held hearings on the bill during which time Arnall spent three days testifying in opposition. He told the committee, "The whole purpose of the Bulwinkle bill is to defeat Georgia's case in the Supreme Court and the federal government case against the AAR." Arnall told the senators that if the bill were passed, "My Georgia case will go out the window." Arnall pleaded with the committee "to let the courts grind on. Do not let the Congress be used as a cat's paw to pull chestnuts out of the fire."[52]

Prior to Arnall's appearance, several southerners had testified in favor of the bill. These included E. L. Hart, chairman of the Atlanta Freight Rate Bureau, and J. V. Norman, chief counsel for the Southern Governors Conference. When asked why so many southerners had testified in favor of the bill, Arnall responded that the South had "Quislings who undertake to speak for the South and speak for their Northern bosses." He accused Hart of deserting Georgia's side because of the economic influence of the railroads." Arnall charged Norman with violating legal ethics by supporting the Bulwinkle bill while at the same time representing the Southern Governors Conference. Arnall told the committee of his intentions to lead an effort to remove Norman from his position with the Southern Governors Conference at the next meeting of that organization. Arnall attributed southern shippers' support of the bill to the fact that this conspiracy "is so broad and has so much economic power that no shipper dare oppose the wishes of the railroads. They are threatened. They are intimidated, and they are frightened." He accused the AAR of having the most powerful lobby in the nation's history and alleged that some of the association's lobbying had been patently unlawful.[53]

As 1946 drew to an end, Special Master Garrison had not made a recommendation to the Supreme Court. He had held lengthy hearings, which began in March 1946 and lasted until August 1946. Arnall did not personally appear before the special master but had a letter introduced into the record as his testimony. Arnall told Garrison that the evidence would prove the existence of a gigantic conspiracy on the part of northern railroads and industries to keep southern manufactured products out of the North.

While Arnall stated in his letter his intention to appear in person at a later stage of the hearing, he never did. By the time Arnall left the governorship, the special master still had not made a recommendation.[54]

In January 1947 the Senate passed a bill, introduced by Senator Clyde M. Reed, which was very similar to the Bulwinkle bill. In the House, Congressman Bulwinkle reintroduced his bill. Although failing to vote on the legislation in 1947, the House passed it the following year with only fifty-three dissenting votes. A concerned Arnall telegraphed Truman to urge him to veto the "immoral monopolistic Bulwinkle-Reed bill." He followed his telegraph with a lengthy letter imploring the president to veto the bill because it "completely cuts the ground out from under Georgia's antitrust case." Arnall further appealed to the president to veto the bill because it was "not fair to change the rules of the game for the benefit of the transportation monopoly in America." He charged the "Republican Congress" with being committed to a policy of exempting big business from antitrust laws. "If you draw the issue with the Republican leadership on this tremendous economic issue," Arnall wrote Truman, "the little people of the United States will sustain you at the polls."[55]

On June 12, 1948, President Truman vetoed the Bulwinkle-Reed bill, contending it would permit the railroads to obtain immunity from the antitrust laws. Arnall praised Truman for his "courageous veto," which was later overridden by Congress. After an effort that lasted five years, the railroads finally had secured the passage of the Bulwinkle bill. However, Arnall downplayed the passage of the Bulwinkle-Reed bill by claiming that rate equality had already been provided by the Interstate Commerce Commission under pressure of the Georgia suit.[56]

Even though the railroads claimed victory in the passage of the bill, they had already suffered a major defeat in the ICC's decision to reduce class rates in the South and West. A federal district court had temporarily enjoined implementation of the ICC decision. In May 1946, however, the district court sustained the ICC's order. The following year the Supreme Court affirmed the district court's ruling. The court agreed with the ICC's conclusion that class rates in existence prior to 1945 had been detrimental to the economic development of the South and West. The last remaining barrier to the ICC's 1945 class rate decision had fallen. Arnall hailed the decision because it meant "that the South is well on its way to readmission to the Union!" At last, Arnall observed, the ICC and the Supreme

Court had recognized the existence of discrimination against the West and the South.[57]

Garrison finally submitted his recommendation to the court on June 12, 1950—five years after his appointment. He concluded that the state had not established that a freight rate conspiracy existed or that northern railroads dominated southern railroads or that injury had been done to Georgia's economy by the defendants. Garrison ruled that the need for injunctive relief for injury arising from an alleged conspiracy had not been established, and therefore, he recommended that the Supreme Court dismiss Georgia's complaint. The court, without official comment, followed Garrison's recommendation.[58]

Two years later the ICC ended the freight rate controversy when it put into effect its 1945 order mandating equality and uniformity in class rates. A reporter for the Atlanta *Constitution* observed that the order ended southern industrial bondage to the North, which had existed since the Civil War. One prominent historian of recent southern history concluded that the decision "removed an irritating obstacle to Southern development." Arnall believed he had performed a major role in bringing about the demise of this "irritating obstacle" because his case had "put the pressure on the Interstate Commerce Commission to equalize freight rates." He considered the rate case a significant accomplishment of his administration because "we brought about the readmission of the South into the Union on the basis of full fellowship and full equality."[59]

Many historians, journalists, and others have concurred in Arnall's assessment of his role in the freight rate controversy. James F. Cook, Jr., in his study of Georgia governors, wrote that the success of the Georgia case ended the discriminatory rates toward the South. Coulter, in his history of Georgia, believed the case "resulted in the South getting its plight prominently before the country, and some good resulted." Historian Numan V. Bartley praised Arnall's "successful fight against discriminatory freight rates." Taylor, in his study of Arnall, concluded that the Georgia case "seems to have played a part in the ICC decision to equalize freight rates." A senior editor of *Reader's Digest*, Eugene H. Methvin, wrote that the nation became "a 'common market' and an area bereft of trade barriers" due to Arnall's fight against unfair rates. In his book entitled *The Revolt of the South and West*, A. G. Mezerik called Arnall's court fight a victory for Georgia, the South, and the West. Stephens Mitchell, brother of Margaret

Mitchell, claimed that one of the most important events that occurred in the South in his lifetime was Arnall's "breaking the freight rate shackles that had kept the South from becoming industrialized."[60]

However, not everyone had praise for Arnall's role in the controversy. Sam Hall Flint questioned Arnall's argument that the Georgia case had goaded the ICC into equalizing freight rates. In support of his argument, Flint noted that the ICC had issued its decision in the important Southern Governors Case in 1937 and that the ICC had started its class rate investigation in 1939 "before any evidence was taken in the Georgia case." Another critic, Robert Lively, believed Arnall's personal assumption of the Georgia case, his "casual dismissal" of the long fight of the southern governors against unfair rates, and Arnall's "police court techniques of impugning the integrity" of those who disagreed with him on the rate question hurt the South's cause. Taylor observed that the Georgia case failed in its immediate aim of ending an alleged rate conspiracy. Two economists at Duke University even contended that freight rates were never "a major barrier to the economic development of the South." According to them, southerners used the freight rate issue to absolve themselves of any responsibility for the lack of industrial development in the South.[61]

Despite arguments minimizing the impact of high freight rates in the South, the fact remained, as the ICC and the Supreme Court finally recognized, that the South had not been treated fairly on the issue of freight rates. In defense of Arnall, he had not originally intended to engage in a solo fight against a freight rate conspiracy before the Supreme Court. He joined others in an unsuccessful effort in 1943 to create a political alliance between western and southern governors to fight the problem. His efforts in 1943 to convince southern governors to exert political pressure as a means of ending unfair rates failed. His plea to southern chief executives to resort to the courts as a means of obtaining justice in the rate-making process also fell on deaf ears. They refused to join him in a court fight, apparently out of concern over fears that a court battle would have an adverse impact on the ICC's investigation of class rates. Growing disillusioned with ICC inaction, Arnall struck out on his own to do battle against the railroads before the Supreme Court.

Less than two months after the Supreme Court granted jurisdiction in the Georgia case, the ICC, which had been investigating class rates since 1939, handed down a decision on class rates favorable to the South. While the Georgia case did not end the freight rate controversy, it is evident that the Supreme Court's acceptance of jurisdiction in the Georgia case, the publicity generated by the case, and Arnall's highly publicized fight against freight rates hastened the demise of a rate system detrimental to the South. Although he cannot be given sole credit for ending southern rate discrimination, Arnall rightly deserves praise for playing a major role in the establishment of freight rate justice for the South.

9

The

Race

Issue

Arnall claimed he had only one difficult problem as governor—the race issue. The young progressive reformer entered the governorship as a segregationist and left the office four years later still of the same persuasion. During those years, however, his version of race relations in the South evolved into one that offered blacks the hope of a better life within the confines of Jim Crow. His stand on allowing blacks to vote in the Democratic primary in 1946 provoked bitter criticism with his political enemies attacking him as a traitor to the white race as a means of diminishing his political popularity. His enlightened view of race relations contributed to his political demise.[1]

According to the 1940 census, Georgia had a population of 3,123,723 of which 34.7 percent was black. In fact, Georgia had the largest black population of any state in the union. Like their counterparts in other southern states, blacks in Georgia had been legally segregated and relegated to second-class citizenship by the turn of the twentieth century. One historian observed that by the time of the Arnall administration, "Georgia's segregated social system had hardened into a rigid caste structure accepted by virtually all whites and substantial numbers of blacks as the ordained and proper way of doing things." Blacks in Georgia, in addition to being segregated, had been disfranchised by the first decade of the twentieth century. While legal segregation remained intact in Georgia until the 1960s, blacks began returning to the voting booths of Georgia in the Arnall administration.[2]

Blacks in Georgia had been enfranchised during the Reconstruction period and constituted a substantial portion of the state's electorate in the latter part of the nineteenth century. However, disfranchisement efforts culminating in 1908 decimated black voting strength. By 1940 the number of blacks voting in Georgia ranged from estimates of ten thousand to twenty thousand. Fraud, intimidation, a cumulative poll tax, a literacy test, and various other means had been used to eliminate the black as a participant in the state's political system. The Democratic party's white primary, however, served as the major means of curtailing black voting.[3]

The first statewide primary in Georgia took place in 1898. Two years later the state Democratic party excluded blacks from participating in its primaries. With the demise of the Populist party in the 1890s and the existence of only a token Republican party, the Democratic party dominated Georgia politics. As a consequence, nomination by the Democratic party constituted election since the primary and not the general election served as the important election in the state. Blacks who survived disfranchisement efforts voted only in general elections or in a few local elections. When Arnall assumed the governorship, blacks lacked the right to participate in political affairs of the state.[4]

Arnall grew up in a segregated society and, like the overwhelming majority of white Georgians, readily accepted segregation, contending that "no man can rise completely above his roots." Arnall, believing that the races preferred segregation even in the absence of Jim Crow laws, expressed the prevailing view of most whites in the South when he told President Roosevelt, "We don't really have any Negro issues in the South. It's white agitators from the North that make the trouble." As a state legislator and state attorney general, Arnall never deviated from southern racial tradition. Even if he had doubts about segregation, political reality precluded a politician in Georgia in the 1930s and the 1940s from challenging the racial order. "Hell, if I had defied Southern [racial] orthodoxy," Arnall observed, "I wouldn't have been elected door keeper."[5]

During his successful gubernatorial campaign in 1942 against Talmadge, the state's best-known advocate of white supremacy, Arnall vigorously emphasized his strong commitment to segregation. "You have to play politics," Arnall recalled, "to get in position to render public service." Talmadge's biographer correctly argued that two racists—Talmadge and Arnall—opposed each other in the 1942 campaign. Lillian Smith, an outspoken Georgia liberal and occasional critic of the governor, noted that Arnall had defended segregation and repudiated racial equality just as vehemently as Talmadge. In fact, the racial rhetoric of the campaign degenerated to the point that the editor of the Augusta *Herald* pleaded with both candidates to stop talking about race, fearing further discussion of the subject could "lead to serious disturbances" in the state.[6]

Despite the plea, both candidates continued to assure the voters of their loyalty to segregation. Arnall even told audiences that whites would always rule Georgia and that no "intelligent or decent type person" believed in racial coeducation in Georgia. On another occasion, Arnall reassured the voters that schools would remain segregated as long as he were governor, as if that were an issue confronting Georgians during World War II. Arnall even made a Talmadge-like statement when he said, "Any nigger who tried to enter the university would not be in existence [the] next day." He stated in one campaign speech that "the sun would not set" on the head of a black who tried to enroll in a white school in Coweta County. Certainly his campaign rhetoric in 1942 revealed a segregationist point of view, but more important, it assured whites that he was just as "safe" on the race issue as Talmadge. For that matter, most whites in Georgia, ranging from conservatives like Talmadge to liberals like Ralph McGill, believed segregation best for the South and for both races. On this subject at least both Arnall, the progressive reformer, and Talmadge, the state's foremost racial demagogue, agreed.[7]

Arnall's reform program lacked specific provisions to benefit the blacks of the state for obvious reasons. Arnall conceded that if he had advocated state action to benefit blacks or to ensure first-class citizenship for them, "I would have been so handcuffed that I could not have done the job which we wanted to do for Georgia and which was done." In his fight to extend voting rights to Georgians in military service, Arnall made it clear that the reform would apply only to white Georgians. He even assured the legislators that the abolishment of the poll tax would not result in increased black voting as long as the state had the white primary. As governor, Arnall never proposed legislation allowing blacks to vote in the state primary election, realizing the unpopularity of such a request.[8]

Once elected, however, some differences between him and Talmadge on the race question emerged. Arnall avoided the use of racial rhetoric, unlike Talmadge. After the completion of the first year of the Arnall administration, the Atlanta *Daily World,* a black newspaper, noted that Arnall had not yet undertaken any specific act to benefit blacks. Nevertheless the *World* concluded, "The mere fact that he does not carry on an active campaign of hate toward them is a real improvement over his predecessor." Benjamin E. Mays, a prominent leader in the Atlanta black community, conceded that Arnall had not waved "the red flag of race" in his administration.[9]

Arnall carefully avoided the race issue in the first two years of his governorship, but he made some statements in June 1945 that led Talmadge to question Arnall's commitment to the "Southern way of life." Arnall had gone to Louisville, Kentucky, to give a speech to a gathering of Kentucky Democrats. During a news conference, a black reporter asked Arnall about opportunities for blacks in Georgia. Arnall responded that his policy was for Georgia blacks to have equal opportunities in education and in earning an income. He further stated that racial problems were only economic problems and concluded, "If there is no economic problem, there is no racial problem." Maintaining that Georgia could not prosper if blacks were held back economically, he conceded that economic equality for blacks could not occur overnight and criticized liberals who tried "to make the world over in a day." Arnall then rhetorically asked: "What the hell difference does it make if you sit down and eat with Negroes, visit with them in their homes, talk with them?" As far as he was concerned, "That just means that they have something to eat, that they have a home, that they have had enough education to carry on a conversation."[10]

Talmadge, who had been unsuccessful in his political clashes with his young political adversary, saw Arnall's enlightened position on race as a weak link in his political armor. He attacked Arnall's racial views as being out of line with the thinking of most white Georgians and accused Arnall of advocating social equality of the races. Clearly Arnall had trod on grounds where none of his predecessors had ventured. He had publicly endorsed the practices of the races eating together, of whites visiting blacks, and the necessity of economic equality of blacks. Gunnar Myrdal's study of blacks in America during this time period concluded that "the main symbol of social equality between the two groups had traditionally been the taboo against eating together." Arnall had publicly challenged that taboo while in Louisville.[11]

The day after his remarks, Arnall sought to clarify his "what the hell" statement by claiming the quotation had been garbled when printed. He contended that what he intended to say was what "difference does it make to them if you sit down and eat with Negroes, visit with them in their homes, talk with them." According to Arnall, it just meant that blacks had "something to eat, a home, enough education to carry on a conversation—

in other words, economic equality." Arnall then expressed pride in the advances of blacks since slavery, even claiming that "Negroes have advanced
farther than any other race in the world." Arnall stated his belief that white
southerners believed blacks should enjoy their constitutional rights, receive
just and fair treatment from the government, and enjoy economic opportunities. He contended that whites rejected social equality as absurd and
injurious to both races. At the same time, he believed that the South's racial
problems would be resolved by understanding, tolerance, education, and
economic prosperity.[12]

The Louisville news conference had resulted in Arnall's most extensive
discussion of race during his governorship. In some respects, Arnall had
simply restated his commitment to segregation. He had however distanced
himself from the racial views of some white Georgians, especially the conservative residents in the rural areas of the state. Few Georgia politicians
had ever praised blacks for their advancement since slavery, endorsed social
intermingling of the races, or called for toleration and understanding in
solving the South's racial problem. With Talmadge in mind, Arnall, in an
article in *Collier's,* condemned racial demagogues in the South and attributed the elections of these "clowns" to bigotry and intolerance.[13]

While Arnall had no intention of raising the issue of blacks voting in
Georgia, some black citizens of the state did in the federal courts. The white
primary in the South had first come under legal attack in the 1920s in a
case involving a Texas law that barred blacks from the state's primaries. The
U.S. Supreme Court in 1927 held the law to be in violation of the Fourteenth Amendment. The Texas Democratic party quickly adopted party
rules excluding blacks from participating in its primaries. Party leaders contended that blacks could be excluded from their party's activities because
their party was a private association and not an instrumentality of the state.
The U.S. Supreme Court upheld the Texas Democratic party's position
in 1935.[14]

However, nine years later, in April 1944, the Supreme Court held in
Smith v. Allwright that the exclusion of blacks from the Texas Democratic party violated the Fifteenth Amendment. The court reasoned that
the Democratic primary was an integral part of the electoral process in
Texas. Even though the party and not the state had excluded blacks, the
court ruled that the state of Texas was involved in the primaries because
of its regulation of the party's primaries. While Governor Arnall remained
silent, southern politicians bitterly attacked the court's decision. U.S. Sena-

tor Claude Pepper of Florida, perhaps the most liberal New Dealer in the South, proclaimed, "The South will allow nothing to impair white supremacy." *Time* concluded that the South with the exception of a "few plaintive newspaper editorial writers" was in "thunderous harmony" on the question of keeping the blacks in their traditional place. Talmadge drew attention to Arnall's silence on the question at a time when the other southern political leaders condemned the decision.[15]

A subcommittee of the state's Democratic party executive committee concluded *Smith v. Allwright* was not applicable to the state since Georgia had not been a party to the case and ruled that the upcoming 1944 Georgia primary would still be for whites only. Nevertheless, Rev. Primus E. King, a black resident of Columbus, attempted to vote in the primary. After election officials refused to allow him to vote, Rev. King filed suit in federal district court seeking to invalidate the state's white primary. Federal District Court Judge T. Holt Davis, rendering his decision in October 1945, ruled the Democratic party's white primary to be unconstitutional. The judge concluded that the primary was an integral part of the state's electoral process.[16]

The Atlanta *Journal,* agreeing with the decision, pointed out that blacks had long been voting in the primaries of several southern states with "no disturbances or perils" to those states' established social order. Other papers, such as the Columbus *Ledger-Enquirer* and the Macon *Telegraph,* expressed agreement with the decision. Talmadge, however, warned that "for the safety and protection of this state . . . the negro should not be allowed to participate in a white primary." Governor Arnall responded to the decision by urging an appeal of the decision to the Fifth Circuit Court of Appeals. Arnall's response brought criticism from the Atlanta *Daily World,* which called it "very surprising to us and we believe to all the liberal forces in this section." The Savannah *Morning News,* however, saw no need for surprise, claiming that Arnall's racial views were not any different from those of the average white citizen of the state.[17]

The Fifth Circuit Court of Appeals, handing down its decision on March 6, 1946, upheld the lower federal court. Judge John Sibley, who wrote the opinion, held that party election rules enforced by state power which excluded blacks violated the Fifteenth Amendment. However, Judge Sibley detected significant differences between the Georgia case and that of Texas in that Georgia did not require party primaries, did not require party candidates to be chosen in a primary, and did not require the state to pay the expense of a primary. Judge Sibley's opinion seemed to leave a way for the white primary in Georgia to be saved by converting the Georgia Democratic party into a private organization with no state regulation.[18]

On March 7, 1946, Speaker Harris called for a special legislative session to repeal the state's primary laws. Talmadge also urged the convening of a special legislative session. As the pressure increased on Arnall to call a special session, the governor remained silent except to say that he would not comment on the case until the Supreme Court had ruled on it. On March 28, 1946, Senate President Frank Gross spoke out against a special session. Gross downplayed the threat to white supremacy by pointing out that whites outnumbered blacks in Georgia. Gross recommended holding off on any possible state action until the Supreme Court had ruled on the appeal. Expressing concern over repealing the state's primary regulations, Gross feared such a move "might be more damaging than the disease." In particular, he expressed fear over the possibility of the county unit system being abandoned if not required by state law.[19]

Governor Arnall telegraphed the Senate president to commend him for his speech. The Atlanta *Constitution* saw this as Arnall's first public expression on the white primary issue. In his Louisville news conference in June 1945, however, Arnall was reported as saying that blacks should have the right to vote just as other citizens. But he had also stated, "If I stumped Georgia and demanded that right for them, it would set everything back fifty years." In his clarification remarks the day following the news conference, Arnall modified his earlier statements, contending Georgians believed blacks could be excluded from Democratic party primaries because the party was a voluntary organization. During deliberations of the Constitutional Revision Commission, Arnall had expressed his opposition to state regulation of primaries being in the state constitution or in state law. The Constitution of 1945 lacked references to state primaries, although the state retained laws regulating primaries. Ironically, Arnall had thus earlier taken a position that Harris and Talmadge were now advocating.[20]

On April 1, 1946, the U.S. Supreme Court refused to review Judge Sibley's decision and Georgians anxiously awaited Arnall's reaction. The invalidation of the white primary presented Arnall with one of the most difficult dilemmas of his administration. How should he respond to the federal courts' mandate? Should he advocate evasion or compliance? Either way, Arnall stood to lose politically. By trying to evade the mandate of the federal courts, he would be aligning himself with his arch political foe—one of the foremost white supremacists in the South. Such a decision would damage Arnall's progressive reputation and diminish his standing in the national Democratic party. By abiding by the decision, Arnall faced the loss of political support from white Georgians opposed to blacks voting in the white primary. It would place him on the defensive on the emotional issue of race and provide Talmadge with an issue that could return him to the governor's office.[21]

On April 4, 1946, Arnall announced his decision on the white primary—one of the most important of his administration—by declaring, "I will not be a party to any subterfuge or 'scheme' designed to nullify the orders of the courts." He further declared it to be the duty of good citizens "to uphold the courts, the Constitution and laws of our land." He warned that the county unit system could be discarded if the law requiring it were repealed and that fraud and corruption would occur in Georgia elections without state regulation. The governor stated his firm opposition to a special session of the legislature and threatened to veto any legislation repealing such laws passed by a self-convened session. After Arnall's decision, the Georgia Democratic party amended its regulations to permit black participation in the 1946 primary. For the first time since 1900, blacks could participate in the Democratic party's primaries. Before Arnall had made his decision, he went to see his "political godfather," James M. Cox, the presidential candidate of the Democratic party in 1920, a former governor of Ohio, and the owner of the Atlanta *Journal*. Arnall recalled the conversation:

> I said, "Governor, the highest court has spoken. I have a chance to dominate Georgia politics for the next forty years simply by saying, to hell with the Court. We are going to run things our way and we're not going to give first-class citizenship to the blacks, and we're not going to let blacks vote in the white primary. We will use any subterfuge we can to prevent that." But I said, "Governor, I can't do that because we have a country of law, and either we must respect the courts or we will have anarchy." And he looked at me, and said, "Ellis, I would have thought nothing of you at all had you tried to defy the court."[22]

Believing the "great mass of Georgia citizens" overwhelmingly supported his stand, Arnall had, nevertheless, made a politically dangerous move by refusing to call a special session to try to save the white primary. Herman Talmadge called it "a political mistake because it was completely out of harmony with the thinking of the people of Georgia at that time."

Arnall conceded that his failure to call a special session was the major blow that caused his loss of political popularity in the state. Blacks constituted a majority in 47 of Georgia's 159 counties and made up 38.2 percent of the potential voting strength in the state. Thanks to Arnall's efforts, Georgia was the only Black Belt state that had neither a poll tax nor legislation to circumvent the federal courts' invalidation of the white primary. By the end of 1946 only one southern state—Texas—had more blacks registered to vote. According to NAACP estimates, Georgia had 150,000 black voters compared to Alabama's 10,000, South Carolina's 5,000, and Mississippi's 5,000.[23]

Arnall's decision received praise from Governor Cox's Atlanta *Journal,* which commended him for his "stand of true statesmanship and common sense." The Columbus *Ledger* called Arnall's decision "sound and ethically honest" and warned that repealing the state's primary laws "would produce a condition of bedlam, and open the way to all sorts of skulldruggery." The Macon *News* agreed with Arnall's stand on the special session and asserted that "there is no middle ground. Either we obey or we defy the law and the Constitution."[24]

Eugene Talmadge disagreed. Two days after Arnall's announcement on the white primary, a politically revived Talmadge entered the 1946 governor's race. He promised the restoration of the Democratic white primary and accused Arnall of robbing the people of their white primary. Talmadge charged Arnall with selling out to the presidential ambitions of Henry Wallace in return for being Wallace's vice presidential candidate as "the champion of the Negro vote." Arnall's stand also brought condemnation from Speaker Harris, who vowed to stump the state either for himself or as a candidate in favor of a white primary. The political alliance between Harris and Arnall, which had been strained by the second term issue, ended over their differences on the white primary. Talmadge, conducting a bitter white supremacist campaign, eventually won the 1946 gubernatorial primary—with white supremacy the major issue in the campaign.[25]

During the last year of his administration, Arnall took on the Ku Klux Klan, the South's most infamous organization opposed to first-class citizenship for black southerners. On the night of May 9, 1946, several hundred members of the Klan gathered on Stone Mountain to burn a cross and to initiate new members. Arnall criticized the Klan for desecrating Stone Mountain and holding the state up to the ridicule of the nation. He asked Attorney General Eugene Cook to advise him as to what action the state could take concerning the activities of the Klan in Georgia. Cook responded by informing the governor of the state's authority to revoke a state-issued charter that had been granted in 1916 if the Klan had violated provisions of its charter. After receiving the opinion, Arnall directed the attorney general to institute legal proceedings to revoke the Klan's charter. Arnall justified the revocation on the basis that the Klan had engaged in unlawful activities, deprived citizens of their constitutional rights, violated state criminal laws, and engaged in political activities. If legal proceedings against the Klan failed, Arnall promised to consider calling a special legislative session to dehood the Klan and to prohibit Klan activities detrimental to the public good. Arnall's attack on the Klan resulted in his receiving anonymous threatening phone calls and a report from the FBI that the Klan had plotted his assassination. Arnall stated that such activities would not stop his "effort to purge the state of this infamous organization which has brought discredit to our State and is a national eyesore."[26]

In the midst of his fight with the Klan, Arnall invited the well-known columnist and commentator Drew Pearson to present his regular radio program from the steps of the state capitol. Arnall introduced Pearson, who had earlier announced his program would be anti-Klan in nature to an audience of two thousand, many of whom were hostile to the columnist. Pearson praised Arnall as "a valiant crusader for good-will among men" and called him one of the nation's greatest governors. In his introductory remarks, Arnall spoke out strongly against racial intolerance and called for a crusade against "fear, bigotry, prejudice, and hate."[27]

In the state's fight against the Klan, Attorney General Cook designated Assistant Attorney General Daniel Duke to head the effort to revoke the Klan's charter. Arnall requested President Truman to allow the Justice Department to assist the state's fight against the Klan by turning over to Duke information it had on Klan activities. The president assured the governor that Department of Justice files on the Klan would be open to the state. In addition, Truman praised Arnall for the "vigorous effort which you have been making and are making against all racist intolerance and hatred." On June 20, 1946, the state filed a suit in Fulton Superior Court to revoke the Klan's charter. A technical error in the state's prosecution resulted in a delay in the court's proceedings. In June 1947, several months after Arnall had left the governorship, the Klan, recognizing the inevitable, voluntarily surrendered its charter. Although the state's official sanction of the Klan had finally been withdrawn, the Klan continued to function with little noticeable change in its activities.[28]

Arnall's fight against the Klan earned him widespread praise in both the state and the nation. However, his acceptance of an award from a liberal organization in the last months of his administration received strong opposition even from some of his most loyal supporters. Clark Foreman, president of the Southern Conference for Human Welfare (SCHW), announced in November 1946 that Governor Arnall would receive the organization's Jefferson Award, an honor given for "outstanding service to the people of the South in the tradition of Thomas Jefferson." Foreman called Arnall's term of office as governor "one of the most vivid pages in the history of Southern Liberalism." Previous recipients of the award included U.S. Supreme Court Justice Hugo L. Black and Frank G. Graham, president of the University of North Carolina.[29]

The SCHW, an organization of liberal southerners committed to improving the South, had been organized in 1938. The organization supported progressive legislation and efforts to improve the economic and social well-being of southerners. From its beginning, the organization drew criticism from conservatives in the South as an organization committed to racial equality. The organization held its first convention in the Birmingham municipal auditorium with delegates ignoring the city's Jim Crow ordinance regulating meeting in public facilities. After city authorities forced the convention to comply with its local segregation ordinance, the organization resolved never again to hold segregated meetings. That stand drew strong criticism from the southern press, leading most of the liberal southern politicians in the organization to end their affiliation with it. Following World War II, the organization took an increasingly militant stand against segregation and came under attack for having communists in its ranks. Thus, the organization that offered Arnall its highest honor stood condemned in the eyes of many southerners as too liberal, too closely affiliated with communism, and a threat to segregation.[30]

Shortly after Foreman's announcement, the Atlanta *Constitution* stated its opposition to Arnall's accepting the award. While praising the SCHW for doing "some few good things," the *Constitution* concluded that the organization was not "trustworthy" because of its "flirting with 'certain commie' personalities." The *Constitution* accused the organization of trying to cash in on Arnall's national reputation. The Columbus *Ledger,* a long-time supporter of the governor, also shared the attitude of the *Constitution*. The Augusta *Chronicle*, another long-time Arnall backer, also urged the governor to refuse the award, which it believed was given in an effort to swing "on to the coattails of a distinguished Georgian who has won a nationwide reputation as a liberal." The *Statesman* saw the award as another example of the governor of Georgia lowering white Georgians into disgrace. Arnall, in the opinion of Talmadge's paper, had become the "Darling of the Race-Mixing Radicals."[31]

On November 25 Arnall moved to distance himself from the SCHW. The governor, admitting that he had agreed to accept the award without consulting his friends and advisors, announced, "I am not familiar with purposes of the conference and my acceptance of the organization's award does not mean I accept the group's ideas." Revealing that several personal friends had advised him to decline the award, Arnall decided to still accept it since he had made a commitment to do so. Talmadge bitterly attacked Arnall's claim of not being familiar with the purpose of the SCHW as "double-talk" that would fail to convince "decent white people." Ironically, one of the members of the SCHW, the liberal Georgian and opponent of white supremacy, Lillian Smith, criticized the SCHW for honoring Arnall, accusing him of being a political opportunist.[32]

The SCHW convention took place in a private meeting hall in New Orleans in November 1946. The conference location had been changed from the municipal auditorium to avoid compliance with the city's segregation ordinance. Nearly one half of the 269 delegates at the conference were blacks with the remaining delegates consisting of a small number of socialists, several communists and liberals. Only two prominent politicians, Senator Pepper and Governor Arnall, attended the conference. In an acceptance speech, Arnall avoided the race issue while calling for more democracy to cure the ills of democracy, for educational reforms, for an extension of public health services, and for an end to the South's colonial status. Arnall's political enemies used the SCHW award and the integrated SCHW convention as further evidence of his racial liberalism.[33]

In addition to recognition from the SCHW, Arnall also received awards from two other organizations. In February 1947 the Council Against Intolerance in America announced Arnall as the recipient of its Thomas Jefferson Award for public service. The council presented the award to Arnall for being most responsible for the advancement of democracy in the nation during 1946. Arnall received the award as a result of a poll of five hundred city newspaper editors and fifteen hundred civic organizations. The same month, Lawrence D. Reddic, curator of the Schomburg Collection of Negro Literature of the New York City Public Library, revealed that Arnall had been selected for inclusion on the collection's Honor Roll of Race Relations. Reddic cited Arnall's "fight for Democracy in Georgia" as the basis for Arnall's selection. Never had a governor of Georgia been so honored.[34]

As the Arnall administration drew to a close, the publisher released the governor's first book, *The Shore Dimly Seen,* in which Arnall devoted an entire chapter to the subject of blacks. He defended the institution of seg-regation and urged the South to provide equal facilities for blacks as man-dated by the separate-but-equal doctrine. Arnall also urged the South not to use segregation as "a device for robbing the Negro, as it has become in the instance of some classes of public transportation." Arnall defended the South's treatment of blacks, claiming the difficulties faced by them were problems common to minority groups throughout the United States and the world. He even claimed that white southerners "in the main, are less resentful of a minority group than any other in America."[35]

In his book, Arnall elaborated on a theme he had raised before—the South's poverty being the cause of white-black problems. Arnall shifted the blame for exploitation of the blacks from white southerners to those outside of the region whom he held responsible for the region's economic exploitation. "In a prosperous South, in a South that did not suffer from colonialism and exploitation," Arnall wrote, "the Negro would prosper and would be able to obtain most of the things he deserved." Arnall believed the blacks would be better off economically if they stayed in the South and concluded that, overall, the South offered blacks more economic oppor-tunities and economic justice than the critics of the South would admit. While Arnall saw economic prosperity as part of the solution to the south-ern race problem, he reasoned, "It is not all of the problem, for part of the answer must be found within the human heart."[36]

The Shore Dimly Seen dealt with three of the major complaints of blacks against the South—poor educational opportunity, violations of civil lib-erties, and deprivation of political rights. Arnall conceded educational opportunities for southern blacks had been inadequate and that higher educational opportunities for them had been neglected. However, Arnall saw the South making progress in providing better educational opportu-nities for blacks. He dismissed the complaint of civil liberties violations as "uncommon" in the South and claimed, "In general, the basic civil liberties of black citizens are respected thoroughly in Georgia." He believed most white southerners favored blacks voting in both general and primary elections with the only obstacle standing between blacks and the voting booth being the literacy test. While favoring the literacy test, Arnall believed it should be enforced evenhandedly and not made a subterfuge to prevent blacks from voting.[37]

Arnall's book ignored the darker side of race relations in the South. White southerners had segregated, disfranchised, and relegated southern blacks to a status of inferiority and second-class citizenship. Southern legislators, not northern economic exploiters, had stripped the southern black of his dignity and his rights. The institution of segregation ended, and blacks returned to the voting booths not because of a rising tide of prosperity, as Arnall predicted, but because of federal intervention. Many disagreed with Arnall's assertion that civil liberties of blacks were only "occasionally" interfered with or that the civil liberties of Georgia's black citizens were "respected thoroughly." Contrary to Arnall's claim that the right of blacks to vote in the South was "now unchallenged," blacks continued to experience resistance to voting in the South. They gained the right to vote in many parts of the South only after passage of the Voting Rights Act of 1965.[38]

Arnall became governor without an agenda to improve the well-being of blacks in the state. During his governorship, he never questioned the necessity of segregation except to call upon the South to provide equal facilities for blacks as mandated by *Plessey v. Ferguson*. Arnall never took the position that blacks should vote in state primaries until the federal courts forced him to make a decision on the issue. Arnall eventually urged Georgians to comply with the federal courts' mandate to allow blacks to vote in the state's primary, resulting in considerable damage to his political standing in the state. His successful fight to do away with the poll tax, his successful effort to lower the voting age, and his acceptance of the federal court's invalidation of the white primary allowed blacks to participate in the state's political process in unprecedented numbers in Georgia in the twentieth century.

Although he received the condemnation of many Georgians for his alleged racial liberalism, Arnall defended segregation and never presented a threat to it. His view of race relations in the South ignored the darker side of a segregated South. He minimized the strong opposition of many whites in the South to blacks voting as well as the indignities experienced by blacks because of the second-class citizenship imposed upon them. To his credit, however, Arnall took on the Klan—the organization that epitomized the worst in race relations in the South. Arnall wanted all Georgians, including blacks, to experience a higher standard of living and a better way of life. He wanted all Georgians to benefit from better educational opportunities and to receive the same level of governmental services as well. Arnall wanted progress for the black citizen of Georgia within the framework of segregation.

10

. . . .

Political

. . . .

Adversities

. . . .

By the summer of 1944 Arnall had established himself as one of the state's most successful chief executives. He had obtained passage of his legislative requests in the 1943 regular legislative session and in two special sessions. Under his leadership, a commission had been created to revise the state's antiquated constitution. Both the state and national press praised the young governor for his accomplishments. He enjoyed widespread popularity in the state and had even been suggested as a presidential candidate. Approaching the halfway mark in his term, Arnall had avoided any major political missteps or defeats. One observer even went so far as to call him "invincible" in Georgia politics.[1]

That invincibility ended in the second half of his term, during which he suffered three major defeats—one in national politics and two on the state level. His first serious political setback occurred at the 1944 Democratic National Convention in Chicago. There Arnall unsuccessfully fought for the renomination of Vice President Henry A. Wallace. In the months that followed, Arnall suffered another political defeat when the legislature, on two separate occasions, failed to pass a constitutional amendment permitting gubernatorial succession. Denied the opportunity to seek a consecutive term, Arnall supported James V. Carmichael's unsuccessful candidacy in the 1946 gubernatorial primary. Shortly before that primary, Arnall's decision to abide by a federal court order to allow black participation in the Democratic party's white primary further undercut his political influence. Arnall no longer appeared invincible.

Arnall did not play a role in either the 1932 or the 1936 presidential elections. He was too busy trying to get elected to the legislature for the first time in 1932 and he was too busy working on behalf of Ed Rivers's gubernatorial campaign in 1936. In the 1940 race, however, he served as state director of the Roosevelt-Wallace clubs in Georgia and made numerous speeches throughout the state on behalf of the national ticket. Arnall enthusiastically favored a third term for Roosevelt, "the man who saved our country from social revolution in 1933." Two years later, in the 1942 gubernatorial election, President Roosevelt gave behind-the-scenes support to Arnall in his race against Talmadge. In that campaign Arnall successfully made Talmadge's long-standing opposition to the president a major issue.[2]

While most observers assumed that Roosevelt would seek a fourth term, he had not made a public statement to that effect. On June 22, 1944, less than a month before the convention, Arnall conferred with the president in the White House. In their conversation, Arnall asked if the president would seek another term. Roosevelt responded that he would serve if nominated. With the approval of the president, Arnall released that information to the press. However, the most important revelation to come out of that meeting concerned the vice presidential nomination. During their conversation, Arnall asked the president if he had a preference for his running mate. Roosevelt replied that he favored the renomination of Wallace. Arnall promised the president to do all that he could to help Wallace gain the vice presidential nomination even though he had never met the vice president.[3]

By supporting the renomination of the vice president, Arnall embarked upon a potentially dangerous course of action. The liberal Wallace had many political enemies, with southern conservatives and urban party leaders heading the list. The former secretary of agriculture had gained the vice presidential nomination in 1940 only after Roosevelt threatened not to run again unless Wallace was on the ticket. Despite Roosevelt's ultimatum, many delegates still opposed him. He received the nomination on the first ballot, with the southern delegates least supportive of his nomination. Wallace's nomination in 1940 was so controversial that he was advised not to give a speech thanking the delegates for nominating him.[4]

Wallace's relationship with his political opposition continued to deteriorate because, in the opinion of John Gunther, the vice president "made little effort to get along with the politicians." Eleanor Roosevelt, a strong supporter of the vice president, conceded that Wallace was "perhaps too idealistic—and that makes him a bad politician." The political bosses in the party distrusted him because of his idealism, his talk of reform, and his lack of interest in their concerns. Wallace frightened conservatives because of his liberalism, his strong support from organized labor, and his racial liberalism. Herman Talmadge contended that Wallace had been unpopular in the South since his days as secretary of agriculture because "he was a damn fool." While conservatives and party bosses had accepted the inevitability of the president's running for a fourth term, they were determined to deny Wallace renomination, especially in light of Roosevelt's failing health.[5]

Despite Wallace's numerous liabilities, Arnall returned to Georgia committed to Wallace. He moved to shore up Wallace's standing in Georgia by portraying the vice president as a friend of the South committed to ending freight rate discrimination. Arnall also tried to convince his fellow Georgians that Wallace had more knowledge of foreign affairs than anyone in government with the exception of the president. "The only criticism I have heard about Wallace," Arnall declared, "is that he is too sincere and too honest." Arnall met Wallace for the first time shortly before the 1944 convention and was "impressed by his courage, simplicity, sincerity, and intense shyness." Arnall, who possessed a gregarious personality, thought Wallace's shyness strange for a politician.[6]

Unknown to Arnall, party leaders had already begun a campaign to dump Wallace by undermining Roosevelt's support of Wallace. These leaders attempted to convince Roosevelt that Wallace's renomination would cause the party to lose the support of several of the major states and possibly cause the president to lose the election. Roosevelt's commitment to Wallace began to weaken. Early in July, several key party leaders met with Roosevelt to discuss the vice presidential nomination. The group finally prevailed upon Roosevelt to drop Wallace and to accept Senator Harry S. Truman as the vice presidential candidate. Unknown to Wallace and Arnall, Roosevelt had abandoned the vice president and had shifted his support to Truman.[7]

As expected, the vice presidential nomination dominated proceedings at the 1944 convention. Arnall, in addition to lining up votes for Wallace, served as a floor manager for the vice president. Prior to the first ballot on the vice presidential nomination, the Georgia delegation caucused to determine its position. The delegation operated under the unit rule by which a majority vote determined the vote of the delegation. Arnall had no concerns over how the vote would go because he, as governor, served as head of the delegation and had stacked the delegation with delegates willing to support Wallace. Prior to the caucus vote, Arnall explained his position to the Georgia delegates: "I know that some of you do not like Mr. Wallace. My own position is not that of being for Mr. Wallace. It is that of being for the President. I could not go halfway with him."[8]

Democratic National Committee Chairman Robert E. Hannagan, a leader in the effort to dump Wallace, unsuccessfully sought to convince Arnall at the convention to switch his allegiance to Truman. Arnall declined to do so, claiming that Roosevelt had asked him to support Wallace. "Now if he wants to call me," Arnall told Hannagan, "and tell me not to [support Wallace], I'll quit." At the time, Roosevelt, who did not attend the convention, was on the West Coast preparing to sail to Hawaii. Roosevelt never called, and Arnall stood by his commitment to the president, still believing Wallace to be Roosevelt's vice presidential choice.[9]

Wallace supporters had packed the convention hall for the vice president's speech seconding Roosevelt's renomination. Arnall recalled, "We had all the galleries stacked and they would holler. We had all the crowd with us." The planned demonstration following Wallace's speech was the most enthusiastic of the convention. The vice president's supporters, believing that his only hope was to capitalize on the enthusiasm at that moment, attempted to place his name in nomination. To block that effort, Hannagan quickly prevailed upon the chairman of the convention to entertain a motion to adjourn the session. The chairman ruled that a motion to adjourn, decided by voice vote, had passed. Arnall, however, believed the motion to adjourn was "overwhelmingly defeated" and complained of the "outrageous tactics" used by Hannagan to adjourn the convention. He believed that Wallace would have won if the delegates had been allowed to vote on the vice presidential nomination at that session.[10]

The following day the convention considered the vice presidential nomination. At the request of the vice president, Arnall gave a seconding speech on behalf of Wallace's renomination, which was interrupted by applause ten times. Arnall called for Wallace's renomination because of his loyalty to the president, his outstanding record as secretary of agriculture, his success in diplomacy, his popularity with the people, and his being the first choice of Roosevelt to be his running mate. Arnall contended that Wallace's renomination would be "reassurance that the Democratic Party remains true to its ideals of progressive liberalism."[11]

The vice president failed to obtain the nomination on the first ballot. Only two southern delegations supported Wallace: Georgia, under the unit rule, cast all her votes for Wallace and the Florida delegation gave Wallace nine votes. On the second ballot, Arnall again cast all of Georgia's votes for Wallace. As the voting on the second ballot progressed, the Wallace candidacy collapsed under an avalanche of delegates switching to Truman. After Truman obtained a number sufficient for nomination, Arnall switched the Georgia vote to Truman, who won the nomination on the second ballot. Following the convention, Roosevelt invited Arnall to the White House where the president apologized for not informing Arnall of his abandonment of Wallace. Wallace praised Arnall for "showing great courage" in delivering the seconding speech.[12]

After the convention, the relationship between Arnall and Wallace grew closer, to the delight of the Talmadgites. Wallace hailed Arnall as an example of an emerging "intelligent constructive liberal leadership in the South" and "one of the pillars of the new liberalism" in the South. Wallace even stayed with the Arnalls in the executive mansion for several days in August, telling reporters that he liked Arnall "very much." Arnall, while visiting the White House in September 1944, returned the compliment by carrying a copy of Wallace's book *Democracy Reborn* with him to indicate to Roosevelt that Wallace was "still tops with the Governor of Georgia." The vice president had inscribed the book, "For my good friend, Ellis Arnall, who is doing so much to bring about the rebirth of democracy." In December 1944 Wallace wrote Arnall that "because of your unique position, you mean more to the liberal cause than you yourself realize."[13]

As Wallace prepared to leave the vice presidency in January 1945, Arnall expressed the hope that the vice president would be called to "broader fields of service." Arnall had already played a part in creating a "broader field" by discussing Wallace's future with President Roosevelt. The president proposed to offer Wallace any position in his next administration with the exception of that of secretary of state. Roosevelt asked Arnall to find out the vice president's preference, which turned out to be the position of secretary of commerce. Arnall returned to the White House and informed the president, who nominated Wallace to that position in January 1945. Arnall urged both of the state's senators to vote to confirm Wallace because he was "my warm personal friend." Conservatives opposed the nomination with Senator George of Georgia leading an effort to reduce the power of the future secretary of commerce by stripping the Commerce Department of its lending agencies. Arnall expressed his opposition to the effort "to take lending agencies away from Commerce and my friend Henry Wallace." Despite Arnall's views, the Georgia congressional delegation supported

George on the issue. The legislation passed with only fourteen dissenting votes in Congress. Shortly thereafter, the Senate confirmed Wallace as
secretary of commerce.[14]

Following the death of Roosevelt in April 1945, Secretary Wallace increasingly spoke out against President Truman's foreign policy, which he
considered too militaristic and too anti-Soviet. In September 1946 Truman
fired Wallace over foreign policy disagreements. Two years later Wallace
ran for president against Truman as a candidate of the Progressive party.
Arnall finally parted company with Wallace over foreign policy issues. Unlike Wallace, Arnall supported the president's foreign policy and deemed
Wallace's views on foreign policy demonstrated "a failure to see the menace of Russian imperialism." Arnall recalled, "My break from Wallace came
when he began to speak well of Russia, and I was of the opinion that this
was a terrible thing to do, and he was against the Truman Doctrine, which
I was strong for." Arnall also differed with Wallace on the issue of a third
party. Always the loyal Democrat, Arnall supported Truman, to whom he
pledged his "full loyalty and active support" in the 1948 campaign. He
called the third party venture of Wallace a mistake because "liberals can
fight more effectively within the major party that traditionally welcomes
them than they can outside."[15]

Arnall drifted away from Wallace for another reason. Wallace had become
an outspoken crusader against segregation—a position that a southern
politician could not publicly embrace at that time if he hoped to remain
in public life. In November 1947 Wallace spoke to integrated audiences
in Macon and Atlanta urging blacks to register to vote and calling for
the demise of segregation. Arnall had publicly opposed Wallace's trip to
Georgia. On this occasion Wallace did not stay with the Arnalls nor did
Arnall attend either of his speeches. Nevertheless, Wallace told reporters,
"Ellis and I have been friends and we'll be friends again—our principles
are the same—I imagine he needs all the friends he can get in Georgia at
this time."[16]

Arnall's political enemies gloated in reminding Georgians of the Arnall-
Wallace relationship and of Wallace's racial liberalism. Talmadge denounced
Arnall for joining up with the communists in supporting "the man from
Iowa who believes in social and political equality with the negroes" and
reminded Georgians that Arnall had supported "that negro lover and sponsor of social equality" for vice president. Talmadge accused Arnall of selling
out the South at the 1944 convention to the "Radical South-haters," who

wanted racial equality, racial intermarriage, and "mixed" schools. Harris
joined in the attack by accusing Arnall of siding with the liberals at the 1944
convention over "the decent white people of Georgia and of the South." In
return, Harris charged that Arnall hoped to obtain the 1948 vice presidential nomination "or else break into the big-time politics in Washington as
an officer in the Cabinet." Herman Talmadge labeled Arnall "a lap dog for
the left-wing element of the national party" and reminded Georgians that
if Arnall had succeeded in renominating Wallace, "the foremost exponent
of Moscow would now be President of these United States." While Arnall
never believed that his relationship with Wallace significantly undermined
his popularity in Georgia, the Talmadge faction correctly believed that it
had and used it as an issue against him.[17]

While Arnall's first major political defeat occurred outside the state, the
second took place in more familiar surroundings—the state legislature. The
revised constitution submitted to the 1945 legislative session included a
provision to allow a governor to succeed himself. The legislature, at Arnall's
request, had postponed consideration of the issue until the 1946 session.
While favoring the removal of the prohibition on the grounds that it was
undemocratic, Arnall had never publicly stated whether he would seek
reelection if given the opportunity. In April 1945 Melvin E. Thompson,
Arnall's executive secretary, publicly stated that the governor would seek
reelection if allowed to do so. "I am as certain of that," Thompson declared,
"as I am that the Allies will win the war." Conceding that Arnall had not
authorized him to make such a statement, Thompson explained, "I think I
am close enough to him to know how he feels on the subject."[18]

Representative Fortson, who had recommended the removal of the limitation to the constitutional commission in 1944, sought to speed up the
legislature's consideration of the issue. On May 15, 1945, he called for the
legislators to convene themselves into a special session to propose a constitutional amendment allowing succession. The state's constitution required
the governor, on the petition of three-fifths of the membership of both
houses, to call a special session. Speaker Harris, who was receiving mention as a possible gubernatorial candidate in 1946, and Senate President
Gross objected to a special session because it might jeopardize the adoption
of the proposed constitution. Arnall himself publicly viewed a special session as "ill-advised." He added, "I do not ask that the rules be changed for
my benefit." Undaunted, Fortson and twenty-four other legislators mailed
convening petitions to their fellow lawmakers. Arnall announced that he

would have nothing to do with the effort. Yet when the campaign seemed to bog down, he directed Thompson to make a few "well-placed" telephone calls to assist the endeavor.[19]

Fortson's effort also received support from the Georgia press. One reporter estimated that 90 percent of the state's newspapers supported the extra session. The Vienna *News* exemplified the views of the pro-session press. After commending Arnall for his progressive accomplishments, it concluded, "We cannot permit him to retire on his laurels yet." The Columbus *Enquirer* expressed another reason for supporting Arnall's reelection. It declared, "if the way is not cleared for the reelection of Ellis Arnall, it is not certain that the red-gallused politician [Talmadge] will not wrangle his way back into the governorship."[20]

Many political observers viewed Talmadge as a possible contender in 1946. As early as February 1945 the former governor expressed his opposition to removing the ban on succession. He accused the Atlanta papers of being the main supporters of the drive for a special session. "Arnall is their tool," Talmadge charged. "They are afraid they will not get another tool in the governor's chair." The possibility of former Governor Rivers entering the 1946 campaign also seemed likely. Rivers had considered running in 1942 but backed Arnall instead out of fear of splitting the anti-Talmadge forces. Reports circulated at least as early as September 1944 of his possible candidacy in 1946. In May 1945 the political editor of the Atlanta *Journal* claimed that Rivers was already actively campaigning.[21]

After receiving the necessary number of petitions from legislators, Arnall called a special session of the General Assembly to convene on May 29, 1945. Speaker Harris promptly announced his opposition, calling it "ridiculous to hold a session of the legislature for the sole purpose of trying to keep Eugene Talmadge from being elected governor of Georgia." In his address to the General Assembly on May 29, Arnall emphasized that he had called the special session at the request of the legislators. He told of his efforts to stay clear of Fortson's campaign to convene a special session. Nevertheless, Arnall attacked the limitation on gubernatorial succession as undemocratic and urged the legislature to "allow the people to decide whether they wanted to retain the limitation." His supporters quickly introduced succession amendments, and on the same day a Senate committee recommended passage.[22]

Harris, appearing before the House committee considering the amendment, expressed opposition. The speaker claimed that until recently Arnall had no intention of seeking reelection. Harris accused James Cox, the owner of the Atlanta *Journal*, of persuading Arnall to seek reelection. Harris denied his opposition stemmed from collusion with Talmadge because "I am not in the good graces of Eugene Talmadge." Harris also denied that he was "double crossing" Arnall on the gubernatorial succession issue, even though Arnall had promised that the constitution would be a "non-political document." Harris accused Arnall supporters, with the governor's knowledge, of injecting the issue of Arnall's succeeding himself into the ratification campaign. Indicating he had been given a "raw deal" by the governor, Harris told the House committee that "I have been out beating the bushes for the new constitution. I have wound up every speech with the assurance that no politics or issues were involved. If you pass this amendment, you'll have given the lie to every speech I've made." Despite Harris's plea, the House committee recommended passage of the amendment.[23]

On the following day, May 30, 1945, Arnall issued a statement attacking opponents of the amendment, whom he called an "unholy alliance of gubernatorial candidates, the railroads, Georgia Power Company, and other public utilities." Arnall reminded the legislature that the leading opponent to the amendment was Speaker Harris, who held his position "because of his friendship with me." Harris angrily denied membership in the "unholy alliance" and declared that Arnall had "blown his top." Harris observed that Arnall was "perfectly satisfied with my services and my statesmanship until this special session." The speaker provoked a speedy retort from the governor, who accused Harris of "singing the song of a defeated candidate for governor."[24]

The Senate, on May 31, 1945, passed the amendment by three votes more than the required two-thirds majority. Attention turned to the House, where Harris on the House floor accused Arnall of trading a Supreme Court justiceship for Senate votes. Arnall labeled the charge "an unadulterated falsehood." Harris responded, "I was a knight in shining armor until I disagreed with the governor." After spirited debate, the House voted on the amendment, which failed by ten votes to receive the required two-thirds majority. "My friends have always known," Arnall stated after the vote, "that I have not desired a successive term." Talmadge, applauding the defeat of the amendment, deemed it the best legislative action taken since the adoption of the Constitution of 1877.[25]

Few believed the issue settled. Fortson served notice that there would be a renewal of the fight at the 1946 legislative session. Arnall assured Georgians that "the fight for liberalism and the people's rights will not die." Several newspapers agreed and urged passage of the amendment in the January session. In July 1945 Arnall stated he might seek reelection if the legislature passed the amendment. If he were not in the race, the governor declared that his support would be for a candidate "who can most easily beat the crowd I beat and who will more nearly carry on the principles of the present administration."[26]

In July 1945 Harris revealed his major reason for opposing the succession amendment by announcing his intent to enter the 1946 governor's race. Harris, who had never run for governor before, was a powerful candidate. The accomplishments of his political career included over two decades of service in the state legislature. During this tenure, he had served as speaker of the House of Representatives under two governors—Rivers and Arnall. Most observers recognized his ability as a political organizer and his political astuteness contributed greatly to Arnall's success in 1942. Harris considered himself to be the logical "progressive" successor to Arnall. In November 1945 Harris unveiled a legislative agenda for the 1946 session consisting of a multimillion dollar expansion of state services. The Atlanta *Constitution* deemed it a bid for Arnall's progressive following.[27]

However, Ed Rivers considered himself the only candidate who could provide Georgia with another four years of progressive leadership. Rivers and Arnall had been political allies since Arnall had entered the legislature in 1933. After becoming governor, Rivers had appointed Arnall state attorney general, and Arnall, when he assumed the governorship, had designated Rivers one of the members of the National Democratic Committee from Georgia. Like Harris, Rivers supported the proposed constitution. Urging its adoption in a speech at Carrollton, Rivers lauded the governor for keeping the banner of liberalism high in Georgia. He spoke of his pleasure in appointing Arnall attorney general during his former administration and in aiding Arnall's campaign in 1942. Arnall likewise complimented Rivers as "a great builder and a man of progressive thought and action."[28]

Rivers possessed one advantage over Harris in soliciting Arnall's support: he had not opposed the special session. According to Rivers, Arnall had asked the former governor to support the amendment in the special session, and Rivers had. In return, Rivers claimed, Arnall promised his support in 1946 if the special session failed to pass the amendment. From Arnall's viewpoint, however, Rivers possessed several disadvantages. The former governor had left office amid corruption charges, had been accused of operating a pardon racket, had been a member of the Ku Klux Klan, and had engaged in Talmadge-like antics while governor. Supporting such a candidate entailed damaging Arnall's progressive image. Moreover, Rivers also had the strong opposition of former governor Cox, whom Arnall considered his political godfather.[29]

The 1946 session of the General Assembly convened in January. "If the General Assembly submits legislation to remove this restriction," Arnall told the legislators, "I will be a candidate." The Senate quickly approved the amendment by a one vote margin over the required two-thirds majority. Speaker Harris, after referring the proposal to a House committee chaired by Representative J. W. Culpepper, an opponent of the amendment, predicted defeat for the amendment if it reached the House floor. Supporters of the amendment feared Culpepper intended to kill it by refusing to call his committee into session. While denying such an intent, Culpepper's committee had not met by the midpoint of the fifteen-day session. Arnall urged the House "to measure up to its responsibility and vote on the amendment one way or the other." A front-page editorial in the Atlanta *Journal* called for the House to "take matters in its own hands if one member, or a small group, attempt to defy the will of the majority." After representatives Fortson and Walter W. Harrison sought to remove the amendment from Culpepper's committee, Harris promised committee action. The House committee finally recommended passage of the amendment.[30]

As the fight progressed, both sides accused the other of improper political pressure. Harris accused Arnall of recklessly trading roads for votes, while Talmadge charged Arnall with promising almost anything in return for support in "this attempt to destroy democracy in Georgia." The governor, in turn, accused his opposition of threatening a county's right to select a senator unless its representative voted against the amendment. At that time senatorial districts consisted of several counties with each having the opportunity to choose the district's senator on a rotation basis. M. L. St. John, a reporter for the Atlanta *Constitution,* called the vote-seeking "the greatest scramble for votes in the history of the Georgia Legislature."[31]

House debate on the amendment occurred on January 25, 1946. Representative Harrison declared gubernatorial hopefuls acted like this was a governor's campaign because they knew that "when the ban is lifted, the people will overwhelmingly re-elect Governor Arnall." During the debate, Harris contended that the original purpose of the amendment had been to keep Talmadge out of the governor's chair. Claiming a recent split had occurred between Rivers and Arnall, Harris declared its purpose now was to keep Rivers out as well. Following the debate, the House voted on the amendment, which again failed to receive a two-thirds majority, this time by eleven votes. Arnall declared that the opposition was based on the knowledge that the people would adopt the constitutional amendment and would reelect him governor. The Atlanta *Journal* credited a Talmadge-Harris-Rivers alliance with the defeat of the amendment. "That we dare say," the *Journal* concluded, "was one of the strangest coalitions in the annals of Georgia politics—three who are notoriously at odds with one another combining to obstruct the popular will." The defeat of the amendment, the editor of the Atlanta *Journal* noted, "caused great exuberance among the Talmadge followers in the state. And one must admit there is justification for their joy." Many observers now considered Talmadge a certain candidate in the upcoming primary.[32]

While Talmadge prepared for the primary, Harris still sought to establish himself as Arnall's progressive successor. He predicted on the day after the amendment's defeat that "the old forces that brought Georgia into disrepute will not be returned to power." The speaker avowed that there would be a candidate pledged to honest and progressive government. As political hopefuls throughout the state began to give consideration to entering the governor's race, the Fifth Circuit Court of Appeals, on March 6, 1946, announced its decision upholding the federal district court's invalidation of the white primary. However, the appellate court's decision seemed to provide a way in which the white primary could be saved. Its salvation required the repealing of all state primary laws and converting the Georgia Democratic party into a private organization with no state regulation. Harris and Talmadge called for a special legislative session to repeal the state's primary laws.[33]

Harris vowed to stump the state for himself or a candidate in favor of a white primary. For Harris the maintenance of white supremacy took precedence over all other issues. The white primary had to be saved. Eugene Talmadge agreed and promised that Georgia would have a white primary as he announced his candidacy for governor. Rivers and Harris had alienated themselves from the governor, and neither would receive his support in the upcoming election. The anti-Talmadge faction, so strong in 1942, stood in shambles in 1946. On the other hand, Talmadge, with the invalidation of the white primary, had been handed a potent political issue.[34]

Harris's candidacy, however, loomed as a serious threat to Talmadge's hoped-for position as champion of the white primary. Even without Arnall's backing, Harris seemed intent upon running and denied reports early in April that he would manage Talmadge's campaign. However, Harris's potential candidacy received a crushing blow on April 16. Seeking reelection to the legislature in the Richmond County primary, Harris was defeated by a candidate of a local reform movement. Arnall's relationship with Harris had so deteriorated that the governor personally went to Richmond County and campaigned against him. With his hopes for the governorship ended, Harris endorsed the candidacy of Talmadge—something he had not done since the 1934 governor's race. Harris attacked Arnall for selling the white people of Georgia "down the river" on the white primary question. "If you want the white primary back," he told a Thomaston audience, "every loyal Georgian will vote for Gene Talmadge."[35]

About that same time James V. Carmichael, who had earlier withdrawn his name from consideration, entered the governor's race as the progressive successor to Arnall. On the white primary question, Carmichael stated, "The decision has been made. I have no power to reverse that decision—nor does any other person in Georgia." Furthermore, he announced his opposition to any scheme repealing the state's primary laws. Former governor Rivers formally announced his candidacy on April 20 and stated, "The Negroes will vote. It is now the law."[36]

As it had in his previous campaign, the press overwhelmingly opposed the Talmadge candidacy. The Atlanta *Daily World* noted that Talmadge had received over 128,000 votes in the 1942 election even with the education issue against him. "Now, on a strictly race issue," the *Daily World* cautioned, "he may even be stronger." The Gainesville *News* predicted that Talmadge would "dwell on the 'nigger' issue." Denouncing Talmadge as a reactionary, the Augusta *Chronicle* declared that his rule had brought shame to Georgia. The Athens *Banner-Herald* assailed Talmadge as the "greatest menace facing Georgia today!" Warning that the state could not stand another Talmadge administration, the Milledgeville *Union-Recorder* added its voice to the opposition. "Georgia has made a lot of progress since Talmadge left office," the Thomaston *Free-Press* declared, "but if he sits in the governor's chair . . . we lose all the ground we made and then some!"[37]

Diametrically opposed to Talmadge in political philosophy stood Rivers, who was one of the state's most liberal governors with Herman Talmadge considering him an "ultra-liberal." Rivers had made two records while serving as governor, one of which consisted of a record of progressive accomplishment. On the other, Rivers had been criticized for his pardoning record, the scandals in the highway department, his removal of the chairman of the highway department, his activities leading to court indictments, and the large debt left in the aftermath of his administration. Many Georgians viewed Rivers, the Macon *Telegraph* noted, as the Warren G. Harding of Georgia politics.[38]

At the beginning of the campaign Carmichael was the least known of the three candidates. When he announced his candidacy, Carmichael was general manager of the Georgia Division of the Bell Aircraft Corporation. He had served in the legislature during the Rivers administration and had supported many of Rivers's legislative measures. However, he had opposed Rivers's proposals to finance the "Little New Deal." In the 1942 governor's race, Carmichael had supported Arnall. More recently, he had served as a member of the Constitutional Revision Commission of 1943–1944. Carmichael's platform promised good government and a debt-free, honest, economical, and progressive administration. He pledged, within state income, to expand the state's welfare and health programs and assured Georgians of no increased taxation without a referendum. In contrast to his opponents, Carmichael received overwhelming support from the press. Not since Reconstruction, proclaimed the Atlanta *Journal,* had there been such unanimity among the press. One editorial contributed this unanimity to the fact that the average editor viewed the race as one between the Arnall type of government and a "retrogression to the dictatorial, corrupt, idiotic type he witnessed under Talmadge and Rivers."[39]

Besides receiving the support of the press, Carmichael, as expected, received the support of Arnall. The governor first endorsed Carmichael's candidacy in letters to several citizens throughout the state. On June 22 Arnall made a statewide radio broadcast on behalf of Carmichael. He dismissed Rivers and Talmadge as "quacks whose bottles contain the poison of hate, disunity, strife, corruption, and extravagance." In another statewide radio address, Arnall urged Georgians to support Carmichael, who was "making the fight for decency and good government in our state." Arnall believed that the voters would not support candidates "who have caused our state to be the target for ridicule and harsh criticism throughout the nation."[40]

In addition to radio speeches, letters, and telephone calls, Arnall also resorted to the traditional practice of governors awarding highway contracts to aid a favorite candidate. Prior to the primary, the State Highway Commission passed a resolution giving the governor, as director of the budget, the power to allot funds for highway construction. Rivers charged this maneuver permitted Arnall to engage in "wholesale road-vote swapping for Carmichael." During the campaign, Rivers produced an affidavit signed by a Calhoun County commissioner, who along with another commissioner, had gone to the governor seeking to have a road built. According to the affidavit, Arnall "stated that if we could and would guarantee that we would carry Calhoun County for Carmichael, we would get the contract." The affidavit further stated that Arnall supporters in McIntosh County had requested a road and "that he was going to let the contract in exchange for McIntosh County voting for Carmichael for Governor." Arnall never denied the allegations.[41]

While Carmichael made the fight for good government, Talmadge, as expected, made the fight to keep Georgia a "white man's state." Talmadge bitterly assailed Arnall as the leader of those who were trying to destroy the southern way of life. "Ellis 'Benedict' Arnall," Talmadge stated, "opened the breach in the dike that has protected Southern manhood, Southern womanhood, and Southern childhood for three quarters of a century." He accused Arnall of going "further than any white man in America to promote it [racial equality] in Georgia." Talmadge predicted that Arnall's betrayal of the white people of Georgia would cause him to be the most despised governor since Rufus Bullock, the Republican governor who served during Reconstruction. Talmadge bitterly attacked Arnall's position that Georgians had to abide by the decision of the federal courts on the white primary and accused Arnall of robbing the white people of their primary.[42]

Rivers had entered the race, some believed, as the strongest candidate. Nevertheless, the Eastman *Times-Journal* declared that the Rivers campaign had "crumbled" in the opinion of most newspapers. The collapse of Rivers's campaign probably stemmed from two factors. Voters were constantly reminded by the press and his opponents of the misfortunes of his former administration. Moreover, most anti-Talmadge voters probably viewed Carmichael as the strongest candidate to prevent Talmadge from returning to the governorship. Whatever the reason for Rivers's loss of momentum, he nevertheless refused to withdraw, leading the press to conclude that he was staying in the race to divide the anti-Talmadge vote.[43]

Although his candidacy was splitting the anti-Talmadge vote, Rivers continued to campaign. Instead of limiting his attacks to Carmichael and Talmadge, Rivers began attacking Arnall, whom he called "the greatest political double-crosser and the rankest ingrate Georgia has ever seen in her public life." Rivers claimed that as late as December 1945 Arnall had promised to support his bid for election in 1946. Rivers charged that under pressure from Cox, Arnall had switched his support to Carmichael. He denounced his former political ally as "the Benedict Arnold of Georgia politics" and confessed that the biggest mistake of his administration was in appointing Arnall attorney general. He called Arnall "the worst product of Riversism." Rivers charged that instead of working for the best interests of the people, Arnall was more "concerned with running over the United States making speeches in a race for the vice-presidency or in building himself up for a federal job."[44]

While several factors accounted for Rivers's obstinate course, revenge seemed the major reason. Rivers knew that by remaining a candidate and dividing the anti-Talmadge vote, he reduced the Arnall-backed candidate's chance of winning. Arnall's support of Carmichael further damaged the strained relationship between the two former political allies. As vice chairman of the House Economy Committee in 1939, Carmichael had played a major role in the committee's investigation that lead to the indictment of several members of the Rivers administration. In addition, the committee's uncovering of waste and extravagance damaged Rivers's efforts to obtain additional revenue sources to finance the "Little New Deal." In response to Rivers's attacks on him, Arnall apologized to the voters for ever having supported Rivers for public office and called him unworthy of political office. While not denying that he had promised his support to Rivers in the 1946 race, Arnall declared that Rivers forfeited his friendship when he joined ranks with Harris and Talmadge to defeat the succession amendment and to defeat Carmichael's election. Arnall's version of his understanding with Rivers pertaining to the 1946 election differed with that of Rivers. According to Arnall, "I never committed myself to him" because "I would have been foolish to have gotten behind a dead pigeon or committed myself to a dead pigeon. . . . Had I thought he could have been elected governor, I would have supported him."[45]

After the long, bitter campaign, Carmichael received 313,389 votes to Talmadge's 297,245 and Rivers's 69,489. Despite Carmichael's majority of over sixteen thousand popular votes, Talmadge won the nomination, thanks to the county unit system. Arnall declared, "Carmichael got the most votes and Talmadge was nominated." Talmadge, however, claimed that he had gotten a majority of the votes of white Georgians. With 105 counties in his column, Talmadge received 242 unit votes while Carmichael received 146 and Rivers only 22. Observers credited two significant factors—the race issue and the presence of Rivers in the campaign—with the county unit election of Talmadge. McGill attributed 98 percent of Talmadge's victory to the race issue. The Augusta *Chronicle* declared Talmadge had conjured up a fear in the minds of Georgians that blacks would run rampant in the state if he were not reelected. The Rome *News-Tribune* editorialized that Talmadge's victory "was based entirely on one issue—that of white supremacy." In the 1942 election Arnall skillfully used the accreditation issue to diffuse Talmadge's white supremacy campaign. Unfortunately for Carmichael, the federal courts, by striking down the white primary prior to the 1946 race, handed Talmadge an issue that he used to revive his sagging political fortunes. Carmichael's acceptance of the court's decision placed him and Arnall on the defensive on the race question in a state clinging to the racial status quo. Carmichael's good government campaign and Arnall's endorsement could not overcome Talmadge's racist appeal, especially in the rural counties.[46]

Several observers attributed Talmadge's victory primarily to Rivers's candidacy. The Atlanta *Journal* believed that 90 percent of the Rivers support would have backed Carmichael in a two-man race with Talmadge. Assuming the validity of this assumption, the Rivers candidacy played a crucial role in Talmadge's election. In nineteen counties the combined Carmichael-Rivers vote exceeded Talmadge's. Nevertheless, Talmadge carried the counties on a plurality basis and received their forty-two unit votes. If Carmichael had been able to obtain those forty-two unit votes plus the twenty-two from counties that Rivers carried, he would have received 210 unit votes and the nomination. In addition to Rivers's presence, Talmadge's victory may be attributed to such factors as the widespread effort to purge blacks from the voter registration rolls and voting irregularities.[47]

As a result of the outcome of the election, the New York *Times* offered its sympathy for "Georgia's misfortune," and the liberal publication *The Nation* expressed its condolences to Georgia. Congressman Eugene Cox, in his keynote address at the Democratic State Convention in October 1946, claimed Arnall was the real loser in the primary. According to Cox, the primary was really "between Gene Talmadge and Ellis Arnall, and like 'Humpty Dumpty,' Ellis had a big fall, and . . . all of the radical jackasses and all of Wallace's men can never put Ellis together again." The Talmadge faithful clapped and cheered.[48]

In the first half of his term, Ellis Arnall seemed to possess the political

Midas touch. He had to his credit a long list of accomplishments and had gained the national reputation of being a progressive reformer. In the process, Arnall found himself in the unusual position for a chief executive of Georgia of being popular both at home and in the national press. He had made great progress in his goal of changing the state's national image from that of a backward state to one of a leader in progressive reform.

Unfortunately, halfway through his administration his political influence underwent a sharp decline. His close association with Wallace, whose liberalism was unpopular in Georgia, damaged him politically, especially among the conservative rural voters of the state. While his support of Wallace enhanced his standing with the liberal wing of the national party, it weakened his political base at home. Arnall's firm support of Wallace at the 1944 convention, which was out of loyalty to President Roosevelt, evolved into a close personal friendship. However, Arnall, the usually shrewd and pragmatic politician, underestimated the negative impact such an association would have on his popularity. Arnall finally ended his political relationship with Wallace, but this break took place after Arnall had left office when the political damage had already been done. In the public mind, Arnall and Wallace had been linked politically and the Talmadgites never let the voters forget it.

Arnall's political influence also suffered because of the legislature's failure to permit gubernatorial succession. He insisted that his fight for succession was based on principle—the people had the right to elect whomever they wanted as governor. The major reason, however, was Arnall's desire for a second term. He enjoyed politics and being governor. While he had been able to accomplish a great deal, Arnall knew that much needed to be done in education, in public health, and in other governmental services. Arnall also wanted to deny his aging political foe, Talmadge, the honor of a fourth term as governor. Arnall failed in his efforts to be allowed to succeed himself, and his foes taunted him for his loss of political clout. Denied the opportunity to run in 1946, Arnall supported a capable but a lackluster Jimmy Carmichael in the primary against a revived Gene Talmadge. Arnall's efforts again resulted in failure, in part due to Rivers's insistence on remaining in the race to divide the anti-Talmadge vote. Rivers's course of action may be attributed to one reason—revenge—because of his accusation that Arnall had reneged on a commitment to support him in the 1946 campaign. It seemed that Arnall had lost his political Midas touch.

As Talmadge prepared to assume the office denied him in 1942, Arnall began to contemplate life outside politics. It seemed that his political battles would soon be over. Before leaving office, however, Arnall unexpectedly found himself embroiled in the most bizarre political controversy in the state's history. Once again, Arnall found himself in a heated political struggle with a Talmadge.

11

The

Three-

Governor

Controversy

Arnall came into the governor's office with a promise of inaugurating a new day in Georgia politics. As his term drew to a close, Arnall's new politics stood on the verge of collapse with the impending restoration of Talmadgeism. His aging political adversary had won the Democratic gubernatorial nomination, and the U.S. Supreme Court refused to overturn a legal challenge to Talmadge's election. However, Eugene Talmadge faced a more serious challenge to his return to the governor's office when he was hospitalized because of a ruptured blood vessel in his stomach. In the general election in November 1946 the ailing Talmadge was officially elected to his fourth gubernatorial term. Several individuals received scattered write-in votes for governor in the election with the majority of these votes going to three persons: Herman Talmadge, 675; James V. Carmichael, 669; and D. Talmadge Bowers, 637.[1]

Voters had also elected Melvin E. Thompson to the lieutenant governorship, an office that had recently been created by the Constitution of 1945. Thompson had not publicly identified himself with any of the gubernatorial candidates during the primary, but he had promised to cooperate with whomever the people elected governor. Thompson had apparently avoided taking a position on the all-important white primary question. However, his major opponent in the race, S. Marvin Griffin, accused Thompson of favoring blacks voting in the state's primaries, and the Atlanta *Daily World* claimed that Thompson had received most of the black vote.[2]

Although Thompson had served as a member of Governor Arnall's official family, first as executive secretary and later as revenue commissioner, Arnall had endorsed Senate President

Gross for the lieutenant governorship. Thompson had first requested Arnall's support in a race for state superintendent of schools. After Arnall agreed to support Thompson for this office, Gross obtained the support of the governor for his campaign for the lieutenant governorship. In the meantime, Thompson changed his mind and decided to run for the state's second highest office. By then Arnall was committed to Gross, who had been instrumental in getting Arnall's legislative program through the Senate. Thus, despite his close political association with Arnall, Thompson ran without the governor's support. Thompson, according to Arnall, worked behind the scenes on behalf of Rivers.[3]

Following his election, Thompson prepared to assume his new responsibilities in January 1947. Talmadge, however, suffered a relapse on November 29 and was hospitalized again. His condition steadily declined, and on the night of December 20 Talmadge went into a coma. On the following day the sixty-two-year-old governor-elect died due to acute hepatitis and hemorrhaging of the stomach and intestinal tract. While in the hospital, Talmadge joked that his illness had divided Georgians with "half of them praying I'll recover and half of them that I won't." In commenting on the death of Talmadge, the Cairo *Messenger* declared Georgia had probably lost one of her "most outstanding politicians since the death of the late Tom Watson." The liberal publication *The Nation,* however, expressed relief that death had prevented Talmadge from becoming governor again. *Time* concluded that only Huey Long and Theodore Bilbo had been more successful than Talmadge in appealing to ignorance and bigotry, though the Savannah *Morning News* pointed out that Talmadge was "looked upon as a real 'champion of the people' by his admirers."[4]

Whatever Eugene Talmadge's place in Georgia history, his death denied him the honor of serving a fourth term as the state's chief executive. But more important, the death of Talmadge raised one of the most crucial questions in Georgia's political history. Who would assume the executive power of the state in January 1947? The Constitution of 1945 failed to specify what action was to be taken when a governor-elect died. Carmichael, a member of the Constitutional Revision Commission, contended that the question had not even been discussed by that body. He insisted that the commission had not planned for the lieutenant governor-elect to automatically be given the post unless the governor's death occurred after the inauguration.[5]

Article V, section 1, of the Constitution of 1945 furnished three possible interpretations as to who Arnall's successor should be. Paragraph 1 provided that the incumbent governor should hold office for four years "and until his successor shall be chosen and qualified." Paragraph 7 stipulated that the lieutenant governor would exercise the executive power in case of the death, resignation, or disability of the governor. Paragraph 4 provided that the person receiving the majority vote in the general election shall be governor and further stipulated that the legislature would choose a governor from the two living candidates having the highest number of votes if a candidate failed to receive a majority of the votes in the general election.

Shortly after Talmadge's funeral, Thompson declared that the people had elected him lieutenant governor for the purpose of succeeding to the governorship in the event of death, disability, or resignation of the governor. As a result of Talmadge's death, Thompson insisted that the people wanted him to assume the executive power of the state. He warned against anyone resorting "to trickery or legal technicalities in order to thwart the expressed will of the people." Arnall, while arguing that he could legally continue in office for another four years, insisted he would not serve another term because of the death of Talmadge. He concurred with Thompson's claim to the governorship and claimed it to be his constitutional duty to remain in office until Thompson had been sworn in as lieutenant governor and could assume the executive power.[6]

Several prominent Talmadge leaders disagreed with the Arnall-Thompson interpretation. They contended that Eugene Talmadge had been elected because of his platform to restore the white primary, retain the county unit system, and expand state services. The Talmadge leaders accused Arnall of trying to dictate his successor in the present situation as he had in the recent primary in order to destroy the white primary. Fortunately, they declared the constitution provided a way for the election of a governor who would carry out Eugene Talmadge's platform. As a result of the death of the governor-elect, the Talmadge leaders claimed, the General Assembly had the duty to elect the next governor from the two candidates receiving the highest number of write-in votes in the general election. The statement asserted that Herman Talmadge, who was in this category, could best implement his father's program because he had written his father's platform and managed his father's campaign. The Talmadge leaders called on all Georgians to join them "in a campaign to obtain the legislative election of Herman Talmadge as governor."[7]

Herman Talmadge issued his first statement on the question on December 27, stating that it was his duty to carry on his father's fight. Talmadge contended that it was mandatory for the General Assembly to elect a governor and attacked Thompson's claim to the governorship. Talmadge charged that the forces that had opposed his father in the primary were using Thompson to destroy the county unit system and the white primary. He accused Rivers, who supported Thompson's claim, Arnall, and the Atlanta *Journal* of joining together "to foist M. E. Thompson on the people of Georgia and destroy forever in this state the white primary." In a telegram sent to members of the legislature, Talmadge charged that Arnall had destroyed the white primary and wanted to abolish the county unit system. Talmadge warned:

> If Ellis Arnall is allowed to dictate his successor he will control the next administration of this state. He will block every vote to restore the Democratic white primary in Georgia. This state will be turned over lock, stock and barrel to the reds and pinks of the East and the Negroes in Georgia. This is a white man's state. It always has been a white man's state and this fight I am making is a white man's fight to keep Georgia a white man's state.[8]

While Thompson and Talmadge argued over who could best carry out Eugene Talmadge's platform, Arnall requested an opinion from the state attorney general as to who should hold the office. Attorney General Cook, who had been appointed to that position to fill a vacancy by Arnall, responded with a ruling early in January upholding Arnall's right and duty to remain in office until his successor qualified. Cook held that Thompson would assume the executive power of the state on his qualification and Arnall's resignation. As for the Talmadge argument, Cook contended that the only duty of the legislature consisted of counting and publishing the results of the general election and declaring who had received a majority of the votes cast. After declaring that Eugene Talmadge had received such a majority, Cook held that state lawmakers could not disregard the outcome of the election simply because the person receiving those votes had died. Talmadge immediately denounced Cook's ruling as a political decision that was not binding on the General Assembly because it was a sovereign body.[9]

On January 11, 1947, Arnall removed himself as a participant in the crisis by announcing his resignation, effective as soon as the lieutenant governor-elect took his oath of office. Talmadge called the resignation "just another effort by Governor Arnall to dictate his successor as governor, in order that he might control him." Nevertheless, Talmadge predicted that Arnall would comply with the constitution when the legislature elected him governor.[10]

While the press tended to favor Thompson's position over that of Talmadge, the latter received some press support. Some of the national press deemed the election more important than just the question of who should occupy the governorship. *The Nation* viewed the fight as determining whether Georgia would "continue to follow the path of industrial and social emancipation that he [Arnall] has laid out for it or slump back into four more years of corrupt cracker government." The New York *Times* viewed the controversy as a struggle between the New South and the Old South with Georgia having to decide "whether to advance along the road to progress or remain sunk in the political morass which breeds Talmadges and Talmadgism, Bilbos and Bilboism."[11]

Since Talmadge based his claim to the governorship on write-in votes received in the general election, speculation naturally arose concerning those votes. Both Harris and Talmadge credited Gibson Greer Ezell, a Talmadge supporter, with the idea of a write-in campaign for Herman Talmadge. According to Talmadge, Ezell had been bothered by the question of what would happen if Eugene Talmadge died before his inauguration. Ezell found that the constitution did not specifically deal with that issue. However, it provided that the General Assembly could elect a governor from the two persons having the highest number of votes if a person failed to receive a majority of the vote in the general election. Therefore, Ezell proposed a write-in campaign for Herman Talmadge in the general election. After hearing Ezell's suggestion, Talmadge raised the question with some of his friends whom he deemed among the best lawyers in the state. They agreed with Ezell that the legislature could choose the next governor from the general election's two highest write-in candidates in the event of the death of the governor-elect. Talmadge explained that "I passed the word to a few reliable friends to arrange some write-in votes for me. You might call it an insurance policy. If I couldn't keep Papa from dying, at least I could keep him from dying in vain."[12]

Although Talmadge and Thompson claimed to be the main contenders for the governorship, other individuals also laid claim to the office. Talmadge Bowers claimed the legislature should elect him governor. Carmichael, one of the three highest recipients of write-in votes in the general election, removed himself from consideration of a legislative election. "I will not seek the office," he stated shortly after Talmadge's death, "and I would not accept it even if I were elected." Carmichael made it clear that he had no intentions of taking any more time from his family or business for another political struggle. With the elimination of Carmichael, the General Assembly, according to the much-publicized Talmadge succession interpretation, had to choose between Bowers or the son of Eugene Talmadge. However, in a little-publicized dinner speech before a group of 250 guests on the eve of the 1947 legislative session, Herman Talmadge, according to a press account of the speech, modified his position by claiming the legislature was not even restricted to write-in candidates but could elect anybody governor.[13]

The General Assembly of Georgia convened on January 13, 1947, and adopted a resolution providing a joint legislative session for the following day for the purpose of opening and publishing the election returns. Prior to the joint session on January 14, a resolution was introduced in the House inviting Talmadge and Thompson to appear and state whether or not they favored a special election to resolve the issue. The House overwhelmingly defeated this resolution. At the designated hour of 10:30 A.M., the senators filed into the House chambers. Turmoil and confusion were rampant, because of the presence of many unauthorized persons on the House floor. When a senator shouted a motion for an executive session, an angry storm of boos shook the hall. No one seconded the motion. The presiding officer, failing to gain order, adjourned the session until two o'clock in the afternoon.[14]

Responding to Talmadge's plea for his friends to come to Atlanta, hundreds of Talmadge supporters had converged upon the capitol. Arnall estimated the number ranged from two to three thousand. Talmadge estimated that there were several thousand in the building, "90 percent of them my friends—some of them armed, some of them drunk." *Newsweek* described the activity of the Talmadgites as "they milled around the Capitol and whooped it up in the galleries and overflowed onto the floor of the General Assembly." Both sides engaged in vigorous lobbying of the beleaguered lawmakers.[15]

As soon as the joint session reconvened, a special election resolution, which had been defeated earlier in the day in the House, was introduced. The presiding officer ruled the resolution out of order. Thereafter, Representative J. Robert Elliott, the Talmadge floor leader in the House, introduced a resolution providing for a committee to tabulate the returns of the general election. The resolution, asking for separate reports to be made for each of the nine state house offices, stipulated that the report on the governor's office be considered first and that no action be taken on other returns until final action had been taken on the election of a governor.[16]

Representatives Adie N. Durden and Charles L. Gowen, who were Thompson supporters, sought to amend Elliott's resolution. The Durden-Gowen amendment provided for the publication of all general election returns before any other business was transacted. If the Durden-Gowen amendment were adopted, Thompson's status changed from lieutenant governor-elect to lieutenant governor with an indisputable constitutional claim to the governorship. Elliott's resolution, on the other hand, sought to keep Thompson in the position of lieutenant governor-elect until after the governorship issue had been settled.[17]

The lawmakers voted on the Durden-Gowen amendment first and defeated it by a vote of 128 to 126, a narrow Talmadge victory. The legislators then passed unanimously Elliott's resolution. The presiding officer appointed a committee to tabulate the results of the governor's election. The tabulating, commencing around four o'clock in the afternoon, took about five hours. The results, to the amazement of Talmadge supporters, showed that Carmichael had received 669 write-in votes, Bowers 637, and Herman Talmadge only 617. With the report of the tabulating committee, Talmadge's hopes of assuming the executive power of the state appeared threatened. According to the much-publicized Talmadge position, the General Assembly had to elect a governor from the two recipients of the highest number of write-in votes in the general election.[18]

Thus, the lawmakers, with Herman Talmadge in third place, had to choose between Bowers or Carmichael, providing neither would turn down such an election. Bowers, as previously noted, had expressed his willingness to being elected governor by the legislature. Carmichael, in his statement on December 21, had expressed his opposition to assuming the governorship by such an election. However, Representative Pierre Howard, Sr., claimed that as soon as the tabulating committee made its report "rumors flew thick and fast that Jimmy Carmichael was on the way to the Capitol to state that he would accept the governorship." Howard, who had supported Carmichael in the primary, rushed to Arnall's office and questioned the governor about the rumor. Howard stated that Arnall confirmed the reports and declared, "We are reversing our position and we are going to elect him [Carmichael] and I will surrender the office of Governor to him." According to Howard, Arnall further stated, "They will have had to vote with us to elect him [Carmichael] governor and if they are stupid enough to elect Bowers, I think I will surrender the office to him." Talmadge also claimed that Arnall had changed his position on the issue of the legislative election following the report of the tabulating committee. Arnall, however, denied the allegation that he had changed his position on legislative election.[19]

As noted earlier, Talmadge had claimed that the legislature could elect anyone governor whether a recipient of write-in votes or not. Whether Talmadge would have attempted to carry out this claim could have proven highly interesting. He did not attempt this, however, because subsequent events moved Talmadge from third place in write-in votes to first. The Telfair County delegation immediately challenged as incorrect the write-in votes for Talmadge from Telfair County. Upon checking the returns, the committee found fifty-eight additional Telfair County write-in votes for Talmadge that had been incorrectly placed in a wrong envelope. This discovery gave Talmadge first place in write-in votes with 675. Now, according to the Talmadge interpretation, he was eligible to be elected governor by the legislature. Talmadge's position was made stronger when Carmichael, according to Ralph McGill, reiterated his opposition to being elected by the legislature.[20]

Resuming the efforts for a Talmadge election, Elliott introduced a resolution declaring that as a result of the death of Eugene Talmadge no person had received a majority of the votes cast for governor. Therefore, since there had been no election, the resolution concluded that the legislature had the duty of electing the next governor. Representative Durden offered a substitute resolution contending Eugene Talmadge had been elected governor and the legislature did not have authority to elect a governor. The lawmakers defeated Durden's resolution, 132 to 118, and adopted Elliott's resolution, 137 to 114. Elliott then nominated Herman Talmadge for a four-year term as governor. At 1:50 A.M., January 15, 1947, 161 legislators elected Talmadge governor. Eighty-seven members of the General Assembly voted against his election by voting "present."[21]

Immediately after the vote, Talmadge took the oath of office and gave an inaugural address that was carried nationally by the radio networks. Following his inaugural address, Talmadge, escorted by a committee of twenty-five legislators, proceeded to the governor's office, where Arnall had been awaiting the outcome of the session. Harris, Eugene Talmadge's widow, and a host of Talmadge supporters also accompanied the newly elected governor. On reaching the executive offices, they found the outer doors locked. Two Talmadge supporters quickly eliminated this obstacle by battering down the doors. The resulting scene was described by Arnall: "A pathway opened in the crowd, and the young son of the dead Governor-elect of Georgia was led through the office on the arm of his chief advisor [Harris]. I remember that his face was ghastly pale, except for a scarlet spot at each cheekbone, and that his companion [Harris] wore a smile of immeasurable elation."[22]

A brief exchange of words ensued. Talmadge, with Harris occasionally whispering in his ear, asked Arnall whether he was aware of the legislature's recent action. Replying that he was, Arnall told the delegation, "The governorship belongs to the people and cannot be decided by the legislature." Arnall further dubbed Talmadge a "pretender" and refused to yield the office of governor to him. Talmadge, declaring his purpose was not to create disorder, turned to walk out of the governor's office. Several of Talmadge's more zealous supporters who had accompanied the newly elected governor threatened to throw Arnall out of the office, but they were restrained by other Talmadgites. One irate Talmadgite, a former bodyguard of Eugene Talmadge, engaged in a brief scuffle with Arnall's chauffeur. Before leaving the capitol, Talmadge urged his supporters to avoid trouble and to go home. By 3 A.M., the Talmadgites had deserted the capitol. Arnall deemed the confrontation historic because "it marked the first attempt in American history to seize the government of a sovereign Commonwealth by force."[23]

After a few hours of sleep, both governors returned to the capitol. Talmadge conducted the state's business in an office formerly occupied by Arnall's executive secretary. Arnall continued to occupy the governor's private office. Talmadge appointed Marvin Griffin, who had been Arnall's adjutant general, to the same position in his administration. Other Talmadge appointments included a commissioner of public safety, a revenue commissioner, a highway director, a labor commissioner, and a parks commissioner. Officials who held those positions in the Arnall administration refused to recognize the new appointments. Arnall tried to conduct business as usual. Among other things, he swore in several justices of the peace, commissioned a new adjutant general, held several news conferences, and made a radio address. As the eventful day of January 15, 1947, ended, Georgians had witnessed the business of the state conducted by two individuals both claiming to be the rightful governor of the state.[24]

Talmadge, deciding one day of dual governorship was enough, ordered the locks changed on the executive offices after Arnall departed. The following day, January 16, Talmadge arrived at seven A.M. and went to work at the desk previously used by Arnall. A large crowd of spectators and newspaper reporters anxiously awaited Arnall's arrival. At 10:30 A.M., Arnall strode into the capitol and proceeded to the executive offices. On reaching the governor's private office, Arnall demanded admission, but was told by Talmadge's executive secretary to wait his turn "like any other private citizen." Arnall turned to the crowd and charged the "military forces of the Pretender" with having removed the executive office locks in "an expert pincer movement." He announced his intentions to remain governor until the lieutenant governor-elect assumed the executive powers. He told his listeners that the central question was "whether democracy will continue or give place to dictatorship, illegality, and force, whether the constitution must yield to threats, force and violence."[25]

Arnall announced he would set up his gubernatorial office at the information booth in the capitol rotunda. Admitting what he was doing was "unpleasant and distasteful," he nevertheless claimed it was his duty to preserve the office for the lieutenant governor. Arnall then invited newspaper reporters to join him at the executive mansion for lunch. The Arnalls had moved out of it prior to the legislative session. Arnall and the invited guests found a welcoming committee of four state highway patrolmen at the mansion who informed him of their orders to prevent his entry. The action of these "storm troopers," Arnall told the reporters, completed the capture of the physical properties of the state government by "military and armed forces."[26]

On January 17, when Arnall returned to the capitol, he found Representative James M. Dykes, a Talmadge follower, sitting at the information booth in the rotunda. Dykes asked if Arnall desired an appointment with Governor Talmadge. "Jimmy, I am the Governor!" Arnall retorted to the approval of a partisan crowd. Dykes retorted that Arnall had "no more right to be Governor than I have. It's my day to play Governor." The crowd booed. Leaving the capitol in order not to create further disturbance, Arnall announced he would move the governor's office, "in exile," to his Atlanta law office in the Candler Building.[27]

At noon the same day, Arnall spoke over a statewide radio network. Declaring he had no personal interest in the lieutenant governor-elect, Arnall admitted he had not even voted for him in the 1946 primary. Arnall even claimed to possess no animosity toward Herman Talmadge even though he was "a puppet in the hands of those who would steal the rights of the people." Arnall explained that his fight had "been and will continue to be for the people and the rights of the people, for democracy as opposed to dictatorship, for law and order as opposed to mob rule, storm troop tactics, thugism and hoodlumism." He urged the people to discuss with their legislators the indignity of being robbed of their rights by a military coup d'etat.[28]

Talmadge emphatically denied using force to secure his election and contended that his election was according to the mandate of the constitution. While claiming no disorder had occurred, he justified his physical taking over of the governor's office by the necessity of insuring that "the functions of our state government might proceed in a lawful and regular democratic manner." Arnall scoffed at Talmadge's claim of "no disorder" and contended that "everyone who knows right from wrong knows that force and violence brought about the seizure of the governorship by a military coup d'etat."[29]

Talmadge's election, which Ralph McGill called "a coup d'etat out of a fiction writer's plot," provoked a vociferous protest throughout Georgia. The Atlanta *Constitution* claimed that public opinion had never been so incensed in all Georgia's modern history. An editorial in the Augusta *Chronicle* called Talmadge's election "one of the most amazing and cynically executed political coup d'etats in the history of the state—indeed, in the history of the nation." The Fitzgerald *Herald* believed the legislature's action had established dictatorship in Georgia, and the editor of the Valdosta *Daily Times* warned that Georgians had just witnessed "the first step away from the democratic way of government." The Washington *Post* agreed, while the Atlanta *Daily World* thought Talmadge's election suggestive of the era of the Divine Right of Kings. The Cedartown *Standard* called on all Georgians to "rise up" against the rule of a clique who "will stop at nothing to perpetuate themselves in power." The Eastman *Times Journal* denounced the legislature's election of "The little king! The little pretender!"[30]

The Peachtree Road Methodist Church in Atlanta condemned "this revolution against law and order." Thirty-six ministers in the Atlanta area denounced the "seizure" of the governor's office and mansion as "dictatorship of the worst order." The Gainesville Ministerial Association joined in the condemnation of Talmadge's election. One irate citizen pleaded for

President Truman to send federal troops to save Georgia from "mob violence in this state." Clark Foreman, president of the Southern Conference for Human Welfare, compared Talmadge's election to Hitler's Munich beer hall putsch. The state commander of the American Legion denounced the "scandalous display of dictatorship now being reflected all over the world from the Georgia Capitol." The liberal Georgia author, Lillian Smith, attacked Talmadge for jeopardizing law and order in the state "by a coup d'etat so violent, so brazen, that it has shocked the entire state."[31]

Over 150 Georgia Tech students, in a letter to the editor of the Atlanta *Journal,* accused Talmadge of "applying himself in true 'Heil Hitler' fashion." In another letter to the editor, one writer threatened to leave the state if "Von Herman" remained governor. Arnall's executive secretary claimed that Arnall had received more than five hundred telegrams and more than fifteen hundred letters commending him on his stand. Even Senator Russell received several letters concerning the controversy. One questioned why Russell sat "calmly by while Herman Talmadge takes the seat of government by force—as Hitler took Germany." One citizen telegraphed Thompson, "The divine right of kings have [*sic*] been left in Europe." Another lamented, "Georgia is as much under the rule of the mob as France was in the days of the French Revolution." One disgusted citizen pleaded with Thompson not to "permit 'HOIMAN THE KING' and his HENCHMEN to steal the Capitol." One citizen complained, "Even Hitler did not get started with such a bang."[32]

Mass meetings protesting Talmadge's election were held all over the state. Four hundred citizens assembled in Lowndes County and passed a resolution censuring the legislature for electing Talmadge. Prior to the meeting, a petition had been circulated calling upon the legislature to adjourn until the gubernatorial question had been settled by the courts. More than one thousand persons signed the petition. In Bartow County a mass meeting, broadcast over twenty-six radio stations, passed resolutions urging the legislature to adjourn until the courts ruled. Over three hundred citizens in Washington County gathered to denounce the "seizure of the state government," while more than four hundred disgruntled residents of Meriwether County adopted a resolution condemning "this revolution against law and order and usurpation of power."[33]

An estimated two thousand people assembled in DeKalb County to pass a resolution censuring Talmadge for "seizing and holding by force Georgia's State Capitol." A Jasper County mass rally assailed the legislature for "trying to set up a dictatorship in Georgia." In Cook County participants in a mass rally passed resolutions protesting "methods employed by the Legislature of Georgia to thwart the will of the citizens of our state." State Representative Walter Harrison, addressing a Jenkins County rally, declared, "Georgians will rise up from the mountains to the sea to make sure that our democratic ways are preserved." Students of West Georgia College marched into Carrollton, protesting Talmadge's election with one carrying a placard asking, "HOW MANY REPRESENTATIVES WERE DRUNK WHEN THE CROWN PRINCE WAS CROWNED?" More than two hundred students at Wesleyan College signed a petition condemning the way in which Talmadge "seized" office, and more than one thousand college and high school students marched on the state capitol and hung an effigy of "King Herman the First" from a statue on the capitol grounds.[34]

Talmadge supporters in turn held mass meetings over the state in favor of the new governor. In Bulloch County a large gathering of Talmadgites held a rally and passed a resolution endorsing the legislature's election of Talmadge. Talmadge supporters in Meriwether County commended the lawmakers for "their staunch and loyal adherence to the Constitution of the State in exercising the prerogatives conferred upon them to elect and declare Herman Talmadge governor." Some 125 Talmadge supporters in Dodge County urged the General Assembly to stay in session, while more than seven hundred persons gathered in DeKalb County and passed a resolution congratulating the legislature "on doing its duty in electing Herman Talmadge." In Washington County three hundred citizens assembled and urged the legislature to stay in session and pass a white primary bill. Talmadge supporters gathered in Savannah to pass resolutions declaring the constitution had to be upheld even if it did not suit some of the people.[35]

Understandably, Arnall came under bitter attack from the Talmadgites. One Talmadge supporter lambasted Arnall as a traitor to the state for his fight against Talmadge. "I imagine that the Lord has repented that He made Ellis Arnall," the Talmadgite concluded. A pro-Talmadge legislator called Arnall's fight against Talmadge a disgrace. One Talmadgite predicted, "Arnall will never again get a state position as he has killed himself in politics completely." Another pleaded with Senator Russell to "please help us stop this Negro-loving man." A pro-Talmadge Atlanta attorney accused Arnall of dragging the state "into mire and filth and disgrace," and a resident of Muscogee County confessed that the "worst mistake I ever made was when I voted for Arnold [*sic*] 4 years ago." At a DeKalb County rally of seven hundred Talmadge supporters, Representative Howard denounced Arnall as a liar who was "getting rich going around defaming the State of Georgia." An associate editor of the Atlanta *Journal* noted that many citizens gnashed their teeth with rage at the mention of Arnall's name.[36]

Talmadge charged that the mass meetings protesting his election were being sponsored by "the same little group" who destroyed the white primary and wanted to destroy the county unit system. Talmadge reminded Georgians that "we whipped this crowd" when Arnall tried to remove the succession prohibition, when he attempted to dictate his successor in the primary, and when the general assembly elected a governor. Talmadge warned that "if they persist in their effort, I shall call for this majority of the WHITE PEOPLE of Georgia to come to Atlanta and show them a real demonstration." Talmadge claimed his office had been deluged with messages from supporters desiring to stage a march on the capitol in support of his election. He admitted, "We can have 25,000 people on the Capitol lawn on 24 hours notice." Nevertheless he announced his disapproval of such an endeavor that might be construed as a threat to intimidate the legislature or the courts.[37]

Many of the mass meetings over the state protesting Talmadge's election called for the controversy to be settled by the courts. An organization founded as a result of such a meeting, the Aroused Citizens of Georgia, called on Talmadge and Thompson to go on record "as recognizing the power and authority of our courts to decide the issue." As early as January 15 Arnall had ordered the attorney general to bring legal action against Talmadge's claim to the governorship. Talmadge, when asked what he would do if the suit went against him, replied, "Nothing. The governorship is exclusively the province of the General Assembly." On another occasion, he declared that the legislature's "action in this matter is not subject to review by the courts, since it would be an encroachment by the judicial branch of the government upon the legislative branch." Harris also boasted that opponents would be unable to unseat Talmadge through court proceedings because "this is one of those situations where the Legislature has jurisdiction and not the courts." Harris even predicted a revolution if the Supreme Court of Georgia ruled against Talmadge. Arnall accused the Talmadgites of fearing resolution of the issue by the judiciary because they knew the judges would rule against them.[38]

Talmadge, on January 18, denied having claimed that he would not abide by a court's decision. At the same time, he reiterated his claim that the

courts had no jurisdiction in the matter. Later that day Thompson, temporarily relegated to a secondary position in the controversy, took the oath as
lieutenant governor. After doing so, he announced his intentions of assuming the executive powers in the capacity of acting governor until the people
could elect themselves a governor in the next general election. Attorney
General Cook immediately recognized Thompson as acting governor.[39]

On hearing of Thompson's qualification, Arnall announced his resignation. Arnall had earlier stated that he had no desire to hold office under a
legal technicality. In addition, Arnall claimed that he "had already booked
lecture engagements all over the United States and was committed to business affairs, so I just couldn't have continued in office if I had wanted to."
Although Arnall had stepped down from the governorship, he nevertheless kept up a barrage of attacks upon Talmadge's election. Speaking to
over two thousand citizens at a gathering in Atlanta, he called the governorship fight a test of whether "nazi methods can be used to seize our
government by force." Arnall assailed "King Herman" for assuming the
governorship "in a manner that would have shamed the Third German
Reich." After leaving the state on a nationwide speaking tour, Arnall predicted the Supreme Court of Georgia would rule against Talmadge's being
the governor.[40]

The issue of who should be governor finally made its way to the state's
highest court. Three suits pertaining to the legislative election had been
filed in superior courts. Two superior court judges upheld Talmadge's election while a third ruled in favor of Thompson. Parties in the three suits
joined together in a petition urging acceleration of a ruling in the dispute
by the consolidation of the three cases and the rendering of a single decision. The Georgia Supreme Court agreed and set March 6 as the date of
oral arguments.[41]

Four days before oral arguments were scheduled to begin, the Atlanta
Journal, in a front-page story under the headline "TELFAIR DEAD WERE
VOTED," revealed the results of its investigation of the write-in vote in
Talmadge's home county of Telfair. According to the Helena precinct tally
sheet, 103 persons had voted in the precinct in the 1946 general election
with the last thirty-four persons voting in alphabetical order. According to
the *Journal,* only two of these voters said they had actually voted. The *Journal,* along with over thirty other papers, called for an investigation. *Time*
magazine praised the *Journal's* story as "one of the year's notable journal-
istic exploits." Talmadge, however, denounced the story as "yellow jour-

nalism of the extreme form" and charged that the *Journal* had waited until the week of oral arguments before the Supreme Court concerning his election in order to influence the court. Talmadge denied being involved in any "electoral chicanery" in Telfair County. He argued that even if those write-in votes were thrown out, the legislature could still elect him because he was "still one of the two top vote-getters in life who was willing to accept election by the General Assembly."[42]

On March 19 the high court, in a five to two decision, upheld Thompson's claim to the governorship. The majority opinion, written by Presiding Justice William H. Duckworth, dealt with two questions: Did the courts have jurisdiction in the dispute and did the General Assembly exceed its authority in electing Talmadge? Counsel for Talmadge argued the courts lacked jurisdiction for two reasons. First, the legislature's election of Talmadge was a "purely political question" over which the courts had no right of review. Second, counsel for Talmadge argued that the legislature, in electing Talmadge, was exercising powers conferred upon it by the constitution, which subsequently removed the action from court jurisdiction.[43]

Despite such argument, Presiding Justice Duckworth held that the court had jurisdiction because the dispute involved interpretation of the constitution as to the authority of the legislature to elect a governor. Duckworth then dealt with the central question of whether the legislature had exceeded its authority in electing Talmadge governor. With one exception, Duckworth noted, the power to elect a governor had been reserved by the constitution for the people. This exception occurred only when the voters failed to cast a majority of their votes in the general election for a gubernatorial candidate. Under such circumstance, and only then, Duckworth held the constitution conferred on the legislature the power to elect a governor. Duckworth therefore held the legislature had erred in assuming this elective power on January 15, 1947, because Eugene Talmadge had received a majority of the votes cast in the 1946 general election. Furthermore, Duckworth ruled that the death of the governor-elect did not change the constitutional duty of the legislature in declaring his election. Duckworth held that any action taken by the legislature in place of this duty was null and void. On the resignation of Governor Arnall, Duckworth declared, Thompson automatically assumed the executive power of the state until the next general election.[44]

The Macon *Telegraph* hailed the decision as a "great victory for constitutional government." The decision, the Eatonton *Messenger* editorialized, spared Georgia the destiny that befell Louisiana under Huey P. Long and Tennessee under Ed Crump. The Columbus *Ledger* proclaimed, "IT IS ILLEGAL TO STEAL." The Gainesville *News* stated that next to Thompson, "former Governor Ellis Arnall is perhaps the happiest man in Georgia." On learning of the decision, Arnall remarked, "Stealing is still unlawful in Georgia." In the same statement, Arnall noted: "There was never a moment's doubt as to the final outcome." Arnall revealed later why he could make such a statement:

> Before I plunged the state into a banana republic war, I wanted to know that I was right. I knew I was right but I wanted it confirmed. So in violation of all law and legal ethics and everything else, I called one of the members of the Supreme Court down to my office and I said, "Look, if I make this fight and am wrong, I am a fool and will have embarrassed the state. If I am right in my view that I am governor for four more years and upon my resignation the lieutenant governor becomes acting governor, I want to know it before I pitch the battle." This dear friend of mine . . . that afternoon came back and said, "I have canvassed the reaction of the court and while they are not committed to this, I believe that a majority of the court supports your view." So I wasn't just shooting in the dark and I felt that I had a right to violate the law and legal ethics because of the principle at stake, the highest office at the gift of the people was at stake, and I wanted to know that my procedure was right before I adopted the view that I did.[45]

Insisting the decision was contrary to the law, Talmadge claimed that all the justices concurring in the majority opinion had, at some time, been appointed to some office either by Arnall or Rivers. Nevertheless, despite his objections to the decision, Talmadge immediately evacuated the governor's office. As he left the capitol, he told reporters, "The court of last resort is the people of Georgia. This case will be taken to the court of last resort." Harris, immediately announcing Talmadge's candidacy for 1948, predicted he would receive the support of three-fourths of the white people.[46]

The sixty-three days of the governorship fight had damaged the state's reputation. "The State of Georgia," the Tifton *Daily Gazette* lamented, "again is the laughing stock of the nation." The Macon *News* called the controversy "the most sordid exhibition in the annals of Georgia's history." *The Nation* contended that the last time the state was so newsworthy was when Sherman invaded the state. According to *Time,* Georgia was getting more publicity than a two-headed calf. A reporter for the Atlanta *Constitution* on assignment in New York City found that "every paper you see is yelling the story of what is going on in Georgia. It is the biggest news in the United States." Another *Constitution* reporter writing from Washington agreed and noted that none of the editorial comment was favorable to the state. The controversy received extensive coverage in national publications such as *Life, Newsweek,* and *Time.* A Gallup Poll revealed that 84 percent of the people surveyed had heard or read about the controversy. A resident of Macon complained, "One can hardly turn on a radio or pick up a magazine without discovering some 'crack' about Georgia's two governors."[47]

The decision of the Georgia Supreme Court ended one of the most controversial and unusual gubernatorial elections in the history of the state. By invalidating Talmadge's legislative election, the court provided Arnall with a significant victory over Herman Talmadge. The victory turned out to be bittersweet, however, in that it would prove to be Arnall's last triumph over Talmadgeism. The court had upheld Thompson's claims to the governorship and denied the office to the Talmadgites for two more years. However, the relationship between the two victors in this battle of constitutional interpretation, Arnall and Thompson, remained somewhat strained even though they were allies in the fight against Herman Talmadge. Arnall had not supported Thompson's successful bid for the state's second highest office and had even publicly acknowledged his support of one of Thompson's opponents.

In retrospect, the blame for the unfortunate power struggle following Gene Talmadge's death could be placed upon the Constitution Revision Commission chaired by Arnall. That body, in its haste to revise the state's fundamental law, had simply borrowed the provisions of the Constitution of 1877 pertaining to the governor's office for inclusion in the Constitution of 1945. If that body had provided a constitutional remedy in the death of a governor-elect, the state would have been spared much tribulation, turmoil, embarrassment, and unfavorable publicity. In defense of the commission, the problem of the death of a governor-elect had never arisen in the state and the issue hardly ranked as a major topic of discussion in political circles prior to Talmadge's death.

Arnall had entered the governorship in 1943 committed to redeeming the state's reputation, which had suffered due to abuses in the Rivers and Talmadge administrations. As governor, Arnall had succeeded to a remarkable degree in cultivating the image of a forward-looking and progressive Georgia, but that image shattered as a result of Eugene Talmadge's election as governor and the tragic controversy that shook the state following his death. At least Arnall could enjoy some satisfaction knowing that Herman Talmadge would not complete his father's term of office.

12

Federal

Service,

Law, and

Business

In the spring of 1946, the editor of the Birmingham *Age-Herald* wrote that Ellis Arnall "had his eyes on Washington, not Atlanta anymore." A columnist in the Atlanta *Constitution* agreed, "Arnall is looking for bigger fields of operation." Many observers of the Georgia political scene and especially those in the Talmadge faction concurred with those sentiments. As early as Arnall's first year in the governorship, he had been mentioned as a potential presidential or vice presidential candidate. However, tradition worked against his receiving the Democratic presidential nomination since a southerner had not been the presidential nominee of either major party since before the Civil War.[1]

However, a vice presidential nomination for Arnall in 1948 loomed as a possibility because of his favorable and widespread national press coverage. An Associated Press writer observed in March 1945 that Arnall had "caught the national spotlight" and that the number of newspaper editorials throughout the country praising Arnall was "almost inexhaustible." National publications such as *Life, American Mercury, Collier's, Saturday Evening Post, Newsweek, Time,* and *New Republic* ran feature articles about Georgia's chief executive. One historian later concluded that "it seemed none came to Georgia but to praise the state and its governor." Arnall's three-year national lecture tour, which ended in 1948, his two best-selling books published prior to the 1948 Democratic National Convention, his prolific writing in numerous national magazines, and his frequent appearances on radio programs during this period confirmed the suspicions of many that Arnall was actively campaigning for his party's 1948 vice presidential nomination. Certainly Arnall's progressive administration, the widespread national media coverage, the three-governors controversy, and his antitrust fight against the railroads had made him one of the best-known southerners in the nation.[2]

A reporter for the Atlanta *Constitution* even claimed that Arnall was the best-known Democrat in the United States. Arnall's standing in the party had reached the point that he had been asked to give the principal address at the Democratic party's 1945 Jefferson Day Dinner in Washington. Arnall received frequent mention as the 1948 Democratic vice presidential nominee at the annual governors conference in 1947. "Hardly a doubt remains in the minds of political observers," a writer in the *American Mercury* concluded, "that Ellis Arnall . . . is playing for the Democratic vice-presidential nomination in 1948." A poll conducted by *Fortune* magazine revealed that Arnall ranked second among voters as their choice for the Democratic party's vice presidential nomination.[3]

Arnall's vice presidential hopes suffered a major blow when President Roosevelt died in 1945. Arnall had supported Vice President Wallace's renomination in 1944 over Truman's bid and he had since publicly disagreed with President Truman on several issues. Arnall had another major liability in that he no longer controlled the machinery of the state Democratic party. While the Georgia Supreme Court had ensured the anti-Talmadge faction's control of the governorship until the 1948 general election, it had left the Talmadge faction in control of the party's machinery. The latter decision meant the party's delegation to the 1948 convention would be composed of Talmadgites who would be hostile to any effort by their arch enemy to gain the vice presidential nomination.[4]

In addition, conservatives across the South were skeptical of Arnall. His support of Wallace at the 1944 convention, his stand on the white primary, the favorable reception of his lecture tour outside the South, and his liberal reputation had alienated many southern conservatives. His solo fight against the railroads before the Supreme Court and his strong rhetoric against the railroads and their allies had angered many southern political leaders who would play a major role at the 1948 convention. Arnall could not count on support of the conservative southern delegates but could probably expect strong opposition from them if he sought the vice presidency. But ultimately, President Truman ended Arnall's vice presidential aspirations in that he wanted Associate Justice William O. Douglas to be his running mate in 1948. After Douglas decided to remain on the court, Truman picked a southerner, Senate minority leader Alben W. Barkley, to be on the ticket with him. Apparently, Truman never considered Arnall. Faced with the threat of a revolt on the part of southern conservatives, Truman needed a conservative southerner like Barkley who could keep them in line.[5]

The likelihood of Arnall's receiving the vice presidential nomination in 1952 appeared even more remote. The Talmadge faction still remained firmly in control of the party machinery in Georgia. Moreover, by 1952 Arnall had been out of the governorship for five years and the anti-Talmadge faction, which he had led to victory a decade earlier, stood in shambles. As in 1948 Arnall lacked the power base in his own state necessary to gain the vice presidential nomination. If Arnall intended to serve his country in national office, it would have to be as a member of Congress or as a presidential appointee. Arnall never seriously contemplated running for Congress because he viewed it as an institution that did not lend itself to the exercise of strong leadership. Instead, he saw congressmen as office holders whose major task was to satisfy constituents' requests. With Arnall's rejection of a congressional career, a presidential appointment remained the only route left for him to undertake federal service.[6]

Roosevelt had planned to nominate Arnall as U.S. attorney general in his fourth term, but the president's death ended that possibility. In September 1945, however, President Truman offered Arnall the position of solicitor general, the second highest position in the Department of Justice. The offer carried with it an understanding that Arnall would be moved up to attorney general to replace Tom C. Clark, who had been promised the first vacancy on the U.S. Supreme Court. Arnall declined the offer, claiming that his wife, pregnant with a second child, refused to move to Washington. Arnall also feared his resignation would "open the door for Talmadge" to return to the governorship.[7]

Early in 1952 speculation arose that Arnall would be appointed special prosecutor in the Department of Justice to investigate widely reported scandals in the Truman administration. In a press conference on January 31, 1952, President Truman denied reports of Arnall's appointment to that position. However, the president told reporters that Arnall would be welcomed in his administration in another capacity "if he wanted to come." The following day, Attorney General J. Howard McGrath announced that the position of special prosecutor would be filled by a New York Republican. On that same day, Arnall met with President Truman in Washington amid growing speculation of Arnall's being offered the position of director of the Office of Price Stabilization. That position had recently become vacant when Michael DiSalle had resigned to run for a U.S. Senate seat from Ohio. Truman offered Arnall the position of OPS director, but he declined it. On reconsideration, however, Arnall reluctantly accepted the nomination with the stipulation that he would serve for only six months. On February 7, 1952, President Truman announced his nomination of Arnall as director of OPS.[8]

Many wondered why Arnall would take a leave of absence from a lucrative law firm, which he had started after leaving the governorship, to assume a difficult and thankless position which paid only sixteen thousand dollars a year. *Time* estimated that Arnall would give up compensation of almost one hundred thousand dollars a year from his legal and business activities to assume the position of OPS director in an administration under attack for alleged corruption, incompetence, and misconduct of the war effort in Korea. Moreover, it seemed unlikely that an increasingly unpopular President Truman could repeat his 1948 upset victory if he decided to seek reelection.[9]

Arnall dismissed political advancement as the reason for accepting the OPS position. Instead he considered his acceptance to be a patriotic response to the country's needs at a time when American troops were fighting communist aggression in Korea. Arnall saw his role as ensuring a strong economy, which was essential to the nation's struggle against communism. He reasoned that someone had to "be ever willing to perform the difficult, tough, unpopular, and thankless tasks necessary to preserve our economic stability and our nation's security." Some months later, Arnall explained his decision to accept his "call to duty" in a speech to the Virginia Federation of Women's Clubs, "I have a selfish interest, as all of us have, in wanting to preserve the value of the dollars I earn."[10]

Despite the public explanation of Arnall's decision, some observers detected other reasons for his decision to accept the OPS directorship. Some believed it reflected Arnall's belief that President Truman would run again and that Arnall had been promised a position other than the OPS directorship in the next Truman administration. *Time* observed, "Some Washington hands think that he [Arnall] believes Truman will run and is simply getting on the bandwagon." Others saw Arnall seizing the opportunity and a chance "to step back into the national limelight before it is too late." The Atlanta *Journal*, while accepting Arnall's explanation, reasoned, "if he has political motives too, he is surely due credit for accepting one of the most hazardous places in government in order to advance them." The Atlanta *Constitution* praised Arnall for his willingness to return to public service at "a considerable personal sacrifice." [11]

Whatever the reason for Arnall's decision, southern senators praised it, for they believed Arnall would be more receptive to eliminating price controls on southern commodities such as textiles, lumber, and cotton than his northern predecessor. Arnall's political enemies in Georgia remained unusually quiet toward the nomination. However, a member of the Talmadge-dominated state House of Representatives jokingly introduced a resolution praising Arnall for his "noble sacrifice," which "has touched the hearts of this Legislature." [12]

On February 12, 1952, the Senate Committee on Banking and Currency held hearings on Arnall's nomination. Arnall, while expressing his strong opposition to a controlled and regimented economy, nevertheless stated his belief that existing economic conditions required price controls to protect the nation from the ravages of inflation, which he deemed the greatest danger to the nation's economy. While promising to decontrol prices on nonessential goods, Arnall told the committee of his reluctance to "hasten headlong into decontrols." However, he favored decontrol as long as the relaxation did not adversely affect the economy. The committee unanimously recommended approval of the nomination to the Senate, which approved the nomination on February 18, 1952, without a dissenting vote. Senator William Benton of Connecticut praised Arnall on the Senate floor for taking one of the toughest jobs in the government and noted, "Few men have come to Washington with a greater breadth of experience." [13]

Arnall became head of one of several agencies that had been created to stabilize the national economy following American intervention in Korea. The Economic Stabilization Agency, created in September 1950, had been given the broad responsibilities of preventing inflation and of stabilizing the economy. The administrator of the Economic Stabilization Agency at the time of Arnall's nomination, Roger L. Putnam, had supervisory responsibility over the Office of Price Stabilization. The Office of Price Stabilization had been created by the ESA administrator in February 1951. When Arnall assumed the directorship of the agency a year later, it had twelve thousand employees scattered throughout fourteen regional and over eighty-five district offices. In addition, the agency had some 550 industry advisory committees with over 7,500 industrialists and businessmen as members. OPS had been given the awesome responsibilities of preventing inflation, preserving the value of the national currency, establishing price ceilings, preventing profiteering, and protecting the public's living standards.[14]

Following the outbreak of the Korean conflict, Congress had enacted the Defense Production Act of 1950, which permitted the federal government to establish price controls. Reluctant at first to impose such controls, the government resorted to indirect controls such as increasing taxes and tightening credit to control inflation. When these efforts proved unsuccessful, the Economic Stabilization Administration created the Office of Price Stabilization to institute a program of price controls over most goods and services.[15]

Arnall, firmly committed to the principles of a capitalistic economy, conceded that the government's interference with the free market violated American tradition. Nevertheless, he defended the governmental intrusion as "needed to avert internal calamity while the nation was mobilizing its strength to forestall international disaster." Arnall rejected the argument that price controls were anti-business since they were "created to aid and help business—not to hurt, impede or strangle it." He assured the business community that OPS was "dedicated to preserving our American way of life—our system of free enterprise." Arnall conceded that he disliked price controls in normal times but argued that the times were not normal. "I believe in free competitive enterprise, but in this grave emergency which confronts our Nation and our people," Arnall declared, "I have come to believe in the urgent need today for more effective controls."[16]

Early in 1952 President Truman requested that the Defense Production Act, due to expire in June, be extended for two more years. He also urged the Congress to repeal several amendments that had been added to the Act in 1951 and that he believed had seriously weakened price controls. In particular, both Truman and Arnall objected to the Capehart amendment, which had been sponsored by Republican Senator Homer E. Capehart, as the most damaging to effective price controls. The amendment allowed manufacturers and processors to obtain higher price ceilings from OPS to cover cost increases that occurred between June 1950 and July 1951. Arnall estimated that price increases of $750 million had occurred because of the amendment.[17]

Arnall supported the president's request for an extension of price control legislation despite the fact that opposition to OPS in general and to price controls in particular was increasing. Some business groups, such as the National Association of Manufacturers and the National Chamber of Commerce, favored the dismantling of the agency. A regional director of OPS warned Arnall of "the increasingly intense effort" of trade and industrial groups to do away with price controls. One irate citizen even telegraphed Arnall that Arnall wanted "to maintain this crazy price controls to give 60,000 Democrats a job." Another wrote, "The doings of your office gives me a laugh"; one disgruntled Texan urged Arnall to immediately close down all OPS offices in the Lone Star State.[18]

Arnall dismissed the criticism of price controls as coming from a small minority who had never supported price controls anyway. He criticized those in the business community wishing to abolish OPS as "short-sighted and ill-advised" and accused them of engaging in a "callous and irresponsible gambling with America's economy and America's security." In March 1952 Arnall told a congressional committee that the overwhelming majority of the American people wanted price controls to continue. Arnall predicted that without them, inflation would undermine the nation's economy and threaten the national defense. He defended OPS, contending it had "saved the American public many millions of dollars, which would have otherwise been lost in a disastrous spiral of inflation." Arnall insisted that the country needed price controls "never more than today" because economic conditions that had led to their creation in 1951 still existed. If the United States dropped its vigilance against inflation, Arnall warned a serious financial disaster could result.[19]

Despite the pleas of Truman and Arnall for a two-year extension of the Defense Production Act, the Senate Banking and Currency Committee voted to extend price controls for only eight months. Moreover, the committee retained the crippling amendments to which both the president and Arnall objected. After adding an amendment removing price controls on fresh fruits and vegetables, the Senate overwhelmingly approved the Banking and Currency Committee's recommendation.[20]

In an effort to obtain a longer extension of the bill, Arnall appeared before the House Committee on Banking and Currency. He argued that an extension of price controls of only eight months was "unrealistic" and would not give a new administration sufficient time to consider properly the important question of price controls. Yielding to Arnall's plea, the House committee recommended a one-year extension of price controls. When the bill reached the House floor, however, the representatives adopted several amendments that further weakened price controls. One amendment removed price controls from all products not rationed or allocated. This amendment, sponsored by Republican congressman Henry D. Talle, would have effectively killed price controls since most products were not rationed or allocated. Arnall recommended abolishing OPS if the Talle amendment remained in the bill. He vigorously protested the amendment to House Speaker Sam Rayburn, contending that it would kill price controls and result in skyrocketing prices.[21]

In June 1952 the House finally passed an extension of the Act that included the Talle amendment. Differences between the House and Senate bills resulted in a conference committee that deleted the Talle amendment but exempted fresh and processed fruit and vegetables from price controls from the ten-months extension of the law. Arnall, who had opposed decontrolling fruits and vegetables, saw the action as further undermining the government's efforts to control inflation. Despite having strong objections to the bill, President Truman signed it. Even Arnall conceded that the legislation "could have been very much worse." At least price controls had been retained for ten more months.[22]

In the midst of House consideration of the extension of the Defense Production Act, Arnall himself became an issue on the floor of the House of Representatives. Republican Congressman Jesse P. Wolcott of Michigan attacked Arnall as "merely a public relations man" who lacked knowledge of the fundamentals of economics. Wayne L. Hays, a Democratic congressman from Ohio, came to Arnall's defense by praising the former governor as one of the best administrators in the federal government. Georgia Congressman Albert S. Camp, who counted Arnall as one of his constituents, also spoke in defense of Arnall, contending that "no man in this country is better versed in price control matters." Arnall also received support from an unlikely source—Georgia Congressman E. Eugene Cox, a staunch Talmadgite. Cox told the House that despite their political differences, Arnall was "the most courteous man I have known in the carrying along of his work in Washington."[23]

Failing to kill OPS outright, opponents of the agency turned to the appropriations process as a way to dismantle it. President Truman pleaded with Congress to give OPS sufficient funds to operate; otherwise, the president warned, the "limited program of controls which this law authorizes will collapse." OPS opponents managed, however, to cut the appropriations for the agency by over 50 percent in spite of the objections of Truman and Arnall. As a result, Arnall had the "unhappy job" of reducing the size of his agency from over twelve thousand employees to five thousand and closing almost half of the district OPS offices. He predicted that by March 1953 the agency would be scaled back to less than fifteen hundred employees. With a weak price-control law and a substantial reduction in appropriations and personnel, Arnall conceded OPS was "having a most difficult time" in carrying out its responsibilities. His argument that prices could be controlled only if the deleted funds were restored fell on deaf congressional ears.[24]

As the cost of food increased due in part to decontrolling vegetable and fruit prices, Arnall called for a special session of Congress to strengthen the government's price-control program. Arnall attributed the rising cost of food to drought, an inadequate price-control law, and the cut in OPS appropriations. On August 6, 1952, Arnall conferred with President Truman to discuss the need for a special session. Arnall's suggestion ran into strong opposition from presidential advisors, political leaders of both parties, and Arnall's immediate boss, Roger Putnam. Senator John J. Sparkman, the Democratic vice presidential candidate, also rejected the idea of a special session in the midst of a presidential campaign. Despite such opposition, Arnall remained committed to the need for a special session. He warned of living costs shooting "sky-high" before Congress reconvened in January 1953. Despite Arnall's pleas, President Truman refused to call a special session.[25]

While struggling with the problem of price controls, the Truman administration faced the possibility of a nationwide steel strike. Contracts between the United Steel Workers Union and the major steel companies had expired at the end of 1951. The steel industry had refused to discuss union demands for increased wages and improved working conditions leading President Truman to refer the issue to the Wage Stabilization Board (WSB), an agency that had been given the responsibility of settling labor disputes affecting national defense. The union, bowing to a presidential request, postponed the threatened strike. At the time Arnall assumed the OPS directorship in February 1952, the WSB had not submitted its wage increase recommendations. Arnall considered the resolution of the steel dispute to be the most difficult task confronting him because of the importance of steel to the national economy. Arnall anticipated requests from the steel industry for price increases if the WSB granted wage increases and predicted the dispute could make his job "awfully uncomfortable."[26]

The WSB, without consulting Arnall, made its recommendations in

March 1952. The board recommended that union members be given an increase of twenty-six cents per hour to be awarded over an eighteen-month period. While the Steel Workers Union threatened a strike if the industry turned down the recommended wage increase, Charles E. Wilson, director of Defense of Mobilization, believed the steel industry would reject the proposed increase. Wilson carried the recommendations to President Truman, who was vacationing in Key West, Florida. Wilson expressed his disagreement with the WSB recommendation, insisting that union members should receive only a cost-of-living increase and that the steel companies should settle for a price increase of approximately three dollars per ton, which they were entitled to under the Capehart amendment. If the steel workers received only a cost-of-living increase, Wilson believed that the steel industry would not seek a price increase beyond that authorized under the Capehart amendment.[27]

According to Wilson, however, Truman did not think a cost-of-living increase sufficient to satisfy the union and insisted that "we would have to go to whatever was needed in preventing a strike." As a result, Wilson left the meeting believing that he had the authority to offer the union more than a cost-of-living increase and to offer the steel companies an increase in price commensurate with the raise offered to the steel workers. Without the concurrence of Arnall or Putnam, Wilson offered the steel companies increases in line with what was granted in wage increases, even though they exceeded OPS standards. In testimony before the Senate Banking and Currency Committee, Arnall informed the committee that Wilson had made the offer to the parties without consulting him. Arnall confessed to being "a little hurt," since "I was naive enough to believe that the man who was supposed to be in charge of the price end of the deal would at least be consulted."[28]

Arnall's mood soon changed from being "a little hurt" to being "upset" that he had not been consulted on the question and that the price increase would be given without regard to OPS standards. Wilson had requested that Arnall, Putnam, and Nathan P. Feinsinger, the chairman of the Wage Stabilization Board, join him for a joint press conference to announce the offer. Arnall called Wilson that night and told him that he would not attend the press conference because "I am not going to sit there and be gagged and muzzled and be pulled along here, as an appendage to what you do, when you haven't consulted me about it." Putnam and Feinsinger also refused to attend the news conference, which was then cancelled. Although Wilson directed Arnall to prepare an order giving the steel companies a price increase to settle the steel controversy, Arnall refused to comply, insisting that the price standard of OPS must apply to all companies regardless of size. He insisted that "big steel is not entitled to a price increase and I'm not going to give them one."[29]

To resolve the issue, Arnall, Wilson, and Putnam met with the president. Arnall told the president that there was "a clash of philosophy here. Charlie is for the big man and I'm for the little man." Arnall objected to Wilson's agreeing to give the steel companies a price increase to which they were not entitled and for doing so without consulting him. Wilson saw his integrity on the line and insisted that the president had authorized him, if need be, to give a price increase beyond that permitted by Capehart's amendment. Truman disagreed and explained that Wilson had "interpreted my willingness to consider an adjustment to cover the actual added costs as a promise to meet the companies' full demands." Wilson offered his resignation, which the president accepted. Truman then offered Arnall Wilson's former job. Arnall declined, telling the president that he would not take the job of the man he forced out of office. Shortly thereafter, Arnall met with representatives of the steel industry and offered them an increase of $4.50 per ton—an increase that exceeded permissible limits under the Capehart amendment. However, Arnall did so at the direction of President Truman and over his objection. The steel companies turned down the Arnall offer.[30]

The industry offered to increase wage and fringe benefits, but the union leadership turned the offer down and scheduled a strike. President Truman reached the decision that the steel mills could not be shut down while the country was fighting a war in Korea. Arnall, among others, recommended to the president that the government take over running the steel mills. President Truman agreed and directed Secretary of Commerce Charles Sawyer to take over the mills and for the army to operate them. The steel companies obtained a ruling from a federal district judge that the president had no legal authority to seize the mills. However, a federal court of appeals overturned that decision and the country awaited the Supreme Court decision on the controversy.[31]

In the meantime, Arnall increasingly assumed the role of major spokesman for the administration in the dispute, expressing his strong opposition to the demands of the steel industry for a twelve-dollar-per-ton price increase. In a speech before the National Press Club shortly after the seizure, Arnall claimed that the increase demanded by the steel industry would probably "set off another spiraling rise in the cost of living." Arnall told his audience, "The steel price line can be substantially held and I intend to hold it." In a speech over national radio, Arnall assured the American people that a price increase as requested by the steel industry would not be granted "while I can raise my voice to prevent it." Arnall warned that prices would increase if he gave in to the steel industry because other industries would seek to increase their prices as well if government yielded to the steel industry's "unrealistic" request for price increases. Such a chain of events, Arnall warned, would lead to the collapse of price controls and an economic crash that would put "smiles on the faces of our enemies in the Kremlin."[32]

In testimony before the Senate Committee on Labor and Public Welfare, Arnall defended the two OPS standards used to determine price increases in the steel industry. Arnall pointed out that the steel companies had never requested a price increase under the standard in the Capehart amendment even though they were entitled to do so. Arnall assured the committee that he was willing to grant the industry the increase which was mandated if it were requested. Arnall also pointed out that the industry could have applied for a price increase under the OPS Industry Earnings Standard, which required prices to be raised for an industry when its returns on the stockholders' investment fell below 85 percent of the level enjoyed in the best three of the four years between 1946 through 1949. Arnall insisted, however, that the steel companies were not entitled to receive an increase in prices under the Industry Earnings Standard because their profits were the highest since World War I. Arnall warned that if OPS "bowed under pressure to Steel, we would be fair game for intimidation by other groups." He stressed the harmful impact the price increase sought by the steel industry would have on the nation's economy. Arnall vigorously opposed giving the steel industry a "special privilege" of a price increase while expecting other industries to comply with OPS standards.[33]

In May 1952 Arnall appeared before the House Committee on Banking and Currency where he vigorously defended the Industry Earning Standard, which he called fair and equitable. Arnall charged that the steel industry, which could not qualify for price increase under the standard, had resorted to attacking it. Arnall further charged that the steel companies' fight was not with the union but with the government because "they figure they have got the government across a barrel, and they are going to extort this price increase, or wreck the economy." During a heated exchange with Congressman Walcott, a member of the committee, Arnall accused the steel industry of wanting "to wreck the Defense Production Act so they could get any price they want." In the midst of Arnall's verbal assault on the steel industry, the U.S. Supreme Court ruled in a six-to-three vote that the president's seizure of the steel mills was unconstitutional. While the steel workers reacted to the decision by striking, negotiations between the two parties continued.[34]

Shortly after the decision, Arnall turned down requests from three steel companies that were seeking price increases of six dollars per ton. He continued to insist that the steel industry should get no more than three dollars a ton as permitted under the Capehart amendment. As the strike continued and its cost mounted, however, some observers began to question Arnall's adamant position. President Truman estimated the strike had cost the country over $40 million in lost wages and production and a total loss to the economy of $2 billion. While expressing sympathy for Arnall's opposition to increasing steel prices, the Atlanta *Constitution* editorialized, "If Mr. Arnall's adamant stand prevents an early settlement, the loss to the country will be greater than if the increases were granted." Indications of the Truman administration's reconsidering the question of steel prices began to surface. In fact, Acting Defense Mobilizer Steelman announced his support for a $5.60 a ton price increase for the industry. Arnall, however, successfully convinced the president not to go along with such an increase and announced the withdrawal of the Steelman offer. Although Arnall had prevented an increase in the steel prices again, the victory proved to be his last against the steel industry.[35]

Steelman met with the president of the steel workers' union and the president of United States Steel and settled the strike by giving union members a pay raise of almost twenty-two cents per hour while the industry gained a price increase of over five dollars a ton. Truman later explained he agreed to a price increase because the steel companies "held all the advantages. If we wanted steel—and we wanted it very badly—it would have to be on the industry's terms." A disappointed Arnall signed the order granting the price increase, making it clear that his signing had been mandated by higher authority. As reports circulated that Arnall would resign in protest, he predicted the increase would trigger a new round of inflation with other industries seeking higher prices and employees seeking higher wages. Arnall lamented that there was little the government could do to hold down prices due to the weakened price control law and OPS's inadequate funding.[36]

Shortly thereafter, Arnall told Truman that he planned to leave his post on September 1. He never attributed his resignation to the price increase but to the fact that he had agreed to serve for only six months. Truman wrote Arnall that "it would materially help our fight to win the coming [presidential] election if you could stay just thirty days longer." Despite the plea, Arnall remained committed to resigning on September 1. A few days later, Truman agreed reluctantly to accept his resignation. The New York *Times* praised Arnall for being an "efficient administrator," whose worse fault was "a chronic addiction to hyperbole." The Washington *Post* credited Arnall for making "a valiant if not always politically successful effort" to fight inflation even though "congressional undercutting of the price control law made his task an all but impossible one." Truman praised Arnall for undertaking a difficult assignment and handling "it with courage, vigor and intelligence." Truman went on to call Arnall an outstanding public servant.[37]

Though he spent only six months as director of OPS, Arnall enjoyed a much longer career as a professional lecturer, speaking in every state in the Union—an activity that none of his predecessors in the governor's office had ever undertaken. The president of the Alkahest Celebrity Bureau, S. Russell Bridges, had prevailed upon Arnall in his last year as governor to join the professional lecture circuit. Arnall received one thousand dollars a lecture. While on tour, he gave three lectures a day and did not leave Atlanta unless a solid week of lectures had been scheduled. Arnall later confessed to having made more money lecturing than "I ever did in anything." His progressive reputation as governor, his well-publicized fight against unfair freight rates, the three governors controversy, his writings, and the radio and television appearances made Arnall a much sought after lecturer. In fact, Bridges claimed that Arnall made more money for him than any other lecturer he ever handled except Winston Churchill. While insisting that the major purpose of the lecture tour was financial, Arnall nevertheless conceded that increasing his national recognition entered into his decision to undertake the lecture tour. His lecturing received widespread praise and acclaim with the exception of criticism from the Talmadge faction. Claiming that he had grown tired of hearing himself talk, Arnall left the lecture circuit in 1948.[38]

Even before he left the governorship, Arnall received numerous business proposals as well as offers from Atlanta and out-of-state law firms. He declined all such offers and planned to start his own law firm. Jack Leban, a New York businessman and friend of the governor, urged him to go into practice with Sol I. Golden, a young and rising Atlanta attorney, who wanted to leave the firm he was with to start his own. Arnall and Golden agreed to establish a new law firm to be located in Atlanta. At Arnall's suggestion, Cleburne E. Gregory, Jr., who had served as an assistant state attorney general in Arnall's administration, became one of the founding partners. The law firm of Arnall, Golden and Gregory officially came into existence on February 1, 1949, and grew into one of the city's largest and most prestigious corporate law firms. The firm specialized in representing clients in the food industry, including the National Frozen Food Association, National Fisheries Institute, National Association of Advanced Foods, National Institutional Food Distributors, Rich Products Corporation, General Foods Corporation, Carnation Company, and Sysco. The firm also represented such well-known clients as Walt Disney Productions, Paramount Pictures, Motion Picture Association of America, Eastman Kodak, Burlington Northern, Rollins, National Distributors, and Canadian Pacific Railroad, as well as a number of foreign clients.[39]

Although the practice of law proved to be Arnall's major interest after leaving the governor's office, Arnall also became prominent in the insurance business. In the last year of his administration, several of Arnall's friends and associates in Newnan organized the Dixie Life Insurance Company and asked Arnall to serve as its president. At first Arnall declined, claiming that he "didn't know anything about life insurance and didn't want to." However, he changed his mind, stating he could not turn down his hometown friends and neighbors who were among the principal financial backers of his 1942 gubernatorial campaign.[40]

Busy with lecturing, writing, and practicing law, Arnall did not devote much time to the Dixie Life Insurance Company, and after three years of operation, the company had not sold a single policy. "Then it hit me like a clap of thunder," Arnall recalled, "that if this thing goes under, it would be no excuse for me to say to the stockholders, 'After all, I'm just lending my name as president.'" Arnall determined the company's problem to be its chief actuary, who had failed to file the required paperwork with the appropriate state agency for policy approvals. Arnall replaced the actuary with a more competent one, and the company began selling policies for the first time. After a few years, the company prospered in selling small weekly premium policies. By 1952 Dixie Life, under Arnall's direction, had excelled in the selling of weekly premium insurance policies. At that time another insurance company, Coastal States Life, was considering selling its weekly premium business. The president of the company, Claude H. Poindexter, approached Arnall about the possibility of Dixie Life purchasing the weekly premium business from his company.[41]

As attorney general, Arnall had crossed paths with Poindexter, who operated a burial association to which families paid a small weekly premium to cover the cost of burial of family members. The funeral home directors, seeing burial associations as a potential economic threat, decided to drive Poindexter out of business. They secured the passage of legislation that crippled the operation of burial associations. Attorney General Arnall had the responsibility of enforcing the legislation. Because of Arnall's diligent efforts, Poindexter converted his funeral business to a life insurance company in 1939. Coastal States Life, with Poindexter as president, eventually became one of the largest life insurance companies in the state. Arnall later claimed that he made Poindexter a millionaire because he had forced him into the life insurance business.[42]

When the two former adversaries met in 1952, Arnall wanted to sell Dixie Life to Coastal States while Poindexter wanted to unload his weekly premium department on Dixie Life. In the end, Arnall prevailed, and Poindexter agreed to take over Dixie Life as a subsidiary of Coastal States with the stipulation that Arnall would become chairman of the board of directors of Coastal States. Arnall agreed and, at the same time, continued to serve as president of Dixie Life. In 1955 Coastal States merged Dixie with two other subsidiaries, and the new company became Columbus National Life Insurance Company with Arnall assuming its presidency. Two years later, however, that company was merged into Coastal States. By 1968 Coastal States passed the milestone of having over one billion dollars of life insurance in force. The company, which had acquired over seventeen insurance companies since its founding in 1939, was ultimately itself acquired by Sun Life Group of America, an insurance holding company of Kaufman and Broad, Inc., of Los Angeles. Arnall continued as chairman of Coastal States and became vice chairman of the Sun Life Group of America directors. By 1985 the companies of Sun Life Group had over a million policy holders with over seven billion dollars of life insurance in force.[43]

Arnall also played a major role, along with Poindexter and Devereaux

McClatchey, in founding the National Association of Life Companies to protect the interests of smaller insurance companies. The organization eventually became the second largest insurance trade association in the United States with headquarters in Washington, D.C., and a membership of over six hundred life insurance companies. Arnall served as the chairman of its board of directors for twenty-five years and was made a lifetime member of its board for his service.[44]

In addition to his activities in the insurance field, Arnall's business career included membership on the board of directors of the First National Bank of Newnan and membership on the board of directors of numerous corporations, including Security Mortgage Investors, Midland Capital, Midland Venture Limited of New York, Atlas Sewing Machine Company, One-Hour Valet of Miami, Florida, Alterman Foods, Simmons Plating Works, Rushton Company, and National Airline Passengers Association. He held the position of chairman of the board of trustees of the Atlanta Americana Hotel Corporation for almost two decades as well as serving as a trustee of the Livingston Foundation, which supports charitable organizations such as the Atlanta Arts Alliance, Atlanta Symphony, and the Atlanta Historical Society. Arnall also served as a trustee of Mercer University, the University of the South, and the Newnan Carnegie Library. As governor, he had the Franklin D. Roosevelt Warm Springs Commission created and served as its vice chairman for many years. He also served as vice chairman of the United States Commission to the United Nations Educational Scientific and Cultural Organizations.[45]

Arnall played an active role in the motion picture industry by serving as president of the Society of Independent Motion Picture Producers from 1948 to 1963. The Society protected the independent motion picture producers from unfair trade practices by exhibitors and major movie studios. Membership in the Society of forty film producers included Samuel Goldwyn, Walt Disney, Mary Pickford, and David O. Selznick. Arnall also served as president of the Independent Film Producers Export Corporation and a member of the board of directors of the Council of Motion Pictures Organizations and the Motion Picture Industry Council. As president of the export corporation, Arnall negotiated trade agreements with foreign countries to allow American movies made by independent producers to be imported and shown in their theaters.[46]

Arnall found time in his busy career to write two best sellers—*The Shore Dimly Seen* published in 1946 and *What the People Want* published in 1948.

In *The Shore Dimly Seen,* Arnall discussed the major accomplishments of his governorship, his views on such subjects as education, the dangers of monopoly, the exploitation of the South, the role of the states, and the race question. *What the People Want* contained Arnall's observations gathered from his national lecture tour in which he discussed the common problems facing the American people and how these problems could be resolved. Both books generally received widespread praise from reviewers. In addition, Arnall contributed articles to numerous national publications, such as the *Yale Review, Virginia Quarterly,* New York *Times Magazine, Atlantic Monthly, New Republic, Nation,* and *Southwest Review.* Such literary endeavors from a politician were unusual in any state and unheard of in Georgia.[47]

After leaving the governorship, Arnall became successful in the fields of writing, lecturing, law, insurance, and business. In retrospect, Arnall observes, "I have always been criticized as being 9/10ths socialist, a progressive, a libertarian and all that kind of stuff, and yet, ironically, I ended up as a rather successful businessman and corporate lawyer." Arnall also proved to be a forceful, articulate, and capable administrator. Unlike his tenure as governor, however, Arnall's stint as OPS director proved to be less successful due to his brief tenure and to the growing opposition to OPS. While Arnall, the successful corporation lawyer and businessman, adamantly believed in capitalism, he defended price controls as a necessary mechanism needed to maintain a healthy economy in the wake of the Korean War.[48]

Never known for timidity in political battle, Arnall forcefully and enthusiastically defended price controls and OPS against an increasing number of political foes. Ultimately, Arnall failed to turn back efforts to cut OPS's appropriations, manpower, and authority. Arnall also failed in his efforts to convince President Truman to convene a special session of Congress to strengthen OPS. For a brief period of time, Arnall held off Big Steel's effort to gain a substantial price increase. President Truman, though, eventually overrode Arnall's objections and yielded to the demands of the steel companies. Despite his lack of success at OPS, Arnall left Washington with the satisfaction of having done his best to serve his country in one of the nation's most difficult and thankless jobs.

13

. . . .

Arnall

. . . .

and

. . . .

State

. . . .

Politics,

. . . .

1947–1962

. . . .

After leaving the governorship in January 1947, Arnall quickly adjusted to private life by practicing corporate law, overseeing a rapidly expanding insurance business, and serving as an executive in the motion picture industry. Yet, the successful lawyer-businessman maintained a keen interest in politics and even contemplated running for governor again on several occasions. However, with an announcement in 1961 of his intentions of never seeking public office again, it appeared that a new generation of Georgia voters would be deprived of the excitement of an Arnall political campaign.

While Arnall successfully made the transition to private life in 1947, acting governor Thompson struggled with his responsibilities as chief executive of the state. One of the most critical decisions that Thompson had to make concerned the Talmadge-sponsored white primary bill which had been signed into law during Talmadge's brief tenure as governor. After the Georgia Supreme Court rejected Talmadge's claim to the governorship, Attorney General Cook ruled that laws passed in the recent session of the legislature had to be submitted to acting governor Thompson for his consideration. Some supporters of Thompson urged him to sign the bill to prevent Talmadge from using it as an issue against him in 1948. The Atlanta *Daily World* claimed that Rivers was foremost among those advocating such a course of action. Thompson had promised prior to the 1947 legislative session to sign a white primary bill if the legislature passed it but, as acting governor, criticized the bill as a threat to honest elections in the state. Arnall agreed and called for anti-Talmadge Democrats to boycott party primaries if Thompson signed it. Thompson sided with Arnall and vetoed the bill. While the Atlanta *Journal* praised the veto as "an act of statesmanly courage," Talmadge promised to restore the white primary if he were elected governor in 1948.[1]

The split in the anti-Talmadge faction allowed Eugene Talmadge to win the 1946 gubernatorial primary. In order to present a united front against Talmadge in the 1948 election, Arnall and Rivers moved toward political reconciliation. The effort began at least as early as March 1947, at a dinner where Rivers called for the anti-Talmadgites to close ranks against Herman Talmadge. While Arnall was out of town, Thompson told the gathering that the former governor had told him that unity should be restored to the anti-Talmadge faction. A year later, in March 1948, Rivers and Arnall attended the state Democratic party's annual Jefferson-Jackson Day Dinner where both publicly complimented each other. In May 1948 the two former governors issued a joint statement declaring that they were "intimate, personal and steadfast political friends who shared the same philosophy of government" and who were united again in their fight for a better Georgia.[2]

Speculations arose as to whom the Arnall-Rivers alliance might support in 1948. Thompson had earlier indicated his intent to seek reelection and most observers believed that he would receive the backing of the two former governors. A question of eligibility prevented a possible Arnall candidacy in 1948 since the constitution stipulated that a governor could not succeed himself until he had been out of office for four years. Arnall claimed lecture and business commitments prevented him from holding the governorship even if he were eligible. Rivers's tattered reputation and his dismal showing in the 1946 race posed as major liabilities to his ever seeking public office again. Rumors circulated that Jimmy Carmichael, the standard bearer of the anti-Talmadge faction in 1946, might run. However, after Carmichael removed his name from consideration, Arnall and Rivers announced their intent to actively support Thompson. Thompson, who had earlier appointed former state highway director John C. Beasley as his campaign manager, quickly appointed Arnall and Rivers to join Beasley as co-campaign managers.[3]

Press reaction was divided on the significance of the political reunion of the two anti-Talmadge leaders. The pro-Talmadge Greensboro *Herald-Journal* deemed the support of the two former governors a political "kiss of death" for Thompson. The Cordele *Dispatch* argued that the two former governors no longer had any influence in state politics and would have little impact on the outcome of the election. The Bainbridge *Post-Searchlight*, whose editor was Marvin Griffin, agreed. The Savannah *Morning News* called the reunion an alliance of "Strange Bed Fellows" consisting of one of the worst governors in the state's history and a "former governor who in the guise of being a 'liberal' went up and down the land with pay denouncing his own state." Another paper, the Albany *Herald,* called the "political firm of Rivers, Arnall & Co." the strangest political alliance in history. The *Herald,* dismissing Arnall as a major factor in the election, contended that he was as "dead politically in Georgia as the proverbial mackerel."[4]

Harris's paper, the Augusta *Courier,* speculated that Arnall's friends "can't figure out how Ellis can be an angel and sleep in the same bed with Ed." The Savannah *Evening Press* wondered how Arnall's "high-minded" supporters were going "to like their political saint forming an alliance with Mr. Rivers." The Atlanta *Journal,* Arnall's strongest supporter in the press, expressed its disdain at the renewed political friendship. Another Arnall supporter, the Columbus *Ledger-Enquirer,* also expressed disappointment over the fact that Arnall had "stooped to such an association." Nevertheless, other papers, such as the Moultrie *Observer* and the Valdosta *Daily Times,* believed the alliance's support beneficial to Thompson.[5]

While Talmadge considered Thompson a weak candidate, he concluded "that to go after M.E. exclusively would have been to make him into a bigger deal than he actually was." Thus Talmadge made the two former governors a major campaign issue. "I didn't know which one was the bride and I didn't know which one was the groom," Talmadge told Georgians, "but I knew who the offspring was." Talmadge called Thompson the proxy candidate of Arnall and Rivers and claimed that this election was the first time "two former governors have ever run for governor without their names on the ticket."[6]

Talmadge, making race the principal theme of his campaign, sought to convince white voters that his opposition would not defend Georgia's "way of life." He condemned Thompson for his veto of the white primary bill and accused Arnall of receiving a medal from the Southern Conference of Human Welfare for killing the white primary in Georgia. Attacking President Truman's civil rights program as "the most dangerous threat to Georgia's way of life since Reconstruction," Talmadge accused his opponents of supporting the president's reelection. Talmadge promised to fight vigorously to defend southern racial traditions. A Talmadge political advertisement bluntly stated: "HERMAN TALMADGE TAKES HIS STAND WITH THE WHITE PEOPLE."[7]

Ellis Arnall's grandfather
Henry C. Arnall. (Courtesy of Bob
Shapiro Photography, Newnan)

Sallie Wynn Arnall and her grandson, Ellis Arnall. (Courtesy of
Bob Shapiro Photography, Newnan)

The home of Ellis Arnall's parents, Joe and Bessie Arnall, 211 Jackson Street, Newnan. (Courtesy of Bob Shapiro Photography, Newnan)

Ellis and Mildred Arnall's home, 213 Jackson Street, Newnan. (Courtesy of Bob Shapiro Photography, Newnan)

Arnall kicking off his 1942 campaign at the Coweta County courthouse, July 4, 1942. (Courtesy of Special Collections Department, Georgia State University)

Above: Part of the crowd at the July 4 rally of Arnall's campaign in Newnan. (Courtesy of Special Collections Department, Georgia State University)

Arnall slicing barbeque to feed the crowd at his kickoff rally. (Courtesy of Wide World Photography)

Arnall campaigning at Cumming during the 1942 election. (Courtesy of Atlanta *Journal-Constitution*)

Arnall speaking before a partisan crowd in front of the Arch at the University of Georgia during the 1942 campaign. (Courtesy of the Atlanta *Journal-Constitution*)

Arnall delivering his inaugural address while a gloomy Eugene Talmadge listens.
(Courtesy of Atlanta *Journal-Constitution*)

Arnall accompanying President Franklin D. Roosevelt on a tour of Fort Benning
in April 1943. (Courtesy of Alvan Arnall)

Governor and Mrs. Arnall launching a liberty ship at Brunswick Shipyards during World War II. (Courtesy of Atlanta *Journal-Constitution*)

Arnall celebrating passage of the amendment in August 1943 lowering the voting age to eighteen. (Courtesy of Atlanta *Journal-Constitution*)

Arnall receiving the results of the vote ratifying the 1945 Constitution. (Courtesy of Atlanta *Journal-Constitution*)

Arnall addressing the legislature in January 1945. The three men behind Arnall are, left to right, Senator Ed Johnson, Senate President Frank C. Gross, and House Speaker Roy V. Harris. (Courtesy of Atlanta *Journal-Constitution*)

Ellis and Mildred Arnall with James M. Cox. (Courtesy of Atlanta *Journal-Constitution*)

Governor Arnall, Alice, and Alvan, Christmas 1946. (Courtesy of Atlanta *Journal-Constitution*)

Ellis and Alvan Arnall greeting Vice President Henry Wallace in Atlanta in 1946. (Courtesy of Atlanta *Journal-Constitution*)

Confrontation between Governor Arnall and Herman E. Talmadge shortly after Talmadge's legislative election as governor on January 15, 1947. (Courtesy of Atlanta *Journal-Constitution*)

Arnall giving a lecture in New York City shortly after the three-governor controversy. (Courtesy of Atlanta *Journal-Constitution*)

Arnall speaking on behalf of Governor Melvin E. Thompson in 1948 campaign. (Courtesy of Atlanta *Journal-Constitution*)

Former governor Arnall being sworn in as director of Office of Price Stabilization in 1952, with Mildred, Alvan, and Alice. (Courtesy of Atlanta *Journal-Constitution*)

Arnall as a successful Atlanta lawyer in the mid-1960s. (Courtesy of Jay:Leviton-Atlanta)

Arnall delivering a speech in Newnan at the beginning of his unsuccessful comeback effort in 1966. (Courtesy of Atlanta *Journal-Constitution*)

Arnall pressing the flesh in 1966. (Courtesy of Jay:Leviton-Atlanta)

Arnall campaigning with Atlanta mayor Ivan Allen, Jr., in 1966. (Courtesy of Jay:Leviton-Atlanta)

Arnall casting ballot in 1966. (Courtesy of Bob Shapiro Photography, Newnan)

Arnall with his first wife, Mildred, in 1966. (Courtesy of Atlanta *Journal-Constitution*)

The opposition—Eugene Talmadge. (Courtesy of Vanishing Georgia Collection, Georgia Department of Archives and History)

The opposition—Herman Eugene Talmadge. (Courtesy of Vanishing Georgia Collection, Georgia Department of Archives and History)

Arnall with his second wife, Ruby, and University of Georgia head football coach Vince Dooley. (Courtesy of Atlanta *Journal-Constitution*)

Four former governors: Herman E. Talmadge, S. Ernest Vandiver, Carl E. Sanders, Lester G. Maddox. (Courtesy of Herb Pilcher, Tifton)

Two former adversaries. (Courtesy of Atlanta *Journal-Constitution*)

Talmadge reminded Georgians of Arnall and Thompson's past association with former Vice President Wallace and their efforts to renominate Wallace in 1944. Talmadge charged that if they had been successful, Wallace would now be president "and we would have a Communist government in this country." Talmadge relished the opportunity to read excerpts from Arnall's seconding speech of Wallace at the 1944 convention. Other Talmadge spokesmen joined in the attack on Arnall's past association with Wallace.[8]

The Talmadge faction also made Arnall's national lecture tour a campaign issue. Talmadge accused Arnall of ridiculing his state for being "ignorant and backward" and "vilifying the people of Georgia who elected him to high office." On another occasion, Talmadge expressed his disgust with "seeing people honored by high office, vilifying our state." He compared Arnall's lecturing to that of "a strange bird befouling his own nest." With great enthusiasm, pro-Talmadge newspapers joined in the assault on Arnall's lecture tour. In particular, the editor of the Greensboro *Herald-Journal,* Carey Williams, Sr., who was a long-time Talmadgite, accused Arnall of having "belittled and blackened" Georgia's reputation from lecture platforms throughout the country.[9]

The *Herald-Journal*'s attack proved too much for the Atlanta *Journal,* which came to the defense of Arnall. The *Journal* charged that the allegation of Arnall's damaging the reputation of the state was a "vicious and indecent falsehood." The Greensboro *Herald-Journal* responded to the *Journal* by citing eleven specific indictments of Arnall to substantiate its allegation. The indictments included quotes from Arnall's seconding speech for Wallace, a speech in Chicago in which he said, "The so-called backwardness of the South stems from the poverty and ignorance of our people," and a speech given at Dartmouth College in which Arnall stated: "The crux of the Negro problem is the fact that the South is so anxious to keep the Negroes in the ditch that it has been in the ditch with them."[10]

The list of indictments also included Arnall's support of the pardoning of Robert Burns, Arnall's receiving a medal from the Southern Conference for Human Welfare, and a quotation from a speech given in New York City where Arnall reportedly said, "We must make this one common country without distinction between race, color, and creed." The Atlanta *Journal* retorted that the *Herald-Journal*'s indictments did not support the charge that Arnall had "belittled and blackened" the name of Georgia while on his lecture tour. Arnall also denied the allegation by declaring that "everywhere I have gone I have done everything I could to uphold the good reputation and dignity of my own state and its institutions." [11]

The Talmadge campaign sought to rally the support of the voters in the rural counties, so crucial to electoral success in the county unit system, by portraying Arnall, Rivers, and Thompson as foes of the county unit system. According to Talmadge, the trio wanted to replace the county unit system with a statewide political machine propped up by the black vote. Talmadge even claimed that a state employee with Arnall's encouragement had filed suit in 1946 against the county unit system. Talmadge further accused Arnall of expressing disappointment after the U.S. Supreme Court refused to overturn the county unit system. The future of the county unit system in Georgia, Talmadge told rural Georgians, depended on his reelection. [12]

During the campaign, Arnall made several speeches on behalf of Thompson to try to persuade voters that Thompson would continue the progress of his administration. He criticized the Talmadge faction's appealing to racial prejudice and claimed that Talmadge lacked the qualities to make a good governor. Arnall denounced his former political ally, Harris, as "the manipulator" who had told Talmadge what to do in the seizure of the governor's office in January 1947. In a radio speech broadcast statewide, Arnall criticized the effort to make Talmadge governor on the basis of the write-in votes as a "dirty, black, nauseating scheme." Arnall responded to the allegation that he had damaged the state's reputation by declaring that "Herman, the puppet, has done more to disgrace and discredit our state than any living Georgian." [13]

Despite the unification of the anti-Talmadge faction, Talmadge won the primary, carrying 130 counties. However, only forty-five thousand popular votes separated the two candidates out of almost seven hundred thousand cast. Several factors accounted for this crucial Talmadge victory. Talmadge proved to be a capable campaigner who retained his father's political support while gaining support from voters who had opposed his father. Thompson proved not to be in the same league as a campaigner as Talmadge, Rivers, and Arnall. In addition, many Georgians who were not Talmadgites disagreed with the state's highest court decision removing Talmadge from office in 1947 and voted for Talmadge for that reason. Even though Thompson attempted to disassociate himself from Truman's civil rights program, Talmadge successfully portrayed Thompson as weak in maintaining the southern way of life. While Thompson campaigned on a record of providing expanded services, Talmadge's campaign emphasized race, and in 1948, racial feelings far outweighed economic consideration among most white voters.[14]

While Arnall had again suffered defeat by a Talmadge, his efforts in the 1948 presidential election proved to be more fruitful. Southern dissatisfaction over Truman's liberal stance on race led to the creation of the States' Rights party, which ran a presidential candidate in 1948. Liberal dissatisfaction with President Truman's foreign policy led to former vice president Wallace's entering the race as the candidate of a third party. In February 1948 Arnall announced that he was a loyal Democrat and would support President Truman. He dismissed the southern opposition as not strong enough to deny Truman renomination. Arnall strongly opposed Wallace's third-party effort, believing liberals could be more effective by remaining in the Democratic party. Arnall conceded that Truman was "not an attractive candidate" and was not perceived as a strong leader. Nevertheless, Arnall believed Truman, a typical American, was electable because Americans "are very likely to vote for one of themselves."[15]

While Arnall's presidential candidate returned to the Oval Office, Talmadge reassumed gubernatorial power and was faced with a difficult choice of either curtailing services or increasing taxes. Talmadge had given his pledge of never raising state taxes without the prior approval of the people in a referendum. Unfortunately for Talmadge, the voters overwhelmingly rejected a tax increase in a referendum in April 1949. Talmadge, refusing to cut state services, called a special legislative session to increase the state excise taxes and corporate property tax. The $23 million tax increase came under substantial criticism and loomed as a potential campaign issue if Talmadge sought reelection in 1950. Other potential problems for Talmadge included reports of a drinking problem as well as failures to keep office appointments and speaking engagements. The Talmadge administration also drew criticism for inadequately funding state services. Harris, along with many leaders in the education and business communities, pressured Talmadge to support a sales tax to adequately pay for state services.[16]

With a rising tide of problems for Talmadge, some observers saw Arnall entering the 1950 governor's race. A reporter for the Atlanta *Journal* wrote in July 1949 that "capitol gossipers are touting him [Arnall] as the gubernatorial candidate of the anti-Talmadge faction." The following month, Arnall told reporters that the people had called him to rid the state of Talmadgeism once before and that "if they want me to do the job again, I will be very happy to try." Arnall believed that Talmadge could be beaten with the violation of his pledge not to raise taxes as his greatest political liability.[17]

Interestingly, a question of eligibility loomed over the potential candidacy of Talmadge in 1950. The state constitution stipulated that a governor could not succeed himself "until after the expiration of four years from the conclusion of his term of office." Could Talmadge, elected to complete his father's term, seek reelection in 1950? Before the 1948 primary, Attorney General Cook issued an unofficial opinion in response to an inquiry from the Associated Press. Cook held that the governor elected in 1948 could not seek reelection in 1950 because that individual would hold the position of governor, not acting governor, and therefore would be limited by the constitutional ban prohibiting gubernatorial succession. Without Talmadge in the race in 1950, the chances of the anti-Talmadge faction regaining the governorship seemed excellent for the first time since 1942. Talmadge, however, had no intention of quietly accepting Cook's opinion, for he had no doubts as to his eligibility. Conceding that a governor was not eligible to succeed himself after serving a four-year term of office, Talmadge argued that he had not served a four-year term but had simply completed a portion of his father's term.[18]

Arnall's potential candidacy also presented a possible eligibility question. In the three governor controversy, Arnall had served five days beyond his four-year term. Because of this, some observers believed that the state constitution prevented Arnall from seeking the governorship in 1950. Early in January 1950 Arnall requested an opinion from Attorney General Cook to resolve the question of his eligibility. Arnall's request drew an immediate response from the pro-Talmadge Savannah *Morning News:* "The Plumed Knight of Georgia . . . is throwing his lance of ambition at the gubernatorial target once more!"[19]

Talmadge responded to Arnall's request by stating that Cook could not render an opinion to a private citizen unless requested to do so by the governor. Again asserting he had no doubts concerning his eligibility, Talmadge refused to ask the attorney general for an opinion. He accused his opposition of being so desperate that they would do anything to keep voters from having the opportunity to vote for him in 1950. Arnall retorted that the governor was "advocating illegality and constitutional violation" just like he had in the three governor controversy. Arnall called on Tal-

madge to settle the issue by requesting a ruling from Cook. Several newspapers also urged such a course of action for Talmadge.[20]

At the moment the anti-Talmadgites appeared to have the upper hand.
If Cook ruled on the question again, they had every reason to believe he
would adhere to his reasoning in his 1948 opinion. The Talmadgites considered Cook part of the anti-Talmadge faction since he had served three years
as Arnall's revenue commissioner and had been appointed to the position
of attorney general by Arnall. In addition, it had been Cook who ruled
prior to the 1947 legislative session that the legislature lacked the authority
to elect a governor. Talmadge could ignore an adverse Cook opinion as he
had in 1947, but such a response would provide the anti-Talmadge faction
with a major issue to use against him.[21]

While Georgians mulled over the controversy, Talmadge made an unex-
pected move. On January 9, 1950, the governor reversed his earlier position
by requesting an opinion from Cook on the eligibility of Arnall and himself. The following day, Cook held that both Arnall and Talmadge were
eligible. Cook upheld Talmadge's eligibility by contending that Talmadge
had never qualified for nor held a four-year term. The attorney general upheld Arnall's eligibility because four years had elapsed since he last held the
office of governor. Cook based his change of mind on two factors. First, he
cited a superior court judge's ruling in 1949 contrary to his 1948 opinion.
He also cited a 1949 Georgia Supreme Court decision in favor of a liberal
construction of eligibility for public office. Clearly Cook had reversed himself on the eligibility of Talmadge to seek the governorship in 1950. Arnall
believed his former revenue commissioner did so in order to seek reelection
in 1950 unopposed by a Talmadge candidate, though Talmadge denied any
deal was made with Cook.[22]

In the aftermath of the opinion, the Macon *Telegraph* urged Arnall to
enter the race as the candidate of "forward-thinking Georgians." It was
time, the *Telegraph* concluded, for patrons of good, progressive government to reunite. Unfortunately for such patrons, Thompson, without consulting anyone else, announced his candidacy for the governorship on January 28, 1950. The Atlanta *Constitution* responded by calling Thompson's
entry, "Fustest with the Leastest." Despite Thompson's entry, the Macon
Telegraph still urged Arnall to enter because "he has the best record of
any recent Georgia governor and that he will again make an outstanding
chief executive." On learning of Thompson's decision, Arnall said that it

"wouldn't do to print" his reaction. Thompson's entry into the race without consulting the leadership of the anti-Talmadge faction irritated Arnall. Several days later Arnall announced that he would not be a candidate in the 1950 gubernatorial primary. He attributed his decision to "political and personal reasons" and added that he would not actively support any candidate in the race.[23]

The Macon *News* expressed regret over Arnall's decision, contending that he would have made "an excellent governor" again, though the *News* concluded, "Ellis Arnall is too progressive and thus too vulnerable to his political enemies." The Albany *Herald* speculated that three major factors derailed an Arnall candidacy—Talmadge's political strength, Arnall's liberalism, and the split within the anti-Talmadge ranks. The Savannah *Morning News* believed Arnall's decision could be traced to his desire to continue his lucrative law practice as well as to continue as head of the Independent Movie Producers of America. Jack Tarver, associate editor of the Atlanta *Constitution,* agreed that Arnall did not want to give up a profitable career. Arnall later claimed that this was the reason he declined to enter the 1950 race.[24]

The Savannah *Morning News,* however, attributed Arnall's decision to the realization that he could not win with the division in the anti-Talmadge faction. Although Talmadge entered the campaign with major political liabilities, Arnall had some heavy political baggage as well. If he entered, the Talmadgites would resurrect the old charges they used against him in 1948—his liberalism, his support of Wallace and Truman, his liberal views on race, his alleged degradation of Georgia from the lecture platform, his association with Rivers, his alleged opposition to the county unit system, and his role in ending the white primary in Georgia.[25]

Even if Thompson could be persuaded to withdraw, Rivers remained as a potential candidate. After Arnall declined to run, Rivers offered himself as the best anti-Talmadge candidate. When Thompson made no effort to withdraw, Rivers, claiming that Talmadge couldn't be defeated by a divided opposition, declined to enter the race. Rivers, like Arnall, refused to support Thompson and eventually supported Talmadge and even introduced him to a Talmadge rally in Columbus as the state's next governor. In addition, Rivers quietly worked to persuade local politicians to support Talmadge. Despite the desertion of the two key leaders of the anti-Talmadge faction, Thompson ran a surprisingly strong campaign. He favored a 2 percent sales tax to finance an expansion of state services and vigorously attacked the Talmadge record. Talmadge nevertheless won convincingly in the county unit vote even though he led Thompson by only eighty-five hundred popular votes. Some even questioned whether all the Thompson votes had been counted. Thompson accused Harris of stealing at least fifty counties from him, but Harris claimed that "it wasn't more than thirty-five."[26]

Arnall's self-imposed silence about state politics ended in 1951 when he expressed his views on the state's sales tax, which had recently been enacted by the legislature. The 3 percent tax had been hailed as a progressive step forward by some, but Arnall denounced it as a "shackle on the state." He predicted the governor chosen in 1954 would be someone who had advocated its repeal or modification. The Atlanta *Journal* called Arnall's remarks unfortunate, claiming the tax allowed for improved state services. Arnall responded to the editorial by pointing out that the voters had overwhelmingly rejected the tax in a referendum in 1949. Contending the tax was regressive in nature, Arnall called for its modification or repeal and predicted it would be the major issue in the 1954 primary.[27]

Arnall's political attention turned to presidential politics in 1952. Even though President Truman was unpopular in Georgia, Arnall remained a firm supporter of Truman and favored the president's reelection. Early in January 1952 Arnall wrote the president, "I admire you sincerely as a wonderful guy and a great American!" Later in January Arnall visited Truman in the White House and told reporters afterward that he believed the president would seek reelection. The following month Arnall predicted the voters would reelect Truman. After Truman decided not to seek reelection, Arnall undertook an eight-state speaking campaign on behalf of the Democratic presidential nominee, Adlai E. Stevenson. Arnall was so confident of a Stevenson victory that he told Ralph McGill that he bet five thousand dollars on Stevenson's victory. When Truman hit the campaign trail on behalf of Stevenson, Arnall telegraphed the president, "The ball started rolling when you hit the campaign trail." Arnall praised Truman for doing his best for the unsuccessful campaign and wired him, "I admire you more than ever."[28]

Early in 1953 Arnall received mention as a possible gubernatorial candidate in 1954. His numerous speaking engagements to civic clubs throughout the state during this period did nothing to dispel such rumors. Among other things, he called for higher teachers' salaries, urged greater financial support for education, complained of the "unjust" sales tax, and criticized the operation of the state merit system. As the year progressed, Arnall became increasingly critical of Talmadge's handling of the state's financial affairs. In August 1953 he complained of the "mess" state finances were in even though the state had its highest income in history. He even suggested that there was talk in the Talmadge administration of selling valuable state property to provide revenue to resolve the state's financial problems. Governor Talmadge angrily denied Arnall's allegation that the state was considering such action to get out of financial trouble. In fact, Talmadge declared that the state had a surplus. Arnall responded by claiming his attacks had "successfully torpedoed the infamous plot" to sell off the state-owned property. He called for "sounder and more business-like policies" to be applied to the state's budgetary process to replace the faulty financial policies of the Talmadge administration, which he accused of being wasteful and extravagant.[29]

In September 1953 Arnall provided another reason to believe he would enter the 1954 primary. In response to a question in a WSB-TV program, Arnall replied, "I am in politics up to my neck, and I am going to run for something." Earlier in the year, Arnall had publicly reminded Talmadge that no outgoing governor had ever been able to name his successor. Arnall predicted there would be only two candidates—one representing the Talmadge faction and one representing the anti-Talmadge faction—in the upcoming primary. He further predicted the major issues to be the sales tax and the extravagance of the Talmadge administration.[30]

Despite his prediction, neither the sales tax nor alleged Talmadge extravagances were major issues in 1954. While the sales tax's unpopularity had faded in light of the increased state services it provided, Talmadge's popularity reached an all time high as he neared the end of his term. If Arnall ran in 1954, he would have a problem of explaining his long-time opposition to a tax that most Georgians had accepted and to a man who was one of the state's most popular governors.[31]

Arnall's prediction that only two candidates would enter the 1954 primary proved inaccurate as well. Nine candidates eventually paid their qualifying fees. Since Talmadge could not succeed himself, an unprecedented fight occurred in the Talmadge faction over gubernatorial succession with three Talmadgites—Lieutenant Governor Griffin, House Speaker Frederick B. Hand, and Agriculture Commissioner Linder—entering the race. The division in the Talmadge faction provided an opportunity to elect an anti-Talmadge candidate if the anti-Talmadgites could rally behind one candidate. However, two anti-Talmadge candidates, former acting governor Thompson and state Representative Charles Gowen, qualified.[32]

In addition to the popular acceptance of the sales tax and the disunity in the anti-Talmadge faction, another factor, perhaps the most important, hindered an Arnall candidacy in 1954. Several months prior to the primary, the U.S. Supreme Court ruled that segregation in the public schools was unconstitutional. All other issues in the upcoming primary proved to be secondary to the issue of which candidate could best protect segregation. Since the days of Eugene Talmadge, the Talmadge faction had claimed the role of defender of white supremacy. Arnall had successfully used the university system accreditation issue to impede Eugene Talmadge's white supremacist campaign, but he had no such issue to deflect the explosive race issue in 1954. While Arnall's liberal reputation precluded him from being considered as the defender of segregation in the eyes of many Georgians, Talmadge's popularity and the *Brown v. Board of Education* decision made the Talmadge faction's candidate an almost certain winner. Therefore Arnall decided not to enter the 1954 race and remained inactive in it except to appear on the same platform with Thompson at a political rally in Newnan. Griffin won the primary after convincing enough voters of his ability to defend segregation and the county unit system from their foes. The lieutenant governor, who supposedly received behind-the-scenes support from Talmadge, won the nomination with only 36 percent of the popular vote.[33]

Later in 1954 Arnall emerged from political obscurity long enough to declare that he was not "out of politics" and that he would reenter the political arena at some future date. Arnall then faded from the political scene until the 1958 gubernatorial primary. In that election Lieutenant Governor S. Ernest Vandiver entered the campaign as the favorite of most Georgians and the political establishment. He had served as Talmadge's campaign manager in 1948 and had spent six years as Talmadge's adjutant general. His close personal and political association with Talmadge and the fact that he was Senator Russell's nephew-in-law made him a formidable candidate. In April 1958 Arnall denied reports that he would enter the race and let it be known that he would support Vandiver's candidacy. In June, however, Arnall revealed that he had been urged by friends to reconsider entering the race. Admitting that he had not yet made up his mind, Arnall believed the people wanted "constructive and dedicated leadership." Several days later, though, Arnall announced his reluctant decision not to seek the governorship. He cited a lack of time necessary to organize an effective statewide campaign as the reason for his decision.[34]

Vandiver ran on a platform promising that the public schools of Georgia would not be desegregated in his administration. Like his predecessors, Talmadge and Griffin, Vandiver threatened to close the public schools rather than to permit them to be integrated. While Talmadge and Griffin never had to consider such a drastic step, Vandiver did. A federal district court ordered the desegregation of the public schools in Atlanta in Vandiver's first year in office. Although the court delayed implementation of the order, a controversy over desegregation raged throughout the state. Massive resistance legislation, which had been enacted in the aftermath of the *Brown* decision, provided for the closing of any public school that was desegregated.[35]

However, the political and business leadership of Atlanta, fearing the economic repercussions of closing the schools, supported keeping their schools open even if they were desegregated. Amid the growing controversy, Arnall took a strong stand in favor of keeping the state's public schools open. He threatened to enter the 1962 gubernatorial primary if the public schools were closed and if no candidate came forth to fight to reopen them. While stating a belief in segregated schools, Arnall declared that the schools should be kept open with as much segregation as possible. In order to achieve such a goal, he favored a pupil placement law, local option on closing schools, and state grants-in-aid to allow students to attend private schools. "If the schools are kept open," Arnall declared, "there is no reason I should re-enter the arena of politics." Arnall warned that the closing of Georgia's public schools would create the greatest mass unemployment in the state's history with thousands of teachers and other school employees unemployed while one million school children stayed at home.[36]

James S. Peters, long-time Talmadge supporter and chairman of the State Board of Education, realized the political consequences of closing the public schools. On December 30, 1959, he wrote a letter to Roy Harris, the foremost opponent of desegregation in the Talmadge faction. Peters predicted that "Ellis and the proponents" of integration would attempt to get the federal courts to integrate the schools in 1961 hoping to force Governor Vandiver to carry out his promise of closing the schools. Peters warned that if the schools were closed, Arnall could campaign on the promise of reopening them and, "we would lose control of the government and entrench Ellis Arnall and the integrationists in the control of the government for decades to come." Harris rejected the possibility of Arnall's returning to the governorship championing open schools, contending that "no human agency can breathe life into his body." In the aftermath of the Peters letter, Arnall reiterated his intention to run for governor if the schools were closed. He reminded Georgians of his election in 1942 on a school issue and declared that this "issue is a much bigger one and much more vital than the 1942 issue."[37]

Perhaps realizing that integration was inevitable, Governor Vandiver accepted the idea of a special committee to hold hearings throughout Georgia to determine the people's wishes toward closing the schools. The committee, chaired by John A. Sibley, held hearings in every congressional district. It recommended the repealing of the massive resistance laws and the adoption of a local option policy allowing each school district to determine whether its schools remained open. At the urging of Governor Vandiver the legislature adopted most of the recommendations of the Sibley committee, which led to the collapse of the resistance movement in Georgia. In May 1961 Arnall announced that he would not run for governor in 1962. In addition, Arnall claimed that his active legal career precluded him from entering the race.[38]

At the same time Arnall threatened to reenter state politics to save the public schools, he also challenged the political establishment's sacred cow —the county unit system of nominating state officials. The nominating system, which was enacted into state law in 1917, ensured rural domination of state politics. Arnall pointed out that while the state was predominantly urban, the county unit system denied the majority of the population an effective voice in nominating state officials. The former governor warned of legal challenges to correct an unjustifiable situation. Arnall even implied that he would file suit himself. While Arnall never did, opponents of the system successfully challenged it in the federal district court in 1962. After declining to enter the 1962 primary, Arnall urged Carl E. Sanders, a young state senator from Augusta, to run for governor against Marvin Griffin's comeback effort. In the midst of the campaign, a federal district court invalidated the county unit system. Sanders overwhelmed Griffin in the 1962 primary. In the same election, voters returned Talmadge to the U.S. Senate for a second term. Interestingly, the first contribution that Talmadge received for his reelection campaign, a five hundred dollar check, came from Arnall.[39]

The years between 1947 and 1962 proved to be difficult years for Arnall in state politics. He witnessed the demise of the anti-Talmadge faction and the emergence of his major political adversary, Herman Talmadge, as the dominant power on the state's political scene. Although receiving mention as a possible candidate in each gubernatorial election held during this time period, Arnall always declined to reenter the arena of electoral politics. A highly successful legal and business career deprived Arnall of the necessary time to engineer a political comeback. Unlike the situation in 1942, Arnall never again had the opportunity to run as the sole candidate of the anti-Talmadge faction. He had witnessed firsthand the devastating effect that a division of the anti-Talmadge vote could have. The collapse of the anti-Talmadge faction in the mid-1950s further undermined Arnall's chances for a political comeback. With each passing year, Arnall's grass-roots contacts, so essential to success in the county unit system, became fewer and fewer. Increased racial tensions in the aftermath of the *Brown* decision also worked against someone of Arnall's liberal reputation among the conservative white rural voters whose support was essential for electoral success under the malapportioned county unit system. The fact that Arnall favored the abolishment of the county unit system had not endeared him to the voters in the rural counties. Nor could Arnall ignore the strength of the powerful Talmadge organization that could be expected to oppose an Arnall candidacy. In May 1961 Arnall, taking into account these numerous obstacles to a political comeback, declared that he would never seek public office again.[40]

14

. . . .

Arnall's

. . . .

Last

. . . .

Hurrah

. . . .

In July 1965 Ellis Arnall once again became a candidate for his state's highest office. Much had changed in Georgia's political environment since Arnall's first campaign for governor twenty-three years earlier. The major bulwarks of the politics of the 1940s—the county unit system, segregation, and black disfranchisement—had collapsed under the pressure of federal intervention. Another landmark of the political old order—Democratic party dominance in national and state elections—faced a growing threat from the Republican party. A Republican presidential candidate actually carried the state in 1964—an event that had never happened before. The Republicans looked to the 1966 election as a golden opportunity to gain control of the governorship, an office that had not been held by a Republican since Reconstruction. Clearly, a political and social upheaval had ushered in a new era for the state.[1]

The most significant change in state politics had been the invalidation of the county unit system of nominating Democratic state office holders by the federal judiciary. The system maximized the influence of rural and small-town residents who were the state's most conservative voters. Each county had unit votes in proportion to representation in the state's malapportioned House of Representatives. By 1960 the eight largest populated counties had 41.3 percent of the state's population but cast only 12 percent of the county unit vote. In contrast, the 121 least populated counties had only 32 percent of the state's population but cast 59 percent of the state's unit votes. For urban residents of Georgia, the county unit system had become intolerable and an obstacle to majority rule government on the state level. The system assured a dwindling rural population of dominance in politics in a state that by 1960 had more urban than rural residents.[2]

Urban citizens had been unsuccessfully challenging the county unit system in the federal courts since the end of World War II. A U.S. Supreme Court decision in 1962, which held that apportionment was a federal constitutional issue, revived the hopes of those opposed to the system. Once again opponents sought to overturn the system in federal court. After a federal district court invalidated the county unit system in April 1962, the state Democratic party's executive committee voted to conduct the 1962 Democratic primary on a popular vote basis. Thus, for the first time since 1908, the voters had the power to determine the outcome of a state primary election on the basis of popular votes. Under such circumstances 1962 seemed an ideal time for the progressive Arnall, whose greatest political strength would be among urban voters, to seek the governorship. State senator Carl E. Sanders, Jr., however, had already entered the campaign as the progressive candidate. In addition, Arnall claimed a busy law practice prevented his undertaking a gubernatorial campaign in 1962.[3]

Sanders, a youthful, handsome, and articulate candidate, ran as a racial moderate who was committed to economic progress, educational improvement, and industrial development. While the older and less physically attractive Marvin Griffin campaigned as the defender of the rural old order, he also had to defend his previous administration against charges of corruption. One historian described the campaign as one in which a "traditional rural-oriented, race-baiting former governor" competed against a "more sophisticated urban-oriented proponent of the new politics." The "new politics" prevailed and Sanders overwhelmed Griffin with 58 percent of the popular vote. Sanders ran well throughout Georgia and would have won even if the county unit system had still been in place, but his greatest support came from the urban-suburban counties.[4]

In addition to the loss of the county unit system, the old regime suffered another crippling blow when the federal judiciary overturned segregation in the public schools. Although the Supreme Court had ruled segregation in state-supported educational systems to be unconstitutional in 1954, Georgia avoided school desegregation until 1961. In that year, a federal district judge ordered the admission of two black students to the University of Georgia. Governor Vandiver, who had won the governorship in 1958 with a pledge to maintain segregated schools, had to choose between closing the university or desegregating it. He chose the latter course.[5]

Shortly thereafter, the Atlanta public schools became the first school system in the state to be desegregated. The pace of desegregation proved to be exceedingly slow. The Civil Rights Act of 1964, though, increased the rate of desegregation by denying federal funds to segregated school systems. The Department of Health, Education, and Welfare drew up desegregation guidelines, which southern school systems had to comply with in order to receive federal funds. The Civil Rights Act of 1964 also authorized the U.S. attorney general to file desegregation suits. By 1966 almost 10 percent of the black students in Georgia attended desegregated schools.[6]

Even before school desegregation, many white Georgians had uneasily watched as the number of black voters steadily increased. Blacks had been legally disfranchised in Georgia since the turn of the century. As late as 1940 only an estimated ten thousand blacks appeared on the state's voting rolls. During the Arnall administration, however, the federal judiciary removed a major obstacle to black voting—the Democratic party's white primary. After this action, the number of black voters increased to over 130,000 in 1946 and had grown to 270,000 by 1964. In the aftermath of the Voting Rights Act of 1965, the number of black voters in Georgia increased to 289,545, a number that constituted 17 percent of the state's electorate in 1966.[7]

As the number of blacks voting in Georgia continued to rise, so did the number of Georgians voting Republican. The Republican party had not experienced significant electoral success in either the South or Georgia until the post–World War II period. The election of 1952, with Dwight D. Eisenhower running as the Republican presidential candidate, established the Republican party as the respectable party among the affluent urban and suburban whites in the South. In the 1964 election Barry M. Goldwater became the first Republican presidential candidate to make the South a major factor in his electoral strategy to gain the presidency. Goldwater's conservatism, his vote against the Civil Rights Act of 1964, and his states' rights platform appealed to conservative southern Democrats. Such prominent conservative Georgia Democrats as Marvin Griffin, Lester Maddox, and Roy Harris supported Goldwater's candidacy. A coalition of white voters in the black belt and in south Georgia, affluent white urbanites, and lower socioeconomic urban whites gave Goldwater 54 percent of the vote in Georgia.[8]

In addition, voters in the state's Third Congressional District chose a Republican, Howard Hollis "Bo" Callaway, to represent them in the U.S.

House of Representatives. Callaway's father had been placed on the Board of Regents by Arnall and had chaired the agriculture panel of the governor's Agricultural and Industrial Board. The younger Callaway became the first Republican to represent the state in the nation's lower house in ninety-two years. A confident Georgia Republican party looked toward the 1966 gubernatorial election as an opportunity to forge a new political order based on the conservative coalition that had supported Goldwater in the 1964 election.[9]

In the aftermath of the substantial changes that had occurred in Georgia since Arnall had left the governor's office, it seemed appropriate that one of Georgia's most progressive governors would seek the state's highest office again. Arnall believed that the times had finally caught up with the views he had expressed two decades earlier. "Everything I advocated," he remarked in March 1964, "was called treasonable at the time and now every one of these things is accepted." Arnall maintained that he finally decided to become a candidate because, "Many of the reforms that I had advocated had come about, such as the right of the black people to vote and first-class citizenship for all of our people. I thought that would be a tremendous voting strength for me." In addition, Arnall believed his successful legal career and business endeavors had allowed him to make "enough money to where I could afford the luxury of getting back into politics."[10]

Arnall faced an electorate in 1966 that had changed significantly since 1942. Then, blacks had been denied the right to vote in Democratic party primaries and the county unit system minimized the more progressive urban vote, allowing the conservative rural and small-town voters to dominate the gubernatorial electoral process. Gubernatorial hopefuls in 1966 had to contend with a substantially different political landscape. The electorate consisted of three large blocs of voters—the conservatives, progressives, and liberals. The conservative coalition consisted principally of the rural and small-town whites, the lower-status urban whites, and the white town residents of south Georgia and the black belt. These voters, making up about 45 percent of the state's electorate, tended to be segregationist in race relations, provincial in outlook, and fundamentalist in religion. They had been most supportive of abandoning public education rather than desegregating their schools. The conservative coalition had consistently supported the Talmadge faction and had enthusiastically backed Goldwater in 1964. The conservatives had been the most staunch defenders in the old regime and had dominated state politics under the county unit system. Even though the unit system had been invalidated, the conservative voters still exercised a great deal of influence in the state politics since they remained the largest bloc of voters in the state.[11]

The other two blocs of voters, the progressives and the liberals, made up about 55 percent of the state's electorate. The progressives, numbering about 30 percent of the state's electorate in the 1960s, consisted primarily of upper-class whites in the state's fifteen urban-suburban counties and in the thirteen town counties of north Georgia. Progressives supported keeping the public schools open, favored economic and civic progress, supported limited government regulation, and favored expanded state services. The liberals, numbering about 25 percent of the state's electorate, consisted primarily of blacks. They held many of the views of the progressives, but also favored school desegregation, supported the federal government's social-welfare programs, and had consistently opposed the Talmadge faction. The liberals and progressives had been least supportive of the old regime. It had been Sanders's strong support from these two blocs of voters, with the backing of many conservatives, that had allowed him to overwhelm Griffin in 1962. In order to win in 1966 Arnall had to run an exceptionally strong race among the liberals and progressives as well as to appeal to the conservatives as Sanders did in 1962.[12]

Arnall's comeback effort faced formidable opposition from former governor Ernest Vandiver, who also wished to return to the governor's office. Vandiver, who left the governorship in 1963, had been prevented from succeeding himself because of the same constitutional prohibition that had denied Arnall a consecutive term. Vandiver appeared early to be the leading candidate in the 1966 gubernatorial campaign. He planned to campaign as a conservative who provided honest and efficient government. Although he had not carried out his pledge to maintain segregated schools, Vandiver believed that he had left office with the public's general approval of the way he handled the desegregation crisis. A poll commissioned by Vandiver in May 1966 indicated that 70 percent of the electorate favored his return to the governor's office. As a well-liked former governor, relative of Senator Russell, and close political associate of Senator Talmadge, Vandiver presented a serious threat to Arnall's comeback effort.[13]

After announcing his candidacy in July 1965, Arnall decided to engage in a vigorous campaign to cut into the commanding lead held by Vandiver. He raised the issue that Vandiver "got elected by lying to the people about how he would prevent integration." Arnall called him a fool for promising to maintain school segregation in his 1958 campaign when he knew that he couldn't carry out that commitment. Arnall attacked Vandiver's claim that taxes had not increased in his administration as "an unadulterated and unmitigated lie" and accused Vandiver of having "one of the most disgraceful records a governor had ever had." In addition, Arnall criticized Vandiver's association with the Louisville and Nashville Railroad Company. He maintained that the state's effort to force the L&N to pay taxes on profits made from its lease of the state-owned Western and Atlantic Railroad ceased when Vandiver became governor. Arnall accused Vandiver of receiving a retainer of thirty thousand dollars per year from the L&N for protecting its interests. Finally, Arnall claimed that Vandiver, while governor, had the route of Interstate 85 changed in order for it to go through his farm near Lavonia. Upset by Arnall's attacks, Vandiver viewed Arnall's bitter campaign against him as an effort to destroy his "image of being honest." [14]

With Arnall trying to cut into Vandiver's commanding lead in the race, a former restaurateur, Lester G. Maddox, announced his entry in the governor's race. Maddox, an outspoken segregationist, based his candidacy on the theme of "constitutional government, free enterprise, God, liberty, and Americanism." Most observers considered Maddox's candidacy a joke. Herman Talmadge observed that prior to 1966 any person who seriously predicted a political future for Maddox would have received a psychiatric examination. Nevertheless, the feisty segregationist entered the primary as one of the South's best-known white supremacists at a time of upheaval in race relations in Georgia.[15]

Born into a low-income blue collar family, Maddox grew up in borderline poverty in Atlanta. Maddox dropped out of school in the tenth grade to work full time to help support his father's family, which included seven children. A firm believer in the work ethic, he finally achieved his longtime goal of owning his own business with the opening of Lester's Grill in 1947. Maddox had never held public office and had the image of being an extremist on the race issue. His interest in politics lead to unsuccessful bids for mayor of Atlanta in 1957 and 1961. The coalition of blacks and affluent whites that dominated Atlanta politics turned back his bids for the mayor's office.[16]

A determined Maddox ran an unsuccessful campaign for lieutenant governor in 1962 against a conservative who portrayed Maddox as an extremist. Nevertheless, Maddox, with little money and no political backing, gained statewide recognition from his unsuccessful race. Two years later Maddox staunchly opposed President Lyndon B. Johnson's candidacy and joined with Gray and Griffin to organize Democrats for Goldwater. He made national headlines with his adamant opposition to the public accommodation section of the Civil Rights Act of 1964. Shortly after the passage of the law, several blacks attempted to desegregate Maddox's restaurant only to be turned away by a gun-toting Maddox. Under federal court order to desegregate, Maddox sold his restaurant and shortly thereafter announced his candidacy for governor. Ironically, Arnall enlisted a mutual friend of his and Maddox to encourage the segregationist to enter the race, seeing Maddox's candidacy as a means of dividing the conservative vote.[17]

Normally the struggle over the governorship would have been settled in the Democratic primary. However, the Republican party posed a threat to Democratic control of that office in 1966. Congressman Callaway became the Republican gubernatorial nominee and gained the endorsement of former governor Griffin. With less than a month before the Democratic primary deadline, it appeared that the conservative Callaway would face either Vandiver, Arnall, or Maddox in the general election. On May 18, 1966, however, Vandiver suddenly withdrew from the campaign on the advice of his physician. Vandiver had suffered a heart attack in 1960 and had recently experienced frequent attacks of angina pectoris. Vandiver pled with Talmadge to enter the race in order to deny Arnall or Maddox the governorship. While Talmadge seriously considered entering the race, he finally decided to remain in the Senate.[18]

With Vandiver and Talmadge out of the race, the owner of the Albany *Herald,* James H. Gray, Sr., entered as the candidate of the Talmadge organization and the conservative alternative to a liberal Arnall. He received the support of Vandiver, Talmadge, Harris, and some key leaders of the Talmadge organization. The Massachusetts-born Gray, who had moved to Albany after World War II, espoused a conservative and segregationist point of view and had supported the Talmadge faction in Georgia politics. Gray had served as chairman of the state party in the Vandiver administration but had publicly disagreed with Vandiver's handling of the school desegregation issue. He had supported Griffin's campaign in 1962 and had been a staunch supporter of Goldwater in 1964. Prior to 1966 Gray had neither held nor sought an elective public position.[19]

Another conservative, Garland T. Byrd, also entered the primary. He had been a supporter of Governor Herman Talmadge while serving in

the legislature and had held an appointive position in the Talmadge administration. Byrd later served as lieutenant governor during the Vandiver
administration. Despite such an association, Byrd's candidacy lacked the
support of the Talmadge organization, perhaps due to his reputation of
being a loser. He had lost a congressional race to Callaway in 1964, had
been defeated earlier in a bid for the office of commissioner of agriculture,
and had dropped out of the 1962 governor's race.[20]

At the last moment state senator James E. Carter, Jr., who had served
two terms in the state's upper house, entered the race. He had previously
announced his candidacy for the congressional seat held by Callaway. After
Vandiver withdrew from the campaign, however, Carter switched to the
gubernatorial race, believing he could best unite the factions of the Democratic party and beat Callaway. Carter rejected classification as the candidate of any faction or political ideology. During the campaign, he called
himself a "middle-of-the-roader." Several state senators who encouraged
Carter to get into the race saw him as a moderate alternative to the other
candidates.[21]

With the withdrawal of Vandiver, Arnall assumed the position of front-
runner in the Democratic primary. He vigorously campaigned on a pledge
to provide dynamic leadership to "move Georgia ahead." Reminding Georgians that once before he had provided such leadership, Arnall emphasized
his record as governor and proposed a platform of action to "move Georgia forward into the 21st Century." As he had in 1942, Arnall emphasized
education in his campaign. He promised to establish a quality education
program that included increasing teachers' salaries beyond the national
average, expanding the university system, improving teacher retirement
benefits, enlarging the state's vocational educational program, improving
the remedial education programs, establishing academies for gifted students, and creating a statewide kindergarten program. In addition, he
promised to improve the state's mental health program, to create state cen-
ters for the treatment of alcoholism, and to build state retirement homes
for the elderly if the private sector failed to keep up with the need.[22]

Other planks in his platform included writing a new constitution, reorganizing and modernizing state government, revising the state's tax system,
increasing the number of state recreation facilities, expanding the State
Ports Authority, and strengthening the state's Veterans' Service Program.
He promised to support a rapid transit system for Atlanta, establish home
rule for local governments, provide more state assistance for dealing with

urban problems, create new sources of revenue for local governments, and lead a program to ensure greater industrial and economic growth. Arnall assured Georgians that, if elected, he would move the state forward "with a program so dynamic, so exciting, so vigorous, that it will capture the imagination of the entire nation." While the other candidates also promised improvement in state services, Arnall contended that he could "best move our state forward with vigor."[23]

Arnall's candidacy enjoyed several advantages. According to the political editor of the Atlanta *Journal*, about three-quarters of the state's daily and weekly newspapers endorsed Arnall's comeback effort. Arnall had strong support from the black community, labor unions, financial interests, and educational groups. Sam Caldwell, a former state commissioner of labor, observed, "Probably, no other campaign has ever produced a candidate with a more powerful show of strength than Ellis Arnall displayed in 1966." Arnall also had the financial resources to run a vigorous campaign. He stated during the campaign, "Whatever it takes in time, money, and effort, we're going to win." Arnall spent over a million dollars of his own money to finance his campaign and borrowed another million as well, making his candidacy one of the best financed in the race. A vigorous campaigner, Arnall enjoyed politics and considered it fun. By the end of August, Arnall had made almost eight hundred speeches in his quest for the nomination. One political observer dubbed him the "Happy Warrior" of Georgia politics who "leaves aides half his age gasping for breath or pleading urgent business back at the air-conditioned hotel." Arnall had no doubts as to his ability to lead, with Eugene Patterson, editor of the Atlanta *Constitution*, observing that Arnall possessed a "monumental self-confidence even for a politician."[24]

Arnall, who had consistently supported the national Democratic party throughout his political career, refused to downplay his loyalty to it in spite of its growing unpopularity in the state. Unlike other southern politicians who were distancing themselves from the national party, Arnall boldly proclaimed, "I am a local Democrat, and a state Democrat, and a national Democrat, and anyone who doesn't like it can go to hell." The former governor conceded that he did not agree with everything that the Democratic party did, but he emphasized that no one was going to drive him out of his political party. Arnall also took the unusual position for a southern politician of defending the national government as "the finest government in the world." He contended that when he heard his opponents "damn the U.S.

government, it makes my blood boil." Such comments made the blood of many conservatives throughout the state boil as well, and it confirmed their suspicions about Arnall.[25]

Many of those who supported Arnall praised his leadership abilities, his progressive platform, and the accomplishments of his term as governor. The Atlanta *Journal* endorsed him because he was "better suited than any of the other Democratic candidates to continue the state on its course of sensible moderation, progress, and general governmental improvement." The Marietta *Daily Journal* supported him because "his administration was one of the most progressive, most responsible, and most productive in the state's history." Governor Sanders later praised him as "one of the smartest guys around," who was an able administrator and who "had a good administration." While Sanders professed neutrality in the campaign, two of his close political associates, J. B. Fuqua and Mills B. Lane, endorsed Arnall. The president of the Georgia State AFL-CIO, W. H. Montague, Sr., hailed Arnall as "the most liberal and farsighted governor that Georgia ever had." His organization, representing 165,000 union members, unanimously endorsed Arnall's candidacy. Other endorsements included one from the Fulton County Citizens Democratic Club, a prominent black political organization.[26]

In spite of his front-runner status, Arnall's campaign did have some major liabilities. In retrospect, former governor Sanders contended that Arnall's liberal reputation constituted his greatest political liability. According to Sanders, "Arnall was pretty well labeled as a rich Atlanta lawyer who . . . had some very liberal political ideas. I think that the political climate in the State of Georgia at that time did not favor that type of candidacy." Talmadge and Arnall's opponents concurred in Sanders's assessment. His opponents also accused Arnall of fiscal irresponsibility. Harris claimed that it was impossible for other candidates to outpromise Arnall. Gray designated Arnall as the "Santa Claus candidate" whose platform could be implemented only with a huge tax increase. Carter accused Arnall of making "wild promises to every pressure group in this state and he knows that he can't fulfill them." Carter predicted that state taxes would double if Arnall were elected.[27]

Sanders pointed out that Arnall had another major problem in that "it's pretty hard for a former governor to resurrect himself after 15 or 20 years." Others believed Arnall's age—fifty-nine—to be a liability, while some observers viewed Arnall's campaign style to be detrimental to his election. Jim

Rankin, writing in the Atlanta *Constitution,* noted that Arnall was a "natural and apparently compulsive orator." However, he observed that some of Arnall's advisers believed that while Arnall's style of campaigning "goes over well on the courthouse steps, it did not ring true under the kleig lights on TV where most of the campaign money is being spent these days." Another observer, Bruce Galphin, contended that Arnall was a disaster on television because "the oratorical style that had wooed them when he beat Ol' Gene Talmadge sounded like a parody on TV." In addition, Galphin concluded that Arnall's bandwagon technique of campaigning, so essential in the days of the county unit system, came across as arrogance.[28]

Ralph McGill agreed. In a letter written during the campaign, McGill told the former governor, "You were the winner in the old days of campaigning when it was done in the style of Gene Talmadge and Ed Rivers, but things are different, and the new generation somehow looks back on that as sort of Cleghorn stuff." Paul Hemphill, a reporter in the Atlanta *Journal,* agreed that Arnall's aggressive campaign style alienated many voters. Carol Dadisman, writing in the Marietta *Daily Journal,* wrote that Arnall's "go to hell" statement "reflected a side of Arnall's personality which turned many voters against him. It dramatized the cocky, flamboyant, almost arrogant attitude which characterized his whole campaign." Dadisman believed that, as a result of this perception of Arnall, many voters turned to other candidates.[29]

Arnall countered the major criticisms of his candidacy in several ways. He dismissed the charge of being liberal, insisting, "I'm just a native-born Georgian running for governor on a Georgia program for Georgia people." He also attempted to address the problem of his campaign style. McGill urged Arnall to "get some real good agency advice" to help him. Arnall conceded that he was flamboyant and egotistical but that he believed that "with some good handling and good support, maybe we can overcome some of my frailties." Arnall agreed to bring in an adviser from New York to help him with his campaigning style. He conceded, however, that the adviser failed in his efforts to remake him into "a real calm super salesman."[30]

Arnall attempted to deflate the charges that his platform would lead to a tax increase by contending that his new programs would cost considerably less than his critics claimed. Arnall promised to get $1.15 of service out of every taxpayer's dollar spent because of his ability as a good administrator. He estimated a savings of over $170 million in his next term by reorganizing state government and revising the state's tax structure. The former governor maintained that his progressive platform could be financed without a tax increase due to the continued growth of state tax revenue. Even if nothing were done to revise the tax system, Arnall claimed his administration would have over one billion dollars in new revenue simply by the growth of the state's tax digest. Finally, Arnall reminded Georgians of his accomplishment of paying off the state debt without increasing taxes in his previous administration. In fact, Arnall claimed to be the only governor who ever paid Georgia out of debt without raising taxes and also to be the most fiscally conservative governor in the state's history.[31]

Arnall lacked the support of several key political leaders who had played a critical role in his defeat of Talmadge in 1942. The anti-Talmadge faction that he had led in the 1940s no longer existed. Harris and James L. Gillis, Sr., chairman of the State Highway Board, as well as other influential members of the Talmadge organization opposed the comeback effort of the aging Talmadge foe. In addition, many of Vandiver's close supporters, resentful of Arnall's abrasive attacks on Vandiver, opposed Arnall. Carter even claimed that Arnall had alienated so many of the state's Democratic leaders that he could not lead a unified party effort against the Callaway challenge. Ironically, Arnall's strong support of the Democratic party constituted a major liability. One observer contended that Arnall "made the mistake of being too much the loyal national Democrat at a time when the role had gone out of style, even in Georgia."[32]

Arnall led in the primary with 29.4 percent of the vote and would have received the nomination prior to 1966. However, during the Sanders administration, the legislature changed the plurality requirement to one requiring a majority vote for nomination. If a candidate failed to receive a majority vote, then a runoff election occurred between the two candidates who had received the highest number of votes. Arnall therefore had to run against the candidate receiving the second highest number of votes. To the surprise of many, Maddox, with 23.5 percent of the vote, was that candidate. Carter came in third with 20.9 percent of the vote, followed by Gray with 19.4 percent, and Byrd with 5.1 percent.[33]

As expected, Arnall's strongest support in the primary came from the fifteen urban-suburban counties, where almost 46 percent of the registered voters of the state resided. In fact, Arnall received almost 54 percent of his total vote from these counties. Arnall also received overwhelming support from blacks—92 percent of the black vote in Atlanta and 84 percent of the black vote in Macon. Of the five candidates, he received the largest percentage of support among upper-class whites in the urban-suburban counties. However, his support declined sharply among lower- and middle-class whites in those counties. He received the lowest percentage of support of all the candidates among the rural and small-town counties. In contrast, Maddox received his greatest support from voters in those counties. Maddox also ran much stronger than his two conservative opponents among the lower- and middle-class whites in the urban-suburban counties. His strong showing with the rural voters and his creditable strength among lower-income whites in the urban-suburban counties enabled him to get in the runoff with Arnall.[34]

Although Arnall led in the primary election results, his showing had to be considered a disappointment. Arnall himself believed that he would have received most of the Carter votes if Carter had not been in the race. Arnall and Carter received 50.3 percent of the total vote in the primary with both receiving their greatest support in the town counties of north Georgia and in the urban-suburban counties. If Carter had not been in the race, Arnall would have received substantial support from those voters who supported Carter, though it seems unlikely that he would have obtained the overwhelming support from Carter supporters necessary to win the nomination. Even without Carter's presence, as Arnall himself conceded, a runoff would have been inevitable.[35]

Arnall immediately sought to strengthen his position in the runoff by seeking Carter's support only to be turned down by Carter who announced his neutrality in the runoff. According to Arnall, Carter had offered his support in return for the chairmanship of the state Democratic party, a condition that Arnall refused. Betty Glad, in her biography of Carter, however, attributed Carter's refusal to endorse Arnall to his desire to avoid alienating conservative voters whom he might need in future elections.[36]

Unlike his primary effort, Arnall's runoff campaign was low-key. In fact, Arnall did not make a speech during that "run-off because I just couldn't imagine the people of Georgia supporting a fellow who was against law and order." The former governor announced shortly after the primary that he would not leave his law office in Atlanta but would do his campaigning by telephone. Arnall admitted to looking past the runoff and toward campaigning against Callaway. Arnall soon changed his position though, calling the runoff election the most crucial election ever held in the state. He now considered a race against Callaway to be a "breeze" but warned that it would be "tough" running against Maddox.[37]

The former governor sought to portray Maddox as a "preacher of fear, distrust and racial extremism" whose nomination would make Georgia the laughing stock of the nation. Arnall warned that if Maddox were elected, Georgia's good image would be damaged, the axe handle and the pistol would become the symbols of state government, and economic development would suffer. He claimed that the only governmental experience that Maddox had was in waving axe handles and pistols and causing civil disturbances. Arnall stressed that "everybody knows that it is important that we maintain a good national image if we are to bring new industry to our state and move Georgia forward." Arnall received the overwhelming endorsement of the press in the runoff, but Maddox's candidacy was viewed by the press as a threat to the well-being of the state.[38]

While Arnall remained in Atlanta, Maddox conducted a vigorous runoff campaign concentrating on the urban areas where his support had been weakest. Maddox claimed that the only issue in the runoff was whether Georgia wanted "some more of the same old dragging and lagging government with more sellouts, SNCC, Great Society, and lawlessness." According to Maddox, Arnall was a socialist and "the granddaddy of forced racial integration." He reminded Georgians that Arnall had supported Henry Wallace, "a socialist and communist sympathizer," for vice president in 1944 and had been given an award by the leftist Southern Conference on Human Welfare.[39]

In the runoff Maddox defeated Arnall with 54.3 percent of the vote. His victory ranks as one of the major political upsets of Georgia politics. Maddox ran strongest in the rural and small-town counties, but he overwhelmed Arnall in the town counties as well. Arnall's vote exceeded that of Maddox only in the fifteen urban-suburban counties. The former governor received over 56 percent of the vote cast in those counties, thanks to the coalition of black and upper-income whites. An Arnall majority of 46,000 in the urban-suburban counties was insufficient to overcome Maddox's 116,000 vote majority he had in the other counties. Maddox also received substantial support in the urban-suburban counties, even outpolling Arnall among the lower- and middle-class white voters.[40]

Several factors contributed to Arnall's defeat by a candidate considered by many to be a political joke and an embarrassment to the state.

Former governor Sanders attributed Maddox's upset election primarily to his "running as a segregationist. Segregation was still a very hot, vital, emotional issue." Neal Pierce contended that Arnall's racial moderation "was out of step with plain Georgia people." Bruce Galphin argued that Arnall's most serious error was that he "assumed that Georgia was basically different from the state of twenty years before. It simply had not altered *that* much. It wasn't ready for Arnall's liberalism." Moreover, according to Matt Williamson, Arnall's strong attacks on Maddox in the runoff "made a martyr of Maddox as a poor man set upon by the important rich man." In addition, Arnall's old political foes supported Maddox to prevent their former adversary from reaching the governorship.[41]

Arnall attributed his defeat to several factors, one of which was Maddox's riding "the crest of the anti-black attitude." Arnall noted that shortly before the primary election, some racial disturbances occurred that intensified racial feelings. In particular, a major racial riot involving Stokely Carmichael occurred in Atlanta just before the primary. Arnall contended, "If it had not been for that I would have won." Both Vandiver and Callaway agreed that the Atlanta riot hurt Arnall's chances in the primary. Roy Wilkins, executive director of the National Association for the Advancement of Colored People, viewed the Atlanta race riot as the key factor in Maddox's nomination. Arnall also contended that his candidacy suffered because many whites "voted against me for having led the fight to give blacks first-class citizenship." The Moultrie *Observer* agreed and attributed Arnall's defeat to a white voter backlash. Carol Dadisman, writing in the Marietta *Daily Journal,* agreed and concluded that Maddox received the nomination "primarily on the strength of symbolism. He was a symbol of anti-administration, anti-forced integration sentiment at a time when these feelings are running high in Georgia."[42]

Arnall and others had clearly underestimated Lester Maddox in 1966. Like Gene Talmadge, Maddox entered the race assured of a hard core of conservative voters and had statewide name recognition. One reporter claimed that Maddox was even better known than the incumbent governor, Carl Sanders. Roy Harris stated, "I was around in the days of Tom Watson and Gene Talmadge and they couldn't match the grassroots movement that developed for this man." Jim Rankin, writing in the Atlanta *Constitution,* contended that none of the candidates could attract as much attention and interest as Maddox. Sam Caldwell observed that Maddox, "the underdog, the ax-handle wielding segregationist, the tireless campaigner with the

antics of a circus clown and the quips of a backwoods humorist, had cap-
tured the imagination of the voters."[43]

Even though Arnall, Gray, and Carter outspent Maddox, the feisty segregationist compensated for a lack of adequate financing by a vigorous personal campaign. Claiming that he slept only five hours a night during the
campaign, Maddox estimated that he traveled over one hundred thousand
miles throughout the state after entering the race in October 1965. Maddox
came across to the common white man as one of them—a God-fearing,
hard-working, honest man who had known poverty and hardship and
could understand their problems. Maddox very effectively used a common-
man image campaign against Arnall—the wealthy Atlanta lawyer.[44]

Another factor to be considered was Republican participation in the
Democratic primary and runoff. Since Georgia did not have closed primaries, there had been speculation that Republicans would vote in the
Democratic primary in order to nominate the weakest candidate to run
against the Republican gubernatorial candidate. The charge of Republican participation intensified after Maddox's victory. The Atlanta *Constitution* charged that some Republicans supported Maddox, believing that he
would be easier than Arnall to defeat. Ralph McGill estimated that at least
seventy-five thousand Republicans voted for Maddox in the runoff. Arnall
attributed his defeat to Republicans who perceived Maddox as the weaker
candidate. Others who believed that Republicans voted for Maddox in the
Democratic primary included Carter, Atlanta Mayor Allen, Atlanta *Constitution* editor Eugene Patterson, former governors Vandiver and Sanders,
and state senator Leroy Johnson.[45]

Callaway, however, denied the charge, stating that a number of his "supporters probably did, but I don't think that there was anything like enough
to change the results." Maddox also rejected the theory of the Republicans aiding in his nomination as an attempt to explain away Arnall's
defeat. While contending that some Republicans did vote in the runoff for
Maddox, Galphin concluded that the extent of the crossover could never
be accurately determined. Bartley concluded that it was doubtful whether
a "purposive Republican cross-over vote had much effect on the outcome
of the election." Williamson failed to find any evidence to indicate a substantial Republican crossover vote. Although some Republicans may have
voted in the runoff for Maddox, it cannot be concluded that they voted in
sufficient strength to nominate Maddox.[46]

With the defeat of Arnall, Maddox, a conservative Democrat, faced Callaway, a conservative Republican, for the governorship. In sharp contrast to Maddox's background, Callaway was born into a wealthy Georgia family of textile mill owners. Though he had supported the Talmadge faction in state politics, Callaway switched parties in 1964 and vigorously supported Goldwater's presidential candidacy. Callaway was elected to the U.S. House of Representatives in 1964 and became the most conservative member of the state's congressional delegation.[47]

Despite the claims of Callaway, many Georgians detected few differences in the political philosophies of the two candidates. Three black leaders— state senator Leroy Johnson, Rev. Samuel Williams, and Hosea Williams— charged that Callaway was "a silk-stocking segregationist who is no better than Maddox." NAACP Executive Director Roy Wilkins announced that his organization could not endorse either candidate because the choice was between the devil and the witch. Dr. Martin Luther King, Jr., president of the Southern Christian Leadership Conference and a native Georgian, also refused to endorse either of the candidates. Asked if he perceived any difference between the candidates, Sanders replied, "Yeah. One was a Democrat and one was a Republican." The Atlanta *Constitution* refused to endorse either candidate, noting "both adhere to the Goldwater type of extreme conservatism which swept Georgia in the 1964 presidential election."[48]

Appalled at the lack of choice confronting the voters in the general election, some Georgians considered the possibility of a write-in campaign. The Georgia Constitution of 1945 provided that the state legislature would elect a governor from the two candidates receiving the highest number of votes if a candidate failed to receive a majority vote in the general election. A biracial gathering of over five hundred people met in Atlanta in October and agreed that a write-in effort was needed. A straw vote of the group favored Lieutenant Governor-elect George T. Smith as the first choice, followed by Arnall and then Carter. While Smith and Carter refused to run as a write-in candidate, Arnall did not. Thus the group of dissident Georgians picked Arnall as their choice and dubbed itself Write-In Georgia, or WIG.[49]

Arnall issued a statement claiming that he would not encourage nor discourage the write-in effort. The former chief executive insisted that he had nothing to do with the write-in effort and attributed it to some of his friends who were angry about Republicans voting for Maddox in the run-off. While Maddox agreed that Arnall did not take an active role in the write-in effort, he maintained that Arnall could have stopped the campaign by refusing to let his name be used. Maddox saw the write-in effort as pulling votes from his campaign. Despite his request to repudiate the effort, Arnall refused. Callaway also viewed the write-in effort as a threat to his candidacy and warned that a large write-in vote could throw the choice of governor into the hands of the Democratically controlled General Assembly, who would "in all probability" elect Maddox. Callaway, like Maddox, believed that Arnall could have stopped the write-in campaign because "without his permission it couldn't happen."[50]

The press generally condemned the write-in effort as a futile gesture. According to the Macon *News,* no major daily newspaper in the state supported the write-in. The two major dailies in the state, the Atlanta *Constitution* and the Atlanta *Journal,* opposed the write-in. Other papers, such as the Dalton *Daily Citizen-News,* Marietta *Daily Journal,* Atlanta *Daily World,* Columbus *Ledger,* and Macon *Telegraph,* opposed the write-in, believing it would result in Maddox's election by the legislature. However, Arnall's hometown newspaper, the Newnan *Times-Herald,* saw the write-in effort as an opportunity for the voters to rectify "that terrible mistake" when "mad Democrats and cross-over Republicans" nominated Maddox.[51]

Division existed in the black political community concerning the write-in effort. The SCLC, citing a policy of noninvolvement in partisan politics, refused to endorse the write-in effort. The Socio-Political Action Commission of the black Baptist Convention of Georgia urged its members not to write-in because "a vote for a write-in candidate is a Maddox vote." Prominent blacks opposed to the write-in included Q. V. Williamson, a member of the Atlanta Board of Aldermen; Jesse Hill, an insurance executive in Atlanta; and Horace Tate, a member of the Atlanta Board of Education. Supporters of the write-in effort in the black community included state Senator Johnson and state representatives Ben Brown and J. D. Grier, Jr., the Rev. Samuel Williams, president of the Atlanta Chapter of the NAACP, and Hosea Williams. In addition, the all-black Atlanta Negro Voters League, the Georgia State Metro Voters League, and the Georgia Association of Democratic Clubs endorsed Arnall's write-in candidacy.[52]

As feared by the opponents of the write-in, neither Maddox nor Callaway received the necessary majority on election day as required by the Georgia constitution because of the write-in campaign. Callaway received 46.6 percent to Maddox's 46.3 percent of the vote cast while the Arnall write-in candidacy received 7.1 percent of the votes. Callaway possessed a thin plurality of 3,039 votes out of almost one million cast. Callaway, like Arnall, ran strongest in the urban-suburban counties, and Maddox ran strongest in the rural and small-town counties. While 63 percent of the write-in votes came from the urban-suburban counties, Arnall's write-in candidacy carried only one county—Liberty—in which blacks made up a majority of the population. Since neither of the candidates received a majority of the vote, the legislature had the responsibility of electing the next governor. Although Callaway had a plurality in the vote count, the legislature, which was overwhelmingly Democratic, elected Maddox as governor. Arnall believed that Callaway would have been elected if it had not been for the write-in vote. However, Arnall did not write his own name in but voted for Maddox because of party loyalty and his belief that the Republican crossover had deprived him of the nomination. In addition, Arnall believed Maddox would be less harmful to the state because of his inexperience, while the more experienced Callaway "could have brought about the enactment of repressive and special interest legislation which would hurt the state for years to come."[53]

Ironically, a reform in the state's election laws requiring a majority vote for nomination prevented one of Georgia's most famous reform governors from obtaining his party's nomination and possibly the governorship in 1966. Too many factors worked against Arnall's effort to obtain the nomination. These included his liberal image, his support of the national Democratic party, a white backlash against federal intrusion that had undermined the state's social and political status quo, the opposition of former political opponents, and a formidable runoff opponent who shocked most political observers with his upset win.

Despite a vigorous and well-financed campaign, Arnall could not overcome a liberal image in a state where most voters found such an image distasteful. If the former governor had been seeking the office of mayor of Atlanta, he would have stood an excellent chance of being elected by that city's coalition of blacks and affluent whites. Unfortunately for Arnall, such a coalition did not dominate state politics as it did the politics of Atlanta in the 1960s. Instead, whites in rural and small-town counties and lower- and middle-class whites in the urban-suburban counties constituted the largest coalition of voters in the state. This conservative coalition carried the state for Goldwater in 1964 and denied the nomination to Arnall in 1966. Arnall effectively used the accreditation issue to defeat Eugene Talmadge in the 1942 primary. Unfortunately, he had no such issue to use against Maddox, who, like Gene Talmadge, clung to the traditional order in a period of significant change in Georgia. Arnall's defeat in the 1966 primary ended his political ambitions. Never again would the gentleman from Coweta seek public office.[54]

15

A
Mover
and a
Shaker

Ellis Arnall's rise to political power is one of the most remarkable chapters in Georgia history. The voters of Coweta County sent him to the legislature when he was only twenty-five. The members of the House of Representatives twice elected him speaker pro tempore—that body's second highest elective position. Governor Ed Rivers appointed his youthful protégé— then only thirty-one years old—to fill a vacancy in the office of state attorney general. With that appointment, Arnall became the youngest attorney general in the nation. After assuming the governorship four years later, he became the nation's youngest chief executive.

Arnall achieved a remarkable record as governor. He came into office with a reform agenda that was added to as his administration evolved. When Arnall left office four years later, most of his reforms had been enacted. One writer in an article for a national publication praised him for "lifting his state from the benightedness of Tobacco Road to the position of runner-up to North Carolina for title of 'most progressive Southern state.'" U.S. Senator Wayne L. Morse commended Arnall for establishing "one of the greatest liberal records of any governor" in recent history. With the assistance of a willing legislature, he attained reaccreditation of the university system, established a teachers retirement system, created a merit system for state employees, established eight constitutional boards, repealed the state's poll tax, reformed the state's penal system, lowered the voting age, revised the state's constitution, and paid off the state's debt. In addition, he led the South's political and legal fight against discriminatory freight rates. To his credit, Arnall restored the tarnished image of Georgia and in the process became an eloquent spokesman for the state and the South.[1]

As a result of Arnall's reform program, the national press found themselves in the unusual position of praising rather than condemning a governor of Georgia. Never had a chief executive of the state received such favorable attention from the national media. Columnist Drew Pearson even called Arnall "the South's greatest leader since the Civil War." The academic community likewise applauded the accomplishments of the Arnall administration. Numan V. Bartley concluded that Arnall's tenure as governor "was the most progressive and probably the most effective in modern Georgia history." James F. Cook contended, "Arnall had compiled a record of progressive reforms unsurpassed by a governor in Georgia's history." V. O. Key, Jr., wrote, "Many Georgians and most outsiders consider his administration (1943–1947) the most competent given the state in several decades." E. Merton Coulter concluded, "Arnall was the most dynamically constructive governor Georgia had within the memory of its oldest inhabitants." Elkin Taylor believed Arnall to be "one of the most noteworthy individuals to come out of the South this century." A survey of Georgia historians in 1985 ranked Arnall first among Georgia governors who served from 1943 to 1983 in the categories of having the most positive national reputation, providing the most effective political leadership, and addressing the major issues of his term of office. Arnall's reputation as a progressive reformer has remained strongly intact in the hands of the academic community.[2]

Arnall entered the governorship as a reformer committed to doing away with "gubernatorial dictatorship" in Georgia. To do so, he obtained the creation of eight constitutional boards in a state where none had existed before. The existing state Board of Regents, the state Board of Education, and the Public Service Commission became constitutional bodies. In addition, five new agencies that had constitutional state boards were created: the Game and Fish Commission, the Board of Pardons and Paroles, the the Board of Corrections, the Veterans Service Board, and the Personnel Board. With the exception of the Game and Fish Commission, Arnall's constitutional boards continue to exist today. Since the Arnall administration, only two additional constitutional state boards have been created: the Transportation Board and the Board of Offender Rehabilitation.[3]

Other legacies of the Arnall administration in state government included the creation of the office of lieutenant governor, the establishment of a merit system for state employees, the creation of a state board of workmen's compensation, the establishment of the Teachers Retirement System, and the creation of the State Ports Authority. To a large extent, the structure of Georgia's modern government came into existence in the Arnall administration.[4]

Arnall willingly gave up gubernatorial control of those governmental activities he deemed "administrative" rather than "political" in nature. His support of constitutional boards did not mean he favored weakening the office of governor. On the contrary, Arnall believed in the concept of strong executive leadership. In his view, removing time-consuming administrative responsibilities such as issuing pardons strengthened the governorship because it allowed a governor to devote more time to more important issues. A strong governor, Arnall clearly enjoyed the role of being the state's chief executive. Ivan Allen, Jr., who served as Arnall's executive secretary, recalled, "He liked to get things done. He had great drive." In addition to his great drive, Arnall possessed other qualities that served him well in the political arena. He was articulate, personable, forceful, intelligent, farsighted, and shrewd.[5]

In some respects, Arnall fit the traditional mode of a Georgia politician. He had a small-town background, earned a law degree from the University of Georgia, came from a prominent family, belonged to a Baptist church, had an outgoing personality, and enjoyed politics. In other respects, however, Arnall seemed out of place in Georgia politics. Highly intelligent, he received an undergraduate degree in Greek from an out-of-state Episcopal liberal arts college. Arnall enjoyed reading poetry and had even written some poems, hardly a typical pastime activity of Georgia politicians. A voracious reader, Arnall possessed a wide range of knowledge that made him a favorite participant on national radio and television game or talk shows. He seemed equally at home campaigning among south Georgia voters or discussing problems of the South in a radio studio in New York City.

Unlike most Georgia politicians of that time, Arnall rose above provincialism and was concerned about what outsiders thought of Georgia and the South. He wrote for national publications, authored two best-selling books, and conducted a national lecture tour—all precedent-setting for a governor of Georgia. Arnall even spoke out in favor of federal aid to education and praised organized labor at a time when both were unpopular in the South. He expressed a strong belief in democratic government and his stand on the poll tax, lowering the voting age, and black voting led to a doubling of the state's electorate. His fight against the Talmadges earned him nationwide praise. "There's nothing wrong with government that a good dose of democracy won't cure" became his favorite motto. His commitment to academic freedom, his efforts to improve the state's inadequate educational system, and his extolling of the importance of education earned him the designation of being an education governor.

As governor, Arnall remained a segregationist and never threatened the "Southern way of life." However, he complied with the federal judiciary's mandate to allow blacks to vote in the state's white primaries at a time when liberal southern politicians either criticized the federal courts or remained silent on the issue. Arnall admitted that the South had not lived up to the equal requirement of the *Plessey v. Ferguson* decision. He believed that blacks should be treated fairly and have equal rights—an unusual position for a southern politician in the 1940s. As the state's chief executive, he talked of first-class citizenship for all of Georgia's citizens. Later, during the state's desegregation crisis in the early 1960s, Arnall came out strongly in favor of keeping the public schools open while many politicians advocated closing them to avoid desegregation.

During the 1940s, southern politicians could be classified into at least three categories—demagogues, conservatives, and liberals. The demagogues, including such politicians as Eugene Talmadge of Georgia and Theodore Bilbo of Mississippi, appealed to the prejudices and passions of the southern masses. While some demagogues such as Talmadge displayed a conservative philosophy toward state taxes, expenditures, and services, others such as Bilbo were liberal except on the race question. The second category, the conservatives, including Walter George of Georgia and John Stennis of Mississippi, possessed a conservative racial and economic philosophy. They represented the views of the economically privileged in southern society and stood as defenders of the status quo. While frowning upon the ranting and raving of the demagogues, they favored limited governmental activity, low taxes, and opposed expansion of state services to improve the lot of the have-nots. The liberals, including Hugo Black of Alabama, Claude Pepper of Florida, and Ed Rivers of Georgia, supported governmental reform, economic development, and expansion of state services. They called for greater intervention by the state to improve the standard of living for the have-nots. Nevertheless, liberals in the South tended to be more conservative in comparison with their liberal counterparts elsewhere. In particular, most southern liberal politicians, including

Arnall, agreed with the conservatives and demagogues on the necessity of segregation.[6]

Arnall entered politics in 1932 as a conservative calling for economy in government and for a reduction of taxes. During his first legislative term, the young representative generally followed the conservative direction of Governor Eugene Talmadge. By his second term, however, Arnall had drifted over to the more progressive camp of House Speaker Ed Rivers. Arnall ran as a reformer in the 1942 gubernatorial race and as governor generally adhered to a progressive point of view. He disliked being called a liberal, believing the term had deteriorated in meaning. He preferred to be called either "a democrat, with a little 'd' " or a libertarian. Arnall realized being tagged a liberal had serious political liabilities in Georgia's conservative political environment. He nonetheless saw his victory in 1942 as part of a "liberal movement" that he believed was sweeping the South and would ultimately become the dominant political force in the region.[7]

Arnall was closely associated with two of the leading national liberal politicians of the 1940s—Franklin D. Roosevelt and Henry A. Wallace. Since the presidential election of 1932, Arnall had supported Roosevelt and the two became close personal and political friends. President Roosevelt offered Arnall the position of solicitor general and even allowed Arnall to announce Roosevelt's decision to seek a fourth term. With substantial risk to this political standing in Georgia, Arnall fought for the renomination of Roosevelt's liberal vice president, Henry Wallace, in 1944. A close personal friendship between Wallace and Arnall continued after their party's 1944 national convention.

Arnall was also closely associated with two of the leading liberals in Georgia—Ed Rivers and Ralph McGill. Rivers played a major role in Arnall's rise to power. He appointed Arnall attorney general and was instrumental in Arnall's victory in 1942. While their political friendship ended temporarily in the heat of the 1946 governor's race, they eventually reconciled their differences and resumed their political friendship. Arnall's friendship with one of the leading liberal newspaper publishers in the South, Ralph McGill, started in the early 1940s. During the 1942 race, McGill, according to his biographer, served as "confidant and counselor" to Arnall. When McGill died in 1969, Arnall wrote his widow, expressing his sorrow in the death of his "loyal friend."[8]

Certainly Arnall embraced many of the tenets of liberalism. He believed in the positive state and subscribed to the concept of state planning, as demonstrated by his Agricultural and Industrial Board. Although wartime conditions and inadequate state revenue hindered the implementation of many of its recommendations, Arnall believed the board had laid the foundation for the state's future growth and improvement. Arnall accepted the liberal view of government's responsibility to meet the needs of its people. Like most southern politicians, Arnall professed a belief in states' rights; however, Arnall believed that states should assume responsibilities for dealing with societal problems. He concluded that state inaction forced federal intervention which resulted in a loss of states' rights. Arnall took pride in the fact that during his administration the state of Georgia acted in a positive, constructive, and responsible manner. Georgia had been first in the nation to lower its voting age to eighteen and to enact a soldier's voting act. Under Arnall's direction, Georgia became the fourth southern state to repeal its poll tax and became the first state to successfully claim that it could seek redress for violations of the Sherman Antitrust Act in the federal courts.

Arnall parted company with the liberals over the issue of centralization of governmental power, believing the best government to be the government closest to the people. He also had misgivings about the growing federal bureaucracy, with its lack of accountability and unresponsiveness. Arnall also differed with liberalism in that he was a fiscal conservative. He ran on a platform in 1942 of not raising taxes, a promise that he kept. Arnall embarked upon an ambitious plan of paying off the state debt, some of which had existed since the 1830s. He accomplished that goal by the use of prudent fiscal management and wartime conditions which held down state spending. Arnall could have diverted the money used to pay off the state's debts to raise the inadequate level of state services. Instead, he believed that a debt-free state could better cope with the post–World War II era. While Arnall managed to increase the level of state spending, inadequate revenue and his refusal to raise taxes precluded a major expansion of state services. Throughout his political career, Arnall opposed a state sales tax as a regressive tax, claiming it to be harmful to lower-income Georgians. As director of the Office of Price Stabilization, Arnall claimed it was his responsibility to look after the interests of the people against the greed of Big Business.

In his classic study of southern politics, V. O. Key detected several major underpinnings of the South's political order in the 1940s, including a low level of white voting, the exclusion of blacks from political participation, and one-party dominance in the South. The economically privileged who generally favored low taxes and minimal expenditure for state services benefited from the weak party system and low voter participation by the have-nots. In addition, Georgia's malapportioned system of nominating state office holders ensured the domination of the most conservative voters in the state—the residents of the thinly populated counties.[9]

Arnall challenged the existing political status quo. His stand on the white primary, unique for a southern politician, allowed blacks to participate in Georgia politics for the first time since their disfranchisement. The addition of black voters to the electorate had the potential of undermining conservative influence in the state. The Talmadgites realized this threat as demonstrated by their frantic efforts to save the white primary and, after its demise, to limit black registration. Arnall's vision of blacks voting freely in Georgia finally came to fruition in the 1960s but only after the intervention of federal authority. Abolishing the poll tax, lowering the voting age, and permitting soldier voting, all of which was due in part to Arnall's leadership, increased the state's low level of white voting participation. Nevertheless, Georgia continued to have a notoriously poor record of voter turnout.

Arnall, the reformer, proved to be a political realist as well. As governor, he never challenged the county unit system of nominating state officers, even though it minimized the political influence of residents in larger populated counties who would more readily support progressive-minded politicians. Arnall realized the hopelessness of challenging the county unit system in the 1940s. By the early 1960s Arnall publicly expressed his opposition to the inequitable system. However, Arnall, always the loyal party man, never questioned the detrimental impact that one-party rule had on Georgia.

Arnall hoped to bring about a change in the economic status quo so that more Georgians could enjoy a higher standard of living. Earl Black and Merle Black concluded in their study of southern politics that there were two approaches that southern politicians used in the twentieth century to change the economic status quo. The first approach, that of neo-populism, called for increased state taxation on the economically privileged to pay for expansion of state services to benefit the have-nots. Arnall rejected neo-populism and embraced the approach of the entrepreneurial individualists who, instead of redistributing scarce resources, "sought to expand the col-

lective wealth of the region . . . through rapid economic development."
Arnall believed that the standard of living for all Georgians could be raised
by economic development.[10]

Arnall embraced Henry W. Grady's view of a New South in which industrialization would bring about an improvement in the region's standard
of living. Arnall envisioned that with increased prosperity the state governments in the South would have additional revenue in which to expand
the level of public services to improve the quality of life for their citizens.
He blamed northern industry for retarding the economic development of
the South by the use of discriminatory freight rates. With the removal of
these rates, Arnall saw the South undergoing economic growth and development. He also saw the South's race problem, which he claimed to be
primarily economic, diminishing with a rising tide of economic prosperity.
Like the Populists, Arnall stressed that the South could not progress while
holding the black man back economically.

Just as spectacular as Arnall's political ascendancy was his political decline. During the first half of his term, Arnall dominated state politics,
but his political influence steadily declined in the last half of his administration. His unsuccessful fight for the renomination of Vice President
Wallace at the 1944 Democratic convention damaged his political standings
in the state. The Talmadge faction used Arnall's association with the liberal Wallace, who was very unpopular in Georgia, as a means of undercutting Arnall's popularity. Although Arnall eventually disassociated himself
from Wallace's controversial foreign policy views, Wallace's hostile attitude
toward segregation, and his third-party candidacy, substantial damage had
been done to the governor's political career.

Arnall's political influence suffered a major blow when the state House
of Representatives twice in the latter half of his term refused to propose
a constitutional amendment allowing gubernatorial succession. Denied
the opportunity to seek a successive term, Arnall unsuccessfully backed
a gubernatorial candidate against Eugene Talmadge and suffered another
political setback. Most damaging of all, Arnall, prior to the 1946 primary,
had taken an unpopular position that blacks should be allowed to vote in
the state's white primary as mandated by the federal judiciary. He believed
that his position on black voting undermined his popularity in the state
more than any other issue. The Talmadge faction convinced many Georgians that their governor posed a threat to the state's segregated way of life.

In addition, Arnall's numerous out-of-state speaking engagements, his two successful books, his numerous articles, and a nationwide lecture tour further damaged him politically. Many Georgians did not want their governors or their former governors discussing problems of the state with outsiders. As Key put it:

A native son's popularity all too often varies inversely with his prestige in the rest of the land. This is especially true when he excited the admiration of the "northern press" and draws plaudits from commentators who annoy the folks back home with meddling observations on southern life. Arnall was accused by his opponents of "smug snobbery" and portrayed as having traded his loyalty to Georgia for the pottage of outside approval.[11]

Arnall left the governorship in 1947, the last of the anti-Talmadgites to be elected to that office. The Talmadge faction, now led by Herman Talmadge, solidified its hold on state politics while the anti-Talmadge faction faded from the scene by the mid-1950s. Like his father, the younger Talmadge promised to maintain and defend white supremacy. However, he differed from his father in that his administration undertook an ambitious program of expanding state services with the passage of a state sales tax. Like Arnall, Herman Talmadge embraced the positive state and saw the need for economic development. Unlike Arnall, though, Talmadge resisted the modernization of Georgia's political system. Forced into political exile by the popularity of Herman Talmadge and the political clout of the Talmadge faction, Arnall diverted his attention and energy toward legal and business endeavors. As the years passed, Arnall's absence from politics resulted in further deterioration of his political influence. Two decades after he had left the office, he made a spirited comeback effort for the governorship. He entered the campaign with an ambitious, progressive platform "to move Georgia into the 21st Century." However, too many obstacles stood in the path of Arnall's unsuccessful effort to return to the governor's office. In particular, many white voters perceived Arnall as being too liberal in a state undergoing a Second Reconstruction.

Arnall, rejected by the voters in 1966, devoted his energies to his legal practice and to his family. His son, Alvan, became a lawyer and joined his father's law firm. Unlike his father, though, Alvan Arnall has never displayed an active interest in politics. His marriage to Carol Marie Lowry gave the former governor two grandchildren, Ashley Carol and Taylor Gibbs. Arnall's daughter, Alice, married Joseph Edward Harty II and their marriage gave Arnall another grandchild, Joseph Edward Harty III. In recent years, Arnall has suffered several family tragedies. Alvan and his wife lost a daughter, Elizabeth Ann, who died in infancy. Mildred Arnall died unexpectedly in June 1980 of a heart attack. Her death, ending a happy marriage of forty-five years, devastated Arnall. He eventually overcame his grief and found, in his opinion, "another wonderful woman." Shortly before Mildred Arnall's death, Arnall had taken her to a Cadillac automobile dealership to purchase her a new car. Arnall later married the attractive red-haired salesperson who had sold Mildred Arnall her last car. Arnall's marriage to Ruby Hamilton McCord, a successful businesswoman in her own right, took place on July 15, 1981, at the Central Baptist Church in Newnan. While Ruby Arnall disliked politics just as much as Mildred Arnall, she tolerated his continued interest in the subject. She did, however, restrict his cigar smoking to one room of their home. The Arnalls eventually sold their home in Newnan and moved to Atlanta where they enjoy an active social life with occasional trips abroad. Within three years after his second marriage, another tragedy struck when Alice died unexpectedly at the age of thirty-eight. Again, Arnall was devastated, but the passage of time healed the loss of his "precious souvenir of the governorship." [12]

Ellis Gibbs Arnall gave the state four years of strong, exciting, and responsible progressive leadership as governor. He once described his concept of being governor by stating, "I am by nature a mover and a shaker. I think holding office, just sitting there keeping the seat warm, would not be much fun." As the state's chief executive, Arnall did more than just keep "the seat warm." He shook the state's political status quo and became the despised political enemy of the defenders of the old order—the Talmadges. His chief political adversary, Eugene Talmadge, represented the values of status quo politics—traditionalism, provincialism, negative government, and white supremacy. Herman Talmadge, with the exception of a belief in the positive state, embraced the political values of his father. Arnall stood for a different Georgia—a new Georgia that looked to the future and not to the past. Arnall believed in progress and spoke of economic development, progressivism, and modernization. He advocated first-class citizenship and economic prosperity for all Georgians, including blacks. He had a vision of Georgia's living up to her motto of being the Empire State of the South and of the South's returning to a position of respectability in the Union as a leader in the practice of the politics of the New South. The tragedy of Arnall's political career is that this capable and forward-looking political leader never held public office in Georgia again. That absence constituted an even greater tragedy for his state.

Notes

1. Newnan-Coweta Historical Society, *A History of Coweta County, Georgia* (Roswell, Ga.: W. H. Wolfe Associates, 1988), p. 7; Mary G. Jones and Lily Reynolds, eds., *Coweta County Chronicles for One Hundred Years* (Atlanta: Stein Publishing Co., 1928), pp. 53–55; John Chamberlain, "Arnall of Georgia," *Life* 19 (August 6, 1945): 72; *Georgia Statistical Abstract, 1965,* ed. David C. Hodge (Athens: Bureau of Business and Economic Research, Graduate School of Business Administration, University of Georgia, 1965), p. 14; James F. Cook, Jr., *Governors of Georgia* (Huntsville, Ala.: Strode Publishers, 1979), pp. 198–201.

2. *History of Coweta County,* p. 191; Newnan *Times-Herald,* April 21, 1987; "Henry Clay Arnall," *Encyclopedia of Biography,* vol. 66 (New York: American Historical Society, 1931), 220–21; Chamberlain, "Arnall of Georgia," p. 72.

3. Ellis Gibbs Arnall, "History of the Arnall Family," (unpublished manuscript), pp. 3–5, 14–16; W. H. Garner, "The J. M. Ellis Family," *Bullock County History* (New York: Herff Jones and Paragon Press, 1937), p. 44; interview with Ellis G. Arnall, Atlanta, Ga., February 2, 1986.

4. Gerald W. Johnson, "Arnall of Georgia—and '48," *American Mercury* 63 (August 1946): 180; Arnall interview, February 2, 1986; interview of Mrs. Georgia Atkinson Bradfield, by Ellis G. Arnall, Ormond Beach, Fla., June 6, 1987. Mrs. Bradfield is the daughter of former governor William Y. Atkinson.

5. Rita Santry McGill, "Miss Maggie—Governor Arnall's First Teacher," Atlanta *Journal Magazine,* June 24, 1945, p. 8; Ellis Arnall to Santa Clause [*sic*], Folder 19, Box 46, Ralph E. McGill Collection, Special Collections, Robert W. Woodruff Library, Emory University, Atlanta, Ga.

6. Arnall interview, February 2, 1986; interview with Ellis G. Arnall, Atlanta, Ga., December 14, 1988.

7. Arnall interview, February 2, 1986; videotape interview with Ellis G. Arnall by Melvin T. Steely and

Theodore B. Fitz-Simons, Georgia Political Heritage Series, Annie Bell Weaver Special Collections, West Georgia College, Carrollton, Ga., 1986.

8. Arnall interview, February 2, 1986.

9. Arnall interview, February 2, 1986; academic information obtained from Arnall's University of the South transcript, Sewanee, Tenn.; "Governor Ellis Gibbs Arnall: An Oral History," interview by James F. Cook, Jr., Government Documentation Project, Georgia State University, Atlanta, August 1988, pp. 7–8.

10. Quotes from Arnall's former classmates at the University of the South obtained from their letters to Thomas Elkin Taylor in his "A Political Biography of Ellis Arnall" (Master's thesis, Emory University, 1959), p. 2; Arnall's extracurricular activities obtained from the 1926, 1927, and 1928 editions of *Cap and Gown*, the annual of the University of the South. Arnall's interest in billiards and his reading of the New Testament in Greek obtained from the Steely and Fitz-Simon interview.

11. Arnall interview, February 2, 1986; Taylor, "A Political Biography of Ellis Arnall," p. 4; Cook, "Arnall: An Oral History," p. 11.

12. *The Pandora, 1931*, University of Georgia annual, pp. 280, 51. The two sections of *The Pandora* "Views of Prominent People" and "Georgia Blackmail" are unnumbered; quotes from Arnall's former law school classmates obtained from their letters to Taylor in his "Political Biography of Ellis Arnall," p. 3.

13. Cook, "Arnall: An Oral History," pp. 9–12; academic information obtained from Arnall's University of Georgia transcript, Athens. Arnall stated in the Cook interview that while in law school he "took M.A. degree work at the University to have something to do." The Registrar's Office at the University of Georgia, however, failed to find any record of Arnall taking any classes other than those in law school.

14. Arnall interview, February 2, 1986; Newnan *Herald,* May 20, September 16, 1932.

15. Arnall interview February 2, 1986; Ellis G. Arnall, *The Shore Dimly Seen* (Philadelphia: J. B. Lippincott, 1946), p. 29.

16. Roy E. Fossett, "The Impact of the New Deal on Georgia Politics, 1933–1941" (Ph.D. dissertation, University of Florida, 1960), pp. 42–45.

17. For the 1932 gubernatorial campaign see William Anderson, *The Wild Man from Sugar Creek: The Political Career of Eugene Talmadge* (Baton Rouge: Louisiana State University Press, 1975), pp. 62–81; Sarah McCulloh Lemmon, "The Public Career of Eugene Talmadge: 1926–1936" (Ph.D. dissertation, University of North Carolina, 1952), pp. 109–37; Willis Anderson Sutton, Jr., "The Talmadge Campaigns: A Sociological Analysis of Political Power" (Ph.D. dissertation, University of North Carolina, 1952), pp. 89–98.

18. Newnan *Herald,* May 20 and December 23, 1932; Arnall interview, February 2, 1986.

19. Newnan *Herald,* September 16, 1932; Arnall interview, February 2, 1986.

20. Arnall interview, February 2, 1986; Ellis G. Arnall, "Governor You Will Be," in *Georgia Governors in an Age of Change: From Ellis Arnall to George Busbee,* ed. Harold P. Henderson and Gary L. Roberts (Athens: University of Georgia Press, 1988), p. 41; Jane Walker Herndon, "Eurith Dickenson Rivers: A Political Biography" (Ph.D. dissertation, University of Georgia, 1974), pp. 68, 89, 96.

21. Arnall, *The Shore Dimly Seen,* pp. 30–31.

22. Georgia General Assembly, *Journal of the House of Representatives* (1933), pp. 15–17; Arnall interview, February 2, 1986.

23. House *Journal* (1933), pp. 276–305.

24. Lemmon, "The Public Career of Eugene Talmadge," pp. 139–43; Arnall interview, February 2, 1986.

25. Atlanta *Constitution,* March 19, 1933; House *Journal* (1933), pp. 1496–98, 1667–72; Georgia General Assembly, *Journal of the Senate* (1933), p. 1127.

26. Herndon, "Eurith Dickenson Rivers," pp. 106–7; Atlanta *Constitution,* March 17, 1933.

27. Atlanta *Constitution,* March 17, February 27, 1933.

28. House *Journal* (1933), pp. 224, 476–77, 566, 1080–81, 635, 310, 326, 364, 459, 524, 601, 720, 826, 1667–72, 1173, 1222, 1149, 1593, 1639, 1753, 1929; Senate *Journal* (1933), pp. 474–75; Atlanta *Constitution,* March 19, 1933; House *Journal* (1933), pp. 308, 1610–28, 1663, 251, 1080–81; Senate *Journal* (1933), p. 986.

29. House *Journal* (1933), pp. 310, 326, 827, 364; Atlanta *Constitution,* January 18, 1933; House *Journal* (1933), pp. 1933–36; Taylor, "A Political Biography of Ellis Arnall," p. 16. For articles of impeachment, see House *Journal* (1933), pp. 1841–56.

30. Atlanta *Journal,* March 19, 26, 1933; Lemmon, "The Public Career of Eugene Talmadge," pp. 151–52; Atlanta *Constitution,* March 20, 1933; The editorials in the Columbus *Enquirer,* Savannah *Morning News,* Macon *Telegraph,* and New York *Times* are quoted in Lemmon, "The Public Career of Eugene Talmadge," pp. 151–52; Newnan *Herald,* March 20, 1933.

31. Lemmon, "The Public Career of Eugene Talmadge," pp. 156–79.

32. Anderson, *The Wild Man from Sugar Creek,* p. 91; Lemmon, "The Public Career of Eugene Talmadge," p. 170.

33. Arnall interview, February 2, 1986; Newnan *Herald,* September 7, 1934; Sutton, "The Talmadge Campaigns," pp. 157–58; the editor of the Athens *Banner* is quoted in the *Statesman,* July 31, 1934.

34. Atlanta *Constitution,* March 17, 1935.

35. Atlanta *Constitution,* January 25, 29, 1935; House *Journal* (1935), pp. 17–19, 706–11.

36. Anderson, *The Wild Man from Sugar Creek,* p. 114; Lemmon, "The Pub-

lic Career of Eugene Talmadge," pp. 184–91; House *Journal* (1935), pp. 1006–9, 2903–7.

37. Atlanta *Constitution*, January 2, March 4, 14, 1935.

38. House *Journal* (1935), pp. 2667, 1981–1982, 2802, 1939–51, 1885, 1829, 92–93, 2667, 2795, 138–41, 150–51, 1845, 2386, 1931, 2802, 2800, 2709, 1983, 827, 2797, 2674, 1769, 1801, 1107, 2803, 1693, 2528, 995, 1020, 1009, 1478, 3107, 1763, 1146, 1451, 2806, 1827, 1751, 1894, 2195, 1981–82, 2795, 2709, 1930–31; Georgia General Assembly, *Acts and Resolutions* (1935), p. 443; Newnan *Herald*, June 12, 1936.

39. House *Journal* (1935), pp. 2803, 2797, 1801, 2582, 1838–48, 1845; Senate *Journal* (1935), p. 1720; Atlanta *Constitution*, March 27, 1935.

40. House *Journal* (1935), pp. 71–72, 2667, 2055, 1100–7, 1693; Senate *Journal* (1935), p. 1398.

41. Newnan *Herald*, November 23, 1934; Atlanta *Constitution*, January 16, 1935; House *Journal* (1935), pp. 1939–51.

42. Arnall interview, February 2, 1986; House *Journal* (1935), pp. 2978, 150–51, 138–41, 1146.

43. House *Journal* (1935), p. 996; Atlanta *Journal*, February 14, 1935; Atlanta *Constitution*, February 15, 1935.

44. Atlanta *Constitution*, February 18, 1935; Newnan *Herald*, February 12, 1935.

45. Atlanta *Journal*, March 14, 1935; Arnall interview, February 2, 1986.

46. Ellis G. Arnall, "Luck, Fate, and Chance" (unpublished manuscript), pp. 11–12; Steely and Fitz-Simons interview with Arnall; Arnall interview, February 2, 1986.

47. Steely and Fitz-Simons interview with Arnall; Arnall, "The Family of Henry Clay Arnall," in *History of Coweta County*, pp. 191–93; Arnall interview, February 2, 1986; Atlanta *Journal*, January 10, 1943.

48. Calhoun *Times* editorial is quoted in Newnan *Herald*, March 1, 1935; Newnan *Herald*, March 22, 29, 1935; Atlanta *Journal*, March 14, 1935; Atlanta *Constitution*, March 1, 1935.

Chapter Two. *This Splendid Young Man*

1. Anderson, *The Wild Man from Sugar Creek*, pp. 157–64.

2. Arnall interview, February 2, 1986; Herndon, "Eurith Dickenson Rivers," p. 167; Fossett, "The Impact of the New Deal," pp. 174, 198.

3. F. N. Boney, "The Politics of Expansion and Secession, 1820–1861," in *A History of Georgia*, Kenneth Coleman, gen. ed. (Athens: University of Georgia Press, 1977), pp. 136–48; Thomas D. Clark and Albert D. Kirwan, *The South Since Appomattox: A Century of Regional Change* (New York: Oxford University Press, 1967),

p. 52; C. Vann Woodward, *Origins of the New South, 1877–1913* (Baton Rouge: Louisiana State University Press, 1951), pp. 81, 105–6, 248–73.

4. V. O. Key, Jr., *Southern Politics in State and Nation* (New York: Alfred A. Knopf, 1949), p. 107; Joseph L. Bernd, "A Study of Primary Elections in Georgia, 1946–1954" (Ph.D. dissertation, Duke University, 1957), p. 23; Numan V. Bartley, *From Thurmond to Wallace: Political Tendencies in Georgia, 1948–1968* (Baltimore: Johns Hopkins University Press, 1970), pp. 24–25.

5. Arnall interview, February 2, 1986.

6. Ibid.; Newnan *Herald*, January 8, 1937.

7. Taylor, "A Political Biography of Ellis Arnall," p. 38; Arnall interview, February 2, 1986.

8. Arnall interview, February 2, 1986.

9. Atlanta *Constitution*, February 4, 1939; *Statesman*, February 14, 1939; Cook, "Arnall: An Oral History," p. 26.

10. Arnall interview, February 2, 1986; Herndon, "Eurith Dickenson Rivers," pp. 252–54; Ivan Allen, Jr., compiler, *The First Year of the State Hospital Authority* (n.p., n.d.), pp. 3–8.

11. Arnall interview, February 2, 1986.

12. Ibid.

13. Arnall interview, February 2, 1986; interview with Herman E. Talmadge, Lovejoy, Georgia, March 24, 1986.

14. Taylor, "A Political Biography of Ellis Arnall," pp. 39–40; Marshall L. Allison, compiler, *Opinions of the Attorney General of Georgia, 1941–1943* (Decatur, Ga.: Bowen Press, n.d.), pp. 68–69.

15. *Opinions* (1941–43), pp. 31–35; Marshall L. Allison, compiler, *Opinions of the Attorney General, 1939–1941* (Atlanta: Curtiss Printing Co., n.d.), p. 99.

16. *Opinions* (1941–43), pp. 35–37; *Opinions* (1939–41), pp. 402–3; *Opinions* (1941–43), pp. 83–85.

17. *Opinions* (1939–41), pp. 507, 148; *Opinions* (1941–43), pp. 69–70.

18. *Acts and Resolutions* (Extraordinary Session, 1937–38), pp. 189–90; *Opinions* (1939–41), p. 74.

19. *Opinions* (1939–41), p. 434; Taylor, "A Political Biography of Ellis Arnall," p. 44; Atlanta *Constitution*, May 23, 1940.

20. Atlanta *Constitution*, May 26, 30, June 13, 11, August 20, 1940.

21. Cook, *Governors of Georgia*, pp. 250–52.

22. Herndon, "Eurith Dickenson Rivers," pp. 207–22, 257–76; Atlanta *Constitution*, May 17, 1939.

23. Atlanta *Constitution*, April 7, 13, 1939; *Opinions* (1939–41), pp. 133–36.

24. Atlanta *Constitution*, September 19, 1939; *Acts and Resolutions* (1937), pp. 53–54.

25. Atlanta *Constitution*, September 21, 1939.

26. Atlanta *Constitution,* October 13, 1939; Herndon, "Eurith Dickenson Rivers," p. 287; Zell Bryan Miller, "The Administration of E. D. Rivers as Governor of Georgia" (Master's thesis, University of Georgia, 1958), pp. 94–95.

27. *Opinions* (1939–41), pp. 244–45.

28. Miller, "The Administration of Rivers," pp. 96–98.

29. Ibid., pp. 100–102; Herndon, "Eurith Dickenson Rivers," pp. 313–16.

30. Atlanta *Constitution,* January 21, March 7, 1940.

31. Herndon, "Eurith Dickenson Rivers," pp. 316–20; Miller, "The Administration of Rivers," pp. 102–13; Atlanta *Constitution,* March 17, 1940; Atlanta *Constitution,* March 21, 1940.

32. There were actually three separate opinions handed down by the Georgia Supreme Court dealing with various aspects of the controversy. See Patten et al. v. Miller, 190 Ga. 105 (1940); Patten et al. v. Miller, 190 Ga. 123 (1940); Patten et al. v. Miller, 190 Ga. 152 (1940); *Opinions* (1939–41), pp. 634–35; Atlanta *Constitution,* May 9, 1940; Herndon, "Eurith Dickenson Rivers," pp. 315–16.

33. Herndon, "Eurith Dickenson Rivers," pp. 322–23; Atlanta *Constitution,* March 13, 23, 1941.

34. Georgia v. Evans et al., 123 F.2d 57 (1941) 57–58; Georgia v. Evans et al., 316 U.S. 159 (1942) 159–63.

35. Arnall interview, February 2, 1986; Georgia v. Evans et al., 316 U.S. 159 (1942); Arnall, *The Shore Dimly Seen,* p. 43.

36. Interview with Ellis G. Arnall, Atlanta, Ga., July 19, 1985; Herndon, "Eurith Dickenson Rivers," p. 336; Atlanta *Journal,* May 1, 1939; Atlanta *Constitution,* October 7, 1939. George Harsh's account of the crime is told in his *Lonesome Road* (New York: W. W. Norton, 1971), pp. 24–30.

37. Atlanta *Constitution,* October 14, 1939; Atlanta *Journal,* May 11, October 7, 1939; Arnall interview, July 19, 1985; unpublished manuscript of the reminiscences of Cleburne E. Gregory, Jr., p. 71. A copy of the manuscript in the possession of his son, C. E. Gregory III.

38. Atlanta *Constitution,* October 11, 1939; Gregory manuscript, p. 71; Atlanta *Journal,* October 12, 1939; for an account of Robert Elliot Burns's view of Georgia justice, see his *I Am a Fugitive from a Georgia Chain Gang!* (New York: Gossett and Dunlap, 1932).

39. Atlanta *Journal,* October 16, 17, 1939.

40. Atlanta *Journal,* October 16, 17, 18, 1939; Atlanta *Constitution,* October 19, 1939; Herndon, "Eurith Dickenson Rivers," p. 337.

41. Atlanta *Constitution,* February 17, 18, March 2, 1940.

42. This conclusion was made after an examination of the two volumes of opinions published while Arnall served as attorney general. These volumes, however, contain only a fraction of the opinions rendered. See the compiler's note on page four in *Opinions* (1939–41).

43. James F. Cook, Jr., "Politics and Education in the Talmadge Era: The Controversy over the University System of Georgia, 1941–1942" (Ph.D. dissertation, University of Georgia, 1972), pp. 63–78, 126–27; Atlanta *Constitution*, June 26, 1941.

44. Arnall's opinion is reprinted in the June 26, 1941 issue of the Atlanta *Constitution*: it was not included in *Opinions* (1941–43); Atlanta *Constitution*, June 27, 1941; Cook, "Politics and Education," pp. 129–32.

45. Atlanta *Constitution*, October 7, 8, 1941.

46. Ibid., December 3, 4, 1941, and January 9, 1942.

47. House *Journal* (1941), pp. 1411–12; Atlanta *Constitution*, July 30, August 19, 1939; Atlanta *Journal*, September 6, 1942; Arnall interview, July 19, 1985.

Chapter Three. *The 1942 Governor's Race*

1. Atlanta *Constitution*, September 9, 1942; Lillian E. Smith, "Democracy Begins at Home: Democracy Was Not a Candidate," *Common Ground* 3 (Winter 1943): 8; Albert B. Saye, *A Constitutional History of Georgia*, rev. ed. (Athens: University of Georgia Press, 1970), pp. 385–86.

2. Atlanta *Constitution*, June 28, November 2, 1941.

3. Department of Archives and History, *Georgia's Official Register* (1939–43), p. 500; Arnall, *The Shore Dimly Seen*, pp. 42–43; Cook, "Politics and Education," p. iii; Anderson, *The Wild Man from Sugar Creek*, p. xiv; Reinhard H. Luthen, *American Demagogues: Twentieth Century* (Boston: Beacon Press, 1954), p. 182; Atlanta *Constitution*, March 25, 1941.

4. James F. Cook, Jr., "The Georgia Gubernatorial Election of 1942," *Atlanta Historical Bulletin* 18 (Spring–Summer 1973): 7; Cook, *Governors of Georgia*, pp. 246–48.

5. Anderson, *The Wild Man from Sugar Creek*, p. 165; Ralph McGill, "How It Happened Down in Georgia," *New Republic* 116 (January 27, 1947): 12; Talmadge interview, March 24, 1986.

6. *Georgia Statistical Abstract, 1965*, p. 13; James F. Cook, Jr., "Eugene Talmadge," in *Dictionary of Georgia Biography*, ed. Kenneth Coleman and Charles Stephen Gurr (Athens: University of Georgia Press, 1983), p. 956; Anderson, *The Wild Man from Sugar Creek*, pp. vii, 42–43.

7. Key, *Southern Politics*, pp. 119–20; Charles Boykin Pyles, "Race and Ruralism in Georgia Elections, 1948–1966" (Ph.D. dissertation, University of Georgia, 1967), pp. 4–9; Saye, *Constitutional History of Georgia*, pp. 356–59, 364.

8. Key, *Southern Politics*, p. 22.

9. Joseph L. Bernd, *Grass Root Politics in Georgia: The County Unit System and the Importance of the Individual Voting Community in Bifactional Elections, 1942–1954*

(Atlanta: Emory University Research Committee, 1960), p. 6; Anderson, *The Wild Man from Sugar Creek*, pp. 200, 229–30, 237–38; Sarah McCulloh Lemmon, "The Ideology of Eugene Talmadge," *Georgia Historical Quarterly* 38 (September 1954): 226–48.

10. Sutton, "The Talmadge Campaigns," pp. 361–62; Lemmon, "The Public Career of Eugene Talmadge," pp. 156–244, 226–48; Ralph McGill, "It Has Happened Here," *Survey Graphic* 30 (September 1941): 453; Key, *Southern Politics*, pp. 116–17; Sutton, "The Talmadge Campaigns," pp. 244–45; Bernd, *Grass Root Politics*, pp. 33–34.

11. Sue Bailes, "Eugene Talmadge and the Board of Regents Controversy," *Georgia Historical Quarterly* 54 (December 1969): 410–12.

12. Cook, "Politics and Education," pp. 63–69; Bailes, "Talmadge and the Regents Controversy," p. 411.

13. Cook, "Politics and Education," pp. 126–33.

14. Anderson, *The Wild Man from Sugar Creek*, pp. 198–99; Talmadge interview, March 24, 1986.

15. Cook, "Politics and Education," pp. 116–18.

16. Ibid., pp. 158–74.

17. Ibid., pp. 189–202. The historian was James F. Cook (p. iii).

18. Ibid., pp. 177–78; Anderson, *The Wild Man from Sugar Creek*, p. 200.

19. Numan V. Bartley, *The Creation of Modern Georgia* (Athens: University of Georgia Press, 1983), p. 180; Cook, "Eugene Talmadge," p. 955.

20. Cook, "Politics and Education," pp. 248–56.

21. Athens *Banner-Herald*, August 2, 1942; Atlanta *Journal*, August 30, 1942; Atlanta *Constitution*, August 28, 1942.

22. Herndon, "Eurith Dickenson Rivers," p. 332; Atlanta *Constitution*, August 3, 1942; Gainesville *News* editorial reprinted in the September 17, 1942 issue of the Atlanta *Journal*; Atlanta *Journal*, August 29, 15, 1942.

23. Lemmon, "The Public Career of Eugene Talmadge," pp. 236–78; Sutton, "The Talmadge Campaigns," pp. 221–22.

24. Atlanta *Journal*, August 19, July 5, 1942; Thomaston *Times* editorial reprinted in the August 28, 1942 issue of the Atlanta *Journal*; Early County *News* editorial reprinted in the June 30, 1942 issue of the Atlanta *Journal*; Americus *Times-Recorder*, July 7, 1942; Moultrie *Observer*, July 27, 1942; Vidalia *Advance*, August 27, 1942; Augusta *Chronicle*, July 28, 1942.

25. Atlanta *Constitution*, August 28, July 6, 7, September 5, 6, 1942.

26. Taylor, "A Political Biography of Ellis Arnall," p. 75; Key, *Southern Politics*, pp. 122–23; Bernd, *Grass Root Politics*, p. 7; Anderson, *The Wild Man from Sugar Creek*, p. 213.

27. Bernd, *Grass Root Politics*, pp. 7–8; Allen Lumpkin Henson, *Red Galluses: A*

Story of Georgia Politics (Boston: House of Edinboro Publishers, 1945), pp. 238–39; Anderson, *The Wild Man from Sugar Creek,* p. 213.

28. Arnall interview, February 2, 1986; Atlanta *Constitution,* November 2, 1941.

29. Arnall, *The Shore Dimly Seen,* p. 42; Arnall interview, February 2, 1986; Elijah W. Maynard to Carlton Mobley, July 9, 1942, Eugene Talmadge Campaign Correspondence, Bibb County folder, Georgia Department of Archives and History, Atlanta; Augusta *Chronicle,* August 2, 1942; political advertisement in Wayne County *True-Citizen,* September 3, 1942.

30. Cook, "Politics and Education," pp. 268–80; Augusta *Chronicle,* August 1, 1942; Cook, "The Georgia Gubernatorial Election of 1942," p. 11; Arnall, *The Shore Dimly Seen,* p. 51; Henson, *Red Galluses,* p. 242.

31. Augusta *Chronicle,* September 1, 1942; Athens *Banner-Herald,* August 2, 1942; Atlanta *Journal,* August 30, 1942; Atlanta *Constitution,* August 28, April 25, 26, 1942; Atlanta *Journal,* July 5, April 5, August 31, 1942.

32. Arnall interview, February 2, 1986; Atlanta *Constitution,* August 16, 1942.

33. Bernd, *Grass Root Politics,* p. 7; Henson, *Red Galluses,* pp. 215–16; Arnall interview, July 19, 1985; Atlanta *Constitution,* November 2, December 7, 1941, and May 31, 1942.

34. Atlanta *Constitution,* January 7, June 25, July 4, 1942; Taylor, "A Political Biography of Ellis Arnall," p. 76; Atlanta *Constitution,* September 6, 1942.

35. Taylor, "A Political Biography of Ellis Arnall," p. 77; Eugene Talmadge to F. M. Reeves, August 10, 1942, Talmadge Campaign Correspondence, Habersham County folder, Georgia Department of Archives and History, Atlanta; Taylor, "A Political Biography of Ellis Arnall," p. 88; Atlanta *Constitution,* May 27, 1945; Steely and Fitz-Simons interview with Arnall; Miller, "Eurith Dickenson Rivers," p. 18; Key, *Southern Politics,* p. 124; Atlanta *Journal,* August 19, 30, 1942.

36. Arnall, *The Shore Dimly Seen,* pp. 42–43; Arnall interview, July 19, 1985.

37. Arnall, *The Shore Dimly Seen,* pp. 44–45; C. E. Gregory in Atlanta *Journal,* September 10, 1942; "Georgia: Change in the Weather," *Time* 40 (July 13, 1942): 19; Atlanta *Constitution,* July 5, 1942.

38. "Arnall: An Oral History," interview by Cook, p. 31; Cook, "The Georgia Gubernatorial Election of 1942," p. 10; Taylor, "A Political Biography of Ellis Arnall," p. 78; Sutton, "The Talmadge Campaigns," p. 274; Bernd, *Grass Root Politics,* p. 9.

39. Atlanta *Journal,* August 19, 1942; Vidalia *Advance,* July 23, 1942; Atlanta *Constitution,* September 9, 1942; Moultrie *Observer,* August 27, 1942; Brunswick News editorial reprinted in the August 24, 1942 issue of the Augusta *Chronicle.*

40. Atlanta *Constitution,* November 2, 1941; Atlanta *Journal,* July 5, 1942.

41. Atlanta *Journal,* July 5, 19, 1942; Ellis Arnall to Joe M. Anderson, August 8, 1942, Talmadge Campaign Correspondence, Wayne County folder, Georgia Department of Archives and History, Atlanta; Atlanta *Journal,* July 19, September 16,

June 28, August 12, July 19, September 1, July 5, 1942; Atlanta *Constitution,* July 12, 1942, and November 2, 1941.

42. James C. Cobb, "Not Gone, But Forgotten: Eugene Talmadge and the 1938 Purge Campaign," *Georgia Historical Quarterly* 59 (Summer 1975): 197–209; Newnan *Herald,* September 12, 1940; Atlanta *Constitution,* February 12, 1942; Atlanta *Journal,* August 16, May 3, 1941; Arnall interview, February 2, 1986.

43. Atlanta *Journal,* August 9, 1942; Atlanta *Constitution,* August 16, 1942; Talmadge political advertisement in Abbeville *Chronicle,* August 13, 1942; Atlanta *Journal,* July 5, 1942; *Statesman,* August 11, September 1, 1942.

44. Eugene Talmadge to Dr. W. H. Powell, July 16, 1942, Talmadge Campaign Correspondence, Jeff Davis County folder, Georgia Department of Archives and History, Atlanta; *Statesman,* July 7, August 18, 11, 25, 28, 1942; Talmadge political advertisement in Abbeville *Chronicle,* September 3, 1942; Douglas *Enterprise,* August 6, 1942; Abbeville *Chronicle,* September 3, 1942; Waycross *Journal-Herald,* July 8, 1942; Savannah *Morning News,* July 15, 1942.

45. Atlanta *Constitution,* August 30, 1942; Atlanta *Journal,* August 18, 1942; *Statesman,* August 25, 1942; Atlanta *Constitution,* July 29, 1942; Atlanta *Journal,* August 13, 1942.

46. *Statesman,* August 25, 11, 1942; Atlanta *Journal,* August 8, July 5, August 18, 1942.

47. Anderson, *The Wild Man from Sugar Creek,* p. 205; Atlanta *Journal,* August 10, May 17, 1942; Atlanta *Constitution,* November 2, 1941; Atlanta *Journal,* August 1, 10, 1942.

48. Athens *Banner-Herald,* August 28, 2, 1942; Atlanta *Constitution,* August 30, 1942; Thomaston *Times* editorial reprinted in the August 28, 1942 issue of the Atlanta *Constitution;* Americus *Times-Recorder,* July 7, 1942. For the editorials of seven other newspapers that attacked Talmadge's use of the race issue, see the editorial page of the June 22, 1942 issue of the Atlanta *Journal.*

49. *Official Register* (1939–43), pp. 653–56.

50. Arnall interview, July 19, 1985; Anderson, *The Wild Man from Sugar Creek,* p. 211; Cook, "The Georgia Gubernatorial Election of 1942," p. 16; Talmadge interview, March 24, 1986; Sutton, "The Talmadge Campaigns," pp. 274–75; telegram from Richard Russell to Ellis Arnall, September 15, 1942, Arnall Political File 1941–45, Richard B. Russell Papers, Russell Memorial Library, University of Georgia, Athens; Eugene Talmadge to E. F. Shelnutt, September 26, 1942, Talmadge Campaign Correspondence, Fulton County folder, Georgia Department of Archives and History, Atlanta; Bernd, *Grass Root Politics,* pp. 47–50; Taylor, "A Political Biography of Ellis Arnall," p. 89.

Chapter Four. *The 1943 Legislative Session*

1. Pittsburg *Courier,* September 19, 1942; Chicago *Defender,* September 19, 1942; Washington *Post,* September 12, 1942; New York *Herald-Tribune,* September 11, 1942; "Exit Gene Talmadge," *Time* 40 (September 21, 1942): 19.

2. Richmond *Times-Dispatch* editorial reprinted in the September 16, 1942 issue of the Atlanta *Journal;* New Orleans *Times-Picayune,* September 12, 1942; "The Shape of Things," *Nation* 155 (September 19, 1942): 223; *People's Voice* editorial reprinted in the September 22, 1942 issue of the *Statesman.*

3. Atlanta *Daily World,* September 11, 1942; Moultrie *Observer,* September 11, 1942; Bartow *Herald,* January 7, 1943; Valdosta *Times,* September 10, 1942; Augusta *Chronicle,* September 11, 1942; Milledgeville *Union-Recorder,* January 7, 1943; Cobb County *Times* editorial reprinted in the September 17, 1942 issue of the Atlanta *Journal.*

4. Interview with Ellis G. Arnall, Atlanta, Ga., December 12, 1985; Arnall's acceptance speech is reprinted in the October 7, 1942 issue of the Atlanta *Journal;* McGill's comments are found in his column in the October 8, 1942 issue of the Atlanta *Constitution.*

5. Atlanta *Constitution,* January 10, 1943; Atlanta *Journal,* January 10, 1943.

6. Atlanta *Journal,* January 10, 1943; *Messages and Addresses: Governor Ellis Arnall, 1943–1946* (Atlanta: Executive Department of the State of Georgia, n.d.), pp. 1–8.

7. *Messages and Addresses,* p. 2; Atlanta *Journal,* January 6, 1943; Macon *Telegraph,* January 12, 22, 1943; Taylor, "A Political Biography of Ellis Arnall," pp. 94–95; House *Journal* (1943), p. 14; Senate *Journal* (1943), p. 8; "Arnall: An Oral History," interview by Cook, pp. 64–65; *Statesman,* January 19, 1943. The office of lieutenant governor, whose occupant would preside over the Senate, was not created until 1945.

8. Senate *Journal* (1943), p. 80; House *Journal* (1943), p. 133; Atlanta *Journal,* February 6, 1943; *Messages and Addresses,* p. 4; House *Journal* (1943), pp. 133–34, 153–55; Senate *Journal* (1943), pp. 105, 160–61.

9. Atlanta *Journal,* January 23, 1943; Atlanta *Daily World,* January 31, 1943; Senate *Journal* (1943), pp. 112–13; Cook, "Politics and Education," pp. 287–89; Atlanta *Journal,* January 31, 1943; *Messages and Addresses,* p. 4; House *Journal* (1943), pp. 197, 327–30; Senate *Journal* (1943), pp. 80–83.

10. *Messages and Addresses,* p. 4; *Acts and Resolutions* (1943), pp. 225, 399–400, 361–63, 142–43; Senate *Journal* (1943), pp. 83, 178, 106–8, 83; House *Journal* (1943), pp. 385–86, 227, 197–98; *Messages and Addresses,* p. 4; Senate *Journal* (1943), pp. 247, 262, 280; House *Journal* (1943), pp. 16, 149, 168.

11. *Acts and Resolutions* (1943), pp. 298–302, 84; Senate *Journal* (1943), pp. 94, 104, 162–63; House *Journal* (1943), pp. 280, 134–36, 185–88; Atlanta *Constitution,* March 19, 1943; *Messages and Addresses,* p. 11; Atlanta *Journal,* February 6, 1943.

12. *Messages and Addresses*, p. 4; Atlanta *Journal*, September 6, 1942; Ellis G. Arnall, "Without a Dissenting Vote," Atlanta *Journal Magazine*, March 7, 1943, p. 1; Senate *Journal* (1943), pp. 125–27, 153–54, 141–45; House *Journal* (1943), pp. 368–69, 358–62; *Acts and Resolutions* (1943), pp. 43–47, 185–95; Atlanta *Journal*, February 9, 10, 1943.

13. *Messages and Addresses*, pp. 5–6; House *Journal* (1943), pp. 1218–38; Senate *Journal* (1943), pp. 933–34; Atlanta *Journal*, March 3, 1943; House *Journal* (1943), pp. 1239–42, 771–74; Senate *Journal* (1943), pp. 185–86, 923–24.

14. *Messages and Addresses*, p. 5; Senate *Journal* (1943), pp. 201–3; House *Journal* (1943), pp. 129–34; *Acts and Resolutions* (1943), pp. 284–88.

15. *Messages and Addresses*, pp. 5–6; Atlanta *Journal*, February 11, 1943; Senate *Journal* (1943), pp. 356–68.

16. Atlanta *Journal*, March 2, 1943; Taylor, "A Political Biography of Ellis Arnall," p. 101; House *Journal* (1943), pp. 912–15.

17. Atlanta *Constitution*, March 4, 1943; Arnall, "Governor You Will Be," pp. 43–44; House *Journal* (1943), pp. 943–45; Atlanta *Journal*, February 13, 1943; U.S. Congress, House, Committee on the Judiciary, Subcommittee No. 1, *Hearings on H.J. Res. 39*, 78th Cong., 1st sess., pp. 6–13.

18. Atlanta *Journal*, August 16, 1942; Senate *Journal* (1943), pp. 581–86; House *Journal* (1943), pp. 1314–16; Macon *Telegraph*, March 1, 1943; Arnall interview, July 19, 1985.

19. House *Journal* (1943), pp. 1381, 1370–72, 585–87, 1318–20; Senate *Journal* (1943), pp. 939–40, 864–65, 383–87, 683–85; Atlanta *Constitution*, January 26, 1943.

20. Cullen B. Gosnell and C. David Anderson, *The Government and Administration of Georgia* (New York: Thomas Y. Crowell Co., 1956), p. 137; Senate *Journal* (1943), pp. 248–49; House *Journal* (1943), 337–38; *Minutes of the Executive Department of the State of Georgia* (1943), files located at the Georgia Department of Archives and History, Atlanta, p. 160.

21. Gosnell and Anderson, *Government of Georgia*, pp. 25–26; Atlanta *Journal*, February 28, 1943; Senate *Journal* (1943), p. 692; House *Journal* (1943), p. 1247.

22. Atlanta *Journal*, March 18, 1943; Atlanta *Constitution*, March 19, 1943; Atlanta *Journal*, March 18, 1943; Senate *Journal* (1943), p. 1008; Walter Davenport, "Unanimous Arnall," *Collier's* 112 (July 24, 1943): 16; Taylor, "A Political Biography of Ellis Arnall," p. 94.

23. Atlanta *Journal*, March 19, 1943; Atlanta *Constitution*, March 19, 1943; Savannah *Morning News*, March 18, 1943; Calhoun *Times*, February 18, 1943; Augusta *Chronicle*, March 18, 1943; Cleveland (Ohio) *Plain Dealer* editorial reprinted in the February 28, 1943 issue of the Atlanta *Journal*.

24. Atlanta *Journal*, March 18, 1943; House *Journal* (1943), pp. 1368–69; Senate *Journal* (1943), p. 681; Franklin D. Burdette, "Lowering the Voting Age in

Georgia," *South Atlantic Quarterly* 44 (July 1945): 304; Ellis G. Arnall, "Admitting Youth to Citizenship," *State Government* 16 (October 1943): 204; Ellis G. Arnall, "Vote the Amendments," Atlanta *Journal Magazine*, July 25, 1943, p. 2.

25. Macon *Telegraph*, July 5, 1943; Arnall, *The Shore Dimly Seen*, p. 53; Atlanta *Constitution*, August 1, 1943; Arnall, "Vote the Amendments," p. 2; Atlanta *Journal* editorial, August 1, 1943.

26. *Official Register* (1945–50), pp. 370–94, 373.

27. Cook, *Governors of Georgia*, pp. 241–42, 250–51.

28. *Acts and Resolutions* (1943), pp. 37, 39, 113–17, 161–70, 212–16; Taylor, "A Political Biography of Ellis Arnall," p. 110.

29. Arnall interview, July 19, 1985; Cook, "Arnall: An Oral History," p. 6.

30. Senator George's comments are found in his letter to the editor, Atlanta *Constitution*, December 10, 1943; Atlanta *Journal*, February 28, 1943 (see the same issue for reprints of editorials from more than twenty out-of-state newspapers praising the Arnall administration); E. Merton Coulter, *Georgia: A Short History*, rev. ed. (Chapel Hill: University of North Carolina Press, 1947), pp. 449–50.

Chapter Five. *Georgia's Smelly Penal Muddle*

1. Taylor, "A Political Biography of Ellis Arnall," p. 117; Valdosta *Daily Times*, September 29, 1943; Augusta *Chronicle*, October 3, 1943; Atlanta *Journal*, April 22, 1943; Meriwether *Vindicator*, April 30, 1943.

2. For a history of the convict lease system, see A. Elizabeth Taylor, "The Origin and Development of the Convict Lease System in Georgia," *Georgia Historical Quarterly* 26 (Spring 1942): 113–28, and "The Abolition of the Convict Lease System in Georgia," *Georgia Historical Quarterly* 26 (Spring 1942): 273–87; Amanda Johnson, *Georgia as Colony and State* (Atlanta: Walter W. Brown Publishing Co., 1938), pp. 666–70, 725–26; Coulter, *Georgia: A Short History*, p. 416.

3. Tarleton Collier, *Georgia Penal System* (Atlanta: Citizens Fact Finding Committee, 1938), pp. 7–9.

4. Burns, *I Am a Fugitive*, pp. 47–55, 170–75, 56–57.

5. Atlanta *Journal*, November 1, 1945; Herndon, "Eurith Dickenson Rivers," pp. 190–95; Tarleton Collier, *Penal System: A Reflection of Our Lives and Our Customs* (Atlanta: Citizens Fact Finding Movement, 1940), p. 4.

6. Atlanta *Constitution*, August 22, 1943; Arnall, *The Shore Dimly Seen*, p. 238.

7. Atlanta *Constitution*, April 19, 1943; Atlanta *Journal*, April 16, 21, 1943.

8. Atlanta *Constitution*, April 27, 1943; Augusta *Chronicle*, April 20, 1943; Atlanta *Constitution*, April 19, 1943.

9. Tattnall *Journal*, April 19, 1943; Atlanta *Constitution*, April 21, 1943.

10. The Senate Committee's report is reprinted in the April 22, 1943 issue of the Atlanta *Journal;* Atlanta *Journal,* April 26, 1943.

11. Executive Department, *Minutes* (1943), pp. 124–25; *Statesman,* May 13, 1943; Atlanta *Journal,* April 25, 1943.

12. Atlanta *Journal,* April 25, 1943.

13. Cartersville *Tribune News,* August 26, 1943; Atlanta *Constitution,* August 21, 1943; Atlanta *Journal,* August 23, 1943.

14. Cartersville *Tribune News,* August 26, September 23, 1943.

15. Executive Department, *Minutes* (1943), p. 231; Atlanta *Constitution,* August 22, 1943.

16. Atlanta *Journal,* September 22, 1943; "Georgia's Middle Ages," *Time* 42 (September 13, 1943): 23; Augusta *Chronicle,* September 14, 1943; Valdosta *Daily Times,* September 9, 1943; Albany *Herald* editorial reprinted in the September 28, 1943 issue of the Atlanta *Constitution.*

17. House *Journal* (Extraordinary Session, 1943), pp. 20–21. The Harris-Gross report, officially entitled *Report to Governor Ellis Arnall on Prison Conditions in Georgia and Southern States,* is reprinted in House *Journal* (Extraordinary Session, 1943), pp. 20–34.

18. House *Journal* (Extraordinary Session, 1943), pp. 22–30, 32–33; Columbus *Ledger-Enquirer,* October 3, 1943.

19. Executive Department, *Minutes* (1943), p. 231; Atlanta *Journal,* August 22, 1943. The Senate Penitentiary Committee's report is reprinted in the September 17, 1943 issue of the Atlanta *Journal.*

20. Atlanta *Constitution,* September 13, 23, 24, 1943.

21. Ibid., September 25, 26, 1943.

22. Executive Department, *Minutes* (1943), p. 232; Atlanta *Journal,* September 26, 1943; Columbus *Enquirer,* September 27, 1943; Thomasville *Times-Enterprise,* September 30, 1943; Augusta *Chronicle,* September 27, 1943; Moultrie *Observer,* September 17, 1943; Albany *Herald,* September 29, 1943.

23. Savannah *Morning News,* September 26, 1943; Macon *Telegraph,* October 11, 1943; *Statesman,* October 7, 1943.

24. *Statesman,* October 7, 1943.

25. *Messages and Addresses,* pp. 18–21.

26. Ibid., pp. 21–22.

27. Ibid., pp. 22–24.

28. Ibid., pp. 19–21, 26.

29. Atlanta *Journal,* September 28, 29, 1943; Atlanta *Constitution,* September 28, 1943; House *Journal* (Extraordinary Session, 1943), p. 53; Senate *Journal* (Extraordinary Session, 1943), p. 29.

30. Atlanta *Constitution,* September 30, 1943; House *Journal* (Extraordinary Ses-

sion, 1943), pp. 39–42; Senate *Journal* (Extraordinary Session, 1943), pp. 22–23; House *Journal* (Extraordinary Session, 1943), p. 54.

31. *Acts and Resolutions* (Special Session, 1943), pp. 2–5.

32. House *Journal* (Extraordinary Session, 1943), p. 60; Atlanta *Constitution,* October 2, 1943; "Georgia Prisons: State Abolished Old Abuses," *Life* 15 (November 1, 1943): 93–99; Atlanta *Journal,* October 3, 1943; *Messages and Addresses,* p. 23; "Arnall: An Oral History," interview by Cook, p. 47.

33. Taylor, "A Political Biography of Ellis Arnall," p. 128; Atlanta *Journal,* October 6, 1943; Arnall interview, July 19, 1985; Atlanta *Journal,* December 27, 1943.

34. Robert A. Garson, *The Democratic Party and the Politics of Sectionalism, 1941–1948* (Baton Rouge: Louisiana State University Press, 1974), pp. 44–47.

35. Senator George's letter is reprinted in Atlanta *Journal,* December 12, 1943; Senate *Journal* (Extraordinary Session, 1944), pp. 5–6, 9–15; Atlanta *Constitution,* January 3, 1944. For press support of the session, see editorials in Atlanta *Constitution,* December 13, 1943; Atlanta *Journal,* January 3, 1944; Columbus *Enquirer,* January 3, 1944; Augusta *Chronicle,* December 13, 1943; Albany *Herald,* January 5, 1944; Valdosta *Daily News,* December 15, 1943; Thomasville *Times-Enterprise,* December 17, 1943; Macon *Telegraph,* January 3, 1944.

36. House *Journal* (Extraordinary Session, 1944), p. 29; Senate *Journal* (Extraordinary Session, 1944), p. 25; *Acts and Resolutions* (Extraordinary Session, 1944), pp. 2–8; Savannah *Morning News,* January 8, 1944; Atlanta *Journal,* January 8, 1944; Atlanta *Constitution,* January 8, 1944; Senate *Journal* (Extraordinary Session, 1944), pp. 28, 5.

37. Augusta *Chronicle,* October 3, 1943; Atlanta *Journal,* December 21, 11, 1943; Arnall interview, March 26, 1987.

38. Atlanta *Journal,* November 1, 1945; Arnall interview, March 26, 1987.

39. *Statesman,* November 8, 1945; Atlanta *Journal,* November 2, 1945.

40. Arnall interview, July 19, 1985.

Chapter Six. *A New Constitution*

1. Saye, *Constitutional History of Georgia,* pp. 388, 393; James M. Burns, J. W. Peltason, and Thomas E. Cronin, *State and Local Politics: Government by the People,* 4th ed. (Englewood Cliffs, N.J.; Prentice-Hall, 1984), p. 62; Arnall, *The Shore Dimly Seen,* pp. 247–49.

2. Alan Conway, *The Reconstruction of Georgia* (Minneapolis: University of Minnesota Press, 1966), pp. 200–215; Mildred Thompson, *Reconstruction in Georgia: Economic, Social, and Political* (New York: Columbia University Press, 1915; reprint,

Savannah: Beehive Press, 1972), pp. 210–18; Amanda Johnson, *Georgia as Colony and State*, pp. 542–47; Saye, *Constitutional History of Georgia*, p. 278.

3. William Y. Thompson, *Robert Toombs of Georgia* (Baton Rouge: Louisiana State University Press, 1966), pp. 241–43; Bartley, *Creation of Modern Georgia*, pp. 77–79; Samuel W. Small, *A Stenographic Report of Proceedings of the Constitutional Convention Held in Atlanta, Georgia, 1877* (Atlanta: Constitutional Publishing Co., 1877), p. 407.

4. *Georgia Political System* (Atlanta: Citizens Fact Finding Movement, 1938), p. 7; Arnall, *The Shore Dimly Seen*, p. 249.

5. Senate *Journal* (1901), pp. 32–33; Senate *Journal* (1902), pp. 22–23; Senate *Journal* (1927), p. 182.

6. Gosnell and Anderson, *Government of Georgia*, p. 26; "A Proposed Constitution for Georgia," *Bulletin of the University of Georgia* 32 (January 1932): ix, 10, 18.

7. House *Journal* (1933), p. 1832; Senate *Journal* (1933), p. 1468; *Executive Minutes January 10, 1933 to December 31, 1933, Eugene Talmadge, Governor, State of Georgia*, p. 88.

8. *Political System: Democracy's First Line of Defense* (Atlanta: Citizens Fact Finding Movement, 1940), p. 23; interview with Ellis G. Arnall, Atlanta, Ga., June 19, 1987.

9. Ellis Arnall, "Writing a New Constitution," Atlanta *Journal Magazine*, January 2, 1944, p. 5; Arnall interview, June 19, 1987.

10. House *Journal* (1943), p. 1247; Senate *Journal* (1943), p. 692; paragraphs 1–2, section 1, Constitution of 1877; Taylor, "A Political Biography of Ellis Arnall," pp. 138–39.

11. Albert B. Saye, ed., *Records of the Commission of 1943–1944 to Revise the Constitution of Georgia*, 2 vols. (Atlanta: n.p., 1946), 1:2–4; Arnall interview, June 19, 1987.

12. *Records of the Commission of 1943–1944*, 1:ix.

13. Ibid., 1:5, 23, 85, 65, 79, 66.

14. Ibid., 1:84–85.

15. Ibid., 1:198–202, 206.

16. Ibid., 2:187–90, 235, 262–69.

17. Ibid., 2:181–82, 231–58.

18. Ibid., 2:225, 294–95; Atlanta *Journal*, September 22, 1944; *Records of the Commission of 1943–1944*, 2:297.

19. *Records of the Commission of 1943–1944*, 1:70–74, 187–90, 209–13; Arnall interview, June 19, 1987. The Georgia Supreme Court invalidated this provision of the constitution in 1946 (Thompson v. Atlantic Coast Line Railroad, 200 Ga. 856).

20. Key, *Southern Politics*, p. 119; *Records of the Commission of 1943–1944*, 1:327–31; Arnall interview, June 19, 1987.

21. Arnall, "Writing a New Constitution," p. 5. Percentage obtained from an ap-

pendix prepared by Ella May Thornton, state librarian, in *Constitution of the State of Georgia of 1877 as Amended Through 1943*, compiled by Attorney General T. Grady Head, p. 150.

22. *Records of the Commission of 1943–1944*, 2:281–87, 301–21.

23. Smith v. Allwright, 321 U.S. 349 (1944); Hugh C. Owen, "The Rise of Negro Voting in Georgia: 1944–1950" (Master's thesis, Emory University, 1951), p. 3.

24. *Records of the Commission of 1943–1944*, 1:112–14; Atlanta *Journal*, May 29, 1944.

25. *Records of the Commission of 1943–1944*, 1:95–101; Arnall interview, July 19, 1985; Atlanta *Constitution*, April 11, 1944.

26. Taylor, "A Political Biography of Ellis Arnall," pp. 147–48; *Records of the Commission of 1943–1944*, 2:336–37.

27. Atlanta *Constitution*, August 15, 1944.

28. Atlanta *Constitution*, November 24, 1944; Atlanta *Journal*, November 19, 1944; Atlanta *Constitution*, November 16, 1944.

29. Atlanta *Constitution*, November 26, 1944; *Records of the Commission of 1943–1944*, 2:338; Atlanta *Journal*, December 3, November 26, 1944; Albany *Herald*, November 30, 1944; Augusta *Chronicle*, December 5, 1944.

30. *Records of the Commission of 1943–1944*, 2:374–79, 408–10, 382, 396–405, 450–51, 448, 444–45.

31. Ibid., 2:478–517, 516–17, 465–67, 471–75.

32. Ibid., 2:533–39.

33. Ibid., 2:467–68, 477, 539–40, 543–46.

34. Atlanta *Journal*, January 8, 1945; Atlanta *Constitution*, January 1, 1945.

35. House *Journal* (1945), pp. 489–90; Senate *Journal* (1945), pp. 599–602, 729–30; House *Journal* (1945), pp. 485–88; Senate *Journal* (1945), pp. 597–99; House *Journal* (1945), p. 949; House *Journal* (1945), pp. 385–86; Senate *Journal* (1945), pp. 469–72, 726.

36. Arnall interview, December 12, 1985; *Records of the Commission of 1943–1944*, 1:342; Taylor, "A Political Biography of Ellis Arnall," p. 165; Senate *Journal* (1945), pp. 944–45, 951.

37. Executive Department, *Minutes* (1945), p. 6; Atlanta *Journal*, January 24, February 5, 1945; House *Journal* (1945), pp. 600–601; Senate *Journal* (1945), p. 411; Atlanta *Journal*, February 28, 1945.

38. Atlanta *Constitution*, December 21, 23, 1944.

39. Atlanta *Constitution*, January 7, 1945. For statements of the senators on the subject, see the Atlanta *Journal* editorial "The Discredited Poll Tax," January 8, 1945. Both opposed federal action to do away with the poll tax that was being discussed in the Congress. Atlanta *Constitution*, January 4, 1945; Atlanta *Journal*, January 8, 1945.

40. *Messages and Addresses,* p. 46; House *Journal* (1945), pp. 28–29; Senate *Journal* (1945), p. 14; Atlanta *Journal,* January 14, 1945; House *Journal* (1945), pp. 169–71.

41. Atlanta *Journal,* January 23, 1945.

42. Savannah *Evening Press* editorial is reprinted in the February 8, 1945 issue of the *Statesman.* Atlanta *Journal,* January 24, 1945; Atlanta *Constitution,* January 24, 1945. The Columbus *Ledger* editorial is reprinted in the January 28, 1945 issue of the Atlanta *Journal.*

43. Senate *Journal* (1945), pp. 141–42; Atlanta *Constitution,* January 25, 1945; Taylor, "A Political Biography of Ellis Arnall," p. 261; Arnall interview, July 19, 1985.

44. House *Journal* (1945), pp. 317–18; Senate *Journal* (1945), pp. 271–75; Senate *Journal* (1945), p. 402; House *Journal* (1945), p. 353; Key, *Southern Politics,* p. 578. The other southern states that had repealed the poll tax were North Carolina in 1920, Louisiana in 1934, and Florida in 1937. Atlanta *Journal,* March 28, 1945; the *Times* and *Tennessean* editorials are reprinted in the February 4, 1945 issue of the Atlanta *Constitution;* the *News and Observer* editorial is reprinted in the February 11, 1945 issue of the Atlanta *Constitution;* "People in the Limelight: Ellis Arnall," *New Republic* 112 (February 12, 1945): 214; Clark Foreman, "Georgia Kills the Poll Tax," *New Republic* 112 (February 26, 1945): 291.

45. The *Morning News* editorial is reprinted in the April 5, 1945 issue of the *Statesman;* Frederick D. Ogden, *The Poll Tax in the South* (University: University of Alabama Press, 1958), pp. 181–87; Arnall interview, February 2, 1986.

46. House *Journal* (1945), pp. 943–51; Senate *Journal* (1945), pp. 723–31; House *Journal* (1945), pp. 93–95, 137–38, 252, 629, 1068, 764; Senate *Journal* (1945), pp. 91–92, 116, 854, 266, 819–30, 861.

47. House *Journal* (1945), pp. 798–99, 977; Senate *Journal* (1945), pp. 927, 943.

48. Atlanta *Journal,* July 4, 1945; Eleanor Williams, *Ivan Allen: A Resourceful Citizen* (Atlanta: Ivan Allen–Marshall Co., 1950), pp. 204, 209; Harold Paulk Henderson, "The 1946 Gubernatorial Election in Georgia" (Master's thesis, Georgia Southern College, 1967), p. 14; Atlanta *Journal,* July 8, 15, 1945.

49. Atlanta *Journal,* July 31, 1945; Milledgeville *Union-Recorder,* August 7, 1945; Winder *News,* July 26, 1945; Augusta *Chronicle,* August 7, 1945; Vienna *News,* August 2, 1945; Valdosta *Daily Times,* July 24, 1945; Fitzgerald *Herald,* July 20, 1945. For additional papers in support, see Brunswick *News,* July 21, 1945; Meriwether *Vindicator,* August 3, 1945; Macon *News,* July 30, 1945; Dalton *News,* July 26, 1945; Augusta *Herald,* July 31, 1945; Atlanta *Daily World,* August 5, 1945. For excerpts of editorials of more than twenty other papers favoring ratification, see C. E. Gregory, Jr.'s editorial columns in Atlanta *Journal* of July 31 and August 1, 1945. For papers in opposition, see Savannah *Morning News,* July 10, 1945; Savan-

nah *Evening Press,* July 25, 1945; Rome *News-Tribune,* July 12, 1945; *Statesman,* July 19, 1945.

50. The names of the organizations supporting ratification are in an editorial in the August 3, 1945 issue of the Atlanta *Journal.*

51. *Statesman,* March 2, November 23, 1944; July 19, 1945; August 24, December 14, 1944; July 13, 1944.

52. Ibid., March 2, 1945.

53. Atlanta *Journal,* July 27, August 3, July 29, 1945.

54. Atlanta *Journal,* July 28, 1945; *Official Register* (1945–50), p. 473; Atlanta *Journal,* August 8, 1945; Saye, *Constitutional History of Georgia,* p. 397.

55. Saye, *Constitutional History of Georgia,* p. 397; Taylor, "A Political Biography of Ellis Arnall," p. 173; Arnall interview, June 19, 1987. For a complete listing of the changes, see Ellis G. Arnall, "Arnall Describes Provisions to Eliminate Dictatorship," Atlanta *Constitution,* April 1, 1945; Saye, *Constitutional History of Georgia,* pp. 397–400; Gosnell and Anderson, *Government of Georgia,* pp. 27–32; Arnall, *The Shore Dimly Seen,* pp. 252–58.

56. Georgia replaced the Constitution of 1945 in 1976.

Chapter Seven. *State Finances and Services*

1. Lamar Q. Ball, *Georgia in World War II: A Study of the Military and Civilian Effort* (1946), pp. 9–10; Coulter, *Georgia: Short History,* p. 452.

2. Atlanta *Constitution,* January 10, 1943; *State Auditor Report* (1942), pp. viii–ix; *State Auditor Report* (1943), p. viii; Atlanta *Journal,* January 10, 1943.

3. *Messages and Addresses,* p. 9; Atlanta *Journal,* January 10, 1943.

4. Arnall interview, July 19, 1985; Arnall, *The Shore Dimly Seen,* pp. 232–33; Ellis G. Arnall, "States Must Pay Debts, Too," Atlanta *Journal Magazine,* December 10, 1944, p. 4; Ellis G. Arnall, "Arnall Cites Needs: Material, Skill, Order," Atlanta *Constitution,* April 1, 1945.

5. Atlanta *Journal,* January 10, 1943; Arnall interview, July 19, 1985; Arnall, "State Must Pay Debts," p. 4; *Georgia Goes Forward: The Record of One Year's Accomplishment* (Athens: Agricultural and Industrial Development Board, April 1945), p. 55.

6. *Messages and Addresses,* p. 12; *Georgia Goes Forward,* p. 55; *State Auditor Report* (Supplement, 1942), p. viii; *State Auditor Report* (Supplement, 1945), p. viii; Department of Education, *Seventy-second and Seventy-third Annual Reports,* p. 263; Department of Education, *Seventy-fourth and Seventy-fifth Annual Reports,* p. 69. The number of teachers includes vocational, evening school, and special program

teachers. If only figures for elementary and high school teachers are used, the decline is 387.

7. *State Auditor Report* (1942), p. 2; *State Auditor Report* (1943), p. 2; *State Auditor Report* (1944), p. 2; *State Auditor Report* (1945), p. 2; *State Auditor Report* (1946), p. 2; *Messages and Addresses*, p. 58.

8. "Arnall: An Oral History," interview by Cook, p. 54; Atlanta *Constitution*, December 16, 1945; *Messages and Addresses*, p. 58; Arnall, *The Shore Dimly Seen*, pp. 234–35. Arnall was strongly committed to paying off the state debt.

State Tax Revenue Spent on Public Debt, 1942–1946

Fiscal year ending June 30	State tax revenue spent on public debt	Percentage of state tax revenue spent on public debt
1942	$382,250	.7
1943	8,237,000	14.4
1944	6,818,000	11.4
1945	5,285,000	9.0
1946	4,295,000	5.1
Total	$24,635,000	

In addition to the $24,635,000 in state tax revenues spent on public debt, $1,521,000 of "undistributed revenue" was carried over from the 1942 fiscal year into the 1943 fiscal year and applied toward debt payment. The Arnall administration thus committed $26,156,000 toward paying off the state debt. Sources: *State Auditor Reports* (1942), p. xi; (1943), p. x; (1944), p. x; (1945), p. x; (1946), p. x.

9. Arnall interview, July 19, 1985; Atlanta *Constitution*, February 27, March 17, 1933; Atlanta *Constitution*, November 2, 1941; *Messages and Addresses*, pp. 3, 43, 59; Robert Preston Brooks, *Financing Government in Georgia, 1850–1944*, University of Georgia Bulletin, no. 5, May 1946 (Athens: University of Georgia, 1946), pp. 34–35.

10. Arnall interview, July 19, 1985; Brooks, *Financing Government*, p. 32; Arnall interview, February 2, 1986.

11. Atlanta *Journal*, March 19, 1944; Ellis G. Arnall, "Facilities for Higher Education Must Be Expanded, Arnall Says," Atlanta *Constitution*, December 24, 1944; *Messages and Addresses*, p. 4.

12. *State Auditor Report* (1942), p. 79; *State Auditor Report* (1946), p. 22; *State Auditor Report* (1942), p. 29; *State Auditor Report* (1946), p. 23; *Messages and Addresses*, p. 103.

13. Oscar H. Joiner, gen. ed., *A History of Public Education in Georgia, 1734–1976* (Columbia, S.C.: R. L. Bryan Co., 1979), pp. 327–28; House *Journal* (1943), pp. 1218–38; Senate *Journal* (1943), pp. 933–34; *State Auditor Report* (1945), p. 487;

State Auditor Report (1947), p. 25; "Retirement Realized," *Georgia Education Journal* 38 (March 1945): 9.

14. Letter from Governor Arnall to J. Harold Saxon, executive secretary of the Georgia Education Association, January 18, 1945, reprinted in U.S. Congress, Senate, Committee on Education and Labor, *Federal Aid to Education: Hearings on S. 181*, 79th Cong., 1st sess., part 1, January 29, 30, 31 and February 1, 2, 8, 1945, pp. 220–21; Ellis G. Arnall, "Federal Aid to Education: A Southern View," *Georgia Education Journal* 37 (October 1943): 10; Atlanta *Constitution*, December 7, 1945.

15. Atlanta *Journal*, April 14, 16, 1944, and October 28, 1945; Taylor, "A Political Biography of Ellis Arnall," p. 181.

16. First Resolution of the 1944 Annual GEA Convention reprinted in *Georgia Education Journal* 37 (May 1944): 16.

17. *Statesman*, April 11, 1946; Atlanta *Constitution*, April 12, 1946; Department of Education, *Seventy and Seventy-first Annual Reports*, p. 263; Department of Education, *Seventy-sixth and Seventy-seventh Annual Reports*, p. 82.

18. Department of Education, *Seventy-fourth and Seventy-fifth Annual Reports*, pp. 5–6; Atlanta *Constitution*, April 12, 1946; Atlanta *Journal* editorial, April 12, 1946; *Annual Report for 1944–1945 by Regents of the University System*, June 30, 1945, p. 6.

19. Department of Education, *Seventy-second and Seventy-third Annual Reports*, p. 263; Department of Education, *Seventy-sixth and Seventy-seventh Annual Reports*, p. 82; *A Study of School Buildings in Georgia [Brief Summary] Program of Educational Development for Georgia* (Athens: Education Panel, Agricultural and Industrial Development Board, February 1945), pp. 4–6; Department of Education, *Seventy-fourth and Seventy-fifth Annual Reports*, pp. 73–76.

20. Arnall, *The Shore Dimly Seen*, pp. 96–97; C. Vann Woodward, *The Strange Career of Jim Crow*, 3d rev. ed. (New York: Oxford University Press, 1974), pp. 145–46.

21. Joiner, *History of Public Education*, pp. 334–38; *Records of the Commission of 1943–1944*, 1:309; Department of Education, *Seventy-second and Seventy-third Annual Reports*, pp. 7–10.

22. Department of Education, *Seventy-second and Seventy-third Annual Reports*, pp. 40–46; Joiner, *History of Public Education*, pp. 349–52; Atlanta *Journal*, June 25, 1945; *Messages and Addresses*, p. 57.

23. *Study of School Buildings*, pp. 1–10; *Annual Report of the Education Panel Program of Educational Development for Georgia*, Education Panel Bulletin No. 12 (Agricultural and Industrial Development Board, August 1945), pp. 8–11; Atlanta *Journal*, August 28, 1945.

24. *Acts and Resolutions* (1946), pp. 713–14; O. C. Aderhold et al., *A Survey of Public Education of Less Than College Grade in Georgia. A Report to the General Assembly of Georgia by Its Special Committee on Education* (Atlanta, January 1, 1947), pp.

13, 15; *Acts and Resolutions* (1949), pp. 1406–22; Joiner, *History of Public Education,* pp. 388–90; Numan V. Bartley, "Race Relations and the Quest for Equality," in *A History of Georgia,* Kenneth Coleman, gen. ed., pp. 377–78.

25. *Twentieth Report of the State Highway Department . . . for the Fiscal Years Ending June 30, 1943, and June 30, 1944,* pp. 3, 5; *Congress and the Nation, 1945–1964: A Review of Government and Politics in the Post-War Years* (Washington, D.C.: Congressional Quarterly, 1965), p. 527. *Messages and Addresses,* p. 61; House *Journal* (1946), pp. 393–94; Senate *Journal* (1946), pp. 263–64.

26. Atlanta *Journal,* July 8, 1946; Atlanta *Constitution,* February 10, 1946; Atlanta *Journal,* March 12, 1946.

27. Atlanta *Constitution,* August 29, 1946; Atlanta *Journal,* August 29, 1946.

28. Atlanta *Journal,* August 30, September 1, 1946; Atlanta *Constitution* editorial, September 4, 1946.

29. *Opinions* (1945–47), pp. 622–24; Atlanta *Journal,* September 4, 1946; Atlanta *Journal* editorial, September 5, 1946.

30. Arnall interview, July 19, 1985; *Acts and Resolutions* (1943), pp. 216–22; Derrell Coolidge Dowdy, "State Highway Administration in Georgia" (Master's thesis, University of Georgia, 1950), pp. 45–48.

31. For a brief summary of Eugene Talmadge's and Ed Rivers's difficulties with the leadership of the department, see Albert Pafford Foster, "The Georgia State Highway Department—Its Origin, Development, and Current Administration" (Master's thesis, Emory University, 1949), pp. 45–48; *Official Register* (1945–50), p. 34; Atlanta *Journal,* December 26, 27, 1944; Senate *Journal* (1945), pp. 791–92.

32. Atlanta *Constitution,* January 4, 9, 1946.

33. Ibid., January 9, 1946.

34. Atlanta *Journal,* January 22, 1946; letter from Arnall to Steve Tate, chairman of the Georgia Highway Commission, February 1, 1946, in February 7, 1946 minutes folder of the Highway Commission, Georgia Department of Archives and History, Atlanta; *Minutes of State Highway Commission of Georgia, April 21, 1943–January 6, 1947,* February 7, 1946 meeting, Department of Transportation, Atlanta, pp. 149–50; Atlanta *Constitution,* February 8, 1946.

35. House *Journal* (1946), pp. 130–32; Senate *Journal* (1946), pp. 295–97, 394–95; *Messages and Addresses,* p. 61; Letter from Arnall to Steve Tate, February 1, 1946 Highway Commission minutes, Department of Archives and History, Atlanta; House *Journal* (1946), p. 525; *Acts and Resolutions* (1950), 1:62–72; *Official Register* (1963–64), p. 1544.

36. *State Auditor Report* (1942), pp. 282, 284; *State Auditor Report* (1946), pp. 404–9; Ellis G. Arnall, "Arnall Cites Georgia's Progress in Caring for Its Distressed," Atlanta *Constitution,* January 7, 1945; *Messages and Addresses,* pp. 115–16; Arnall, "Arnall Cites Georgia's Progress."

37. *Messages and Addresses,* p. 61; House *Journal* (1946), pp. 230–33; Senate *Journal* (1946), pp. 222–23; *Official Register* (1945–50), p. 565; *Statesman,* September 19, October 10, 1946.

38. Arnall, "Arnall Cites Georgia's Progress."

39. Senate *Journal* (1946), pp. 452–55; Atlanta *Constitution,* December 20, 1945; House *Journal* (1946), p. 129; Senate *Journal* (1946), p. 362; Atlanta *Journal,* December 12, 1945.

40. Atlanta *Constitution,* March 18, 1945; Senate *Journal* (1946), p. 406. The reports of the committees on the various state institutions are in Senate *Journal* (1946), pp. 406–55; Atlanta *Journal,* February 4, 1945.

41. *Georgia Goes Forward,* p. 40.

42. Atlanta *Journal,* August 29, October 21, 1945.

43. Atlanta *Constitution,* November 16, 1945; Atlanta *Journal,* November 6, December 14, 1945.

44. *Messages and Addresses,* pp. 59–61; House *Journal* (1946), p. 524; *Acts and Resolutions* (1946), pp. 787–90.

45. Herndon, "Eurith Dickenson Rivers," p. 175; Gosnell and Anderson, *Government of Georgia,* p. 336; *Messages and Addresses,* p. 6; Ellis G. Arnall, "Governor Arnall Points the Way to Greater Progress in Georgia," *Georgia Progress,* September 15, 1944.

46. *Acts and Resolutions* (1943), pp. 113–17; Atlanta *Journal,* January 23, 1944; *State Auditor Report* (1942), p. 29. "Financial Statement of Agricultural and Industrial Development Board, April 1, 1944–June 30, 1946" is in *Headlining Georgia's Progress: A Report on the Work of the Agricultural and Industrial Development Board,* September 1, 1946, p. 29. *Georgia Goes Forward,* pp. 12–15; *State Auditor Report* (Supplement, 1946), p. vii; *State Auditor Report* (Supplement, 1942), p. viii. The board divided itself into eight panels—agriculture, education, government, health, industry, public works, and forestry as well as one for trade, commerce, and business.

47. Ellis G. Arnall, "5 State Agencies Devoting Talent to Task of Making Farming Pay," Atlanta *Constitution,* January 14, 1945; *Georgia Goes Forward,* pp. 20–21.

48. Cason J. Callaway, *A Broader Plan for the 100 Georgia Better Farms, Inc.* (mimeographed report); newspaper editorials quoted in *Headlining Georgia's Progress,* p. 8.

49. *Georgia Goes Forward,* pp. 28–30; *Headlining Georgia's Progress,* pp. 9–10; Joiner, *History of Public Education,* pp. 387–88; chapter 1 of *Survey of Public Education: Annual Report of the Education Panel* (1945), p. 5. The results of the four studies are summarized in *Annual Report of the Education Panel* (1945).

50. *Georgia Goes Forward,* pp. 41–43; *Headlining Georgia's Progress,* p. 15; *Georgia Progress,* November 15, 1944.

51. *Georgia Progress*, January 1, 1945; *Georgia Goes Forward*, pp. 47–50.

52. *Messages and Addresses*, p. 56; *Georgia Progress*, July 1, 1946; *Georgia Progress*, December 1, 1945; Atlanta *Journal*, June 28, 1945.

53. Frederick R. Harris, Inc., *The Port of Savannah, Report to the Agricultural and Industrial Development Board of Georgia* (New York, 1945); Frederick R. Harris, Inc., *The Port of Brunswick, Report to the Agricultural and Industrial Development Board of Georgia* (New York, 1945); *Georgia Goes Forward*, p. 58; Senate *Journal* (1945), p. 861; House *Journal* (1945), p. 764; *Acts and Resolutions* (1945), pp. 464–80; *Georgia Progress*, December 1, 1944.

54. Letter from Arnall to Chairman Blanton Fortson, August 22, 1946, reprinted in *Headlining Georgia's Progress*, p. 2; *Acts and Resolutions* (1945), pp. 1252–54; Gosnell and Anderson, *Government of Georgia*, p. 336; Taylor, "A Political Biography of Ellis Arnall," p. 207; *Acts and Resolutions* (1949), p. 249; "Arnall: An Oral History," interview by Cook, p. 61.

55. U.S. Congress, House Judiciary Committee, Subcommittee No. 1, *Hearings on H.J. Res. 39*, 78th Cong., 1st sess., October 20, 1943, serial 6, p. 9; *Messages and Addresses*, pp. 1, 164; Arnall, *The Shore Dimly Seen*, p. 229; Arnall, *What the People Want*, p. 37; Atlanta *Constitution*, July 2, 1945; *Messages and Addresses*, pp. 71–72.

56. Arnall, *What the People Want*, p. 37; *Messages and Addresses*, pp. 164, 28.

Chapter Eight. *The Freight Rate Controversy*

1. National Emergency Council, *Report on Economic Conditions of the South* (Washington, D.C.: 1938), p. 1; Woodward, *Origins of the New South*, pp. 291–320; George Brown Tindall, *The Emergence of the New South, 1913–1945* (Baton Rouge: Louisiana State University Press, 1967), pp. 443–72.

2. Arnall, *The Shore Dimly Seen*, p. 168; David M. Potter, "The Historical Development of Eastern-Southern Freight Rate Relationships," *Law and Contemporary Problems* 12 (Summer 1947): 420–28; William H. Joubert, *Southern Freight Rates in Transition* (Gainesville: University of Florida, 1949), pp. 8–21.

3. Potter, "Historical Development," pp. 430–32; Joubert, *Freight Rates*, pp. 40–51.

4. *Letter from the Board of Investigation and Research Transmitting a Summary Report on Its Study of Interterritorial Freight Rates*, 78th Cong., 1st sess., House document 145, pp. 1–4; Tennessee Valley Authority, *Regionalized Freight Rates: Barrier to National Productiveness*, 78th Cong., 1st sess., House document 137, pp. 12–13, 23.

5. J. Haden Alldredge, *The Interterritorial Freight Rate Problem of the United States*, 75th Cong., 1st sess., House document 264, p. 13.

6. Ibid., pp. 15–17; *Regionalized Freight Rates*, p. 4.

7. Frank L. Barton, "Economic Efforts of Discriminatory Freight Rates," *Law and Contemporary Problems* 12 (Summer 1947): 513; John H. Goff, "The Interterritorial Freight-Rate Problem and the South," *Southern Economic Journal* 6 (April 1940): 450–51.

8. Jonathan Daniels, *A Southerner Discovers the South* (New York: Macmillan, 1938), p. 266; Ellis G. Arnall, "The Freight Rate Cartel," *New Republic* 112 (April 16, 1945): 497; Ellis G. Arnall, "The South's Readmission to the Union," lecture given to the Atlanta Historical Society, February 2, 1982; Ellis G. Arnall, "The Unknown South: Our Last Frontier," New York *Times Magazine*, July 15, 1945, pp. 12–13, 28.

9. Carl Brent Swisher, *American Constitutional Development*, 2d ed. (Cambridge: Riverside Press, 1954), pp. 406–19; U.S. Congress, House, Committee on the Judiciary, *Study of Monopoly Power, Hearings Before the Subcommittee on Study of Monopoly Power of the Committee on the Judiciary*, 81st Cong., 1st sess., 1949, serial 14, part 1, p. 266; Arne C. Wiprud, *Justice in Transportation: An Exposé of Monopoly Control* (Chicago: Ziff-Davis Publishing Co., 1945), pp. 48–49.

10. Potter, "Historical Development," pp. 432–33, 437.

11. Coulter, *Georgia: A Short History*, p. 452; "The Freight-Rate Battle," *Fortune* 13 (October 1944): 149; Alldredge, *Interterritorial Freight Rate Problem*, p. iv; Tennessee Valley Authority, *Supplemental Phases of the Interterritorial Freight Rate Problem of the United States*, 76th Cong., 1st sess., House document 271, pp. v–viii; Wiprud, *Justice in Transportation*, pp. ix–xvii; Henry Wallace, "Transportation Problems," speech given by the vice president in Dallas, Texas, October 20, 1943, reprinted in *Congressional Record*, 78th Cong., 1st sess., pp. 8610–13; Robert A. Lively, *The South in Action: A Sectional Crusade Against Freight Rate Discrimination* (Chapel Hill: University of North Carolina Press, 1949), p. 25.

12. *Southern Class Rate Investigations*, 1925, 100 I.C.C. 513, supplemented by 109 I.C.C. 300, 113 I.C.C. 200, and 128 I.C.C. 567; Robert A. Lively, "The South and Freight Rates: Political Settlement of an Economic Argument," *Journal of Southern History* 14 (August 1948): 362; Lively, *The South in Action*, p. 19.

13. Herndon, "Eurith Dickenson Rivers," pp. 296–97; Lively, *The South in Action*, pp. 21–22.

14. State of Alabama et al. v. New York Central Railroad Co. et al., 135 I.C.C. 255, 257–59.

15. Ibid., pp. 308–11.

16. Ibid., pp. 312–19.

17. Lively, *The South in Action*, pp. 26–27; U.S. Congress, House, Committee on Interstate and Foreign Commerce, *Hearings Before a Subcommittee of the House Committee on Interstate and Foreign Commerce, Omnibus Transportation Bill*, 76th Cong., 1st sess., 1939; U.S. Congress, Senate, Committee on Interstate Commerce, *Freight Rate Discriminations, Hearings Before a Subcommittee of the Senate Committee on Interstate Commerce, Omnibus Transportation Bill*, 76th Cong., 1st sess., 1939.

18. *Supplemental Phases of the Interterritorial Freight Rate Problem,* pp. xiii–xiv, 27–32.

19. Frank L. Barton, "Background of the Class-Rate Investigation," *Southwestern Social Science Quarterly* 21 (December 1940): 205–8; Joubert, *Freight Rates,* pp. 337–41.

20. Alabama v. New York Central Railroad, pp. 319–27, 268–306, 331–32; Lively, *The South in Action,* p. 46.

21. Alabama v. New York Central Railroad, pp. 329–30; Lively, *The South in Action,* p. 48.

22. Joubert, *Freight Rates,* pp. 340–46.

23. Ibid., pp. 365–69.

24. Lively, *The South in Action,* pp. 53–56.

25. *Minutes of the Meeting of the Southern Governors Conference,* March 25–26, 1943, pp. 9–10; Taylor, "A Political Biography of Ellis Arnall," p. 241.

26. *Minutes of the Southern Governors Conference,* p. 9; Ellis G. Arnall, "What the South Asks," Atlanta *Journal Magazine,* May 2, 1943, p. 2.

27. *Messages and Addresses,* pp. 69–70; Atlanta *Journal,* June 24, 1943.

28. Atlanta *Journal,* September 18, 1943; Atlanta *Constitution,* September 19, 1943. The reporter was Lamar Q. Ball.

29. Atlanta *Journal,* September 19, 1943; January 18, 1944.

30. Atlanta *Journal,* January 18, 1944; Arnall, *The Shore Dimly Seen,* p. 167; Atlanta *Constitution,* May 18, 1945.

31. Arnall, *The Shore Dimly Seen,* p. 180.

32. Executive Department, *Minutes,* May 27, 1944, pp. 57–58.

33. Atlanta *Journal,* May 28, 1944; Arnall interview, July 19, 1985; Arnall, *The Shore Dimly Seen,* pp. 180–81; Lively, *The South in Action,* p. 69; Atlanta *Journal,* May 21, 1945; Atlanta *Constitution* editorial, March 27, 1945.

34. Atlanta *Journal,* May 28, 29, 1944; Georgia v. Pennsylvania Railroad Co. et al., 331 U.S. 788 (1947). Alabama's position is stated in *Motion of the State of Alabama for Leave to File Petition of Intervention, Petition of Intervention and Brief, Georgia v. Pennsylvania Railroad Co. et al.,* in *U.S. Supreme Court, Transcripts of Records and File Copies of Briefs, 1950,* vol. 13, case 10, original, part 2.

35. *Motion for Leave to File Amended Bill of Complaint and Amended Bill of Complaint, Georgia v. Pennsylvania Railroad Co. et al.,* in *U.S. Supreme Court, Transcripts of Records and File Copies of Briefs, 1950,* vol. 12, case 10, original, part 1, 10–15.

36. Ibid., pp. 22–23.

37. *Plaintiff's Trial Brief for the Court, Georgia v. Pennsylvania Railroad Co. et al.,* reprinted in U.S. Congress, Senate, *Regulation of Rate Bureaus, Conferences and Associations, Hearings Before the Senate Committee on Interstate Commerce on H. R. 2536,* 79th Cong., 2d sess., 1946, pp. 530–31, 545–46.

38. *Brief for the United States Amicus Curiae as to Jurisdiction, Georgia v. Pennsylva-*

nia Railroad Co. et al., in *U.S. Supreme Court, Transcripts of Records and File Copies of Briefs*, 1950, vol. 12, case 10, original, part 1, 2–17.

39. Arnall interview, July 19, 1985; Atlanta *Journal*, January 1, 1945; Taylor, "A Political Biography of Ellis Arnall," p. 249; Atlanta *Constitution*, January 3, 1945.

40. Atlanta *Journal*, January 3, 1945; New York *Times*, January 3, 1945; Arnall's concluding statement is quoted in Arne C. Wiprud, *The Search for Wider Horizons* (Richmond: William Byrd Press, 1970), p. 75.

41. Atlanta *Journal* editorial, January 3, 1945; Atlanta *Constitution*, January 3, 1945; Sam Hall Flint, "The Great Freight Rate Fight," *Atlanta Historical Journal* 28 (Summer 1984): 19; Taylor, "A Political Biography of Ellis Arnall," p. 248; letter from President Roosevelt to Ellis Arnall reprinted in Atlanta *Constitution*, January 14, 1945.

42. New York *Times*, March 27, 1945; Georgia v. Pennsylvania Railroad Co. et al., 324 U.S. 401 (1945), 462, 453, 455.

43. Atlanta *Constitution*, March 27, 1945; Arnall, *The Shore Dimly Seen*, p. 182; Atlanta *Journal*, March 27, 1945.

44. New York *Times*, March 27, 1945; "For the South—Arnall," *Time* 25 (April 9, 1945): 69; Atlanta *Journal*, April 22, 1945; Taylor, "A Political Biography of Ellis Arnall," p. 253; Atlanta *Journal* editorial, March 27, 1945; Atlanta *Constitution* editorial, March 27, 1945.

45. New York *Times*, December 18, 1945.

46. Lively, *The South in Action*, pp. 65–67; Wiprud, *Justice in Transportation*, pp. 87–95.

47. United States v. Association of American Railroads et al., 4 F.R.D. 510 (1945); Atlanta *Journal*, May 11, 1945.

48. *Southern Class Rate Investigations*, 262 I.C.C. 447, 447–49.

49. Atlanta *Constitution*, May 20, 1945; New York *Times*, May 20, 1945; Birmingham *News* editorial quoted in Lively, *The South in Action*, p. 69; Atlanta *Journal* editorial, May 21, 1945; Ralph Smith in Atlanta *Journal*, May 21, 1945.

50. Letter from Arnall to President Truman, October 11, 1945, Official File of Harry S. Truman, Truman Library, Independence, Mo.; President Truman to Arnall, October 17, 1945, Official File of Harry S. Truman, Truman Library.

51. Atlanta *Journal*, October 5, 1945; U.S. Congress, House, Committee on Interstate and Foreign Commerce, *Application of Antitrust Laws to Agreements in Furtherance of the National Transportation Policy, Hearings Before a Subcommittee of the House Committee on Interstate and Foreign Commerce on H.R. 2536*, 79th Cong., 1st sess., 1945, pp. 379–81, 3–5; "Bulwinkle Bill Receives Overwhelming Support," *I.C.C. Practitioners Journal* 12 (November 1945): 144–45; U.S. Congress, *Congressional Record*, 79th Cong., 1st sess., p. 11777.

52. *Regulation of Rate Bureaus, Conferences, and Associations*, pp. 423, 551.

53. Ibid., pp. 475–76, 420, 457–58, 482, 461, 480–82.

54. U.S. Supreme Court, *Report of the Special Master, Georgia v. Pennsylvania Railroad Co. et al.*, October term, 1949, 1:2; U.S. Supreme Court, *Georgia v. Pennsylvania Railroad Co. et al.*, transcript of *Report of Proceedings Had Before Lloyd K. Garrison, Special Master* (Washington, D.C.: H. S. Middlemiss, Official Reporter), 1:22, 25.

55. *Congressional Record*, 80th Cong., 1st sess., p. 7215; *Congressional Record*, 80th Cong., 2d sess., pp. 5647–48; telegram from Arnall to President Truman, May 17, 1948, Official File of Harry S. Truman, Truman Library, Independence, Mo.; letter from Arnall to President Truman, June 1, 1948, Official File of Harry S. Truman, Truman Library.

56. *Public Papers of the Presidents of the United States, Harry S. Truman, Containing the Public Messages, Speeches, and Statements of the President January 1 to December 31, 1948* (Washington, D.C.: U.S. Government Printing Office, 1964), pp. 330–32, telegram from Arnall to Truman, June 14, 1948, Official File of Harry S. Truman, Truman Library, Independence, Mo.; *Congressional Record*, 80th Cong., 2d sess., pp. 8435, 8633–34; Arnall, "The South's Readmission to the Union."

57. New York *Times*, December 22, 1945; State of New York et al. v. United States, 65 F. Supp 856; New York et al. v. United States et al., 331 U.S. 284 (1947), pp. 284–87; Arnall, "One Country: Equal Rights," *Nation* 164 (May 31, 1947): 650.

58. *Report of the Special Master*, 1:14–16, 156, 175–77, 201; Georgia v. Pennsylvania Railroad Co. et al., 340 U.S. 889 (1950).

59. Albert Riley in Atlanta *Constitution*, May 30, 1952; Tindall, *Emergence of the New South*, p. 602; Cook, "Arnall: An Oral History," p. 43.

60. Cook, *Governors of Georgia*, p. 257; Coulter, *Georgia: A Short History*, p. 453; Numan V. Bartley, "Politics and Government in the Postwar Era," in *A History of Georgia*, Coleman, gen. ed., p. 389; Taylor, "A Political Biography of Ellis Arnall," p. 266; Eugene H. Methvin, "Ellis Arnall: The South's Dragon-Slaying Hero," Atlanta *Journal-Constitution*, March 8, 1987; A. G. Mezerik, *The Revolt of the South and West* (New York: Duell, Sloan and Pearce, 1946), pp. 113–14; Arnall, "The South's Readmission to the Union." Others complimentary of Arnall's role in ending rate discrimination included Zell Miller, *Great Georgians* (Franklin Springs, Ga.: Advocate Press, 1983), p. 22; Frederick Allen and Bill Shipp, political reporters for the Atlanta newspapers, Atlanta *Constitution*, January 5, 1981, and Atlanta *Journal-Constitution*, March 8, 1987; Celestine Sibley, "Once They Heard the Cheers: Southern as a Cotton Patch," Atlanta *Weekly*, October 30, 1983, p. 15.

61. Flint, "Great Freight Rate Fight," p. 19; Lively, *The South in Action*, pp. 88–89; Calvin B. Hoover and B. U. Ratchford, *Economic Resources and Policies of the South* (New York: Macmillan, 1951), p. 78.

Chapter Nine. *The Race Issue*

1. "Arnall: An Oral History," interview by Cook, p. 70.

2. U.S. Bureau of the Census, *Sixteenth Census of the United States, 1940*, Population vol. 2, *Characteristics of the Population*, Part 2, *Florida–Iowa* (Washington, D.C.: U.S. Government Printing Office, 1943), p. 186; U.S. Bureau of the Census, *Statistical Abstract of the United States, 1946*, p. 42; Bartley, "Race Relations and the Quest for Equality," in *A History of Georgia*, Coleman, gen. ed., p. 361.

3. Dewey W. Grantham, Jr., "Georgia Politics and the Disfranchisement of the Negro," *Georgia Historical Quarterly* 32 (March 1, 1948): 1–21; Owen, "Rise of Negro Voting," pp. 1–11.

4. Lynwood M. Holland, *The Direct Primary in Georgia* (Urbana: University of Illinois Press, 1949), pp. 50–54.

5. Arnall interview, February 2, 1986; Arnall, *The Shore Dimly Seen*, pp. 105–6; John Gunther, *Inside U.S.A.* (New York: Harper and Brothers, 1947), pp. 776–77; Arnall interview, February 2, 1986.

6. Arnall interview, February 2, 1986; Anderson, *The Wild Man from Sugar Creek*, p. 205; Smith, "Democracy Begins at Home," pp. 9–10; Anderson, *The Wild Man from Sugar Creek*, p. 210. The Augusta *Herald* editorial is quoted in Benjamin E. Mays, *Born to Rebel: An Autobiography* (New York: Charles Scribner's Sons, 1971), p. 221.

7. Smith, "Democracy Begins at Home," p. 10; Atlanta *Constitution*, May 17, 1942; Harold H. Martin, *Ralph McGill, Reporter* (Boston: Little, Brown and Co., 1973), pp. 81–85. In an editorial McGill declared, "The South knows that a dual system is the only workable system" (Atlanta *Constitution*, August 4, 1946).

8. "Arnall: An Oral History," interview by Cook, pp. 65–66; Atlanta *Journal*, January 28, 1944, and January 23, 1945.

9. Atlanta *Daily World*, January 1, 1944; Mays, *Born to Rebel*, p. 22.

10. Louisville *Times*, June 26, 1945.

11. *Statesman*, July 5, 1945; Gunnar Myrdal, *An American Dilemma: The Negro Problem and Modern Democracy*, Twentieth Anniversary Edition (New York: Harper and Row, 1962), p. 608.

12. Atlanta *Journal*, June 27, 1945.

13. For Eugene Talmadge's views of blacks, see Sutton, "The Talmadge Campaigns," pp. 69–71; Ellis Arnall, "Revolution Down South," *Collier's* 116 (July 28, 1945): 17.

14. Arnall interview, February 2, 1986; Nixon v. Herdon, 273 U.S. 536 (1927); Grovey v. Townsend, 295 U.S. 45 (1935).

15. Smith v. Allwright, 321 U.S. 349 (1944); "The South: Time Bomb," *Time* 43 (April 17, 1944): 20–21; *Statesman*, April 13, 1944.

16. Atlanta *Journal*, June 7, 1944; King v. Chapman et al., 62 F. Supp. 639 (1945), 650.

17. Atlanta *Journal*, October 14, 1945; Columbus *Ledger-Enquirer*, October 21, 1945; Macon *Telegraph*, October 21, 1945; *Statesman*, October 18, 1945; Atlanta *Journal*, October 13, 1945; Atlanta *Daily World*, October 16, 1945; Savannah *Morning News*, October 19, 1945.

18. Chapman et al. v. King, 154 F.2d 460 (1946), 463–64.

19. Atlanta *Constitution*, March 8, 1946; Henderson, "The 1946 Gubernatorial Election in Georgia," p. 26; Arnall, *The Shore Dimly Seen*, p. 59; Atlanta *Journal*, March 16, 1946; Atlanta *Constitution*, March 29, 1946.

20. Atlanta *Constitution*, March 29, 1946; Louisville *Times*, June 26, 1945; Atlanta *Journal*, June 27, 1945; *Records of the Commission of 1943–1944*, 1:112–13; Atlanta *Journal*, May 29, 1944.

21. Chapman et al. v. King, 327 U.S. 800 (1946).

22. Atlanta *Constitution*, April 5, 1946; Holland, *The Direct Primary*, p. 85; Owen, "Rise of Negro Voting," p. 4; "Arnall: An Oral History," interview by Cook, pp. 66–67.

23. Arnall, *The Shore Dimly Seen*, pp. 59–60; Taylor, "A Political Biography of Ellis Arnall," p. 277; Talmadge interview, March 24, 1986; Arnall interview, February 2, 1986; *Sixteenth Census*, 2:216–25; Key, *Southern Politics*, p. 523.

24. Atlanta *Journal*, April 5, 1946; Columbus *Ledger*, April 17, 1946; Macon *News*, April 8, 1946.

25. Savannah *Morning News*, April 7, 1946; Atlanta *Journal*, May 19, 1946; Macon *Telegraph*, April 16, 1946; Henderson, "The 1946 Gubernatorial Election in Georgia," pp. 42–66.

26. Atlanta *Constitution*, May 10, 1946; Atlanta *Journal*, May 20, 30, 1946; Ellis Arnall, "My Battle Against the Klan," *Cornet* 20 (October 1946): 7; New York *Times*, June 22, 1946; Atlanta *Journal*, May 30, 1946; Atlanta *Constitution*, June 22, 1946.

27. Atlanta *Journal*, July 22, 1946; Atlanta *Daily World*, July 28, 1946.

28. Clement Charlton Mosley, "Invisible Empire: A History of the Ku Klux Klan in Twentieth-Century Georgia, 1915–1965" (Ph.D. dissertation, University of Georgia, 1968), p. 140; Atlanta *Journal*, September 26, 1946; Atlanta *Constitution*, June 21, 1946; Mosley, "Invisible Empire," p. 143.

29. Atlanta *Constitution*, November 18, 1946.

30. Thomas A. Krueger, *And Promises to Keep: The Southern Conference for Human Welfare, 1938–1948* (Nashville: Vanderbilt University Press, 1967), pp. 20–39, 149–51, 145.

31. Atlanta *Constitution*, November 19, 1946; Columbus *Ledger*, November 20, 1946; Augusta *Chronicle*, November 22, 1946; *Statesman*, December 5, 1946.

32. Atlanta *Constitution,* November 26, 1946; *Statesman,* December 5, 1946; Morton Sosna, *Southern Liberals and the Race Issue: In Search of the Silent South* (New York: Columbia University Press, 1977), p. 194; Lillian Smith, "Pay Day in Georgia," *Nation* 164 (February 1, 1947): 119.

33. Krueger, *Promises to Keep,* pp. 152–53; New Orleans *Times-Picayune,* December 1, 1946; New York *Times,* December 1, 1946.

34. Atlanta *Constitution,* February 17, 10, 1947.

35. Arnall, *The Shore Dimly Seen,* pp. 83–106.

36. Ibid., pp. 90–91, 101, 106.

37. Ibid., pp. 96–97, 99, 104, 99.

38. On the question of rights of blacks in the South during this period see part 6 of Myrdal, *An American Dilemma,* pp. 523–69, and Ann Wells Ellis, "The Commission on Interracial Cooperation, 1919–1944: Its Activities and Results" (Ph.D. dissertation, Georgia State University, 1976), pp. 59–145. On the question of black voting, see Owen, "Rise of Negro Voting"; Steven F. Lawson, *Black Ballots: Voting Rights in the South, 1944–1967* (New York: Columbia University Press, 1976); and Ira De A. Reid, "Georgia's Negro Vote," *Nation* 163 (July 6, 1946): 12–14.

Chapter Ten. *Political Adversities*

1. Sylvester *Local* editorial suggesting Arnall as a presidential candidate reprinted in the Atlanta *Journal,* February 3, 1944; Taylor, "A Political Biography of Ellis Arnall," p. 291.

2. Bernd, "Primary Elections," pp. 23–28; Anderson, *The Wild Man from Sugar Creek,* pp. 157–64; Arnall interview, February 2, 1986; Newnan *Herald,* September 8, 1940; Atlanta *Constitution,* September 8, 1940; Atlanta *Constitution,* November 2, 1941, February 12, 1942; Atlanta *Journal,* May 3, August 16, 1942.

3. Arnall, *The Shore Dimly Seen,* pp. 290–92.

4. Edward L. Schappmeier and Frederick H. Schappmeier, *Henry A. Wallace of Iowa: The Agrarian Years, 1910–1940* (Ames: Iowa State University Press, 1968), pp. 260–71; J. B. Shannon, "Presidential Politics in the South," *Journal of Politics* 10 (August 1948): 472–73; James F. Byrnes, *All in One Lifetime* (New York: Harper Brothers, 1958), p. 124.

5. John Gunther, *Roosevelt in Retrospect: A Profile in History* (New York: Harper and Row, 1950), p. 348; Eleanor Roosevelt, *This I Remember* (New York: Harper and Brothers, 1949), p. 220; Herman Eugene Talmadge, *Talmadge: A Political Legacy, a Politician's Life, a Memoir* (Atlanta: Peachtree Publishers, 1987), p. 67.

6. Atlanta *Journal,* July 2, 1944; Arnall, *What the People Want,* p. 94.

7. Edward L. Schappmeier and Frederick H. Schappmeier, *Prophet in Politics:*

Henry A. Wallace and the War Years, 1940–1965 (Ames: Iowa State University Press, 1970), p. 102; Leon Friedman, "Election of 1944," in *History of American Presidential Elections, 1789–1968*, ed. Arthur M. Schlesinger, Jr. (New York: Chelsea House Publishers, 1971), 4:3023–24; Norman D. Markowitz, *The Rise and Fall of the People's Century: Henry A. Wallace and American Liberalism, 1941–1948* (New York: Free Press, 1973), pp. 102–3; Henry A. Wallace, *The Price of Vision: The Diary of Henry A. Wallace, 1942–1946*, ed. John Morton Blum (Boston: Houghton Mifflin Co., 1973), pp. 365–67.

8. Arnall interview, February 2, 1986; Atlanta *Journal*, July 19, 1944. A portion of Arnall's address before the Georgia caucus is reprinted in Ralph McGill's column, "Ralph McGill Is Proud of the Georgia Delegation," Atlanta *Constitution*, July 20, 1944.

9. Arnall interview, February 2, 1986.

10. Schappmeier and Schappmeier, *Prophet in Politics*, pp. 107–8; Arnall interview, February 2, 1986; Atlanta *Journal*, July 21, 1944; Markowitz, *American Liberalism*, pp. 110–11.

11. *Official Report of the Proceedings of the Democratic National Convention . . . July 19th to July 21st, inclusive, 1944* (N.p. 1944), p. 79.

12. *Proceedings of the Democratic National Convention*, pp. 256, 257, 270; Atlanta *Journal*, July 22, 1944; Arnall interview, February 2, 1986; Henry Wallace to Ellis Arnall, July 22, 1944, Henry A. Wallace Collection, University of Iowa Libraries, Iowa City.

13. Atlanta *Constitution*, July 30, 1944; Henry Wallace to Ellis Arnall, July 22, 1944, Henry A. Wallace Collection, University of Iowa Libraries, Iowa City; Atlanta *Journal*, August 17, 1944; Ellis Arnall to Henry Wallace, September 25, 1944, and Henry Wallace to Ellis Arnall, December 22, 1944, Ellis Arnall File, Franklin D. Roosevelt Papers, Franklin D. Roosevelt Library, Hyde Park, N.Y. The inscription is from Arnall's copy of Henry A. Wallace, *Democracy Reborn* (New York: Russell Lord, Reynal and Hitchcock, 1944).

14. Telegram from Ellis Arnall to Henry Wallace, January 19, 1945, Henry A. Wallace Collection, University of Iowa Libraries, Iowa City; Arnall, *What the People Want*, p. 96; telegrams from Arnall to Senators Richard B. Russell and Walter F. George, Ellis Arnall File, Henry A. Wallace Collection, University of Iowa Libraries; Schappmeier and Schappmeier, *Prophet in Politics*, pp. 121–24.

15. Markowitz, *American Liberalism*, pp. 178–93; Harry S. Truman, *Memoirs*, vol. 2 (Garden City, N.J.: Doubleday, 1955), pp. 555–61; Arnall, *What the People Want*, p. 98; Arnall interview, February 2, 1986; telegram from Ellis Arnall to Harry S. Truman, December 30, 1947, in Personal File of Harry S. Truman, Harry S. Truman Library, Independence, Mo.; Arnall, *What the People Want*, p. 97.

16. Schappmeier and Schappmeier, *Prophet in Politics*, p. 115; *Statesman*, November 27, 1947.

17. *Statesman,* June 27, July 27, August 31, 1944; Augusta *Courier,* March 8, 1948; Talmadge, *Talmadge,* p. 68; *Statesman,* July 22, 1948.

18. *Records of the Commission of 1943–1944,* 2:225–26, 294, 545–46; Atlanta *Journal,* February 28, April 25, 1945.

19. Atlanta *Journal,* May 15, 1945; Atlanta *Constitution,* May 19, 1945; Atlanta *Journal,* May 16, 1945; Taylor, "A Political Biography of Ellis Arnall," p. 298.

20. C. E. Gregory, Jr., in Atlanta *Journal,* May 29, 1945. For over fifty editorials supporting the session, see Atlanta *Journal,* May 20–29, 1945. Vienna *News* and Columbus *Enquirer* editorials reprinted in Atlanta *Journal,* May 28, 1945.

21. Atlanta *Constitution,* September 23, 1944; *Statesman,* February 1, May 31, 1945; Miller, "The Administration of Rivers," p. 144; Atlanta *Constitution,* September 23, 1944; Atlanta *Journal,* May 23, 1945.

22. Atlanta *Journal,* May 25, 1945; Executive Department, *Minutes* (1945), pp. 96–97; Senate *Journal* (May 1945), p. 12; House *Journal* (May 1945), p. 10; Atlanta *Constitution,* May 30, 1945.

23. Atlanta *Journal,* May 30, 1945; Atlanta *Constitution,* May 30, 31, 1945.

24. Atlanta *Constitution,* May 31, 1945.

25. Senate *Journal* (May 1945), pp. 20–23; Atlanta *Journal,* June 1, 1945; House *Journal* (May 1945), p. 26; Senate *Journal* (May 1945), pp. 25–26; Atlanta *Constitution,* June 1, 1945; *Statesman,* June 7, 21, 1945.

26. Atlanta *Constitution,* June 2, 1945; Atlanta *Journal,* June 11–13, 1945; *Statesman,* June 21, 1945; Atlanta *Journal,* July 15, 18, 1945.

27. Atlanta *Constitution,* July 27, 1945; *Official Register* (1945–50), p. 179; Atlanta *Constitution,* May 27, 1945; Miller, "The Administration of Rivers," p. 18; Key, *Southern Politics,* p. 124; Bernd, "Primary Elections," p. 31; Atlanta *Constitution,* August 1, November 16, 1945.

28. Taylor, "A Political Biography of Ellis Arnall," pp. 7–8; Athens *Banner-Herald,* June 17, 1946; Lanier County *Times,* August 2, 1945.

29. Bernd, *Grass Root Politics,* p. 10; Herndon, "Eurith Dickenson Rivers," pp. 322–31; Miller, "The Administration of Rivers," pp. 135–44; Luther Harmon Zeigler, Jr., "Senator Walter George's 1938 Campaign," *Georgia Historical Quarterly* 43 (December 1959): 333–34; Arnall interview, February 2, 1986; Herndon, "Eurith Dickenson Rivers," p. 354.

30. Atlanta *Journal,* January 14, 1946; Executive Department, *Minutes* (1946), p. 15; Senate *Journal* (1946), pp. 37–39; House *Journal* (1946), p. 125; Atlanta *Constitution,* January 16, 17, 19, 1946; Atlanta *Journal,* January 22, 1946; Atlanta *Constitution,* January 24, 1946.

31. Atlanta *Constitution,* January 18, 1946; *Statesman,* January 17, 1946; Atlanta *Constitution,* February 1, January 25, 1946.

32. Atlanta *Constitution,* January 26, 1946; House *Journal* (1946), p. 386; Atlanta *Constitution,* January 26, 1946; Atlanta *Journal,* January 22, February 1, 1946.

33. Atlanta *Constitution*, January 27, 1946; Chapman et al. v. King, 154 F.2d 460 (1946); Atlanta *Constitution*, March 16, 1946; *Statesman*, March 21, 28, 1946; Atlanta *Constitution*, March 19, 28, 1946.

34. Macon *Telegraph*, April 6, 1946; Savannah *Morning News*, April 7, 1946.

35. Atlanta *Constitution*, April 10, 1946; Augusta *Chronicle*, April 17, 18, 1946; Arnall interview, December 12, 1985; Macon *Telegraph*, May 26, 1946.

36. Cobb County *Times*, April 18, 1946; Atlanta *Constitution*, May 12, 1946; Lanier County *Times*, April 15, 1946; Augusta *Chronicle*, April 21, 1946.

37. Atlanta *Journal*, July 7, 1946; Atlanta *Daily World*, April 9, 1946; Gainesville *News*, April 11, 1946; Augusta *Chronicle*, May 1, 1946; Athens *Banner-Herald*, July 11, 1946; Milledgeville *Union-Recorder*, April 18, 1946; Thomaston *Free-Press*, April 9, 1946.

38. Herndon, "Eurith Dickenson Rivers," p. 42; Talmadge, *Talmadge*, p. 58; Miller, "The Administration of Rivers," pp. 11–144 passim; Henderson, "The 1946 Gubernatorial Election in Georgia," p. 36; Macon *Telegraph*, June 9, 1946.

39. Sutton, "The Talmadge Campaigns," pp. 285–86; Atlanta *Journal*, April 16, 1946; *Records of the Commission of 1943–1944*, 1:iii; Atlanta *Constitution*, May 12, 1946; Atlanta *Journal*, June 23, 1946; Vincent Jones editorial in the Jackson *Progress-Argus* reprinted in the Atlanta *Journal*, June 10, 1946.

40. Savannah *Morning News*, May 22, 1946; Atlanta *Constitution*, June 23, July 7, 1946.

41. Arnall interview, February 2, 1986; Taylor, "A Political Biography of Ellis Arnall," pp. 192–94.

42. Atlanta *Constitution*, June 16, 1946; Savannah *Morning News*, July 2, 1946; Atlanta *Constitution*, June 26, 1946; Savannah *Morning News*, May 19, 1946.

43. Atlanta *Constitution*, July 3, 1946; Atlanta *Journal*, July 5, 1946; Eastman *Times-Journal*, June 20, 1946; Atlanta *Journal*, July 10, 1946; Atlanta *Constitution*, July 1, 1946; Americus *Times-Recorder*, July 2, 1946; Macon *Telegraph*, July 4, 1946; Valdosta *Daily Times*, July 5, 1946; Griffin *Daily News*, July 9, 1946.

44. Atlanta *Journal*, June 21, 23, 25, 27, 1946; Atlanta *Constitution*, May 24, 1946; Atlanta *Journal*, July 9, 1946; Atlanta *Constitution*, July 9, 1946.

45. Herndon, "Eurith Dickenson Rivers," pp. 263–68; Sutton, "The Talmadge Campaigns," pp. 285–86; Valdosta *Daily Times*, June 27, 1946; Arnall interview, February 2, 1986.

46. *Official Register* (1945–50), pp. 486, 490–93; Atlanta *Constitution*, July 19, 1946; *Statesman*, July 25, August 6, 1946; Atlanta *Constitution*, July 19, 1946; Augusta *Chronicle*, July 19, 1946; Rome *News-Tribune* editorial reprinted in Savannah *Morning News*, July 20, 1946.

47. "Condolences to the State of Georgia," *Nation* 63 (July 27, 1946): 86–87; "The Majority Loses," *New Republic* 115 (July 29, 1946): 92–93; Atlanta *Journal*, July 18, 1946; *Official Register* (1945–50), pp. 490–93. Sutton and Carmichael's

campaign manager accepted this assumption. Sutton, "The Talmadge Campaigns," pp. 335–36; Bernd, "Primary Elections," pp. 75–87. Harris attributed Talmadge's victory, among other factors, to Rivers's presence in the race. Atlanta *Journal,* July 18, 1946. Belvin deemed Rivers's presence "made it possible for Talmadge, supported by a hard-core section of the electorate which favored his racial views, to carry counties in which the majority did not see race as the primary issue." William L. Belvin, Jr., "The Georgia Gubernatorial Primary of 1946," *Georgia Historical Quarterly* 50 (March 1966): 51. Bartley concluded that Rivers's entry into the race "very probably" cost Carmichael the election. Bartley, *Creation of Modern Georgia,* p. 188. Herndon believed that Rivers's presence in the race was a major factor in Talmadge's victory. Herndon, "Eurith Dickenson Rivers," p. 368. Taylor concluded, however, that it was "impossible to say who would have won in a two-man Talmadge-Carmichael race." Taylor, "A Political Biography of Ellis Arnall," p. 368. Herman Talmadge believed that his father would have received most of Rivers's votes if Rivers had not been in the race. Herman E. Talmadge interview, March 24, 1986, Lovejoy, Ga. For a discussion of the purge effort, see Joseph L. Bernd, "White Supremacy and the Disfranchisement of Blacks in Georgia, 1946," *Georgia Historical Quarterly* 66 (Winter 1982): 492–513, and Howard Lawrence Preston, "The Georgia Gubernatorial Campaign and Democratic Primary Election of 1946" (Master's thesis, Atlanta University, 1971), pp. 72–86.

48. New York *Times,* July 19, 1946; "Condolences," p. 86; Atlanta *Constitution,* October 10, 1946.

Chapter Eleven. *The Three-Governor Controversy*

1. *Official Register* (1945–50), p. 486; Atlanta *Constitution,* August 3, 4, 1946; Truman et al. v. Duckworth et al., 329 U.S. 675 (1946); Atlanta *Constitution,* October 5, 8, 1946.

2. Senate *Journal* (1947), pp. 34–35; *Official Register* (1945–50), pp. 486, 543; Hartwell *Sun,* July 5, 1946; Augusta *Chronicle,* April 16, 1946; *Georgia Voter: Facts About Candidates Offering for State Positions,* compiled by Georgia League of Women Voters, reprinted in Cartersville *Daily Tribune News,* July 4, 1946; letter from S. Marvin Griffin to John Etheridge, July 12, 1946, S. Marvin Griffin Collection, Baker County folder, Bainbridge College Library, Bainbridge, Ga.; Atlanta *Daily World,* March 20, 1947.

3. Arnall interview, December 12, 1985; Bernd, "White Supremacy and Disfranchisement," p. 508.

4. Atlanta *Journal,* December 21, 1946; Atlanta *Constitution,* December 22, 1946; Talmadge, *Talmadge,* p. 57; Cairo *Messenger,* December 27, 1946; Augusta *Chronicle,* December 22, 1946; "Eugene Talmadge," *Nation* 163 (December 28,

1946): 743; "Georgia: Death of the Wild Man," *Time* 48 (December 30, 1946): 18; Savannah *Morning News,* December 22, 1946.

5. Cobb County *Times,* December 23, 1946.

6. Savannah *Morning News,* December 24, 1946; Americus *Times-Recorder,* December 24, 1946.

7. Atlanta *Journal,* December 27, 1946.

8. Atlanta *Constitution,* December 28, 1946; Valdosta *Daily Times,* January 2, 11, 1947; Atlanta *Constitution,* January 12, 1947; Atlanta *Journal,* January 13, 1947; Herman E. Talmadge to Leon F. Beddingfield, date not given, 1947 correspondence, Dooley County folder, Melvin E. Thompson Papers, Archives of Contemporary South Georgia History, Valdosta State College Library, Valdosta, Ga.

9. *Attorney General Opinions* (August 1945–December 1947), pp. 303–5; Atlanta *Constitution,* January 5, 1947; Talmadge to Beddingfield, 1947 correspondence, Dooley County folder, Thompson Papers, Valdosta State College Library, Valdosta, Ga.

10. Atlanta *Journal,* January 12, 1947; Savannah *Morning News,* January 12, 1947.

11. For some editorials supporting Herman Talmadge's claim, see Greensboro *Herald-Journal,* January 3, 1947; Douglas *Enterprise,* January 2, 1947; Washington *News-Reporter,* December 26, 1946. For some editorials in opposition see Lanier County *Times,* January 9, 1947; Augusta *Chronicle,* December 29, 1946; Savannah *Morning News,* December 15, 1946; "Herman the Pretender," *Nation* 164 (January 25, 1947): 90; New York *Times,* January 13, 1947.

12. Henderson, "The 1946 Gubernatorial Election in Georgia," pp. 83–84; author's interview with Herman E. Talmadge, Government Documentation Project, Georgia State University, Atlanta, 1987, pp. 30–32; Charles Myer Elson, "The Georgia Three-Governor Controversy of 1947," *Atlanta Historical Journal* 20 (Fall 1976): 75; Talmadge, *Talmadge,* pp. 74–75.

13. Valdosta *Daily Times,* January 1, 1947; Atlanta *Constitution,* December 22, 1946, January 14, 1947.

14. House *Journal* (1947), p. 13; Senate *Journal* (1947), p. 12; House *Journal* (1947), p. 27; Atlanta *Constitution,* January 15, 1947.

15. Atlanta *Constitution,* January 11, 1947; Arnall, *What the People Want,* p. 14; Talmadge interview, Georgia Government Documentation Project, p. 32; "Wool Hat Rebellion," *Newsweek* 29 (January 27, 1947): 21; Talmadge interview, Government Documentation Project, p. 36.

16. Senate *Journal* (1947), pp. 20–21.

17. Ibid., p. 21.

18. Senate *Journal* (1947), p. 24; Atlanta *Journal,* January 15, March 2, 1947.

19. *Statesman,* January 30, 1947; Talmadge, *Talmadge,* p. 86; Arnall interview, December 12, 1985; Atlanta *Journal,* January 22, 1947.

20. Atlanta *Journal,* January 15, March 2, 1947; Atlanta *Constitution,* January 16, 1947.

21. Senate *Journal* (1947), pp. 25–33.

22. Talmadge interview, Government Documentation Project, p. 32; House *Journal* (1947), pp. 36–45; Atlanta *Journal,* January 15, 1947; Atlanta *Constitution,* January 15, 1947; Arnall, *What the People Want,* pp. 11–12.

23. Savannah *Morning News,* January 15, 1947; Atlanta *Constitution,* January 15, 1947; Atlanta *Journal,* January 15, 1947; "Wool Hat Rebellion," p. 23; Arnall, *What the People Want,* p. 12.

24. Atlanta *Journal,* January 15, 1947; Augusta *Chronicle,* January 16, 1947; Atlanta *Journal,* January 15, 1947; Atlanta *Constitution,* January 16, 1947.

25. Talmadge interview, Georgia Government Documentation Project, p. 33; Atlanta *Journal,* January 16, 1947.

26. Atlanta *Journal,* January 16, 1947.

27. Atlanta *Constitution,* January 18, 1947.

28. Atlanta *Journal,* January 17, 1947.

29. Savannah *Morning News,* January 20, 1947; Atlanta *Journal,* January 22, 1947.

30. McGill, "How It Happened Down in Georgia," p. 12; Atlanta *Constitution,* January 23, 1947; Augusta *Chronicle,* January 16, 1947; Fitzgerald *Herald,* January 15, 1947; Valdosta *Daily Times,* January 17, 1947; Washington *Post* editorial quoted in Atlanta *Constitution,* January 21, 1947; Atlanta *Daily World,* January 16, 1947; Cedartown *Standard* editorial quoted in A. G. Mezerick, "Georgians Have Had Enough," *Nation* 164 (February 15, 1947): 174–75; Eastman *Times Journal,* January 23, 1947.

31. Valeria Wise, secretary, Quarterly Conference of Peachtree Road Methodist Church to M. E. Thompson, January 23, 1947, 1947 correspondence, Fulton County folder, Thompson Papers, Valdosta State College Library, Valdosta, Ga.; "Church Groups Assail Talmadge," *Christian Century* 164 (February 19, 1947): 242; Macon *Telegraph,* January 21, 1947; W. D. Carswell to President Harry S. Truman, January 20, 1947, copy in Herman Talmadge 1947 File, Russell Papers, Richard B. Russell Memorial Library, University of Georgia, Athens; Atlanta *Daily World,* February 23, 1947; Valdosta *Daily Times,* January 20, 1947; Smith, "Pay Day in Georgia," p. 118.

32. Atlanta *Journal,* January 21, 19, 1947; Valdosta *Daily Times,* January 20, 1947; Marie Adams to Richard B. Russell, January 20, 1947, Herman Talmadge 1947 File, Russell Papers, Richard B. Russell Memorial Library, University of Georgia, Athens; R. E. Hood to M. E. Thompson, December 31, 1946, 1947 correspondence, Glynn County folder, Thompson Papers, Valdosta State College Library, Valdosta, Ga.; W. Millican to M. E. Thompson, January 17, 1947, 1947 correspondence, DeKalb County folder, Thompson Papers, Valdosta State College Library;

A. B. Moss to M. E. Thompson, January 23, 1947, Floyd County folder, Thompson Papers, Valdosta State College Library; Cleveland L. Adams to Rep. Tom Morgan, January 20, 1947, Troup County folder, Thompson Papers, Valdosta State College Library.

33. Valdosta *Daily Times,* January 20, 1947; Cartersville *Daily Tribune News,* January 24, 1947; Sandersville *Progress,* January 30, 1947; Meriwether *Vindicator,* January 24, 1947.

34. DeKalb *New Era,* January 23, 1947; Atlanta *Journal,* January 20, 1947; Valdosta *Daily Times,* January 24, 1947; Atlanta *Journal,* January 22, 1947; Carroll County *Georgian,* January 23, 1947; Macon *Telegraph,* January 21, 1947; Atlanta *Constitution,* January 22, 1947.

35. Bulloch *Times,* February 6, 1947; Meriwether *Vindicator,* January 31, 1947; DeKalb *New Era,* January 30, 1947; Sandersville *Progress,* January 30, 1947.

36. Della Edward to M. E. Thompson, February 13, 1947, General Files, Thompson Papers, Valdosta State College Library, Valdosta, Ga.; M. E. Thompson to Representative M. A. Kenimer, January 28, 1947, General Files, Thompson Papers, Valdosta State College Library (Representative Kenimer's response is written on the Thompson letter); C. J. Woodell to M. E. Thompson, January 18, 1947, 1947 correspondence, Emmanuel County folder, Thompson Papers, Valdosta State College Library; Ralph L. Bridges to Richard B. Russell, January 27, 1947, Herman Talmadge 1947 File, Russell Papers, Richard B. Russell Memorial Library, University of Georgia, Athens; Walter H. Butler to M. E. Thompson, January 16, 1947, Fulton County folder, Thompson Papers, Valdosta State College Library; J. R. Burt to M. E. Thompson, January 20, 1947, Muscogee County folder, Thompson Papers, Valdosta State College Library; Atlanta *Journal,* January 30, 1947; Morgan Blake, Atlanta *Journal,* February 9, 1947.

37. Atlanta *Constitution,* January 21, 1947; Atlanta *Journal,* January 23, 1947; Augusta *Chronicle,* January 25, 1947; Senate *Journal* (1947), p. 63; Atlanta *Constitution,* January 24, 1947.

38. "Aroused Citizens of Georgia," Resolutions folder, General Files, Thompson Papers, Valdosta State College Library; Executive Department, *Minutes* (1947), p. 1; Atlanta *Journal,* January 17, 16, 1947; Roy V. Harris to Ed Stephens, January 31, 1947, 1947 correspondence, Richmond County folder, Thompson Papers, Valdosta State College Library; Roy V. Harris to Thomas J. Tucker, January 31, 1947, Richmond County folder, Thompson Papers, Valdosta State College Library; Atlanta *Journal,* January 22, 1947.

39. Atlanta *Constitution,* January 19, 1947; Savannah *Morning News,* January 20, 1947; Executive Department, *Minutes* (1947), p. 2; Atlanta *Journal,* January 19, 1947; Savannah *Morning News,* January 19, 1947; Executive Department, *Minutes* (1947), pp. 3–4, 12.

40. "Arnall: An Oral History," interview by Cook, pp. 74–75; Atlanta *Journal,* January 22, 1947; Savannah *Morning News,* January 29, 1947.

41. Judge Walter C. Hendrix ruled in favor of Talmadge in *Arnall (M. E. Thompson) v. Talmadge,* 1693 Henry Superior Court (1947), and Judge Bond Almand did likewise in *Fulton National Bank of Atlanta v. Talmadge et al.,* 1698 Henry Superior Court (1947), while Judge Claude H. Porter ruled in favor of Thompson in *Thompson v. Byers et al.,* Floyd Superior Court, January term, 1947; Savannah *Morning News,* February 19, 1947.

42. Atlanta *Journal,* March 2, 3, 9, 6, 1947; "Southern Exposure," *Time* 49 (March 17, 1947): 45; Joseph L. Bernd, "Corruption in Georgia's Primaries and Elections, 1938–1950" (Master's thesis, Boston University, 1953), p. 88; Atlanta *Constitution,* March 3, 1947; Talmadge, *Talmadge,* p. 92.

43. Thompson, Lieutenant Governor, et al. v. Talmadge, 201 Ga. 871, 890 (1947). For an in-depth discussion of Talmadge's and Thompson's legal arguments, see chapters 4–5 of James B. Sanders, "The Georgia Gubernatorial Controversy of 1947," manuscript of thesis submitted for master's degree, Emory University (a copy is in Melvin E. Thompson Papers, Special Collections, Robert W. Woodruff Library, Emory University, Atlanta, Ga.). See also Alfred O. Canon, "The Law of Gubernatorial Succession with Special Reference to Georgia" (Master's thesis, Duke University, 1949).

44. Thompson v. Talmadge, pp. 876–90.

45. Macon *Telegraph,* March 20, 1947; Eatonton *Messenger,* March 20, 1947; Columbus *Ledger,* March 20, 1947; Gainesville *News* editorial of March 20, 1947, in Scrapbook 5, Melvin E. Thompson Papers, Special Collections, Emory University, Atlanta, Ga.; Atlanta *Journal,* March 19, 1947; Arnall interview, December 12, 1985.

46. "Georgia: 'Honey, Pack Up,'" *Newsweek* 29 (March 31, 1947): 23; "Untangled," *New Republic* 116 (March 31, 1947): 9.

47. Tifton *Daily Gazette* editorial reprinted in Atlanta *Journal,* January 19, 1947; Macon *News* editorial quoted in "Georgia: Votes Dimly Seen," *Newsweek* 20 (February 3, 1947): 21; "Georgia Is More Newsworthy Now," *Nation* 164 (February 8, 1947): 141; "Double Trouble," *Time* 49 (February 3, 1947): 20; Harold Martin in Atlanta *Constitution,* January 19, 1947; Gladstone Williams in Atlanta *Constitution,* January 17, 1947; "Another Talmadge Takes Over Georgia," *Life* 22 (January 27, 1947): 21–25; "Wool Hat Rebellion," pp. 21–24; "Strictly from Dixie," *Time* 49 (January 27, 1947): 20–21; William P. Hansen and Fred L. Israel, eds., *The Gallup Poll: Public Opinion, 1935–1971* (New York: Random House, 1972), 1:627; letter from Ernestine Hooker to M. E. Thompson, January 20, 1947, 1947 correspondence, Bibb County folder, Melvin E. Thompson Papers, Valdosta State College Library, Valdosta, Ga.

Chapter Twelve. *Federal Service, Law, and Business*

1. Birmingham *Age-Herald* editorial reprinted in *Statesman*, May 30, 1946; Thomas L. Stokes in Atlanta *Constitution*, March 1, 1946; Talmadge interview, March 24, 1986; Augusta *Courier*, November 10, 1947; Atlanta *Constitution*, September 18, November 7, 1943; Sylvester *Local* editorial reprinted in Atlanta *Journal*, February 3, 1944; Theodore C. Sorensen, "Election of 1960," in *History of American Presidential Elections*, 4:3345–46.

2. John Chadwick in Atlanta *Journal*, March 20, 1945; Chamberlain, "Arnall of Georgia," pp. 68–76; Johnson, "Arnall of Georgia—and '48," pp. 177–83; Davenport, "Unanimous Arnall," p. 16; Rufus Jarman, "Georgia's New Peach," *Saturday Evening Post* 216 (August 28, 1943): 6; "Arnall Sweeps Out," *Newsweek* 25 (February 19, 1945): 48; Foreman, "Georgia Kills the Poll Tax," pp. 291–92; Coulter, *Georgia: A Short History*, pp. 449–50.

3. M. L. St. John in Atlanta *Constitution*, February 13, 1946; Atlanta *Constitution*, July 4, 1945; Johnson, "Arnall of Georgia," p. 177; Taylor, "A Political Biography of Ellis Arnall," p. 348; Ronald F. Stinnett, *Democrats, Dinners, and Dollars* (Ames: Iowa State University Press, 1987), pp. 25, 168–69; "The Fortune Survey: The Political Mood—Summer 1947," *Fortune* 36 (September 1947): 5–6.

4. Taylor, "A Political Biography of Ellis Arnall," pp. 343–46; Thompson, Lieutenant Governor, et al. v. Talmadge, 201 Ga. 871 (1947); Morris v. Peters, 203 Ga. 364 (1948). See also Henderson, "The 1946 Gubernatorial Election in Georgia," pp. 130–31.

5. Arnall interview, February 2, 1986; Truman, *Memoirs*, 2:189–91; Richard S. Kirkendall, "Election of 1948," in *History of American Presidential Elections*, 4:3119.

6. Arnall interview, February 2, 1986.

7. Atlanta *Constitution*, November 5, 1944; Charlie Brown, *Charlie Brown Remembers Atlanta* (Columbia, S.C.: R. L. Bryan Co., 1982), p. 324; Arnall interview, February 2, 1986.

8. Atlanta *Constitution*, February 1, 1952; *Public Papers of the Presidents of the United States, Harry S. Truman, Containing the Public Messages, Speeches, and Statements of the President January 1, 1952 to January 20, 1953* (Washington, D.C.: U.S. Government Printing Office, 1966), p. 132; Atlanta *Journal*, February 1, 1952; Arnall interview, February 2, 1986; *Public Papers, 1952*, p. 140.

9. Atlanta *Constitution*, February 8, 1952; "New Boss for OPS," *Time* 59 (February 18, 1952): 20.

10. Atlanta *Journal*, February 8, 1952; transcript of the speech by Arnall before Virginia Federation of Women's Clubs, April 24, 1952, in Office of Price Stabilization, Central Files 1952–53, Box 650, Record Group 295, National Archives, Washington, D.C.

11. "New Boss for OPS," p. 20; Atlanta *Journal* editorial, February 8, 1952; Atlanta *Constitution* editorial, February 9, 1952.

12. Atlanta *Constitution,* February 9, 1952; Atlanta *Journal,* February 10, 1952.

13. U.S. Congress, Senate, Committee on Banking and Currency, *Hearings on Nomination of Ellis G. Arnall to be Director of the Office of Price Stabilization,* 82d Cong., 2d sess., February 12, 1952, pp. 3, 4, 7, 1; Atlanta *Constitution,* February 13, 1952; *Congressional Record,* 82d Cong., 2d sess., February 18, 1952, p. 1067, and March 6, 1952, p. 1906.

14. *United States Government Organization Manual, 1952–1953* (Washington, D.C.: General Services Administration, n.d.), pp. 334–43; U.S. Congress, House, Committee on Banking and Currency, *Defense Production Act Amendments of 1952, Hearings on H.R. 6546,* 82d Cong., 2d sess., 1952, part 2, p. 1493; *Organization Manual,* p. 337.

15. Office of Price Stabilization, *The First Year of Price Stabilization in a Defense Economy, Operations of the Office of Price Stabilization, January 1951 to January 1952* (Washington, D.C.: Office of Price Stabilization, n.d.), 1:1–6. A copy may be found in OPS, Central Files 1952–53, Box 508, RG 295, NA.

16. *The First Year of Price Stabilization,* 1:1; transcript of Arnall's speech to the National Conference of Business Paper editors, June 18, 1952, and transcript of Arnall's speech over CBS Radio, August 28, 1952, may be found in OPS, Central Files 1952–53, Box 650, RG 295, NA.

17. *Public Papers, 1952,* pp. 145–50; Ellis G. Arnall, "How You Can Fight Inflation," Atlanta *Journal-Constitution Magazine,* May 5, 1952, p. 34.

18. U.S. Congress, Senate, Committee on Banking and Currency, *Defense Production Act Amendments of 1952, Hearings on S. 2594 and S. 2645,* 82d Cong., 2d sess., 1952, Part 1, pp. 153–54; Taylor, "A Political Biography of Ellis Arnall," pp. 351–52; Joseph M. McDonough to Arnall, February 28, 1952, OPS, Central Files 1952–53, Box 586, RG 295, NA; C. P. Overmyer to Arnall, June 25, 1952, OPS, Central Files 1952–53, Box 587, RG 295, NA; Walter B. Carson, Sr. to Arnall, July 14, 1952, OPS, Decentralized Files of Various Directors of OPS, Box 694, RG 295, NA.

19. Transcripts of Arnall's speech to the 15th Annual Super Market Institute, May 13, 1952, and Arnall's speech to National Wholesale Frozen Food Distributors, March 5, 1952, in OPS, Central Files 1952–53, Box 650, RG 295, NA; *Hearings on S. 2594 and S. 2645,* p. 154; Arnall to Senator Lyndon B. Johnson, May 28, 1952, OPS, Central Files 1952–53, Box 587, RG 295, NA; transcript of Arnall's speech to the Atlanta Lawyers' Club, April 11, 1952, in OPS, Central Files 1952–53, Box 650, RG 295, NA.

20. Arnall to Senator Burnet R. Maybank, May 20, 1952, and Arnall to Senator Maybank, May 28, 1952, OPS, Central Files 1952–53, Box 404, RG 295, NA; New

York *Times,* May 14, 1952; *Congress and the Nation, 1945–1964,* p. 361; *Congressional Record,* 82d Cong., 2d sess., June 12, 1952, p. 7108.

21. *Defense Production Act Amendments of 1952, Hearings on H.R. 6546,* 82d Cong., 2d sess., 1952, part 2, p. 1504; *Congress and the Nation, 1945–1964,* p. 361; U.S. Congress, House, Committee on Appropriations, *The Supplemental Appropriation Bill for 1953, Hearings Before Subcommittees of the Committee on Appropriations, Emergency Agencies,* 82d Cong., 2d sess., 1952, part 2, p. 467; New York *Times,* June 24, 1952.

22. *Congressional Record,* 82d Cong., 2d sess., June 26, 1952, pp. 8202–3, 8208; New York *Times,* June 27, 1952; *Public Papers, 1952,* pp. 453–54; New York *Times,* July 2, 1952.

23. *Congressional Record,* 82d Cong., 2d sess., June 26, 1952, pp. 8176–77, 8178, 8183–84.

24. *Public Papers, 1952,* p. 454; Arnall to Thomas D. Alesandro, mayor of Baltimore, August 20, 1952, OPS, Decentralized Files of Various Directors of OPS, Box 695, RG 295, NA; Arnall to J. Elmer Mulford, August 1, 1952, OPS, Decentralized Files of Various Directors of OPS, Box 694, RG 295, NA; Atlanta *Constitution,* August 9, 1952.

25. Washington *Post,* August 7, 1952; Atlanta *Constitution,* August 6, 7, 1952; New York *Times,* August 9, 1952; Washington *Post,* August 11, 1952; New York *Times,* September 2, 1952.

26. Maeva Marcus, *Truman and the Steel Seizure Case: The Limits of Presidential Power* (New York: Columbia University Press, 1977), pp. 58–62; Atlanta *Constitution,* February 15, 1952.

27. Grant McConnell, *The Steel Seizure of 1952,* Interuniversity Case Program, Case Series No. 52 (University: University of Alabama Press, 1960), pp. 24–25; Marcus, *Steel Seizure Case,* p. 65; Atlanta *Constitution,* March 27, 1952; Charles E. Wilson, "Charles E. Wilson's Own Story of Break with Truman," *U.S. News and World Report* 32 (May 2, 1952): 11–12.

28. Wilson, "Wilson's Own Story," p. 12; *Hearings on S. 2594 and S. 2645,* 82d Cong., 2d sess., part 4, p. 2000.

29. *Hearings on S. 2594 and S. 2645,* part 4, p. 2000; Arnall interview, February 2, 1986; U.S. Congress, House, Committee on Banking and Currency, *Defense Production Act Amendments of 1952, Hearings on H.R. 6546,* 82d Cong., 2d sess., part 1, pp. 205–6.

30. *Hearings on S. 2594 and S. 2645,* p. 206; Arnall interview, July 19, 1985; Wilson, "Wilson's Own Story," p. 12; Truman, *Memoirs,* 2:469; Arnall interview, February 2, 1986; Marcus, *Steel Seizure Case,* pp. 74–75; McConnell, *Steel Seizure,* pp. 31–32; *Hearings on H.R. 6546,* part 1, p. 221.

31. Marcus, *Steel Seizure Case,* p. 73; Truman, *Memoirs,* 2:469–70; Arnall interview, February 2, 1986; *Public Papers, 1952,* pp. 246–50; Youngstown Sheet and

Tube Co. v. Sawyer, 103 F. Supp. 569 (1952); Marcus, *Steel Seizure Case*, p. 129; Youngstown Sheet and Tube Co. v. Sawyer, 197 F.2d 582 (1952).

32. A transcript of Arnall's speech to National Press Club, April 16, 1952, OPS Central Files 1952–53, Box 650, RG 295, NA; a transcript of Arnall's radio speech of April 18, 1952, OPS, Central Files 1952–53, Box 650, RG 295, NA.

33. U.S. Congress, Senate, Committee on Labor and Public Welfare, *National and Emergency Labor Disputes, Hearings Before Committee on Labor and Public Welfare and Its Subcommittee on Labor and Labor Management Relations on S. 2999 and S. 3016*, 82d Cong., 2d sess., 1952, pp. 129–31, 150.

34. *Hearings on H.R. 6546*, part 1, pp. 28–29, 220; Youngstown Sheet and Tube Co. v. Sawyer, 343 U.S. 579 (1952); McConnell, *Steel Seizure*, pp. 478–50.

35. Atlanta *Constitution*, July 15, 1952; Truman, *Memoirs*, 2:477; editorial, Atlanta *Constitution*, July 16, 1952; Taylor, "A Political Biography of Ellis Arnall," pp. 358–59; Washington *Post*, July 19, 1952.

36. New York *Times*, July 25, 1952; Truman, *Memoirs*, 2:477; Washington *Post*, July 31, 1952; New York *Times*, July 31, 1952; Atlanta *Constitution*, July 31, 1952; Arnall to John Meskimen, August 15, 1952, OPS Decentralized Files of Various Directors of OPS, Box 697, RG 295, NA.

37. Arnall interview, February 2, 1986; Atlanta *Constitution*, August 27, 1952; President Truman to Arnall, August 8, 1952, Personal File, Truman Papers, Truman Library, Independence, Mo.; Arnall to President Truman, August 14, 1952, and President Truman to Arnall, August 26, 1952, Official File, Truman Papers, Truman Library; editorial, New York *Times*, August 13, 1952; editorial, Washington *Post*, August 11, 1952; President Truman to Arnall, August 26, 1952, Official File, Truman Papers, Truman Library.

38. "Arnall: An Oral History," interview by Cook, pp. 78–80; Arnall interview, December 12, 1985; Arnall interview, February 2, 1986; Talmadge interview, March 24, 1986; Atlanta *Constitution*, February 10, 1946; "Arnall: An Oral History," interview by Cook, pp. 79–80, 57; Arnall, "Along the Way," p. 16; Arnall, "Luck, Fate, and Chance," pp. 1–2.

39. Arnall interview, February 2, 1986; Arnall, "Along the Way," pp. 10, 12, 23.

40. Rufus Jarman, *The History of Coastal States Life* (Atlanta: Coastal States Life Insurance Co., 1974), p. 227.

41. Ibid., pp. 227–29.

42. J. C. McAuliffe, *The Story of Coastal States Life*, rev. ed. (Atlanta: Coastal States Life Insurance Co., 1965), pp. 8–36; "Arnall: An Oral History," interview by Cook, pp. 89–90.

43. Jarman, *History of Coastal States*, pp. 228–29; Arnall, "Along the Way," p. 18.

44. "Arnall: An Oral History," interview by Cook, p. 91.

45. Arnall, "Along the Way," pp. 15–18.

46. Ibid., pp. 9–10; Arnall to author, October 19, 1988; Taylor, "A Political

Biography of Ellis Arnall," p. 366; Arnall to President Truman, May 9, 1950, Official File, Truman Papers, Truman Library, Independence, Mo.

47. For reviews of *The Shore Dimly Seen,* see W. B. Hamilton, New York *Times,* November 17, 1946; E. R. Embree, *Book Week,* November 17, 1946, p. 3; and Hodding Carter, *Saturday Review of Literature* 29 (November 9, 1946): 13. For reviews of *What the People Want,* see Tarleton Collier, New York *Herald-Tribune Weekly Book Review,* June 13, 1948; Warren Moscow, *Saturday Review of Literature* 31 (June 12, 1948): 13; and Richard Watts, Jr., *New Republic* 118 (June 21, 1948): 24.

48. "Arnall: An Oral History," interview by Cook, p. 88.

Chapter Thirteen. *Arnall and State Politics, 1947–1962*

1. House *Journal* (1947), pp. 369–70; Senate *Journal* (1947), pp. 231–32; *Opinions* (1945–47), pp. 305–9; Savannah *Morning News,* January 14, 1947; Executive Department, *Minutes* (1947), pp. 19–20; Savannah *Morning News,* March 26, 1947; Atlanta *Daily World,* March 20, 1947; Atlanta *Journal,* March 26, 1947; Valdosta *Daily Times,* March 29, 1947; Atlanta *Journal,* March 28, 1947; Atlanta *Constitution,* March 28, 1947.

2. Atlanta *Constitution,* March 21, 1947; Atlanta *Journal,* March 28, May 26, 1948.

3. Talmadge, *Talmadge,* p. 98; Arnall interview, December 12, 1985; Atlanta *Journal,* May 28, 1948; Atlanta *Constitution,* June 23, 1948.

4. Greensboro *Herald-Journal,* July 30, 1948; Cordele *Dispatch,* May 28, 1948; Bainbridge *Post-Searchlight,* June 10, 1948; Savannah *Morning News,* May 27, 1948; Albany *Herald,* May 27, June 23, 1948.

5. Augusta *Courier,* July 5, 1948; Savannah *Evening Press,* May 26, 1948; Atlanta *Journal,* August 1, 1948; Columbus *Ledger-Enquirer,* May 30, 1948; Moultrie *Observer,* May 27, 1948; Augusta *Chronicle,* May 29, 1948; Valdosta *Daily Times,* June 25, 1948.

6. Talmadge, *Talmadge,* p. 99; Atlanta *Journal,* August 1, 1948; *Statesman,* July 29, 1948.

7. Bernd, "Primary Elections," pp. 126–27; *Statesman,* July 29, 1948; Atlanta *Journal,* August 1, 1948; Henderson, "The 1946 Gubernatorial Election in Georgia," p. 15; Atlanta *Constitution,* August 1, 1948; political advertisement for Talmadge in Douglas *Enterprise,* September 2, 1948.

8. Augusta *Courier,* August 2, 1948; *Statesman,* July 29, August 18, 1948.

9. Atlanta *Journal,* July 2, 1948; Atlanta *Constitution,* July 18, 1948; Atlanta *Journal,* July 18, August 11, 1948; Talmadge interview, March 24, 1986; Albany *Journal* and Gordon County *News* editorials reprinted in *Statesman,* July 22, 1948; Greensboro *Herald-Journal,* July 30, 1948.

10. Atlanta *Journal*, August 1, 1948; Greensboro *Herald-Journal*, August 6, 1948.

11. Greensboro *Herald-Journal*, August 6, 1948; Atlanta *Journal*, August 10, July 30, 1948.

12. *Statesman*, August 19, 1948.

13. Atlanta *Journal*, July 20, 30, 1948.

14. *Official Register* (1945–50), p. 577; Joseph L. Bernd, "Georgia Static and Dynamic," in *The Changing Politics of the South*, ed. William C. Havard (Baton Rouge: Louisiana State University Press, 1972), pp. 315–16; Talmadge interview, Government Documentation Project, p.41; Bernd, *Grass Root Politics*, pp. 13–14.

15. Atlanta *Journal*, February 5, June 14, 1948; Ellis G. Arnall, "The Democrats Can Win," *Atlantic Monthly* 182 (October 1948): 36; Ellis G. Arnall, "Should We Have a Third Party?," *New Republic* 115 (December 30, 1946): 914–15; Ellis G. Arnall, "Practical Program for Progressives," *Nation* 155 (June 12, 1948): 655; Arnall, "Democrats Can Win," pp. 33, 37–38; *Official Register* (1945–50), p. 610.

16. Bernd, "Primary Elections," pp. 158–65.

17. Augusta *Courier*, August 15, 1949; Ken Turner in Atlanta *Journal*, July 24, 1949; Atlanta *Journal*, August 8, 1949.

18. Atlanta *Constitution*, May 2, 1948; Savannah *Morning News*, January 4, 1950; *Statesman*, January 5, 1950.

19. Atlanta *Constitution*, January 2, 1950; Savannah *Morning News*, January 3, 1950.

20. Savannah *Morning News*, January 4, 1950; Macon *Telegraph*, January 7, 1950; Augusta *Chronicle*, January 7, 1950.

21. Talmadge interview, Government Documentation Project, p. 45.

22. *Statesman*, January 12, 1950; *Opinions* (1950–51), pp. 6–8; Arnall interview, February 2, 1986; Atlanta *Constitution*, January 15, 1950; Talmadge interview, Government Documentation Project, pp.87–88; Bernd, "Primary Elections," p. 166.

23. Macon *Telegraph*, January 12, 1950; Atlanta *Constitution*, January 29, 1950; Macon *Telegraph*, January 31, 1950; Atlanta *Journal*, January 31, 1950; interview with Ellis G. Arnall, Atlanta, Ga., March 28, 1988; Atlanta *Journal*, February 9, 1950.

24. Macon *News*, February 10, 1950; Albany *Herald*, February 10, 1950; Savannah *Morning News*, February 10, 1950; Atlanta *Constitution*, February 11, 1950; Arnall interview, February 2, 1986.

25. Savannah *Morning News*, February 10, 1950.

26. Atlanta *Constitution*, March 9, May 25, 1950; Bernd, "Static and Dynamic," p. 321; Bernd, "Corruption in Georgia Primaries and Elections," pp. 105–23; Robert Sherrill, *Gothic Politics in the Deep South: Stars of the New Confederacy* (New York: Grossman Publishers, 1968; Ballantine Books, 1969), pp. 57–58; *Official Register* (1945–50), p. 681; Bernd, *Grass Root Politics*, pp. 14–15; interview of Melvin E.

Thompson by Gene-Gabriel Moore in *Georgia Governors in an Age of Change*, ed. Henderson and Roberts, p. 72.

27. Atlanta *Journal*, August 7, 8, 16, 1951.

28. Ellis Arnall to President Truman, January 22, 1952, Personal File, Truman Library, Independence, Mo.; Atlanta *Journal*, January 31, February 25, August 18, 1952; Ralph E. McGill to James M. Cox, November 1, 1952, Folder 15, Box 51, Ralph McGill Collection, Robert W. Woodruff Library, Emory University, Atlanta; Ellis Arnall to President Truman, November 5, 1950, Personal File, Truman Library.

29. Atlanta *Journal-Constitution*, February 8, 1953; Atlanta *Journal*, February 27, March 17, 18, June 9, August 18, 27, 1953.

30. "Press Gallery," WSB-TV, September 9, 1953. A transcript may be found in Arnall Political File 1952–54, Richard B. Russell Papers Collection, Russell Library, University of Georgia, Athens; Atlanta *Journal-Constitution*, July 26, 1953, January 20, 1954.

31. Cook, *Governors of Georgia*, pp. 267–68; Jack Bass and Walter DeVries, *The Transformation of Southern Politics: Social Change and Political Consequences Since 1945* (New York: Basic Books, 1976), p. 137; Bernd, "Primary Elections," pp. 263–64.

32. Bernd, "Primary Elections," pp. 259, 261.

33. Brown v. Board of Education of Topeka, 347 U.S. 483 (1954); Bartley, *From Thurmond to Wallace*, pp. 26–27; Arnall interview, March 28, 1988; Robert W. DuBay, "Marvin Griffin and the Politics of the Stump," in *Georgia Governors in an Age of Change*, ed. Henderson and Roberts, pp. 105; *Official Register* (1953–54), p. 620.

34. Atlanta *Journal-Constitution*, October 3, 1954; Atlanta *Constitution*, April 18, June 13, 1954; Atlanta *Journal-Constitution*, June 8, 1958; Atlanta *Constitution*, June 17, 1958.

35. Pyles, "Race and Ruralism," pp. 102–3; Earl Black, *Southern Governors and Civil Rights: Racial Segregation as a Campaign Issue in the Second Reconstruction* (Cambridge: Harvard University Press, 1976), pp. 66–68; Bartley, "Race Relations," in *History of Georgia*, Coleman, gen. ed., pp. 364–67; Paul Douglas Bolster, "Civil Rights Movements in Twentieth-Century Georgia" (Ph.D. dissertation, University of Georgia, 1972), pp. 161–62.

36. Numan V. Bartley, *The Rise of Massive Resistance: Race and Politics in the South During the 1950's* (Baton Rouge: Louisiana State University Press, 1969), pp. 332–33; Atlanta *Journal*, April 9, 13, June 26, 1959.

37. Peters's letter is reprinted in Atlanta *Journal-Constitution*, January 17, 1960; Columbus *Ledger-Enquirer*, January 17, 1960; Atlanta *Constitution*, January 19, 1960.

38. S. Ernest Vandiver, "Vandiver Takes the Middle Road," in *Georgia Governors in an Age of Change*, ed. Henderson and Roberts, pp. 159–60; Bartley, *Massive*

Resistance, pp. 334–35; Bartley, *Creation of Modern Georgia,* pp. 195–96; Atlanta *Constitution,* May 27, 1961; Arnall interview, December 12, 1985.

39. Atlanta *Journal,* April 9, 15, 1959, and June 8, August 11, 1960; Arnall interview, December 12, 1985; Sanders v. Gray, 203 F. Supp. 158 (1962); *Official Register* (1961–62), p. 1436; Talmadge, *Talmadge,* p. 140. Talmadge first won election to the U.S. Senate in 1956.

40. Atlanta *Constitution,* May 27, 1961.

Chapter Fourteen. *Arnall's Last Hurrah*

1. Atlanta *Constitution,* July 23, 1965.

2. Saye, *Constitutional History of Georgia,* pp. 357–59, 364; Key, *Southern Politics,* pp. 117–24; Louis T. Rigdon II, *Georgia's County Unit System* (Decatur, Ga.: Selective Books, 1961), p. 40; *Georgia Statistical Abstract, 1968* (Athens: Bureau of Business and Economic Research, Graduate School of Business Administration, University of Georgia, 1968), p. 13.

3. Baker v. Carr, 369 U.S. 186 (1962); Rigdon, *Georgia's County Unit System,* pp. 42–63; Sanders v. Gray, 203 F. Supp. 158 (1962); Gray v. Sanders, 372 U.S. 368 (1963); Arnall interview, December 12, 1985.

4. James F. Cook, "Carl Sanders and the Politics of the Future," in *Georgia Governors in an Age of Change,* ed. Henderson and Roberts, p. 172; Bernd, "Static and Dynamic," pp. 334–35; Bartley, *From Thurmond to Wallace,* p. 60. Robert W. Dubay concluded that the Griffin administration was "one of the most corrupt, amoral, mismanaged, and inefficient administrations in Georgia history." Dubay, "Marvin Griffin and the Politics of the Stump," p. 108.

5. Brown v. Board of Education of Topeka, 347 U.S. 483 (1954); Vandiver, "Vandiver Takes the Middle Road," in *Georgia Governors in an Age of Change,* ed. Henderson and Roberts, pp. 159–62.

6. Lawrence R. Hepburn, "Public Education," in *Contemporary Georgia,* ed. Lawrence R. Hepburn (Athens: Carl Vinson Institute of Government, University of Georgia, 1987), pp. 199–200; U.S. Commission on Civil Rights, *Southern School Desegregation, 1966–1967* (Washington, D.C.: U.S. Government Printing Office, 1967), p. 6.

7. J. Morgan Kouser, *The Shaping of Southern Politics: Suffrage Restrictions and the Establishment of the One-Party South, 1880–1910* (New Haven: Yale University Press, 1974), pp. 209–23; Owen, "Rise of Negro Voting," p. 11; Henderson, "The 1946 Gubernatorial Election in Georgia," pp. 25, 61; 1964 estimates made by the Voter Education Project of the Southern Regional Council in *VEP NEWS,* April 1968, p. 3; 1966 estimates from Voter Education Project of the Southern Regional

Council, *Voter Registration in the South, Summer 1966* (Atlanta: Southern Regional Council, 1966).

8. Numan V. Bartley and Hugh D. Graham, *Southern Politics and the Second Reconstruction* (Baltimore: Johns Hopkins University Press, 1975), p. 86; Donald S. Strong, *The 1952 Presidential Election in the South* (University: Bureau of Information, University of Alabama, 1956), p. 382; Bernard Cosman, *Five States for Goldwater: Continuity and Change in Southern Presidential Voting Patterns* (University: University of Alabama Press, 1966), pp. 40–41, 62; Bartley, *From Thurmond to Wallace,* pp. 60–65.

9. Matt Winn Williamson, "Contemporary Tendencies Toward a Two-Party System in Georgia" (Ph.D. dissertation, University of Virginia, 1969), p. 92; *Official Register* (1945–50), p. 308; Callaway, *A Broader Plan.*

10. Atlanta *Journal,* March 22, 1964; interview with Ellis G. Arnall, Atlanta, Ga., May 6, 1981.

11. Bartley, *From Thurmond to Wallace,* pp. 24, 104. I am using Bartley's classifications of the Georgia electorate. He warned that they should "be regarded with the greatest caution" since they were "crude and general groupings." In addition, Bartley cautioned that many factors influenced individual voting. Nevertheless, he concluded that the "consistency of these alignments suggests that they are substantially the voting foundation upon which political competition in Georgia rests." Bartley, *From Thurmond to Wallace,* p. 106.

12. Bartley, *From Thurmond to Wallace,* pp. 45, 105–6; Numan V. Bartley and Hugh D. Graham, *Southern Elections: County and Precinct Data, 1950–1972* (Baton Rouge: Louisiana State University Press, 1978), pp. 363–64.

13. A survey of those attending the 1965 annual Georgia Press Association Convention picked Vandiver as the leading candidate by a substantial majority, Atlanta *Constitution,* July 19, 1965; Atlanta *Constitution,* July 21, 1965; interview with S. Ernest Vandiver, Jr., Lavonia, Ga., May 23, 1981.

14. Atlanta *Constitution,* November 18, August 24, September 2, November 6, 1965; Vandiver interview, May 23, 1981.

15. Atlanta *Constitution,* September 15, 1965; Sherrill, *Gothic Politics in the Deep South,* p. 288; Talmadge, *Talmadge,* p. 305; Bartley and Graham, *Southern Politics,* p. 113.

16. Lester Garfield Maddox, *Speaking Out: The Autobiography of Lester Garfield Maddox* (Garden City, N.J.: Doubleday, 1975), pp. 1–17, 35–36; Bartley, *From Thurmond to Wallace,* p. 47.

17. Bruce Galphin, *The Riddle of Lester Maddox* (Atlanta: Camelot Publishing Co., 1968), pp. 42–46; Maddox, *Speaking Out,* p. 48; Lester G. Maddox, "A Chance for the Truth," in *Georgia Governors in an Age of Change,* ed. Henderson and Roberts, pp. 211–12; Galphin, *The Riddle of Lester Maddox,* p. 73; Maddox, *Speaking Out,* pp. 65–70; Arnall interview, December 14, 1988.

18. Atlanta *Journal,* February 17, 1966; Vandiver interview, May 23, 1981; Atlanta *Constitution,* May 19, 24, 1966; interview with Herman E. Talmadge, Lovejoy, Ga., April 21, 1981. For a discussion of why Talmadge decided to stay in Washington see Henderson, "The 1966 Gubernatorial Election in Georgia," pp. 67–72.

19. Augusta *Chronicle,* May 24, 1966; interview with James H. Gray, Sr., Albany, Ga., May 14, 1981; Vandiver interview, May 23, 1981; Talmadge interview, April 21, 1981; Sharon Thomason, "James Gray—Albany's Mr. Power," *Brown's Guide to Georgia* 6 (March–April 1978): 76–78; Bainbridge *Post-Searchlight,* August 25, 1966; Galphin, *The Riddle of Lester Maddox,* pp. 75–76.

20. Atlanta *Journal,* May 24, 1966; *Official Register* (1945–50), p. 187; interview with Garland T. Byrd, Butler, Ga., May 5, 1981; Vandiver interview, May 23, 1981; Talmadge interview, April 21, 1981; Williamson, "Contemporary Tendencies," pp. 87–93; Henderson, "The 1966 Gubernatorial Election in Georgia," p. 89.

21. Jimmy Carter, *Why Not the Best?* (Nashville: Broadman Press, 1975), pp. 80–97; Americus *Times-Recorder,* June 13, 1966; Atlanta *Constitution,* September 1, 1966; Atlanta *Journal,* June 3, 1966. These senatorial colleagues of Carter included Brooks Pennington, Robert Smalley, Bobby Rowan, and Ford Spinks.

22. Arnall's platform may be found reprinted in Atlanta *Constitution,* July 18, 1966.

23. Atlanta *Journal,* July 18, 10, June 4, 1966. For Maddox's platform, see Albany *Herald,* August 22, 1966, and his autobiography, *Speaking Out,* p. 74. For Gray's platform, see Atlanta *Journal,* June 5, 1966. Byrd saw the HEW school desegregation guidelines as the "overriding issue" of the campaign, Augusta *Herald,* September 5, 1966. For Carter's and Byrd's platforms, see Henderson, "The 1966 Gubernatorial Election in Georgia," pp. 137, 145.

24. Atlanta *Journal,* September 20, 1966; Arnall interview, May 6, 1981; Atlanta *Constitution,* July 18, 27, 1966; Atlanta *Journal,* August 31, 1966; Jim Rankin in Atlanta *Constitution,* July 27, 1966; Eugene Patterson in Atlanta *Journal-Constitution,* June 12, 1966. Arnall's anticipated strong support among black voters faced a serious threat when state senator Leroy Johnson, the first black to serve in the legislature in the twentieth century, contemplated entering the race. Johnson finally decided not to run and actively supported Arnall. Atlanta *Journal,* June 1, 1966; Atlanta *Journal-Constitution,* June 5, 1966; Arnall interview, December 14, 1988.

25. Atlanta *Constitution,* July 7, 1966; Savannah *Morning News,* May 10, 1966; Athens *Banner-Herald,* July 7, 1966.

26. Atlanta *Journal,* September 12, 1966; Macon *Telegraph,* September 31, 1966; Marietta *Daily Journal,* September 1, 1966; Sanders interview, June 11, 1981; Atlanta *Constitution,* July 13, 1966; Sanders interview, June 11, 1981; W. H. Montague, Sr., to [no first name given] Conway, July 6, 1966, Box 333, Folder 10, Ellis G. Arnall Write-In Campaign Records, Southern Labor Archives, Special Col-

lections, Georgia State University, Atlanta; Atlanta *Journal,* June 19, 1966; Atlanta *Daily World,* September 13, 1966.

27. Sanders interview, June 11, 1981; Vandiver interview, May 23, 1981; Talmadge interview, April 21, 1981; Atlanta *Journal,* April 21, 1981; Atlanta *Journal,* September 18, 1966; Augusta *Courier,* May 9, July 25, 1966; Gray interview, May 14, 1981; Atlanta *Constitution,* June 22, August 16, 1966; Augusta *Courier,* August 15, 1966; Albany *Herald,* August 2, 1966; Augusta *Chronicle-Herald,* August 21, 1966; Americus *Times-Recorder,* September 10, 1966.

28. Sanders interview, June 11, 1981; interview with Ford Spinks, Tifton, Ga., April 24, 1981; Atlanta *Constitution,* July 27, 1966; Galphin, *The Riddle of Lester Maddox,* p. 110.

29. McGill to Arnall, May 25, 1966, Ralph E. McGill Collection, Box 15, Special Collections, Robert W. Woodruff Library, Emory University, Atlanta; Atlanta *Journal,* September 26, 1966; Marietta *Daily Journal,* October 2, 1966.

30. McGill to Arnall, May 25, 1966, McGill Collection, Woodruff Library; Arnall to Ralph McGill, June 4, 1966, Box 15, McGill Collection, Woodruff Library. "Extemporaneous Remarks Made by Former Governor Arnall Before Members of the Fulton County Campaign Speakers Bureau," August 1, 1966; a transcribed copy of those remarks may be found in Ellis G. Arnall Write-In Campaign Records, Southern Labor Archives, Special Collections, Georgia State University. The "native-born Georgian" quote may be found on page 19, and his remarks about his campaign style may be found on pages 21–22 of the transcript.

31. Atlanta *Journal,* August 28, 1966; Atlanta *Constitution,* August 9, 1966; Valdosta *Daily Times,* September 3, 1966; Athens *Banner-Herald,* August 14, 1966.

32. Bernd, *Grass Root Politics,* p. 10; Atlanta *Journal-Constitution,* September 4, 1966; Talmadge interview, April 21, 1981; Vandiver interview, May 23, 1981; Jimmy Carter to Walter Harrison, September 5, 1966, Box 332, Folder 2, Ellis G. Arnall Write-In Campaign Records, Southern Labor Archives, Special Collections, Georgia State University; Bernd, "Static and Dynamic," p. 341.

33. *Official Register* (1965–66), p. 1738; Sanders interview, June 11, 1981; Bartley and Graham, *Southern Elections,* pp. 363–64.

34. Bartley and Graham, *Southern Elections,* pp. 363–64; *Official Register* (1965–66), pp. 1736–38.

35. Bartley and Graham, *Southern Politics,* p. 114; Arnall interview, May 6, 1981; Bartley and Graham, *Southern Elections,* pp. 100–103; *Official Register* (1965–66), pp. 1736–38; Arnall interview, May 6, 1981.

36. Macon *Telegraph & News,* September 18, 1966; Arnall interview, May 6, 1981; Augusta *Chronicle,* September 10, 1981; Betty Glad, *Jimmy Carter in Search of the Great White House* (New York: W. W. Norton, 1980), p. 106.

37. Arnall interview, May 6, 1981; Macon *Telegraph & News,* September 18, 1966; Macon *Telegraph,* September 23, 1966.

38. Atlanta *Journal,* September 21, 1966; Atlanta *Constitution,* September 23, 27, 1966; Atlanta *Journal,* September 26, 1966; Atlanta *Constitution,* September 22, 1966. See, for example, the editorials in the following: Atlanta *Journal,* September 21, 1966; Macon *Telegraph,* September 27, 1966; Madison *Madisonian,* September 22, 1966; Milledgeville *Union-Recorder,* September 22, 1966; Coffee County *Progress,* September 22, 1966.

39. Williamson, "Contemporary Tendencies," p. 148; Atlanta *Journal,* September 23, 1966; Atlanta *Constitution,* September 21, 27, 1966.

40. *Official Register* (1965–66), pp. 1777–79; Bartley and Graham, *Southern Elections,* pp. 100–103. Arnall received 72 percent of the upper income white vote and over 99 percent of the black vote in Atlanta. In contrast Maddox carried the lower and middle income vote in his hometown. Bartley and Graham, *Southern Elections,* p. 363.

41. Sanders interview, June 11, 1981; Neal R. Pierce, *The Deep South States of America: People, Politics and Power in the Seven Deep South States* (New York: W. W. Norton, 1974), p. 315; Galphin, *The Riddle of Lester Maddox,* pp. 114–15; Williamson, "Contemporary Tendencies," p. 162; interview with Lester G. Maddox, Atlanta, Ga., May 5, 1981; Vandiver interview, May 23, 1981.

42. Arnall interview, May 6, 1981; Ivan Allen, Jr., *Notes on the Sixties* (New York: Simon and Schuster, 1971), pp. 174–92; Arnall interview, May 6, 1981; Vandiver interview, May 23, 1981; Albany *Herald,* September 29, 1966; Athens *Banner-Herald,* October 24, 1966; Arnall interview, May 6, 1981; Moultrie *Observer,* September 30, 1966; Marietta *Daily Journal,* September 29, 1966.

43. Sanders interview, June 11, 1981; Reese Cleghorn, "Meet Lester Maddox of Georgia, Mr. White Backlash," New York *Times Magazine,* November 6, 1966, p. 27; Atlanta *Constitution,* July 29, 1966; Savannah *Morning News,* October 16, 1966; Atlanta *Constitution,* July 28, 1966; Sam Caldwell, *Caldwell Conspiracy* (Lakemont, Ga.: Copple House, 1987), p. 75.

44. Atlanta *Constitution,* July 27, 1966; Rex Reed, "Lester Maddox as a Leader of Men," *Esquire* 68 (October 1967): 120; Pyles, "Race and Ruralism," p. 197.

45. See comments by Travis Stewart, executive director of the State Democratic party in Atlanta *Constitution,* September 8, 1966, and Charles Pou, political editor of the Atlanta *Journal,* August 10, 1966; Atlanta *Constitution,* September 20, 1966; Atlanta *Journal-Constitution,* November 13, 1966; Arnall interview, May 6, 1981; Carter, *Why Not the Best?,* p. 98; Allen, *Notes on the Sixties,* p. 139; Atlanta *Constitution,* October 2, 1966; Vandiver interview, May 23, 1981; Sanders interview, June 11, 1981; Atlanta *Daily World,* December 15, 1966; Henderson, "The 1966 Gubernatorial Election in Georgia," pp. 184–88.

46. Telephone interview with Howard H. Callaway, Denver, Col., May 8, 1981; Maddox, *Speaking Out,* p. 84; Galphin, *The Riddle of Lester Maddox,* p. 115; Bartley, *From Thurmond to Wallace,* pp. 74–75; Williamson, "Contemporary Tendencies,"

p. 159. In the author's interviews with Arnall and in Cook's interview with the former governor, Arnall insisted that Republican participation in the run-off resulted in his defeat. In a letter written after the run-off, however, Arnall stated that he had offered the state constructive, progressive leadership which "a majority of the people, aided and abetted by the Republicans who invaded our Democratic Primary, did not choose." Arnall to Rev. John B. Morris, October 21, 1966, John B. Morris Collection, Richard B. Russell Memorial Library, University of Georgia.

47. Robert Sherrill, "Nixon's Man in Dixie: Bo Callaway Tries to Find the Republican Votes in Wallace Country," New York *Times Magazine,* September 15, 1968, pp. 42–43; Bill Schemmel, "Bo Callaway's Alive and Well," *Georgia* 17 (March 1973): 30; *Biographical Directory of the American Congress, 1774–1971* (Washington, D.C.: U.S. Government Printing Office, 1971), p. 694; Callaway interview, May 8, 1981; Bartley, *From Thurmond to Wallace,* p. 76; *Congressional Quarterly Almanac, 89th Congress, 2d Session . . . 1966* (Washington, D.C.: *Congressional Quarterly,* 1967), pp. 998, 1020; Henderson, "The 1966 Gubernatorial Election in Georgia," pp. 191–92. For a discussion of the Callaway-Maddox race, see Henderson, "The 1966 Gubernatorial Election in Georgia," pp. 188–226, and Billy Burton Hathorn, "The Frustration of Opportunity: Georgia Republicans and the Election of 1966," *Atlanta History* 31 (Winter 1987–88): 37–52.

48. Atlanta *Journal,* November 5, 1966; Atlanta *Constitution,* October 24, 1966; Atlanta *Daily World,* October 21, 1966; Sanders interview, June 11, 1981; Atlanta *Constitution,* November 3, 1966.

49. Galphin, *The Riddle of Lester Maddox,* pp. 124–27; Atlanta *Constitution,* October 5, 1966.

50. Atlanta *Journal,* October 5, 1966; Arnall interview, May 6, 1981; Maddox, *Speaking Out,* pp. 85–86. Despite Arnall's denial, Vandiver and Gray believed he played an active role in the write-in effort. Vandiver interview, May 23, 1981, and Gray interview, May 14, 1981; Atlanta *Constitution,* November 8, 1966; Macon *Telegraph,* October 8, 1966; Callaway interview, May 8, 1981.

51. Macon *News,* November 4, 1966; Atlanta *Journal-Constitution,* October 23, 1966; Dalton *Daily Citizen-News,* October 17, 1966; Marietta *Daily Journal,* October 14, 1966; Atlanta *Daily World,* November 3, 1966; Columbus *Ledger,* October 10, 1966; Macon *Telegraph,* November 8, 1966; Newnan *Times-Herald,* October 13, 1966.

52. Atlanta *Constitution,* October 14, 1966; Atlanta *Daily World,* October 13, 1966; Atlanta *Journal-Constitution,* October 30, 1966; Atlanta *Daily World,* October 7, 1966; Atlanta *Journal-Constitution,* October 30, 1966; Galphin, *The Riddle of Lester Maddox,* p. 146; Atlanta *Constitution,* October 29, 1966; Macon *Telegraph & News,* November 6, 1966.

53. *Official Register* (1965–66), p. 1788. Lieutenant Governor Peter Zack Geer, the presiding officer of the joint session of the legislature that met to certify the

results of the 1966 general election, ruled the 17,228 write-in votes from Fulton County and the 1,118 write-in votes from Cobb County out of order because they had not been submitted with the other votes by the election officials of those counties. Thus, officially, Arnall received only 52,831 write-in votes. See House *Journal* (1967), pp. 49–50. The write-in figure used by the author, however, included the Fulton County and Cobb County write-in votes and the write-in votes from each county obtained from the *General Election Returns, 1966* located in the Georgia Department of Archives and History; *Official Register* (1965–66), pp. 1777–79, 1786–88; *General Election Returns, 1966;* House *Journal* (1967), p. 50; Senate *Journals* (1967), pp. 18–20; "Arnall: An Oral History," interview by Cook, pp. 97–98.

54. Arnall continued to have a keen interest in politics. In 1970 he wrote Carter, who had defeated Sanders for the Democratic gubernatorial nomination, that he was supporting him in the general election. Carter solicited Arnall's advice and support when he sought the Democratic presidential nomination in 1976. Arnall endorsed Carter's candidacy and made speeches for him during the Florida and Pennsylvania primaries. Arnall to Carter, September 25, 1970, and Carter to Arnall, April 17, 1975, letters in the possession of Arnall. Arnall's campaigning for Carter is discussed in Arnall's unpublished manuscript "Along the Way," pp. 28–29.

Chapter Fifteen. *A Mover and a Shaker*

1. The writer is John Chamberlain, "Arnall of Georgia," p. 69. *The Future of Liberal Government: A Radio Discussion by Ellis Arnall, Ernest Colwell, and Wayne Morris,* University of Chicago Round Table, broadcast by NBC, May 26, 1946, p. 7; a transcript is in Arnall Political File 1945–49, Russell Papers, Russell Memorial Library, University of Georgia.

2. The Pearson quote is taken from a one-page advertisement on behalf of *The Shore Dimly Seen* in the New York *Times Book Review,* November 17, 1946, p. 27; Bartley, *From Thurmond to Wallace,* p. 81; "Arnall: An Oral History," interview by Cook, p. viii; Key, *Southern Politics,* p. 128; Coulter, *Georgia: A Short History,* p. 449; Taylor, "A Political Biography of Ellis Arnall," p. 378. The results of the Georgia Association of Historians Survey of Georgia Governors, May 1985, may be found in the appendix of *Georgia Governors in an Age of Change,* ed. Henderson and Roberts, pp. 305–11.

3. Edwin L. Jackson and Mary E. Stakes, *Handbook of Georgia State Agencies,* 2d ed. (Athens: University of Georgia Press, 1988).

4. Ibid.

5. Interview with Ivan Allen, Jr., Atlanta, Ga., March 28, 1988.

6. Chester M. Morgan, *Redneck Liberal: Theodore G. Bilbo and the New Deal* (Baton Rouge: Louisiana State University Press, 1985); Frances Butler Simkins and

Charles Pierce Roland, *A History of the South,* 4th ed. (New York: Alfred A. Knopf, 1972), pp. 523–50; Alan Brinkley, "The New Deal and Southern Politics," in *The New Deal and the South,* ed. James C. Cobb and Michael V. Namorato (Jackson: University Press of Mississippi, 1984), pp. 97–115.

7. Arnall, *What the People Want,* pp. 45–46; Arnall, *The Shore Dimly Seen,* p. 87; Ellis G. Arnall, "Memo to Southern Liberals," *Southwest Review* 33 (Winter 1948): 4; Ellis G. Arnall, "Arnall Sees Hope in Southern Liberalism," New York *Times Magazine,* February 2, 1947, p. 48.

8. Martin, *Ralph McGill,* p. 80; Ellis Arnall to Mary Lynn McGill, February 4, 1969, Ralph E. McGill Collection, Robert W. Woodruff Library, Emory University.

9. Key, *Southern Politics,* pp. 491–508, 298–311, 117–24.

10. Earl Black and Merle Black, *Politics and Society in the South* (Cambridge: Harvard University Press, 1987), pp. 27–29.

11. Key, *Southern Politics,* p. 128. In the preface to a biography of Helen Douglas Mankin, Arnall wrote about the provincialism of southern politics in the 1940s by stating, "The more popular you were in the South, the more unpopular you were in the rest of the nation—and vice versa." Lorraine Nelson Spritzer, *The Belle of Ashby Street: Helen Douglas Mankin and Georgia Politics* (Athens: University of Georgia Press, 1982), p. ix.

12. Arnall interview, February 2, 1986; "Arnall: An Oral History," interview by Cook, p. 106.

Bibliography

Primary Sources

INTERVIEWS BY AUTHOR

Allen, Ivan, Jr. Atlanta, Ga., March 28, 1988.
Arnall, Ellis G. Atlanta, Ga., May 6, 1981.
———. Atlanta, Ga., July 19, 1985.
———. Atlanta, Ga., December 12, 1985.
———. Atlanta, Ga., February 2, 1986.
———. Atlanta, Ga., March 26, 1987.
———. Atlanta, Ga., June 19, 1987.
———. Atlanta, Ga., March 28, 1988.
———. Atlanta, Ga., December 14, 1988.
Byrd, Garland T. Butler, Ga., May 5, 1981.
Callaway, Howard H. Denver, Col. (telephone interview), May 8, 1981.
Gray, James H., Sr. Albany, Ga., May 14, 1981.
Maddox, Lester G. Atlanta, Ga., May 5, 1981.
Sanders, Carl E., Jr. Atlanta, Ga., June 11, 1981.
Spinks, Ford. Tifton, Ga., April 24, 1981.
Talmadge, Herman E. Lovejoy, Ga., April 21, 1981.
———. Lovejoy, Ga., March 24, 1986.
———. Government Documentation Project. Georgia State University, Atlanta, 1987.
Vandiver, S. Ernest, Jr. Lavonia, Ga., May 23, 1981.

OTHER INTERVIEWS

Arnall, Ellis G. Interview by Melvin T. Steely and Theodore B. Fitz-Simons, Georgia Political Heritage Series, Annie Bell Weaver Special Collections, West Georgia College, Carrollton, Ga., 1986.
———. "Governor Ellis Gibbs Arnall: An Oral History." Interview by James F. Cook, Jr. Georgia Government Documentation Project, Georgia State University, Atlanta, August 1988.
Bradfield, Mrs. Georgia Atkinson. Interview by Ellis G. Arnall. Ormond Beach, Florida, June 6, 1987.

SPECIAL COLLECTIONS

Arnall, Ellis G. Write-in Campaign Records. Southern Labor Archives. Special
Collections, Georgia State University, Atlanta.

Griffin, S. Marvin Collection. Bainbridge College Library, Bainbridge, Ga.

McGill, Ralph E. Collection. Special Collections. Robert W. Woodruff Library,
Emory University, Atlanta, Ga.

Morris, John B. Collection. Richard B. Russell Memorial Library, University of
Georgia, Athens.

Roosevelt, Franklin D. Papers. Franklin D. Roosevelt Library, Hyde Park,
New York.

Russell, Richard B. Papers. Richard B. Russell Memorial Library, University of
Georgia, Athens.

Talmadge, Eugene. Campaign Correspondence, 1942. Georgia Department of
Archives and History, Atlanta.

Thompson, Melvin E. Papers. Archives of Contemporary South Georgia History.
Valdosta State College Library, Valdosta, Ga.

————. Papers. Special Collections, Robert W. Woodruff Library, Emory
University, Atlanta, Ga.

Truman, Harry S. Papers. Harry S. Truman Library, Independence, Mo.

Wallace, Henry A. Collection. University of Iowa Libraries, Iowa City.

AUTOBIOGRAPHIES, COLLECTED WORKS,
AND REMINISCENCES

Allen, Ivan, Jr., compiler. *The First Year of the State Hospital Authority.* N.d., n.p.

————. *Notes on the Sixties.* New York: Simon and Schuster, 1971.

Arnall, Ellis G. "Along the Way." Unpublished manuscript.

————. "Governor You Will Be." In *Georgia Governors in an Age of Change: From
Ellis Arnall to George Busbee,* ed. Harold P. Henderson and Gary L. Roberts, pp.
40–46. Athens: University of Georgia Press, 1988.

————. "History of the Arnall Family." Unpublished manuscript.

————. "Luck, Fate, and Chance." Unpublished manuscript.

————. "Odds and Ends." Unpublished manuscript.

————. *The Shore Dimly Seen.* Philadelphia: J. B. Lippincott, 1946.

————. *What the People Want.* Philadelphia: J. B. Lippincott, 1947. Reprint, New
York: Acclaim Publishing, 1966.

Brown, Charlie. *Charlie Brown Remembers Atlanta.* Columbia, S.C.: R. L. Bryan
Co., 1982.

Burns, Robert Elliott. *I Am a Fugitive from a Georgia Chain Gang!* New York:
Gossett and Dunlap, 1932.

Byrnes, James F. *All in One Lifetime.* New York: Harper Brothers, 1958.

Caldwell, Sam. *The Caldwell Conspiracy.* Lakemont, Ga.: Copple House, 1987.

Cap and Gown. University of the South Annuals, 1926, 1927, 1928.

Carter, Jimmy. *Why Not the Best?* Nashville: Broadman Press, 1975.

Daniels, Jonathan. *A Southerner Discovers the South*. New York: Macmillan, 1938.

Georgia Political System. Atlanta: Citizens Fact Finding Movement, 1938.

Gregory, Cleburne E., Jr. Unpublished manuscript of reminiscences. Collection of C. E. Gregory III.

Harsh, George. *Lonesome Road*. New York: W. W. Norton, 1971.

Maddox, Lester G. "A Chance for the Truth." In *Georgia Governors in an Age of Change: From Ellis Arnall to George Busbee,* ed. Harold P. Henderson and Gary L. Roberts, pp. 211–29. Athens: University of Georgia Press, 1988.

———. *Speaking Out: The Autobiography of Lester Garfield Maddox*. Garden City, N.J.: Doubleday, 1975.

Mays, Benjamin E. *Born to Rebel: An Autobiography*. New York: Charles Scribner's Sons, 1971.

The Pandora. University of Georgia Annual. 1931.

Roosevelt, Eleanor. *This I Remember*. New York: Harper and Row, 1950.

Roseman, Samuel I. *Working with Roosevelt*. New York: Harper Brothers, 1952.

Talmadge, Herman Eugene. *Talmadge: A Political Legacy, a Politician's Life, a Memoir*. Atlanta: Peachtree Publishers, 1987.

Truman, Harry S. *Memoirs*. 2 vols. Garden City, N.J.: Doubleday, 1955.

Vandiver, S. Ernest. "Vandiver Takes the Middle Road." In *Georgia Governors in an Age of Change: From Ellis Arnall to George Busbee,* ed. Harold P. Henderson and Gary L. Roberts, pp. 157–66. Athens: University of Georgia Press, 1988.

Wallace, Henry A. *Democracy Reborn*. New York: Russell Lord, Reynal and Hitchcock, 1944.

———. *The Price of Vision: The Diary of Henry A. Wallace, 1942–1946*. Ed. John Morton Blum. Boston: Houghton Mifflin Co., 1973.

PERIODICALS AND NON-GOVERNMENTAL REPORTS

"Another Talmadge Takes Over Georgia." *Life* 22 (January 27, 1947): 21–25.

Arnall, Ellis G. "Admitting Youth to Citizenship." *State Government* 16 (October 1943): 203–4.

———. "Arnall Cites Georgia's Progress in Caring for Its Distressed." Atlanta *Constitution,* January 7, 1945.

———. "Arnall Cites Needs: Material, Skill, Order." Atlanta *Constitution,* April 1, 1945.

———. "Arnall Describes Provisions to Eliminate Dictatorship." Atlanta *Constitution,* January 21, 1945.

———. "Arnall Sees Hope in Southern Liberalism." New York *Times Magazine,* February 2, 1947, p. 10.

———. "Coweta County's Two Governors." In *History of Coweta County*, pp. 138–39. Roswell, Ga.: W. H. Wolfe Associates, 1988.

———. "The Democrats Can Win." *Atlantic Monthly* 182 (October 1948): 33–38.

———. "Facilities for Higher Education Must Be Expanded, Arnall Says." Atlanta *Constitution*, December 24, 1944.

———. "The Family of Henry Clay Arnall." In *History of Coweta County*, pp. 191–93. Roswell, Ga.: W. H. Wolfe Associates, 1988.

———. "Federal Aid to Education: A Southern View." *Georgia Education Journal* 37 (October 1943): 10–11.

———. "5 State Agencies Devoting Talent to Task of Making Farming Pay." Atlanta *Constitution*, January 14, 1945.

———. "The Freight Rate Cartel." *New Republic* 112 (April 16, 1945): 497–98.

———. "Governor Arnall Points the Way to Greater Progress in Georgia." *Georgia Progress*, September 15, 1944.

———. "How You Can Fight Inflation." Atlanta *Journal-Constitution Magazine*, May 5, 1952, p. 7.

———. "The 'Loan Shark' Racket." Atlanta *Journal Magazine*, March 9, 1941, p. 5.

———. "Memo to Southern Liberals." *Southwest Review* 33 (Winter 1948): 1–4.

———. "My Battle Against the Klan." *Cornet* 20 (October 1946): 3–8.

———. "One Country: Equal Rights." *Nation* 164 (May 31, 1947): 650–51.

———. "Practical Program for Progressives." *Nation* 155 (June 12, 1948): 653–56.

———. "Revolution Down South." *Collier's* 116 (July 28, 1945): 17.

———. "Should We Have a Third Party?" *New Republic* 115 (December 30, 1946): 914–15.

———. "The South's Readmission to the Union." Lecture given to the Atlanta Historical Society, February 2, 1982.

———. "States Must Pay Debts, Too." Atlanta *Journal Magazine*, December 10, 1944, p. 4.

———. "The Unknown South: Our Last Frontier." New York *Times Magazine*, July 15, 1945, p. 12.

———. "Vote the Amendments." Atlanta *Journal Magazine*, July 25, 1943, p. 2.

———. "What the South Asks." Atlanta *Journal Magazine*, May 2, 1943, p. 2.

———. "Without a Dissenting Vote." Atlanta *Journal Magazine*, March 7, 1943, p. 1.

———. "Writing a New Constitution." Atlanta *Journal Magazine*, January 2, 1944, p. 5.

"Arnall Sweeps Out." *Newsweek* 25 (February 19, 1945): 48.

Barton, Frank L. "Background of the Class-Rate Investigation." *Southwestern Social Science Quarterly* 21 (December 1940): 197–209.

———. "Economic Efforts of Discriminatory Freight Rates." *Law and Contemporary Problems* 12 (Summer 1947): 507–31.

"Bulwinkle Bill Receives Overwhelming Support." *I.C.C. Practitioners Journal* 12 (November 1945): 144–45.

Burdette, Franklin D. "Lowering the Voting Age in Georgia." *South Atlantic Quarterly* 44 (July 1945): 300–307.

Callaway, Cason J. *A Broader Plan for the 100 Georgia Better Farms, Inc.* N.p., n.d.

Carter, Hodding. Review of *The Shore Dimly Seen* by Ellis G. Arnall. *Saturday Review of Literature* 29 (November 19, 1946): 13.

Chamberlain, John. "Arnall of Georgia." *Life* 19 (August 6, 1945): 69–75.

"Church Groups Assail Talmadge." *Christian Century* 164 (February 19, 1947): 242.

Cleghorn, Reese. "Meet Lester Maddox of Georgia, Mr. White Backlash." New York *Times Magazine,* November 6, 1966, pp. 27–29.

Collier, Tarleton. *Georgia Penal System.* Atlanta: Citizens Fact Finding Committee, 1938.

———. *Penal System: A Reflection of Our Lives and Our Customs.* Atlanta: Citizens Fact Finding Movement, 1940.

———. Review of *What the People Want* by Ellis G. Arnall. New York *Herald-Tribune Weekly Book Review,* June 13, 1948, p. 3.

"Condolences to the State of Georgia." *Nation* 63 (July 27, 1946): 86–87.

Davenport, Walter. "Unanimous Arnall." *Collier's* 112 (July 24, 1943): 16.

"Double Trouble." *Time* 49 (February 3, 1947): 20.

Embree, E. R. Review of *The Shore Dimly Seen* by Ellis G. Arnall. *Book Week,* November 17, 1946, p. 3.

"Eugene Talmadge." *Nation* 163 (December 28, 1946): 743.

"Exit Gene Talmadge." *Time* 40 (September 21, 1942): 19.

Foreman, Clark. "Georgia Kills the Poll Tax." *New Republic* 112 (February 26, 1945): 291–92.

"For the South—Arnall." *Time* 25 (April 9, 1945): 69.

"The Fortune Survey: The Political Mood—Summer 1947." *Fortune* 36 (September 1947): 5.

"The Freight-Rate Battle." *Fortune* 130 (October 1944): 149.

"Georgia: Change in the Weather." *Time* 40 (July 13, 1942): 19.

"Georgia: Death of the Wild Man." *Time* 48 (December 30, 1946): 18.

"Georgia: 'Honey, Pack Up.'" *Newsweek* 29 (March 31, 1947): 23.

"Georgia Is More Newsworthy Now." *Nation* 164 (February 8, 1947): 141.

Georgia League of Women Voters. "Georgia Voter: Facts About Candidates Offering for State Positions." Reprinted in Cartersville *Daily Tribune News,* July 4, 1946.

Georgia Political System. Atlanta: Citizens Fact Finding Movement, 1938.

"Georgia Prisons: State Abolished Old Abuses." *Life* 15 (November 1, 1943): 93–99.

"Georgia's Middle Ages." *Time* 42 (September 13, 1943): 23.

"Georgia: Votes Dimly Seen." *Newsweek* 20 (February 3, 1947): 21.

Goff, John H. "The Interterritorial Freight-Rate Problem and the South." *Southern Economic Journal* 6 (April 1940): 449–78.

Hamilton, W. B. Review of *The Shore Dimly Seen* by Ellis G. Arnall. New York *Times Book Review,* November 17, 1946, p. 1.

"Herman the Pretender." *Nation* 164 (January 25, 1947): 90.

Jarman, Rufus. "Georgia's New Peach." *Saturday Evening Post* 216 (August 28, 1943): 6.

Johnson, Gerald W. "Arnall of Georgia—and '48." *American Mercury* 63 (August 1946): 177–83.

Lively, Robert A. "The South and Freight Rates: Political Settlement of an Economic Argument." *Journal of Southern History* 14 (August 1948): 357–84.

McGill, Ralph. "How It Happened Down in Georgia." *New Republic* 116 (January 27, 1947): 12–14.

———. "It Has Happened Here." *Survey Graphic* 30 (September 1941): 449–553.

———. "Ralph McGill Is Proud of the Georgia Delegation." Atlanta *Constitution,* July 20, 1944.

McGill, Rita Santry. "Miss Maggie—Governor Arnall's First Teacher." Atlanta *Journal Magazine,* June 24, 1945, p. 8.

Maddox, Lester G. "A Chance for the Truth." In *Georgia Governors in an Age of Change: From Ellis Arnall to George Busbee,* ed. Harold P. Henderson and Gary L. Roberts. Athens: University of Georgia Press, 1988.

"The Majority Loses." *New Republic* 115 (July 29, 1946): 92–93.

Mezerick, A. G. "Georgians Have Had Enough." *Nation* 164 (February 15, 1947): 174–75.

Moscow, Warren. Review of *What the People Want* by Ellis G. Arnall. *Saturday Review of Literature* 31 (June 12, 1948): 13.

"New Boss for OPS." *Time* 59 (February 18, 1952): 20.

"People in the Limelight: Ellis Arnall." *New Republic* 112 (February 12, 1945): 214.

Political System: Democracy's First Line of Defense. Atlanta: Citizens Fact Finding Movement, 1940.

Potter, David M. "The Historical Development of Eastern-Southern Freight Rate Relationships." *Law and Contemporary Problems* 12 (Summer 1947): 416–89.

"A Proposed Constitution for Georgia." *Bulletin of the University of Georgia* 32 (January 1932): ix–51.

Reed, Rex. "Lester Maddox as a Leader of Men." *Esquire* 68 (October 1967): 120.

Reid, Ira De A. "Georgia's Negro Vote." *Nation* 163 (July 6, 1946): 12–14.

"Retirement Realized." *Georgia Education Journal* 38 (March 1945): 9.

"The Shape of Things." *Nation* 155 (September 19, 1942): 221–24.

Smith, Lillian E. "Democracy Begins at Home: Democracy Was Not a Candidate." *Common Ground* 3 (Winter 1943): 7–10.

———. "Pay Day in Georgia." *Nation* 164 (February 1, 1947): 118–19.

"Southern Exposure." *Time* 49 (March 17, 1947): 45.

Southern Regional Council. *Voter Registration in the South, Summer 1966.* Atlanta: Southern Regional Council, 1966.

"The South: Time Bomb." *Time* 43 (April 17, 1947): 20–21.

"Strictly from Dixie." *Time* 49 (January 27, 1947): 20–21.

"Untangled." *New Republic* 116 (March 31, 1947): 9.

Voter Registration in the South, Summer 1966. Atlanta: Southern Regional Council, 1966.

Watts, Richard, Jr. Review of *What the People Want* by Ellis G. Arnall. *New Republic* 118 (June 21, 1948): 24.

Wilson, Charles E. "Charles E. Wilson's Own Story of Break with Truman." *U.S. News and World Report* 32 (May 2, 1952): 11–12.

"Wool Hat Rebellion." *Newsweek* 29 (January 27, 1947): 21–24.

COURT CASES

Arnall (M. E. Thompson) v. Talmadge, 1693 Henry Superior Court (1947).

Baker v. Carr, 369 U.S. 186 (1962).

Brown v. Board of Education of Topeka, 347 U.S. 483 (1954).

Chapman et al. v. King, 154 F.2d 460 (1946).

Chapman et al. v. King, 327 U.S. 800 (1946).

Fulton National Bank of Atlanta v. Talmadge et al., 1698 Henry Superior Court (1947).

Georgia v. Evans et al., 316 U.S. 159 (1942).

Georgia v. Evans et al., 123 F.2d 57 (1941).

Georgia v. Pennsylvania Railroad Co. et al., 324 U.S. 401 (1945).

Georgia v. Pennsylvania Railroad Co. et al., 331 U.S. 788 (1947).

Georgia v. Pennsylvania Railroad Co. et al., 340 U.S. 889 (1950).

Gray v. Sanders, 372 U.S. 368 (1963).

Grovey v. Townsend, 295 U.S. 45 (1935).

King v. Chapman et al., 62 F. Supp. 639 (1945).

Morris v. Peters, 203 Ga. 364 (1948).

New York et al. v. United States et al., 331 U.S. 284 (1947).

Nixon v. Herdon, 273 U.S. 536 (1927).

Patten et al. v. Miller, 190 Ga. 105 (1940).

Patten et al. v. Miller, 190 Ga. 123 (1940).

Patten et al. v. Miller, 190 Ga. 152 (1940).

Reynolds v. Sims, 377 U.S. 533 (1964).

Sanders v. Gray, 203 F. Supp. 158 (1962).

Sawyer v. Youngstown Sheet and Tube Co., 197 F.2d 582 (1952).

Smith v. Allwright, 321 U.S. 349 (1944).

State of New York et al. v. United States, 65 F. Supp. 856 (1946).

Thompson v. Atlantic Coast Line Railroad, 200 Ga. 856 (1946).

Thompson v. Byers et al., Floyd Superior Court, January term, 1947.

Thompson, Lieutenant Governor, et al. v. Talmadge, 201 Ga. 871 (1947).

Truman et al. v. Duckworth et al., 329 U.S. 675 (1946).

United States v. Association of American Railroads et al., 4 F.R.D. 510 (1945).

Wesberry v. Sanders, 376 U.S. 1 (1964).

Wood v. Arnall, 189 Ga. 362 (1939).

Youngstown Sheet and Tube Co. v. Sawyer, 103 F. Supp. 569 (1952).

Youngstown Sheet and Tube Co. v. Sawyer, 343 U.S. 579 (1952).

NEWSPAPERS

Abbeville *Chronicle.*

Albany *Herald.*

Americus *Times-Recorder.*

Athens *Banner-Herald.*

Atlanta *Constitution.*

Atlanta *Daily World.*

Atlanta *Journal.*

Augusta *Chronicle.*

Augusta *Courier.*

Augusta *Herald.*

Bainbridge *Post-Searchlight.*

Bartow *Herald.*

Birmingham *Age-Herald.*

Brunswick *News.*

Bulloch *Times.*

Calhoun *Times.*

Carroll County *Georgian.*

Cartersville *Daily Tribune News.*

Charlotte (North Carolina) *Observer.*

Chicago *Defender.*

Cleveland (Ohio) *Plain Dealer.*

Cobb County *Times.*

Coffee County *Progress.*

Columbus *Enquirer.*

Columbus *Ledger.*

Cordele *Dispatch.*

Dalton *News.*

DeKalb *New Era.*

Douglas *Enterprise.*

Early County *News.*

Eastman *Times Journal.*

Fitzgerald *Herald.*

Gainesville *News.*

Georgia *Progress.*

Greensboro *Herald-Journal.*

Griffin *Daily News.*

Hartwell *Sun.*

Jackson *Progress-Argus.*

Lanier County *Times.*

Louisville (Kentucky) *Defender.*

Louisville (Kentucky) *Times.*

Macon *News.*

Macon *Telegraph.*

Madison *Madisonian.*

Marietta *Daily Journal.*

Meriwether *Vindicator.*

Milledgeville *Union-Recorder.*
Moultrie *Observer.*
Nashville *Tennessean.*
Newnan *Herald.*
Newnan *Times-Herald.*
New Orleans *Times-Picayune.*
New York *Herald-Tribune.*
New York *Post.*
New York *Times.*
Pittsburg *Courier.*
Richmond (Virginia) *Times-Dispatch.*
Rome *News-Tribune.*
Sandersville *Progress.*
Savannah *Evening Press.*
Savannah *Morning News.*

Statesman.
Sylvester *Local.*
Tattnall *Journal.*
Thomaston *Free-Press.*
Thomaston *Times.*
Thomasville *Times-Enterprise.*
Tifton *Daily Gazette*
Valdosta *Daily Times.*
Vidalia *Advance.*
Vienna *News.*
Washington *News-Reporter.*
Washington *Post.*
Waycross *Journal-Herald.*
Wayne County *True-Citizen.*
Winder *News.*

FEDERAL GOVERNMENT DOCUMENTS

Alldredge, J. Haden. *The Interterritorial Freight Rate Problem of the United States.* 75th Cong., 1st sess., 1937. House document 264.

Biographical Directory of the American Congress, 1774–1971. Washington: U.S. Government Printing Office, 1971.

Brief for the United States Amicus Curiae as to Jurisdiction, Georgia v. Pennsylvania Railroad Co. et al. In *U.S. Supreme Court, Transcripts of Records and File Copies of Briefs, 1950.* Vol. 12. Case 10. Original, Part 1.

Letter from the Board of Investigation and Research Transmitting a Summary Report on Its Study of Interterritorial Freight Rates. 78th Cong., 1st sess., 1943. House document 145.

Motion for Leave to File Amended Bill of Complaint and Amended Bill of Complaint, Georgia v. Pennsylvania Railroad Co. et al. In *U.S. Supreme Court, Transcripts of Records and File Copies and Briefs, 1950.* Vol. 12. Case 10. Original, part 1.

Motion of the State of Alabama for Leave to File Petition of Intervention, Petition of Intervention and Brief, Georgia v. Pennsylvania Railroad Co. et al. In *U.S. Supreme Court, Transcripts of Records and File Copies of Briefs, 1950.* Vol. 13. Case 10. Original, part 2.

National Emergency Council. *Report on Economic Conditions of the South.* Washington, D.C.: U.S. Government Printing Office, 1938.

Office of Price Stabilization. *The First Year of Price Stabilization in a Defense Economy. Operations of the Office of Price Stabilization, January 1951 to January 1952.* Washington, D.C.: Office of Price Stabilization, n.d.

Plaintiff's Trial Brief for the Court, Georgia v. Pennsylvania Railroad Co. et al.

Reprinted in U.S. Congress, Senate, *Regulation of Rate Bureaus, Conferences and Associations, Hearings Before the Senate Committee on Interstate Commerce on H.R. 2536*. 79th Cong., 2d sess., 1946, pp. 499–548.

Public Papers of the Presidents of the United States, Harry S. Truman, Containing the Public Messages, Speeches, and Statements of the President, January 1 to December 31, 1948. Washington, D.C.: U.S. Government Printing Office, 1964.

Public Papers of the Presidents of the United States, Harry S. Truman, Containing the Public Messages, Speeches, and Statements of the President, January 1, 1952 to January 20, 1953. Washington, D.C.: U.S. Government Printing Office, 1966.

Southern Class Rate Investigations, 1925. 100 I.C.C. 513.

Southern Class Rate Investigations, 262. I.C.C. 447.

State of Alabama et al. v. New York Central Railroad Company et al. 135 I.C.C. 255.

Tennessee Valley Authority. *Regionalized Freight Rates: Barrier to National Productiveness*. 78th Cong., 1st sess. House document 137.

———. *Supplemental Phases of the Interterritorial Freight Rate Problem of the United States*. 76th Cong., 1st sess. House document 271.

U.S. Bureau of the Census. *Sixteenth Census of the United States: 1940*. Population vol. 2, *Characteristics of the Population*. Part 2, *Florida–Iowa*. Washington, D.C.: U.S. Government Printing Office, 1943.

———. *Statistical Abstract of the United States, 1946*. Washington, D.C.: U.S. Government Printing Office, 1946.

U.S. Commission on Civil Rights. *Southern School Desegregation, 1966–1967*. Washington, D.C.: U.S. Government Printing Office, 1967.

U.S. Congress. *Congressional Record*. 79th Cong., 1st sess., December 10, 1945.

———. *Congressional Record*. 79th Cong., 2d sess., July 27, 1946.

———. *Congressional Record*. 82d Cong., 2d sess., February 18, March 6, June 12, and June 26, 1952.

———. House. Committee on Appropriations. *The Supplemental Appropriation Bill for 1953. Hearings Before Subcommittees of Committee on Appropriations, Emergency Agencies*. 82d Cong., 2d sess., 1952.

———. House. Committee on Banking and Currency. *Defense Production Act Amendments of 1952, Hearings on H.R. 6546*. 82d Cong., 2d sess., 1952, part 1.

———. House. Committee on Banking and Currency. *Defense Production Act Amendments of 1952, Hearings on H.R. 6546*. 82d Cong., 2d sess., 1952, part 2.

———. House. Committee on Interstate and Foreign Commerce. *Application of Antitrust Laws to Agreements in Furtherance of the National Transportation Policy, Hearings Before a Subcommittee of the House Committee on Interstate and Foreign Commerce on H.R. 2536*. 79th Cong., 1st sess., 1945.

———. House. Committee on Interstate and Foreign Commerce. *Hearings Before a Subcommittee of the House Committee on Interstate and Foreign Commerce, Omnibus Transportation Bill*. 76th Cong., 1st sess., 1939.

———. House. Committee on the Judiciary Subcommittee No. 1. *Hearings on H.J. Res. 39.* 78th Cong., 1st sess., 1943.

———. House. Committee on the Judiciary. *Study of Monopoly Power, Hearings Before the Subcommittee on Study of Monopoly Power of the Committee on the Judiciary.* 81st Cong., 1st sess., 1949. Serial 14, part 1.

———. Senate. Committee on Banking and Currency. *Defense Production Act Amendments of 1952, Hearings on S. 1594, S. 2645.* 82d Cong., 2d sess., 1952, part 1.

———. Senate. Committee on Banking and Currency. *Hearings on Nomination of Ellis G. Arnall to be Director of the Office of Price Stabilization.* 82d Cong., 2d sess., 1952.

———. Senate. Committee on Education and Labor. *Federal Aid to Education, Hearings on S. 181.* 78th Cong., 1st sess., 1945.

———. Senate. Committee on Interstate Commerce. *Freight Rate Discriminations, Hearings Before a Subcommittee of the Senate Committee on Interstate Commerce, Omnibus Transportation Bill.* 76th Cong., 1st sess., 1939.

———. Senate. Committee on Labor and Public Welfare. *National and Emergency Labor Disputes, Hearings Before Committee on Labor and Public Welfare and Its Subcommittee on Labor and Labor Management Relations on S. 2999 and S. 3016.* 82d Cong., 2d sess., 1952.

United States Government Organization Manual, 1952–1953. Washington, D.C.: General Services Administration, n.d.

U.S. Office of Price Stabilization. Central Files, 1952–53, Record Group 295. National Archives, Washington, D.C.

———. Decentralized Files of Various Directors of OPS, Record Group 295. National Archives, Washington, D.C.

U.S. Supreme Court. *Georgia v. Pennsylvania Railroad Co. et al. Transcript of Report of Proceedings Had Before Lloyd K. Garrison, Special Master.* 22 vols. Washington, D.C.: H. S. Middlemiss, Official Reporter.

———. *Report of the Special Master, Georgia v. Pennsylvania Railroad Co., et. al.* 3 vols. October term, 1949. Case 10. Original.

Wallace, Henry A. "Transportation Problems." Speech given by the vice president in Dallas, Texas. October 20, 1943. Reprinted in *Congressional Record,* 78th Cong., 1st sess., pp. 8610–13.

STATE GOVERNMENT DOCUMENTS

Aderhold, O. C., et al. *A Survey of Public Education of Less Than College Grade in Georgia: A Report to the General Assembly of Georgia by Its Special Committee on Education.* Atlanta, January 1, 1947.

Agricultural and Industrial Development Board. *Annual Report of the Education*

*Panel Program of Educational Development for Georgia, Education Panel Bulletin
No. 12.* August 1945.
———. *Georgia Goes Forward: The Record of One Year's Accomplishment.* Athens,
April 1945.
———. *Headlining Georgia's Progress: A Report on the Work of the Agricultural and
Industrial Development Board.* September 1, 1946.
Arnall, Ellis G. University of Georgia transcript, Athens.
———. University of the South transcript, Sewanee, Tenn.
Board of Regents of the University System of Georgia. *Annual Reports.* 1942–47.
Department of Archives and History. *General Election Returns 1966:
Governor-Appling County Through Worth County.*
———. *Georgia's Official Register.* 1939–43, 1945–50, 1953–54, 1961–62, 1963–64,
1965–66.
Department of Audits. *State Auditor Reports.* 1942–47.
———. *State Auditor Reports Supplements.* 1942–47.
Department of Education. *Annual Reports.* 1941–48.
Department of Public Health. *Annual Reports.* 1945–46.
Department of Law. *Attorney General Opinions.* 1939–49.
Department of Transportation. *Minutes of State Highway Commission of Georgia.*
April 21, 1943–January 6, 1947.
Education Panel, Agricultural and Industrial Board. *A Study of School Buildings in
Georgia [Brief Summary] Program of Educational Development for Georgia.*
Athens, February 1945.
Executive Department. *Messages and Addresses: Governor Ellis Arnall, 1943–1946.*
N.p., n.d.
———. *Minutes.* 1933, 1943–47.
General Assembly. *Acts and Resolutions.* 1943–49.
———. *Journals of the House of Representatives.* 1933, 1935, 1941, 1943–47, 1967.
———. *Journals of the Senate.* 1901, 1902, 1927, 1933, 1935, 1941, 1943–47, 1967.
Harris, Frederick R., Inc. *The Port of Brunswick. Report to the Agricultural and
Industrial Development Board of Georgia.* New York, 1945.
———. *The Port of Savannah. Report to the Agricultural and Industrial Development
Board of Georgia.* New York, 1945.
Head, T. Grady, compiler. *Constitution of the State of Georgia of 1877 as Amended
Through 1943.*
"A Proposed Constitution for Georgia." *Bulletin of the University of Georgia* 32
(January 1932).
"Report to Governor Ellis Arnall on Prison Conditions in Georgia and Southern
States." House *Journal,* pp. 20–34. Extraordinary Session, 1943.
Saye, Albert B., ed. *Records of the Commission of 1943–1944 to Revise the
Constitution of Georgia.* 2 vols. Atlanta, n.d.

Small, Samuel W. *A Stenographic Report of Proceedings of the Constitutional Convention Held in Atlanta, Georgia, 1877.* Atlanta: Constitutional Publishing Co., 1877.
Southern Governors Conference. *Minutes.* March 25–26, 1943.
State Highway Department. *Annual Reports.* 1943–48.

Secondary Sources

DISSERTATIONS AND THESES

Bernd, Joseph L. "Corruption in Georgia Primaries and Elections, 1938–1950." Master's thesis, Boston University, 1953.
———. "A Study of Primary Elections in Georgia, 1946–1954." Ph.D. dissertation, Duke University, 1957.
Bolster, Paul Douglas. "Civil Rights Movements in Twentieth-Century Georgia." Ph.D. dissertation, University of Georgia, 1972.
Bussell, Hazel Varnum. "Selected Aspects of Negro Education in Georgia from 1935 to 1952." Master's thesis, University of Georgia, 1955.
Canon, Alfred O. "The Law of Gubernatorial Succession with Special Reference to Georgia." Master's thesis, Duke University, 1949.
Cook, James F., Jr. "Politics and Education in the Talmadge Era: The Controversy Over the University System of Georgia, 1941–1942." Ph.D. dissertation, University of Georgia, 1972.
Dowdy, Derrell Coolidge. "State Highway Administration in Georgia." Master's thesis, University of Georgia, 1950.
Ellis, Ann Wells. "The Commission on Interracial Cooperation, 1919–1944: Its Activities and Results." Ph.D. dissertation, Georgia State University, 1976.
Fossett, Roy E. "The Impact of the New Deal on Georgia Politics, 1933–1941" Ph.D. dissertation, University of Florida, 1960.
———. "A Study of the Relationship of the Constitutional Boards and Executive Offices of Georgia to the Governor and General Assembly." Master's thesis, Emory University, 1949.
Foster, Albert Pafford. "The Georgia State Highway Department—Its Origin, Development, and Current Administration." Master's thesis, Emory University, 1949.
Henderson, Harold Paulk. "The 1946 Gubernatorial Election in Georgia." Master's thesis, Georgia Southern College, 1967.
———. "The 1966 Gubernatorial Election in Georgia." Ph.D. dissertation, University of Southern Mississippi, 1982.
Herndon, Jane Walker. "Eurith Dickenson Rivers: A Political Biography." Ph.D. dissertation, University of Georgia, 1974.

Lemmon, Sarah McCulloh. "The Public Career of Eugene Talmadge: 1926–1936." Ph.D. dissertation, University of North Carolina, 1952.

Miller, Zell Bryan. "The Administration of E. D. Rivers as Governor of Georgia." Master's thesis, University of Georgia, 1958.

Mixon, Val Gene. "The Growth of the Legislative Powers of the Governor of Georgia: A Survey of the Legislative Program of Governor Herman Talmadge, 1949–1954." Master's thesis, Emory University, 1959.

Mosley, Clement Charlton. "Invisible Empire: A History of the Ku Klux Klan in Twentieth-Century Georgia, 1915–1965." Ph.D. dissertation, University of Georgia, 1968.

Owen, Alice W. "The County Unit System as an Integral Part of the Georgia Primary Election System." Master's thesis, Emory University, 1934.

Owen, Hugh C. "The Rise of Negro Voting in Georgia: 1944–1950." Master's thesis, Emory University, 1951.

Preston, Howard Lawrence. "The Georgia Gubernatorial Campaign and Democratic Primary Election of 1946." Master's thesis, Atlanta University, 1971.

Pyles, Charles Boykin. "Race and Ruralism in Georgia Elections, 1948–1966." Ph.D. dissertation, University of Georgia, 1967.

Sanders, James B. "The Georgia Gubernatorial Controversy of 1947." Manuscript of thesis submitted for master's degree, Emory University.

Sutton, Willis Anderson, Jr. "The Talmadge Campaigns: A Sociological Analysis of Political Power." Ph.D. dissertation, University of North Carolina, 1952.

Taylor, Thomas Elkin. "A Political Biography of Ellis Arnall." Master's thesis, Emory University, 1959.

Williamson, Matt Winn. "Contemporary Tendencies Toward a Two-Party System in Georgia." Ph.D. dissertation, University of Virginia, 1969.

BOOKS

Anderson, William. *The Wild Man from Sugar Creek: The Political Career of Eugene Talmadge*. Baton Rouge: Louisiana State University Press, 1975.

Ball, Lamar Q. *Georgia in World War II: A Study of the Military and Civilian Effort*. N.p., 1946.

Bartley, Numan V. *From Thurmond to Wallace: Political Tendencies in Georgia, 1948–1968*. Baltimore: Johns Hopkins University Press, 1970.

———. *The Creation of Modern Georgia*. Athens: University of Georgia Press, 1983.

———. *The Rise of Massive Resistance: Race and Politics in the South During the 1950's*. Baton Rouge: Louisiana State University Press, 1969.

Bartley, Numan V., and Hugh D. Graham. *Southern Elections: County and Precinct Data, 1950–1972*. Baton Rouge: Louisiana State University Press, 1978.

———. *Southern Politics and the Second Reconstruction*. Baltimore: Johns Hopkins University Press, 1975.

Bass, Jack, and Walter DeVries. *The Transformation of Southern Politics: Social Change and Political Consequences Since 1945*. New York: Basic Books, 1976.

Bernd, Joseph L. *Grass Root Politics in Georgia: The County Unit System and the Importance of the Individual Voting Community in Bifactional Elections, 1942–1954*. Atlanta: Emory University Research Committee, 1960.

Black, Earl. *Southern Governors and Civil Rights: Racial Segregation as a Campaign Issue in the Second Reconstruction*. Cambridge: Harvard University Press, 1976.

Black, Earl, and Merle Black. *Politics and Society in the South*. Cambridge: Harvard University Press, 1987.

Brooks, Robert Preston. *Financing Government in Georgia, 1850–1944*. University of Georgia Bulletin, no. 5, May 1946. Athens: University of Georgia, 1946.

Burns, James M., J. W. Peltason, and Thomas E. Cronin. *State and Local Politics: Government by the People*. 4th ed. Englewood Cliffs, N.J.: Prentice-Hall, 1984.

Clark, Thomas D., and Albert D. Kirwan. *The South Since Appomattox: A Century of Regional Change*. New York: Oxford University Press, 1967.

Coleman, Kenneth, gen. ed. *A History of Georgia*. Athens: University of Georgia Press, 1977.

Congress and the Nation, 1945–1964: A Review of Government and Politics in the Post-War Years. Washington, D.C.: Congressional Quarterly, 1965.

Congressional Quarterly Almanac, 89th Congress, 2d sess. . . . 1966. Washington, D.C.: Congressional Quarterly, 1967.

Conway, Alan. *The Reconstruction of Georgia*. Minneapolis: University of Minnesota Press, 1966.

Cook, James F., Jr. *Governors of Georgia*. Huntsville, Ala.: Strode Publishers, 1979.

Cosman, Bernard. *Five States for Goldwater: Continuity and Change in Southern Presidential Voting Patterns*. University: University of Alabama Press, 1966.

Coulter, E. Merton. *Georgia: A Short History*. Rev. ed. Chapel Hill: University of North Carolina Press, 1947.

Galphin, Bruce. *The Riddle of Lester Maddox*. Atlanta: Camelot Publishing Co., 1968.

Garson, Robert A. *The Democratic Party and the Politics of Sectionalism, 1941–1948*. Baton Rouge: Louisiana State University Press, 1974.

Georgia Statistical Abstract, 1965. Ed. by David C. Hodge. Bureau of Business and Economic Research, Graduate School of Business Administration. Athens: University of Georgia, 1965.

Georgia Statistical Abstract, 1968. Bureau of Business and Economic Research, Graduate School of Business Administration. Athens: University of Georgia, 1968.

Glad, Betty. *Jimmy Carter in Search of the Great White House*. New York: W.W. Norton, 1980.

Gosnell, Cullen B., and C. David Anderson. *The Government and Administration of Georgia*. New York: Thomas Y. Crowell Co., 1956.

Grantham, Dewey W. *The Life and Death of the Solid South: A Political History*. Lexington: University of Kentucky Press, 1988.

Gunther, John. *Inside U.S.A.* New York: Harper and Brothers, 1947.

————. *Roosevelt in Retrospect: A Profile in History*. New York: Harper and Row, 1950.

Hansen, William P., and Fred L. Israel, eds. *The Gallup Poll, Public Opinion, 1935–1971*. Vol. 1. New York: Random House, 1972.

Havard, William C., ed. *The Changing Politics of the South*. Baton Rouge: Louisiana State University Press, 1972.

Henderson, Harold P., and Gary L. Roberts, eds. *Georgia Governors in an Age of Change: From Ellis Arnall to George Busbee*. Athens: University of Georgia Press, 1988.

Henson, Allen Lumpkin. *Red Galluses: A Story of Georgia Politics*. Boston: House of Edinboro Publishers, 1945.

Hepburn, Lawrence R., ed. *Contemporary Georgia*. Athens: Carl Vinson Institute of Government, University of Georgia, 1987.

Holland, Lynwood M. *The Direct Primary in Georgia*. Urbana: University of Illinois Press, 1949.

Hoover, Calvin B., and B. U. Ratchford. *Economic Resources and Policies of the South*. New York: Macmillan, 1951.

Jackson, Edwin L., and Mary E. Stakes. *Handbook of Georgia State Agencies*. 2d ed. Athens: University of Georgia Press, 1988.

Jarman, Rufus. *The History of Coastal States Life*. Atlanta: Coastal States Life Insurance Co., 1974.

Johnson, Amanda. *Georgia as Colony and State*. Atlanta: Walter W. Brown Publishing Co., 1938.

Joiner, Oscar H., gen. ed. *A History of Public Education in Georgia, 1734–1976*. Columbia, S.C.: R. L. Bryan Co., 1979.

Jones, Mary G., and Lily Reynolds, eds. *Coweta County Chronicles for One Hundred Years*. Atlanta: Stein Publishing Co., 1928.

Joubert, William H. *Southern Freight Rates in Transition*. Gainesville: University of Florida, 1949.

Key, V. O., Jr. *Southern Politics in State and Nation*. New York: Alfred A. Knopf, 1949.

Kouser, J. Morgan. *The Shaping of Southern Politics: Suffrage Restrictions and the Establishment of the One-Party South, 1880–1910*. New Haven: Yale University Press, 1974.

Krueger, Thomas A. *And Promises to Keep: The Southern Conference for Human Welfare, 1938–1948.* Nashville:·Vanderbilt University Press, 1967.

Lamis, Alexander P. *The Two-Party South.* New York: Oxford University Press, 1984.

Lawson, Steven F. *Black Ballots: Voting Rights in the South, 1944–1967.* New York: Columbia University Press, 1976.

Lively, Robert A. *The South in Action: A Sectional Crusade Against Freight Rate Discrimination.* Chapel Hill: University of North Carolina Press, 1949.

Luthen, Reinhard H. *American Demagogues: Twentieth Century.* Boston: Beacon Press, 1954.

McAuliffe, J. C. *The Story of Coastal States Life.* Rev. ed. Atlanta: Coastal States Life Insurance Co., 1965.

McConnell, Grant. *The Steel Seizure of 1952.* Interuniversity Case Program. Case Series No. 52. University: University of Alabama Press, 1960.

Marcus, Maeva. *Truman and the Steel Seizure Case: The Limits of Presidential Power.* New York: Columbia University Press, 1977.

Markowitz, Norman D. *The Rise and Fall of the People's Century: Henry A. Wallace and American Liberalism, 1941–1948.* New York: Free Press, 1973.

Martin, Harold H. *Ralph McGill, Reporter.* Boston: Little, Brown and Co., 1973.

Mezerik, A. G. *The Revolt of the South and West.* New York: Duell, Sloan and Pearce, 1946.

Miller, Zell Bryan. *Great Georgians.* Franklin Springs, Ga.: Advocate Press, 1983.

Morgan, Chester M. *Redneck Liberal: Theodore G. Bilbo and the New Deal.* Baton Rouge: Louisiana State University Press, 1985.

Myrdal, Gunnar. *An American Dilemma: The Negro Problem and Modern Democracy.* Twentieth Anniversary Edition. New York: Harper and Row, 1962.

Newnan-Coweta Historical Society. *A History of Coweta County, Georgia.* Roswell, Ga.: W. H. Wolfe Associates, 1988.

Official Report of the Proceedings of the Democratic National Convention . . . July 19–July 21, 1944. N.p. 1944.

Ogden, Frederick D. *The Poll Tax in the South.* University: University of Alabama Press, 1958.

Petersen, Svend. *A Statistical History of the American Presidential Elections.* New York: Frederick Unger Publishing Co., 1963.

Pierce, Neal R. *The Deep South States of America: People Politics and Power in the Seven Deep South States.* New York: W. W. Norton, 1974.

Rigdon, Louis T., II. *Georgia's County Unit System.* Decatur, Ga.: Selective Books, 1961.

Saye, Albert B. *A Constitutional History of Georgia.* Rev. ed. Athens: University of Georgia Press, 1970.

Schappmeier, Edward L., and Frederick H. Schappmeier. *Henry A. Wallace of Iowa: The Agrarian Years, 1910–1940.* Ames: Iowa State University Press, 1968.
———. *Prophet in Politics: Henry A. Wallace and the War Years, 1940–1965.* Ames: Iowa State University Press, 1970.

Schlesinger, Arthur M., Jr. *History of American Presidential Elections, 1789–1968.* 4 vols. New York: Chelsea House Publishers, 1968.

Sherrill, Robert. *Gothic Politics in the Deep South: Stars of the New Confederacy.* New York: Grossman Publishers, 1968; Ballantine Books, 1969.

Simkins, Frances Butler, and Charles Pierce Roland. *A History of the South.* 4th ed. New York: Alfred A. Knopf, 1972.

Sosna, Morton. *Southern Liberals and the Race Issue: In Search of the Silent South.* New York: Columbia University Press, 1977.

Spritzer, Lorraine Nelson. *The Belle of Ashby Street: Helen Douglas Mankin and Georgia Politics.* Athens: University of Georgia Press, 1982.

Stinnett, Ronald F. *Democrats, Dinners, and Dollars.* Ames: Iowa State University Press, 1987.

Strong, Donald S. *The 1952 Presidential Election in the South.* University: Bureau of Information, University of Alabama, 1956.

Swisher, Carl Brent. *American Constitutional Development.* 2d ed. Cambridge: Riverside Press, 1954.

Thompson, Mildred. *Reconstruction in Georgia: Economic, Social, and Political.* New York: Columbia University Press, 1915. Reprint, Savannah: Beehive Press, 1972.

Thompson, William Y. *Robert Toombs of Georgia.* Baton Rouge: Louisiana State University Press, 1966.

Tindall, George Brown. *The Disruption of the Solid South.* Athens: University of Georgia Press, 1972.
———. *The Emergence of the New South, 1913–1945.* Baton Rouge: Louisiana State University Press, 1967.

Williams, Eleanor. *Ivan Allen: A Resourceful Citizen.* Atlanta: Ivan-Allen-Marshall Co., 1950.

Wiprud, Arne C. *Justice in Transportation: An Exposé of Monopoly Control.* Chicago: Ziff-Davis Publishing Co., 1945.
———. *The Search for Wider Horizons.* Richmond: William Byrd Press, 1970.

Woodward, C. Vann. *Origins of the New South, 1877–1913.* Baton Rouge: Louisiana State University Press, 1951.
———. *The Strange Career of Jim Crow.* 3d rev. ed. New York: Oxford University Press, 1974.

PERIODICALS

Bailes, Sue. "Eugene Talmadge and the Board of Regents Controversy." *Georgia Historical Quarterly* 54 (December 1969): 409–23.

Bartley, Numan V. "Politics and Government in the Postwar Era." In *A History of Georgia,* Kenneth Coleman, gen. ed., pp. 388–405. Athens: University of Georgia Press, 1977.

———. "Race Relations and the Quest for Equality." In *A History of Georgia,* Kenneth Coleman, gen. ed., pp. 375–87. Athens: University of Georgia Press, 1977.

Belvin, William L., Jr. "The Georgia Gubernatorial Primary of 1946." *Georgia Historical Quarterly* 50 (March 1966): 37–53.

Bernd, Joseph L. "Georgia Static and Dynamic." In *The Changing Politics of the South,* ed. William C. Havard, pp. 294–365. Baton Rouge: Louisiana State University Press, 1972.

———. "White Supremacy and the Disfranchisement of Blacks in Georgia, 1946." *Georgia Historical Quarterly* 66 (Winter 1982): 492–513.

Boney, F. J. "The Politics of Expansion and Secession, 1820–1861." In *A History of Georgia,* Kenneth Coleman, gen. ed., pp. 129–204. Athens: University of Georgia Press, 1977.

Brinkley, Alan. "The New Deal and Southern Politics." In *The New Deal and the South,* ed. James C. Cobb and Michael V. Namorato, pp. 97–115. Jackson: University Press of Mississippi, 1984.

Cobb, James C. "Not Gone, But Forgotten: Eugene Talmadge and the 1938 Purge Campaign." *Georgia Historical Quarterly* 59 (Summer 1975): 197–209.

Cook, James F., Jr. "Carl Sanders and the Politics of the Future." In *Georgia Governors in an Age of Change,* ed. Harold P. Henderson and Gary L. Roberts, pp. 169–84. Athens: University of Georgia Press, 1988.

———. "Eugene Talmadge." In *Dictionary of Georgia Biography,* ed. Kenneth Coleman and Charles Stephen Gurr, pp. 954–57. Athens: University of Georgia Press, 1983.

———. "The Georgia Gubernatorial Election of 1942." *Atlanta Historical Bulletin* 18 (Spring–Summer 1973): 7–19.

Daniel, Frank. "He Won a 40-Year Battle for the South." Atlanta *Journal-Constitution,* February 3, 1963.

Dubay, Robert W. "Marvin Griffin and the Politics of the Stump." In *Georgia Governors in an Age of Change,* ed. Harold P. Henderson and Gary L. Roberts, pp. 101–12. Athens: University of Georgia Press, 1988.

Elson, Charles Myer. "The Georgia Three-Governor Controversy of 1947." *Atlanta Historical Journal* 20 (Fall 1976): 72–95.

Flint, Sam Hall. "The Great Freight Rate Fight." *Atlanta Historical Journal* 28 (Summer 1984): 5–22.

Freidel, Frank. "Election of 1932." In *History of American Presidential Elections, 1789–1968*, ed. Arthur M. Schlesinger, Jr., vol. 3, pp. 2707–39. New York: Chelsea House Publishers, 1971.

Friedman, Leon. "Election of 1944." In *History of American Presidential Elections, 1789–1968*, ed. Arthur M. Schlesinger, Jr., vol. 4, pp. 3009–38. New York: Chelsea House Publishers, 1971.

Garner, W. H. "The J. M. Ellis Family." *Bullock County History*, p. 44. New York: Herff Jones and Paragon Press, 1937.

"Georgia Association of Historians Survey of Georgia Governors, May 1985." In *Georgia Governors in an Age of Change*, ed. Harold P. Henderson and Gary L. Roberts, pp. 305–11. Athens: University of Georgia Press, 1988.

Grantham, Dewey W., Jr. "Georgia Politics and the Disfranchisement of the Negro." *Georgia Historical Quarterly* 32 (March 1, 1948): 1–21.

Hathorn, Bill Burton. "The Frustration of Opportunity: Georgia Republicans and the Election of 1966." *Atlanta History* 31 (Winter 1987–88): 37–52.

"Henry Clay Arnall." *Encyclopedia of Biography*, vol. 66, pp. 220–21. New York: American Historical Society, 1931.

Hepburn, Lawrence R. "Public Education." In *Contemporary Georgia*, ed. Lawrence R. Hepburn, pp. 172–214. Athens: Carl Vinson Institute of Government, University of Georgia, 1987.

Kirkendall, Richard S. "Election of 1948." In *History of American Presidential Elections, 1789–1968*, ed. Arthur M. Schlesinger, Jr., vol. 4, pp. 3099–3145. New York: Chelsea House Publishers, 1971.

Lemmon, Sarah McCulloh. "The Ideology of Eugene Talmadge." *Georgia Historical Quarterly* 38 (September 1954): 226–48.

Methvin, Eugene H. "Ellis Arnall: The South's Dragon-Slaying Hero." Atlanta *Journal-Constitution*, March 8, 1987.

Schemmel, Bill. "Bo Callaway's Alive and Well." *Georgia* 17 (March 1973): 30.

Shannon, J. B. "Presidential Politics in the South." *Journal of Politics* 10 (August 1948): 474–89.

Sherill, Robert. "Nixon's Man in Dixie: Bo Callaway Tries to Find the Republican Votes in Wallace Country." New York *Times Magazine*, September 15, 1968, p. 32.

Sibley, Celestine. "Once They Heard the Cheers: Southern as a Cotton Patch." Atlanta *Weekly*, October 30, 1983, pp. 15–17.

Sorensen, Theodore C. "Election of 1960." In *History of American Presidential Elections, 1789–1968*, ed. Arthur M. Schlesinger, Jr., vol. 4., pp. 3449–3469. New York: Chelsea House Publishers, 1971.

Taylor, A. Elizabeth. "The Abolition of the Convict Lease System in Georgia." *Georgia Historical Quarterly* 26 (Spring 1942): 273–87.

————. "The Origin and Development of the Convict Lease System in Georgia." *Georgia Historical Quarterly* 26 (Spring 1942): 113–28.

Thomason, Sharon. "James Gray—Albany's Mr. Power." *Brown's Guide to Georgia* 6 (March–April 1978): 74–78.

Zeigler, Luther Harmon, Jr. "Senator Walter George's 1938 Campaign." *Georgia Historical Quarterly* 43 (December 1959): 333–52.

Index

Accountants, 13

Adams, G. C., 10

Agricultural and Industrial Development Board, 57, 104, 111–14, 247–48

Agriculture, 6, 111–12, 116

Agriculture Department, 47

Alabama, 126, 145

Albany *Herald*, 68, 70, 87, 210, 216

Aliens, 22

Allen, Ivan, Jr., 238, 245

Allen, Ivan, Sr., 93

Allredge, J. Haden, 121

American Civil Liberties Union, 22

American Legion, 9, 182

American *Mercury*, 92, 191

Americus *Times-Recorder*, 40, 49

Anti-Talmadge Democrats, 8, 18, 29, 43, 50, 163, 166, 167, 169, 191, 192, 208, 209, 212, 214, 215, 216, 218–19, 222, 234, 251

Antitrust laws, 125, 126, 127, 128, 129–30, 131, 133

Arnall, Alice Slemons (daughter), 15, 252

Arnall, Alvan Slemons (son), 15, 251–52

Arnall, Ann Miles Gibbs (great-grandmother), 1

Arnall, Ashley Carol (granddaughter), 251–52

Arnall, Bessie Lena Ellis (mother), 2, 3, 6, 7, 15

Arnall, Carol Marie Lowry (daughter-in-law), 251–52

Arnall, Elizabeth Ann (granddaughter), 252

Arnall, Ellis Gibbs, 252–53, 306–7 (n. 54); childhood, 2–3, 6; college and law school, 3–5, 256 (n. 13); ambition to be governor, 4–5, 6, 7, 29; runs for legislature, 5–7, 152–53; elected House speaker pro tempore, 7–8, 11, 243; as legislator, 8–10, 11–15, 16, 53, 247; clashes with Talmadge, 11–12, 29–31, 32, 66, 70–71, 75, 76, 140, 148, 157–58, 162, 166; marriage, 15–16; in 1936 campaign, 17; as assistant attorney general, 18; as attorney general, 19–22, 23, 24, 25–29, 30, 31–32, 37, 205, 243, 247; 1942 gubernatorial campaign, 33, 34, 40, 41, 42–48, 49–50, 138–39, 247; meetings with Roosevelt, 47, 52, 124, 153;

Arnall, Ellis Gibbs (*continued*)
    elected governor, 50, 51–52, 243;
    reforms in first year as governor, 52–
    62, 168–69, 243–44; prison reform,
    63, 64–65, 66–67, 69–70, 71–72,
    73, 74–76; and soldiers' voting
    rights, 74; and constitutional
    revision, 77, 78, 79, 80–84, 85, 86–
    88, 89, 90–92, 93, 94–95, 96; and
    state debt, 97–100, 111, 248;
    expansion of state services, 101–4,
    105–8, 109, 110–12, 113, 114–15,
    244–46, 247–48, 249–50; and
    freight rates, 116, 118, 119, 123–26,
    127–29, 130–36; and racial issues,
    137, 138–41, 142, 143–51, 246–47,
    249, 250; campaigns for Roosevelt
    and Wallace, 152–53, 154–56, 157–
    58, 169, 247; and gubernatorial
    succession amendment, 158–63, 169;
    and 1946 gubernatorial campaign,
    161–62, 164, 165–67, 169, 171–72,
    247; in three-governors controversy,
    173, 174–75, 176, 177–78, 179–81,
    182, 183–84, 185, 186–87, 188–89;
    seeks vice-presidential nomination,
    190–92; lecture tour, 190, 203, 207,
    211, 245, 251; directs Office of Price
    Stabilization, 192–94, 195–203,
    207; law firm, 204; insurance
    business, 204–6; writing, 206–7,
    245; and 1948–62 gubernatorial
    campaigns, 208, 209–10, 211–12,
    213–16, 217–18, 219–22; 1966
    gubernatorial campaign, 223, 224,
    226, 227–28, 229, 230–37, 238,
    239–42, 251, 304 (n. 40), 305
    (n. 46)
Arnall, Frank Marion, II (brother), 2
Arnall, H. C., Merchandise Company,
    1, 3
Arnall, Henry Clay (grandfather),
    1–2, 3
Arnall, John Gholston (great-
    grandfather), 1, 6
Arnall, Joseph Gibbs (father), 2, 3, 6
Arnall, Mildred Delaney Slemons (first
    wife), 15, 252
Arnall, Ruby Hamilton McCord
    (second wife), 252
Arnall, Sarah Catherine (grand-
    mother), 2
Arnall, Taylor Gibbs (grandson),
    251–52
Arnold, David J., 81
Aroused Citizens of Georgia, 184
Associated Press, 89, 190, 214
Association of American Railroads,
    126–27, 130, 131, 132
Association of American
    Universities, 39
Association of County
    Commissioners, 95
Athens *Banner-Herald*, 11, 164
Atkinson, William Yates, Jr., 44
Atkinson, William Yates, Sr., 1, 63
Atlanta, 220, 228, 230, 234–35, 237
Atlanta *Constitution*, 9, 38, 59, 65, 73,
    74, 86, 112, 124, 134, 190, 191, 202,
    215; praise for Arnall, 16, 19, 29, 31,
    194; and 1942 campaign, 33, 34, 46;
    and Arnall's governorship, 106, 125–
    26, 128, 129, 143, 147, 161; and
    three-governors controversy, 181,
    188; and 1966 campaign, 232–33,
    238, 239, 240
Atlanta *Daily World*, 51, 54, 139–40,
    142, 164, 171, 181, 208, 240
Atlanta *Journal*, 16, 27, 63, 90, 142,
    144, 159, 162, 208–9, 210, 211, 213,
    217; and 1942 campaign, 40, 45;
    and Arnall's governorship, 58, 59–

60, 62, 70, 73, 101, 106; praise for
Arnall, 74, 75, 91, 102, 128, 129, 131,
145, 193–94; and constitutional
revision, 86, 87, 88, 93, 94; and 1946
campaign, 163, 165, 168, 174; and
three-governors controversy, 182,
184, 185–86; and 1966 campaign,
231, 232, 240
Atlanta League of Women Voters, 85
Atlanta Negro Voters League, 240
Attorney generalship, 55–56
Augusta *Chronicle*, 68, 70, 74, 164, 168,
181; and 1942 campaign, 40, 42, 46,
49, 63; and Arnall's governorship,
52, 59, 65, 148; praise for Arnall,
87, 93
Augusta *Courier*, 210
Augusta *Herald*, 138–39
Automobile tags, 8, 11

Bainbridge *Post-Searchlight*, 209–10
Bane, Frank, 80
Banking Commission, 81
Baptist Convention of Georgia, 240
Barkley, Alben W., 191–92
Bartley, Numan V., 134, 238, 244,
301–2 (n. 11)
Bartow County, 182
Bartow *Herald*, 51–52
Beard, Charles A., 91
Beasley, John C., 209–10
Beaver, Sandy, 39, 41, 43, 49
Bell Aircraft Corporation, 165
Benton, William, 194
Biddle, Francis, 94, 127
Bilbo, Theodore, 172, 175, 246
Birmingham, Ala., 147
Birmingham *Age-Herald*, 190
Birmingham *News*, 131
Black, Earl, 249
Black, Hugo L., 92, 147, 246

Black, Merle, 249
Blacks: education, 21–22, 48–49, 54,
102–3, 225; disfranchisement, 56,
73–74, 84, 90, 94, 96, 137–38, 141–
42, 168, 223; Arnall and opportunity for, 102–3, 139–42, 149–51,
211, 248–49, 250, 252; voting
rights, 142–43, 144, 145, 148, 150–
51, 152, 157, 171, 225, 226, 227,
245–46, 250; and desegregation,
229; and 1966 election, 234–35,
237, 240, 241
Board of Corrections, 82, 86, 87,
88–89, 95, 244
Board of Education, 30, 38, 46, 54, 59,
60, 61, 103, 112, 244
Board of Offender Rehabilitation, 244
Board of Pardons and Paroles, 55, 59,
60, 61, 75, 244
Board of Prisons, 69–70
Board of Public Welfare, 108–9
Board of Regents, 11–12, 29–30, 36–
37, 38, 39, 42, 43, 46, 53–54, 59, 60,
61, 244
Bowers, D. Talmadge, 171, 175, 176,
177–78
Bridges, S. Russell, 203
Broughton, J. Melville, 126
Brown, Ben, 240
Brown, Maggie, 2
Brown v. Board of Education (1954),
219, 220, 222
Brunswick, 92, 113
Brunswick *News*, 46
Budget Bureau, 101
Bulloch County, 183
Bullock, Rufus B., 77, 166
Bulwinkle, Alfred L., 129, 130,
131–32, 133
Burns, Robert Elliott, 28, 64,
74–75, 211

Byrd, Garland T., 229–30, 234

Cairo *Messenger*, 172
Caldwell, Harmon W., 37, 39, 49
Caldwell, Millard, 125
Caldwell, Sam, 231, 237
Calhoun County, 166
Calhoun *Times*, 16, 38, 59
Callaway, Cason J., 112
Callaway, Howard Hollis, 225–26,
  229, 230, 234, 235–36, 237, 238,
  239, 240–41
Camp, Albert S., 197
Camp Dixie for Boys, 3
Canada, 121
Candler, Allen D., 78
Capehart, Homer E., 195
Capehart amendment (Defense
  Production Act), 195, 199, 200,
  201, 202
Carmichael, James V., 81, 85, 87, 172,
  209; 1946 gubernatorial campaign,
  152, 164, 165, 166, 167–68, 169, 171,
  175–76, 177–78
Carmichael, Stokely, 237
Carson, Fiddlin' John, 34–35
Carter, James E., Jr., 230, 232, 234,
  235, 238, 239, 306–7 (n. 54)
Cartersville work camp, 67–68, 76
Cedartown *Standard*, 181
Chain gangs, 64
Chatham County, 44
Chattanooga *Times*, 91
Chicago, Ill., 152
Chicago *Defender*, 51
Churchill, Winston S., 203
Citizens Fact Finding Movement,
  78, 79
Civil liberties, 149–50
Civil Rights Act (U.S., 1964), 225, 229

Clark, Tom C., 192
Clay, A. W., 67
Clay, Ryburn G., 67, 106
Clemency power, 39–40, 46, 55, 61, 65
Cleveland (Ohio) *Plain Dealer*, 59
Coastal States Life, 205
Cobb County *Times*, 38, 52
Coca-Cola Company, 45
Cocking, Walter D., 29, 30, 32, 36–38,
  42, 48
Collier's, 58, 141
Collins, M. D., 20–21, 24, 30–31, 101,
  102, 112
Columbus *Enquirer*, 68, 70, 159
Columbus *Ledger*, 91, 145, 147–48,
  187, 240
Columbus *Ledger-Enquirer*, 68–69,
  142, 210
Columbus National Life Insurance
  Company, 205
Commerce Department, 113–14
Constitution of 1868, 77
Constitution of 1877, 19, 21, 22, 24,
  39, 49, 60–61, 77–78; amendments,
  33, 54, 55, 56, 59–60, 77, 78, 79, 84;
  revision of, 58, 79–81, 82, 83–84,
  85, 94, 95, 96, 160, 188
Constitution of 1945, 103, 143, 171,
  214, 239, 243; ratification, 92, 93–
  96; gubernatorial succession
  amendment, 158–61, 250; and
  three-governors controversy,
  172–73, 175, 183, 186
Constitutional boards, 46, 54, 55, 57–
  58, 59, 60–62, 81–82, 243, 244,
  245
Convict leasing, 63, 64, 71
Cook, J. Eugene, 106, 145–46, 174,
  185, 208, 214–15
Cook, James F., Jr., 134, 244

Cook County, 183
Cordele *Dispatch*, 40, 209–10
Corrections Department, 72, 73
Coulter, E. Merton, 62, 134, 244
Council Against Intolerance in
America, 148
Council of Motion Pictures
Organizations, 206
Counties, 86, 94–96, 110, 162
County unit system, 35, 41, 43, 96,
143, 167–68, 217, 223–24, 226–27;
as campaign issue, 94, 95, 173, 174,
212; Arnall and, 144, 221, 249
County work camps, 64, 71–72
"Courthouse rings," 41
Coweta County, 1, 5, 6, 7, 8, 139, 243
Coweta Fertilizer Company, 1–2
Cox, E. Eugene, 168, 197
Cox, James M., 144, 160, 162, 167
Cracker party, 44
Crump, Ed, 186–87
Culpepper, J. W., 162

Dadisman, Carol, 233, 237
Dalton *Daily Citizen-News*, 240
Daniels, Josephus, 91–92
Dartmouth College, 211
Davis, T. Holt, 142
Deaver, Bascom S., 25, 26
Defense Production Act (U.S., 1950),
195, 196–97, 201–2
DeKalb County, 182, 183–84
Democracy, 46, 148
Democracy Reborn (Wallace), 156
Democratic party, 17, 52, 192, 209;
Arnall and, 16, 44, 123, 144, 191,
213, 231, 234; 1944 National
Convention, 152, 154–56, 157–58,
169; 1948 National Convention,
191; Republican challenge to, 223,

229, 230, 238. *See also* Anti-
Talmadge Democrats; County unit
system; Election campaigns; White
primary
Desegregation, 220–21, 224–25,
227–28, 229, 246
DiSalle, Michael, 193
Disney, Walt, 206
Dixie Life Insurance Company, 204–5
Dodd, Walter F., 80
Dodge County, 183
Douglas, William O., 128, 191
Duckworth, William H., 186
Duke, Daniel, 146
Durden, Adie N., 177, 178
Duvall, W. R., 65
Dyer, Stonewall H., 5, 7, 10, 13, 27
Dykes, James M., 90–91, 180

Eastman *Times-Journal*, 166, 181
Eatonton *Messenger*, 186–87
Economic development, 116–17, 118,
119, 122, 123, 127–28, 130, 133, 135,
249–50, 251, 252
Economic Stabilization
Administration, 194, 195
Education, 100–101, 102–4, 149, 230.
See also Public schools
Education Department, 21, 92, 100
Eisenhower, Dwight D., 225
Election campaigns: 1932 legislative,
5–8; 1936 gubernatorial, 17, 18;
1940 presidential, 153; 1942 gubernatorial, 33–35, 40–50, 51, 138–39,
153; 1946 gubernatorial, 101–2, 109,
137, 144, 145, 152, 159, 161, 163–68,
169, 171–72, 174, 175, 176–77, 185–
86, 209–10, 288–89 (n. 47); 1948
gubernatorial, 209–13; 1948 presidential, 213; 1950 gubernatorial,

Election campaigns (*continued*)
213–17; 1952 presidential, 217; 1954
gubernatorial, 217–19; 1958 gubernatorial, 219–20; 1962 gubernatorial, 220; 1966 gubernatorial, 226,
227–28, 229–42, 304 (n. 40), 305
(n. 46)
Elliott, J. Robert, 56, 59, 176–77, 178
Ellis, J. M., and Sons Company, 2
Ellis, Joseph Mathew, 2, 6
Evans, Hiram W., 26, 32, 125
Executive Democratic Committee, 41
Ezell, Gibson Greer, 175

Farmers markets, 13
Farmers Warehouse Company, 1–2
Federal-Aid Highway Act (U.S.,
1944), 104–5
Federal Bureau of Investigation, 146
Federal Communications Com-
mission, 31
Federal Emergency Relief Admin-
istration, 14
Feinsinger, Nathan P., 199
Felton, Rebecca L., 63
Fitzgerald *Herald*, 93–94, 181
Flint, Sam Hall, 128, 135
Florida, 155–56
Folsom, James E., 126
Foreman, Clark, 92, 147, 182
Fortson, Ben W., Jr., 72, 82, 90,
158–59, 160, 162
Fortson, Blanton, 113
Fortune, 191
Frankfurter, Felix, 27
Freeman, Alvan, 5
Freight rate controversy, 116–36, 154,
243, 250
Fulbright, J. William, 129

Fulton County Citizens Democratic
Club, 232
Fuqua, J. B., 232
Future, 31

Gainesville Ministerial
Association, 181
Gainesville *News*, 39, 164, 187
Gallogly, Richard G., 27–28
Gallup Poll, 188
Galphin, Bruce, 233, 237, 238
Game and Fish Commission, 61, 244
Garrison, Lloyd K., 129, 132–33, 134
Gasoline tax, 24, 52, 97, 107
Geer, Peter Zack, 306 (n. 53)
General Appropriations Act (1937),
23–24
George, Walter F., 44, 62, 74, 119,
156–57, 246
Georgia, 6, 27, 140, 149–50, 168, 175,
243–44, 248, 252–53; state agencies,
13, 23–24, 54–55, 57–58, 60–62;
state debt, 48, 52, 97, 98, 99, 106,
111, 243, 248, 274 (n. 8); merit
system, 58, 82, 87–89, 243, 244–45;
freight rate lawsuit, 125, 126–27,
128, 129, 130–31, 132, 133, 134, 135–
36; population, 137; campaign
primary laws, 137–38, 142–43, 144,
145; Democratic Convention
delegation, 154–56; three-governors
controversy and, 187–89; and
desegregation, 224
Georgia Association of Democratic
Clubs, 240
Georgia Better Farms Program, 112
Georgia Committee for Good
Government, 59–60
Georgia Education Association, 43,
101

Georgia Education Journal, 101
Georgia General Assembly, 10, 22, 23,
   84, 86, 194, 208, 223, 234; Arnall in,
   5, 7, 8–10, 11–14, 31, 53, 243; and
   highway department, 8–9, 57, 105,
   106–8; taxation, 9, 12, 89–91, 217;
   representation in, 35, 223; 1943
   session, 53–59, 60, 61, 62, 106; and
   public schools, 53–54, 55, 104, 221;
   prison reform, 63, 65, 66, 69, 72–73,
   76; soldiers' voting act, 74; constitutional revision, 79, 80, 83, 88–89,
   92–93; and state services, 108–10,
   111, 113; and gubernatorial succession, 152, 158, 159, 160–61, 162–
   63, 250; election of governor, 173–
   75, 176–78, 180, 181, 182–83, 184,
   185, 186, 188, 215, 239, 240, 241
Georgia League of Women Voters,
   86, 88
Georgia Power Company, 45, 160
Georgia Progress, 113
Georgia Railroad Company, 83
Georgia School of Technology, 39,
   43, 182
Georgia State AFL-CIO, 232
Georgia State Metro Voters
   League, 240
Georgia Supreme Court, 26, 95, 184,
   185–87, 188, 191, 208, 212, 215
Georgia Teachers College, 36, 38
Gholston, J. Knox, 106–8
Gillis, James L., Sr., 234
Glad, Betty, 235
Golden, Sol I., 204
Goldwater, Barry M., 225, 226, 229,
   239, 241
Goldwyn, Samuel, 206
Government, 6, 9, 12, 22, 23; Arnall's
   conception of, 7, 13, 111, 233–34;

state agencies, 13, 23–24, 54–55, 57–
   58, 60–62; local, 83–84, 86, 87, 88,
   95–96, 101; expansion of state
   services, 97, 98, 100, 114–15,
   244–45; railroad regulation, 118
Gowen, Charles L., 177, 218–19
Grady, Henry W., 250
Graham, Frank G., 147
Graves, Bibb, 118, 120
Graves, W. Brooke, 80
Gray, James H., Sr., 229, 232, 234, 238
Grayson, Spencer M., 88, 90, 91
Great Depression, 6, 12, 104
Greensboro *Herald-Journal*, 209–10,
   211
Gregory, Cleburne E., Jr., 28, 67, 86,
   93, 204
Grice, Warren, 85
Grier, J. D., Jr., 240
Griffin, S. Marvin, 171, 179, 209–10,
   225, 301 (n. 4); 1954 campaign, 218,
   219, 220; 1962 campaign, 221, 224,
   227, 229
Gross, Frank C., 53, 59–60, 74, 89, 90,
   143, 158, 171–72; and penal system
   reform, 67, 68–69, 72; and constitutional revision, 80, 82, 87, 88, 93
Gubernatorial succession, 214; in
   constitutional revision, 82–83, 88,
   89; amendment attempt, 152,
   158–61, 162–63, 167, 169, 250
Gunther, John, 153

Haas, Beatrice H., 80, 81, 83, 85
Hamilton, Sylla, 36, 37
Hand, Frederick B., 218
Hannagan, Robert E., 155
Harding, Warren G., 165
Hardman, Lamartine G., 78
Harris, Roy V., 12, 59–60, 74, 225,

Harris, Roy V. (*continued*)
229, 232, 234, 237; Arnall and, 8,
44, 53, 164, 210, 212; and taxation,
9, 89, 110, 111; support of Talmadge, 18, 178–79, 184, 187, 212,
213, 217; and penal system reform,
67, 68–69, 72, 73; and constitu-
tional revision, 80, 82, 83, 87–88, 93,
107, 108; and white primary, 143,
145; and gubernatorial succession,
158, 159–60, 161, 162–63; 1946
gubernatorial campaign, 161, 163–
64; and desegregation, 220–21
Harrison, Walter W., 162, 183
Harsh, George R., 27
Hart, E. L., 132
Harty, Joseph Edward, II, 252
Harty, Joseph Edward, III, 252
Hawes, Peyton S., 107
Hays, Wayne L., 197
Head, T. Grady, 69, 125, 127
Health Board, 110
Hearst, William Randolph, 14
Helena precinct, 185
Hemphill, Paul, 233
Henson, Allen L., 43
Highway Board, 57, 106, 107, 108
Highway construction, 98, 104–6,
165–66
Highway Department, 8–9, 10, 23,
24–25, 26, 29, 32, 38, 61, 106–8;
work camps, 67–68, 71
Hill, B. Warren, 107
Hill, Jesse, 240
Hill, Lister, 121, 129
Hill Law Club, 5
Hopkins, Harry, 119
Hospital Authority, 19–20, 109
Hospitals, 110
Howard, Pierre, Sr., 177–78, 183–84

Howell, Clark, 18

*I Am a Fugitive from a Georgia Chain
Gang* (Burns), 64
Income tax, 12
Independent Film Producers Export
Corporation, 206
Independent Movie Producers of
America, 216
Industrialization, 111–12, 113, 116–17,
120, 122, 134–35, 250
Inflation, 194–95, 196, 197, 202, 203
Interstate Commerce Act (U.S., 1887),
118, 120, 121, 130
Interstate Commerce Commission
(ICC), 118–22, 123, 124–25, 126,
127, 128, 129, 130–31, 133–34, 135

Japan, 40
Jasper County, 182–83
Jefferson, Thomas, 147
Jenkins County, 183
Johnson, Gerald W., 92
Johnson, Leroy, 238, 239, 240, 303
(n. 24)
Johnson, Linton S., 31
Johnson, Lyndon B., 229
Junior Chamber of Commerce, 14–15,
31, 124
Jury service, 86

Kaufman and Broad, Inc., 205
Kennedy, J. Henry, 66
Kentucky, 117
Key, V. O., Jr., 18, 36, 41, 244,
248–49, 251
King, Rev. Martin Luther, Jr., 239
King, Rev. Primus E., 142
Korean War, 193, 194, 195, 200, 207
Kuhn, Loeb and Company, 131

Ku Klux Klan, 26, 125, 145–47, 151, 161–62

Lane, Mills B., 232
Lawrence, Roland H., 65–66
Law School Honor Court, 5
League of Women Voters, 84, 85, 86, 88
Leban, Jack, 204
Liberty County, 241
Lieutenant governorship, 11, 17, 89, 95, 171–72, 173, 244–45
Life, 73, 188
Linder, Tom, 41, 218
Liquor fee, 100, 110–11
Literacy test, 150
"Little New Deal," 17, 23, 60, 165, 167
Lively, Robert, 135
Long, Huey P., 172, 186–87
Louisiana, 186–87
Louisville and Nashville Railroad Company, 228
Louisville *News*, 141
Lovett, Herschel, 56
Lowndes County, 182

McClatchey, Devereaux, 205–6
McClure, John E., 31
McCord, Ruby Hamilton, 252
McDonald, George T., 106
McGill, Ralph E., 39, 139, 178; and Arnall, 31, 62, 217, 233, 247; on election campaigns, 34, 44, 52, 168, 181, 238
McGinty, John R., 90
McGinty, Roy, 16
McGrath, J. Howard, 192
McIntosh County, 166
MacIntyre, Hugh J., 81

Macon, 234–35
Macon *News*, 145, 187, 216, 240
Macon *Telegraph*, 57, 60, 70, 74, 142, 165, 186, 215, 240
Maddox, Lester G., 225, 228–29, 234, 235, 236–41, 242, 304 (n. 40)
Mann, Royal K., 66
Manufacturing, 117–18, 120, 121, 124, 132
Marietta *Daily Journal*, 232, 240
Martin, Jess, 28
Maverick, Maury, 129
Maybank, Burnet T., 126
Mays, Benjamin E., 140
Mercer University, 3
Meriwether County, 182, 183
Meriwether *Vindicator*, 38, 63
Methvin, Eugene H., 134
Mezerik, A. G., 134
Milledgeville State Hospital, 19–20, 109
Milledgeville *Union-Recorder*, 52, 93, 164
Miller, M. L., 24, 25–26
Minimum Foundation for Education Act (1949), 104
Mississippi, 145
Mitchell, Margaret, 134–35
Mitchell, Stephens, 134–35
Mobley, Carlton, 30
Montague, W. H., Sr., 232
Moore, Wiley L., 73
Morgan, Arthur E., 119
Morgan, J. P., and Company, 131
Morse, Wayne L., 243
Motion Picture Industry Council, 206
Motor vehicle licenses, 9, 12–13
Moultrie *Observer*, 40, 46, 51, 70, 210, 237
Myrdal, Gunnar, 140

Nashville *Tennessean*, 91
Nation, 51, 168, 172, 175, 187
National Association for the Advance-
ment of Colored People, 145, 239
National Association of Attorneys
General, 27, 32
National Association of Life Com-
panies, 205–6
National Association of Manufac-
turers, 195–96
National Chamber of Commerce,
195–96
National Emergency Council, 116
National Governors Conference, 123
National Guard, 11, 25, 38
National Press Club, 200–201
New Deal, 12, 17, 18, 23, 36, 40, 47, 74
New Jersey, 82
Newnan, Daniel, 1
Newnan, Ga., 1, 45
Newnan Banking Company, 1–2
Newnan Board of Aldermen, 6
Newnan Central Baptist Church, 2, 3
Newnan *Herald*, 10, 16, 18
Newnan High School, 3
Newnan *Times-Herald*, 240
New Orleans, La., 148
New Orleans *Times-Picayune*, 51
New Republic, 92
New South, 250, 252–53
Newsweek, 176, 188
New York Southern Society, 74–75
New York *Times*, 10, 128, 168,
175, 203
Norman, J. V., 132
North Carolina, 243
North Georgia Vocational School, 103

O'Daniel, W. Lee, 28
Office of Price Stabilization, 192–93,
194–96, 197–98, 199–200, 201,
202–3, 207, 248
Official Territory, 117, 118, 120,
121, 130
Ogden, Frederick D., 92

Pan-Hellenic Council, 5
Patterson, Eugene, 231, 238
Peachtree Road Methodist Church,
181
Pearson, Drew, 146, 244
Pennsylvania Railroad Company, 125
Pension system, 12
People's Voice, 51
Pepper, Claude D., 91, 92, 141–42,
148, 246
Personnel Board, 82, 86, 95, 244
Peters, James S., 37, 220–21
Pickford, Mary, 206
Pierce, Neal, 237
Pittman, Marvin S., 29, 30, 32,
36–38, 42
Pittman, Claude, 67, 72
Pittsburg *Courier*, 51
Planning Board, 57, 111
Plessy v. Ferguson (1896), 150, 246
Poindexter, Claude H., 205–6
Poll tax, 21, 85, 88; repeal of, 89–92,
93, 139, 145, 150, 243, 245–46,
248, 249
Poll Tax in the South (Ogden), 92
Populist party, 17, 138, 250
Ports Authority, 92, 113, 244–45
Price controls, 194, 195–97, 198, 201,
202–3, 207
Prison system, 13, 63–73, 74–76,
82, 243
Professional examining boards, 57–58
Progressive party, 157
Property tax, 9

Public health system, 110, 112–13
Public institutions, 109–10
Public schools, 38, 95–96; segregation, 21–22, 48–49, 102–3, 137, 139, 226, 246; Arnall's reforms, 100, 102–3, 104; desegregation, 219, 220–21, 224–25, 246
Public Service Commission, 11, 38, 58, 61, 244
Public transportation, 149
Public Welfare Department, 108
Public Works Administration, 12
Putnam, Roger L., 194, 198, 199, 200

Race, 63; Arnall and, 14, 21–22, 49, 137, 138–41, 145–51, 222, 237, 250; Talmadge and, 36, 38, 48–49, 50, 94, 138–40, 210; as campaign issue, 50, 157–58, 164, 166, 168, 210, 212–13, 219; Maddox and, 228; Atlanta riot, 237. *See also* Blacks; Segregation; White primary; White supremacy
Railroads: freight rates, 117, 118–19, 120, 122, 135–36; Georgia's lawsuit against, 125–29, 130–31, 132, 133, 134
Rainey, Clem R., 66
Raleigh *News and Observer*, 91–92
Ramspeck, Robert, 121
Rankin, Jim, 232–33, 237
Raw materials, 116, 118, 127
Rayburn, Sam, 197
Reconstruction, 77, 137, 165, 166, 223
Reconstruction Finance Corporation, 19–20, 93
Reddic, Lawrence D., 149
Redwine, Charles, 17
Reed, Clyde M., 133
Reidsville prison break, 64–66, 76
Reorganization Act (1931), 31

Republican party, 133, 138, 223, 225–26, 229, 238
Revolt of the South and West (Mezerik), 134
Richmond County, 44, 164
Richmond *Times-Dispatch*, 51
Rivers, Eurith D., 7, 9, 78, 174, 187, 208, 212, 216, 233, 246; Arnall and, 8, 17, 28–29, 32, 48, 152–53, 209–10, 243, 247; and New Deal, 12, 17, 23, 60; as governor, 18, 19, 22, 23–26, 27–28, 39, 57, 58, 64, 67, 111, 120, 188; in 1942 campaign, 43–44, 159; and constitutional revision, 93, 95; in 1946 campaign, 159, 161–63, 164–65, 166–68, 169, 172, 288–89 (n. 47)
Roberts, Columbus, 43–44
Rome *News-Tribune*, 168
Roosevelt, Eleanor, 91, 119, 153
Roosevelt, Franklin D., 12, 19–20, 40, 53, 58–59, 73, 92, 114, 138; Arnall's support for, 29, 47, 153, 169, 247; meetings with Arnall, 47, 52, 124, 156; and freight rate controversy, 116, 119, 121, 124, 125, 128; in 1944 campaign, 153, 154, 155, 156; death, 157, 191, 192
Rosenwald, Julius, 37
Rosenwald Fund, 37–38, 48
Russell, Richard B., Jr., 50, 219, 227; as senator, 17, 34, 41, 119, 182, 183; as governor, 27, 60, 64

St. John, M. L., 162
Sales tax, 9, 12, 23, 99, 100, 216–17, 219, 248, 251
Sanders, Carl E., Jr., 221, 224, 227, 232, 237, 238, 239
Sanford, Steadman V., 39, 43, 49

Savannah, 92, 113, 183
Savannah *Evening Press*, 90, 210
Savannah *Morning News*, 59, 70, 74, 92, 112, 142, 172, 210, 214, 216
Sawyer, Charles, 200
Saye, Albert B., 95
Schomburg Collection of Negro Literature, 149
School for Mental Defectives, 109
Segregation, 223; public schools, 21–22, 48–49, 102–3, 137, 139, 226, 246; Arnall and, 138–39, 141, 147, 149, 150–51, 157, 237, 246–47, 250; held unconstitutional, 219, 224–25. *See also* Desegregation
Selznick, David O., 206
Sherman Antitrust Act (U.S., 1890), 26–27, 119, 129–30, 248
Shore Dimly Seen (Arnall), 149–50, 206–7
Sibley, John A., 142–43, 221
Smith, George T., 239
Smith, Hoke, 18, 94
Smith, Lillian E., 33, 138, 148, 182
Smith, Marion, 102
Smith v. Allwright (1944), 84, 85, 141–42
Snelling, Charles M., 78
Society of Independent Motion Picture Producers, 206
Soldiers' voting rights, 73–74, 139, 248, 249
South, 248–49, 252–53; freight rates and development, 116–17, 118, 119–21, 122–23, 124, 127–28, 129, 133–36, 154, 243, 250; race relations, 137, 138, 139, 141–42, 149–51, 211, 246; conservatism in, 191, 213, 225
South Carolina, 129, 145
Southeastern Association of Railroads and Utilities Commissions, 119–20

Southern Association of Colleges and Secondary Schools, 39, 48, 54
Southern Christian Leadership Conference, 240
Southern Conference for Human Welfare (SCHW), 147, 148, 210, 211, 236
Southern Governors Conference, 120, 123, 125–26, 132
Southern Railway and Steamship Association, 117
Southern States Industrial Council, 123
Southern Territory, 117, 118, 119, 120
Southern Traffic League, 119–20
Soviet Union, 157
Sparkman, John J., 198
Stark, W. W., 56
State Rights party, 213
Statesman, 148
States' rights, 14, 73–74, 101, 114, 124, 225, 248
Steel industry, 198, 199–202, 207
Stennis, John, 246
Stephens, Alexander H., 52
Stevenson, Adlai E., 217
Stewart, A. Thomas, 129
Stone Mountain, 145
Student Political League, 42–43
Sumners, Hatton W., 80
Sun Life Group of America, 205

Talle, Henry D., 197
Talmadge, Eugene, 19, 23, 53, 60, 62, 114, 192, 237, 246, 247, 252; 1932 gubernatorial campaign, 6, 7, 18; as governor, 1933–37 term, 8, 9, 10–11, 13, 26, 27, 58, 59, 79; clashes with Arnall, 11–12, 29–31, 32, 66, 70–71, 75, 76, 140, 148, 157–58, 162, 166; 1936 Senate campaign,

17, 40; elected governor in 1940, 20, 33; University accreditation controversy, 29–31, 36–39, 40, 41, 43, 48, 50; and gubernatorial succession, 33, 138–39, 160; 1942 gubernatorial campaign, 33–36, 39–42, 43, 44, 45, 46–49, 56; and white supremacy, 48–49, 138–39, 141, 142, 143–44, 145, 166, 168; loss of 1942 primary, 50, 51, 52, 153, 233, 234, 241–42; and constitutional revision, 58, 79, 90, 92, 93, 94–95, 109; as governor, 1941–43 term, 99, 100, 101, 106, 111, 123; 1946 gubernatorial campaign, 101–2, 105, 109, 145, 159, 163–64, 165, 166, 167–68, 169, 171, 174, 186, 209, 250, 288–89 (n. 47); death, 172, 173, 175, 178, 188–89

Talmadge, Herman E., 154, 164, 222, 227, 228, 252; on Eugene Talmadge, 20, 34, 37, 41; and Arnall, 105, 158; as governor, 113–14, 213, 218, 251; and white primary, 144, 208–9, 210; 1946 write-in campaign, 171, 173–75, 176, 177; elected governor by legislature, 178–83, 184–86, 187, 188, 189; 1948 gubernatorial campaign, 210–11, 212–13; 1950 gubernatorial campaign, 213–15, 216–17; as senator, 221, 229

Tarver, Jack, 86, 216

Tate, Horace, 240

Tattnall State Prison, 64–66, 69

Taxation, 165, 195, 228, 249; Eugene Talmadge and, 6, 47; Arnall and, 7, 12, 52, 53, 54–55, 97, 99–100, 110–11, 115, 232, 233–34, 248; sales tax, 9, 12, 23, 99, 100, 216–17, 219, 248, 251; gasoline tax, 24, 52, 97, 107; constitution and, 78, 83, 95–96, 103;

Herman Talmadge and, 213–14. *See also* Poll tax

Taylor, Thomas Elkin, 50, 61, 95, 128, 134, 135, 244

Teachers Retirement System, 55, 59, 92, 100–101, 243, 244–45

Teachers' salaries, 23, 24–25, 43, 92, 101–2, 111

Telfair County, 60, 95, 178, 185–86

Tennessee, 119, 186–87

Tennessee Valley Authority, 117, 119, 121

Texas, 28, 84–85, 141–42, 145

Thomaston *Free-Press*, 164

Thomaston *News*, 40

Thomaston *Times*, 49

Thomasville *Times-Enterprise*, 70

Thompson, Melvin E., 44, 100, 158, 159; as lieutenant governor, 171–72; claims governorship, 173–74, 175, 176, 177, 182, 185, 186, 187, 188; as governor, 208–9, 210; gubernatorial campaigns, 212–13, 215–16, 218–19

Thrasher, B. E., Jr., 86, 99, 105–6

Three-governors controversy, 171–89, 214

Tifton *Daily Gazette*, 187

Time, 51, 67–68, 129, 142, 172, 185, 187–88, 193

Toombs, Robert A., 52, 77

Trade, 124, 134

Training School for Black Girls, 109

Training School for White Girls, 109

Transportation Act (U.S., 1940), 122

Transportation Board, 244

Transportation industry, 129–30

Trucking companies, 129–30

Truman, Harry S., 146, 181–82; and freight rate controversy, 131, 133; vice-presidential nomination, 154,

Truman, Harry S. (*continued*)
155, 156; and Arnall, 157, 191–93,
203, 217; and price controls, 195,
197, 198; steel industry struggle,
199, 200, 202, 207; and civil rights,
210, 212, 213
Truman Doctrine, 157
Tuten, Andrew J., 30–31

Union Springs, Ga., 2
United States: Justice Department,
119, 127, 129–30, 146, 192; War
Department, 129; Commerce
Department, 156–57; Health,
Education, and Welfare
Department, 225
U.S. Congress, 58–59, 73–74, 156–57,
192, 239; and highway construction,
104–5; and railroad freight rates,
118–19, 121, 122, 129, 130, 131–32,
133; and price controls, 194, 195,
196–97, 198, 199, 201, 207
U.S. Constitution, 22, 57, 83, 145;
Fifteenth Amendment, 84, 141, 142;
Fourteenth Amendment, 141
U.S. Supreme Court, 22, 27, 83; and
white primaries, 84, 141–42, 143;
and railroad regulation, 118, 119,
125, 126, 127–28, 129, 130–31, 132,
133–34, 135–36, 191; and steel
industry seizure, 200, 202; and
county unit system, 212, 224; and
school segregation, 219, 224
United States v. Cooper Corporation, 27
United States Steel, 202
United Steel Workers Union, 198, 199,
200, 202
University of Georgia, 12, 22, 100;
Arnall at, 4, 5; accreditation controversy, 30, 36, 39, 41, 42, 43, 48, 50,

53–54, 168, 219, 241–42, 243;
segregation, 48–49, 224
University of the South, 4
Utility rates, 11

Valdosta *Daily Times*, 52, 63, 68, 93,
181, 210
Vanderbilt University, 4
Vandiver, S. Ernest, Jr., 219, 229, 230,
234, 237, 238; and school
desegregation, 220, 221, 224,
227–28
Veterans Service Board, 95, 244
Veterans Department, 88
Veterans Hospital, 56–57
Vidalia *Advance*, 40, 46
Vienna *News*, 93, 159
Vinson, Carl, 119
Virginia Federation of Women, 193
Vocational education, 103–4
Voter registration, 91
Voting rights: eighteen-year-olds, 55,
56–57, 59, 60, 62, 150, 243, 245–46,
248, 249; soldiers, 73–74, 139, 248,
249; secret ballot, 86; blacks, 137–
38, 141–45, 150–51, 152, 157, 168,
225, 226, 245–46, 249, 250. *See also*
White primary
Voting Rights Act (U.S., 1965),
150, 225

Wage Stabilization Board, 198–99
Wallace, Henry A., 94, 119, 145;
dropped from 1944 ticket, 152, 153–
56; Arnall and, 154–55, 156, 158,
169, 191, 211, 213, 236, 247, 250; as
commerce secretary, 156–57
War plants, 123
War Production Board, 130
Washington County, 182, 183

Washington *Post*, 51, 181, 203
Watkins, Edgar, 85
Watson, Thomas E., 34, 35, 63,
  172, 237
Wesleyan College, 183
Western and Atlantic Railroad, 228
Western Governors Conference, 124
West Georgia College, 183
WGST radio, 31
What the People Want (Arnall),
  206, 207
White primary, 138; held
  unconstitutional, 84–85, 141–44,
  163, 225; Arnall and, 90, 137, 139,
  141, 142, 143–45, 150, 152, 191, 246,
  249, 250; Talmadge and, 145, 163–
  64, 166, 168, 173; Thompson and,
  171, 174, 208–9, 210
Whites, 226, 227, 236, 248–49; poll
  tax and, 90; Arnall and, 102, 139,
  141, 149, 150–51, 235, 237, 241,
  248, 251; and Republican party, 225
White supremacy, 17, 141–42, 143;
  Eugene Talmadge and, 35, 49, 50,
  51, 94, 138, 145, 163, 168, 219;
  Herman Talmadge and, 251

Whitley, John E., 28–29
Wilkins, Roy, 237, 239
Williams, Carey, Sr., 211
Williams, Hosea, 239, 240
Williams, Rev. Samuel, 239, 240
Williamson, Matt, 237, 238
Williamson, Q. V., 240
Wilson, Charles E., 199–200
Winder *News*, 93
Wolcott, Jesse P., 197
Women, 86
Wood, John S., 18–19
Worker compensation, 244–45
World Court, 14
World War II, 40, 53, 97, 98,
  99–100, 104
Write-In Georgia, 239–40
WSB-TV, 218

Yeomans, Manning J., 18–19
Yeomans, Margaret, 19

Zoning laws, 95